A Quietist Jihadi

Since '9/11', the Jordanian Abu Muhammad al-Maqdisi (b. West Bank, 1959) has emerged as one of the most important radical Muslim thinkers alive today. While al-Maqdisi may not be a household name in the West, his influence amongst like-minded Muslims stretches across the world, from Jordan – where he lives today – to Southeast Asia. His writings and teachings on Salafi Islam have inspired terrorists from Europe to the Middle East, including Abu Musʿab al-Zarqawi, the former leader of al-Qaʿida in Iraq, and Ayman al-Zawahiri, Osama Bin Laden's successor as the head of al-Qaʿida Central.

This groundbreaking book, which is the first comprehensive assessment of al-Maqdisi, his life, ideology and influence, is based on his extensive writings and those of other jihadis, as well as on interviews that the author conducted with (former) jihadis, including al-Maqdisi himself. It is a serious and intense work of scholarship that uses this considerable archive to explain and interpret al-Maqdisi's particular brand of Salafism. More broadly, the book offers an alternative insider perspective on the rise of radical Islam, with a particular focus on Salafi opposition movements in Saudi Arabia and Jordan.

Joas Wagemakers is an assistant professor in the Department of Islam and Arabic at Radboud University Nijmegen, the Netherlands.

A Quietist Jihadi

The Ideology and Influence of Abu Muhammad al-Maqdisi

JOAS WAGEMAKERS
Radboud University Nijmegen

CAMBRIDGE
UNIVERSITY PRESS

CAMBRIDGE UNIVERSITY PRESS
Cambridge, New York, Melbourne, Madrid, Cape Town,
Singapore, São Paulo, Delhi, Mexico City

Cambridge University Press
32 Avenue of the Americas, New York, NY 10013-2473, USA

www.cambridge.org
Information on this title: www.cambridge.org/9781107606562

First published 2012

Printed in the United States of America

A catalog record for this publication is available from the British Library.

Library of Congress Cataloging in Publication data

Wagemakers, Joas, 1979–
A quietist jihadi : the ideology and influence of Abu Muhammad
al-Maqdisi / Joas Wagemakers.
p. cm.
Includes bibliographical references and index.
ISBN 978-1-107-02207-2 (hardback) – ISBN 978-1-107-60656-2 (paperback)
1. Maqdisi, Abu Muhammad, 1959– 2. Salafiyah. 3. Jihad. 4. Islam and state.
5. Muslim scholar – Jordan. I. Title.
BP80.M3255W34 2012
297.8′1092–dc23 2011039454

ISBN 978-1-107-02207-2 Hardback
ISBN 978-1-107-60656-2 Paperback

Contents

Preface

Like many good ideas, the one to write the PhD thesis on which this book is based started over dinner. In 2005, the co-supervisor of my thesis, Roel Meijer, and I were at a restaurant discussing my intention to write a dissertation about radical Islam in the Middle East, but I was not entirely sure what to do yet. Roel, who was quite aware of my fascination with the dynamics of Islamist ideology, suggested I do something with Jihadi-Salafism. Although I do not recall his mentioning the name 'Abu Muhammad al-Maqdisi', of whom I had never heard at the time, I distinctly remember his saying: 'Perhaps you should check out this website.' The URL he suggested was, of course, www.tawhed.ws, al-Maqdisi's website and the biggest online library of Jihadi-Salafi literature. When I got home and found it, I was immediately struck by the huge number of sources available, and I just knew I had to do something with this site. This book is the product of the idea that was born that night.

My fascination with ideology and its development and flexibility is rooted in an inexplicable interest in beliefs and dogmas I have had for a long time. For years I have been intrigued by the intricate details of theological and ideological debates, whose participants often claim to be the only true followers of a certain tradition, all the while quoting the same books and scholars but coming up with entirely different practical solutions. This interest was, of course, directed towards Islamic and Islamist thought during my studies at university. In that sense, this book is something I had long wanted to write, probably even before I realised it myself.

Dinners and long-held fascinations aside, however, it should also be mentioned that this book would probably not have been written had it not been for the terrorist attacks of 11 September 2001 in the United States. Not only were thousands in New York, Washington, D.C. and Pennsylvania murdered in these attacks, but they also had a deep impact on the lives of millions of others affected by the attacks' foreign and domestic policy implications and – importantly – on academia. The aftermath of '9/11', as my generation will always remember it, spawned a great number of think tanks, centres and institutes dedicated to the study of terrorism and – in this case – its radical Islamist underpinnings. In a way, this book is also a result of this trend, although I feel slightly uneasy putting it like that. While I am certainly very interested in radical Islam and terrorism, I have never considered myself a 'terrorism analyst'. This is not to suggest that there is anything wrong with terrorism analysts; many of them do an excellent job of keeping us safe and writing first-class publications. It is just that I have always been more interested in the words and ideas than in the guns and bombs, and would have been happy to apply my time to non-radical beliefs and ideologies. I therefore also hope that this book will not be viewed as dealing only with terrorism and radicalisation – although these subjects are certainly mentioned in the pages to come – but really as an effort to dissect the contents, (ideological) context and impact of Abu Muhammad al-Maqdisi's ideas.

Combining my fascination for ideas with my realisation that this book would not have seen the light of day without '9/11' turned out to be much easier than I had initially thought. As someone who was profoundly shocked and filled with abhorrence by the attacks in 2001, I assumed it would be difficult ever to talk to al-Maqdisi, who so openly applauded this wanton killing and generally held beliefs that were diametrically opposed to my own. It turned out, however, that this was not the case. Not only was al-Maqdisi a very friendly and hospitable person – his radical beliefs notwithstanding – but meeting the man whose ideas have occupied such a major part of my life over the past few years was quite exciting, and ensured that we had a connection that overcame any ideological animosity I had for him. It would be wonderful if this book could in some way contribute to a greater understanding of radical Islam as my reading of al-Maqdisi's work helped me understand him better. While a better grasp of Jihadi-Salafism can be used for various purposes – both good and evil, depending on one's perspective – a bit more understanding is never wasted, especially in today's world. That would definitely be a nice result of an idea that simply started over dinner.

Acknowledgements

One of the many great pleasures of writing a book is that you can do it on your own, free to set your own agenda and work according to your own timetable. Still, throughout the course of doing research and writing these chapters, I have had a lot of help from many people who must be mentioned here. First, I would like to thank the Institute of Historical, Literary and Cultural Studies (HLCS) at Radboud University, Nijmegen, for awarding me a grant that allowed me to do this research. I am grateful for this opportunity and, considering how much I enjoyed doing my research, I still have a hard time believing that HLCS not only enabled me to do it but even paid me for it into the bargain.

I would also like to thank the two supervisors of my PhD thesis that underlies this book, Harald Motzki and Roel Meijer. They gave me the freedom to do research without having to report on my findings every two weeks, and were always willing to comment on my work – including the articles I continued to bother them with – and their advice was very useful and has improved my writing considerably. The two different kinds of research that Harald and Roel represent – philological research on the beginnings of Islam and historical research on contemporary Islamism and the modern Middle East, respectively – have both greatly contributed to this book in their own ways. If, after reading this book, anyone should remark that traces of Motzki and Meijer can clearly be seen in its text, I would consider it a great compliment.

I should also mention the Department of Islam and Arabic at Radboud University, Nijmegen. Shortly after I started working there, we were told that the department would be dissolved, but because of the tireless efforts of several people, particularly Lieke de Jong and Kees Versteegh, we survived. Even throughout this difficult period it was always a joy to work at this department, and I would like to thank all of my colleagues there for creating such a pleasant working environment. The same can be said of my colleagues of the research project on Salafism in which I participated, Carmen Becker, Martijn de Koning, Roel Meijer, Zoltan Pall and Din Wahid, whose research was not only very interesting but also provided me with new perspectives on my own work. I should especially mention Martin van Bruinessen, who often took time out of his busy schedule to listen to our stories and whose extensive experience and judicious advice were useful to all of us.

Several people, including Joseph Alagha, Egbert Harmsen, Thomas Hegghammer, Stéphane Lacroix, Marie Juul Petersen, Madawi al-Rasheed, Guido Steinberg and Quintan Wiktorowicz, have given me some excellent advice on field work in the countries that I visited and often shared contacts that allowed me to get started, for which I thank them all. I am also grateful to Hasan Abu Haniyya, Mohamed-Ali Adraoui, David Commins, Bernard Haykel, Will McCants, Saud al-Sarhan and Paul Schrijver, who have contributed indirectly to this book by commenting on articles I wrote or by providing me with certain documents that I was unable to find myself.

In England, I was always welcomed by my friends Dave and Christine Miller and their sons Daniel and Andrew. Although my support for Arsenal sometimes clashed with their preference for Tottenham Hotspur, we had some very good times together, and I thank them for their hospitality and great sense of humour. In Jordan, I benefited greatly from the personnel at the Institut français du Proche-Orient (IFPO) in Amman, particularly Leila El Jechi, who always had time for my questions. Similarly, my stay in Saudi Arabia would have been much less effective without the help of the staff at the King Faisal Center for Research and Islamic Studies (KFCRIS) in Riyadh, especially Yahya b. Junayd and Awadh al-Badi, whose advice and contacts helped me find the literature and people I was looking for. I am thankful for all of their help, and hope I will be able to benefit from their expertise again in the future.

During my field work, I talked to lots of people. Many of them are mentioned in this study, but some would only be interviewed on the condition of anonymity, which, of course, I respect. I thank all the people I interviewed for their time and expertise, particularly Abu Muhammad al-Maqdisi, who was kind enough to welcome me into his home and give me the best meal I had in all of my stay in Jordan. Without all of them, this book would obviously not have been the same. Several people have also been of tremendous help for me in locating other people. I would especially like to thank Marwan Shahada, who proved indispensable and sacrificed a lot of his time to help me; Fu'ad Husayn, whose car will never be the same again after driving me through the hilly Jordanian countryside; and Hasan Abu Haniyya, from whose insights and experiences I benefited a great deal. Moreover, he and his wife, Huda, never failed to welcome me into their home for a chat. I am grateful for all of their help and hospitality.

Several researchers and visitors to the countries I went to for my field work, including Romain Caillet, Pascal Debruyne, Christopher Parker, Mohammed Sbitli, Ora Szekely and Erin Walsh, made my time in Jordan and Saudi Arabia much more interesting and a lot more fun. We had some good discussions about our work and all kinds of other things I have fond memories of, and I would like to thank them all. Once back home, I found several experts willing to read early drafts of this work. These include Egbert Harmsen, Thomas Hegghammer, Stéphane Lacroix, Madawi al-Rasheed and Jillian Schwedler, whose comments improved the relevant chapters, even if I did not adopt all of their suggestions. I thank them for all their work and efforts. Suffice it to say, all mistakes in this book are mine alone.

There are also several people to whom thanks are due for their special help, such as my colleagues Jan Hoogland and Everhard Ditters, as well as my friend Steven Boogaard, for their efforts to solve my computer-related problems, and Asad Jaber, for teaching me the basics of Palestinian Arabic. At Cambridge University Press, Marigold Acland, Joy Mizan and manuscript editor Ronald Cohen guided me through the process of turning my dissertation into a book that is not just interesting but will also actually be read, and for this I thank them.

Perhaps somewhat strangely, I would also like thank the people behind AccuRadio.com and AccuJazz.com – whoever they are – for ensuring that writing this book was not only an interesting but also a swinging affair. One of the few things I did not like about my research was typing out interviews, not in the least because it kept me from listening to AccuRadio.com's wonderful music. I am not much of a rebel, and perhaps my only act of rebellion during my research was playing AccuRadio.com's fantastic selection of bluegrass music at full blast from my laptop at the King Faisal Center in Riyadh on a Friday afternoon, which may well have been the very first time that the sounds of the American South were heard in that building.

Finally, I cannot finish these acknowledgements without mentioning my wife, who not only had to manage on her own and take care of our son when I was away for what ultimately amounted to several months of field work, but also spent many an evening alone while I was working in my study. I thank her for all the patience and the loving way in which she accepted my oft-broken promises to be downstairs 'in five minutes' time'. My wife and I were blessed with two wonderful children during the course of my research. As anyone who has gone through the same experience will tell you, raising small children on top of a full-time job that includes teaching and writing a book – particularly with all the sleepless nights, of which I have had my fair share – does not exactly contribute to a good working environment. Still, I would not have missed it for the world, as my wife and children have provided me with a deep sense of happiness throughout the past few years. And that happiness has been the best working environment any researcher could ask for.

Glossary

Note: Several of the terms mentioned here have multiple meanings. I have chosen to focus only on those meanings used in this study.

ʿadāwa – hostility. A word used in Q. 60: 4 – a very important verse in al-Maqdisi's writings – and often equated with disavowal (*barāʾ*, q.v.). See also *baghḍāʾ*.

ahl al-ḥadīth – an early-Islamic trend and precursor to Salafism (q.v.) that relied heavily on *ḥadīth*s (q.v.) in establishing its rulings. There are also modern-day movements bearing this name or similar ones.

ahl al-Sunna wa-l-jamāʿa – the branch of Islam that claims to follow the example of the Prophet (Sunna) and belong to the group (*jamāʿa*) that, according to a *ḥadīth* (q.v.), will be saved from hellfire. The term is applied by Salafis (q.v.) to themselves, but is also used by Sunni Muslims in general. See also *al-firqa al-nājiya*, *al-ṭāʾifa al-manṣūra*.

amīr **(pl. *umarāʾ*)** – leader. The term can refer to a prince, the commander of an army unit or the leader of a group. See also *imāra*.

anṣār al-ṭawāghīt – lit. 'the helpers of the idols'. The term is used by al-Maqdisi to refer to the group of politicians, diplomats and military men and women who support, defend or directly help a regime based on laws other than Islamic ones. The term '*anṣār*' has a positive connotation for Muslims since it is also the word used to refer to the people from Medina who helped the Prophet Muhammad in his time of need. Al-Maqdisi implicitly seems to juxtapose this with the *anṣār al-ṭawāghīt*. See also *ṭāghūt*.

ʿaqīda – creed. This is a highly important term for Salafis (q.v.) since they attach great value to following the right path.

***aṣl* (pl. *uṣūl*)** – root, core or basis. Salafis (q.v.) use the term to refer to the part of religion (*aṣl al-dīn*) that is so important that it forms the basis of Islam. Some Salafis (including al-Maqdisi) believe that a violation of parts of the *aṣl al-dīn* (such as a denial of God's existence) immediately turns a Muslim into an unbeliever (*kāfir*, q.v.).

***aṣnām* (sing. *ṣanam*)** – idols. Sometimes applied by Jihadi-Salafis, including al-Maqdisi, to rulers who do not govern on the basis of Islamic law (*sharīʿa*, q.v.). See also *ṭāghūt*.

baghḍāʾ – hatred. A word used in Q. 60: 4 – a very important verse in al-Maqdisi's writings – and often equated with *barāʾ* (q.v.). See also *ʿadāwa*.

barāʾ – see *al-walāʾ wa-l-barāʾ*.

bayʿa – an oath of allegiance. The term is used in Bayʿat al-Imam, the name wrongly applied to al-Maqdisi's group in Jordan before he went to prison in 1994.

***bidʿa* (pl. *bidaʿ*)** – innovation. Salafis (q.v.) regard *bidaʿ* as undesirable and wrong since they are considered illegitimate additions to Islam that compromise the religion's supposed purity.

***bughāt* (sing. *bāghin*)** – rebels against the leadership of (parts of) the Muslim world. They are considered a category of people that may be fought by means of jihad, but should not be equated with non-Muslims (*kuffār* (sing. *kāfir*, q.v.)).

***dāʿin* (pl. *duʿāt*)** – a caller to Islam. See also *daʿwa*.

dār al-ḥarb/dār al-kufr – the abode of war/the abode of unbelief. The terms traditionally referred to the parts of the world that were not under Muslim control and had no peace agreement or truce with the abode of Islam (*dār al-Islām*, q.v.). Al-Maqdisi distinguishes the *dār al-kufr al-aṣliyya* (the original abode of unbelief) from the *dār al-kufr al-ḥāditha* (the new abode of unbelief). The former refers to the parts of the world that are traditionally not under Muslim control, such as Western Europe and the Americas, while the latter term denotes the parts of the Muslim world that are controlled by supposed apostates (*murtaddūn*, q.v.). Al-Maqdisi sees the entire world as *dār al-kufr*, divided only between the original and new ones. See also *dār al-Islām/dār al-īmān*.

dār al-Islām/dār al-īmān – the abode of Islam/the abode of faith. The terms refer to the parts of the world that are under Muslim control. According to al-Maqdisi, these areas do not exist today since no country is ruled entirely in accordance with Islamic law (*sharīʿa*, q.v.). See also *dār al-ḥarb/dār al-kufr*.

da'wa – the call to Islam. This is part of the preferred method (*manhaj*, q.v.) of engaging with society for quietist Salafis (q.v.) but is also an important part of al-Maqdisi's.

dawla – state, caliphate.

farḍ 'alā l-'ayn – individual duty. Used in this study with regard to jihad, where it refers to the duty that is incumbent upon every Muslim. Scholars disagree on when jihad becomes an individual duty, but many claim that this happens in a situation when the *dār al-Islām* (q.v.) is attacked. See also *farḍ 'alā l-kifāya.*

farḍ 'alā l-kifāya – collective duty. Used in this study with regard to jihad, where it refers to the duty that is incumbent upon only a limited group of Muslims to be sufficient. Scholars disagree on when jihad becomes a collective duty, but many claim that this happens in a situation when Muslims attack the *dār al-ḥarb* (q.v.). See also *farḍ 'alā l-'ayn.*

fiqh – Islamic jurisprudence. This term plays a minor role in Salafism (q.v.) and the writings of al-Maqdisi. See also *fuqahā'.*

al-firqa al-nājiya – the saved sect, the group that, according to a *ḥadīth* (q.v.), will be saved from hellfire. Salafis (q.v.) believe that they are part of this group. See also *ahl al-Sunna wa-l-jamā'a*, *al-ṭā'ifa al-manṣūra.*

***fitna* (pl. *fitan*)** – chaos, strife. Quietist Salafis (q.v.) often describe Jihadi-Salafis as causing *fitna* through their jihad and excommunication (*takfīr*, q.v.) of Muslim rulers. Al-Maqdisi, however, claims that the greatest *fitna* is caused by abandoning the unity of God (*tawḥīd*, q.v.) through – amongst other reasons – ruling on the basis of laws other than those of Islamic law (*sharī'a*, q.v.).

fuqahā' – (sing. *faqīh*) – scholars of Islamic jurisprudence (*fiqh*, q.v.).

ghulāt – exaggerators, extremists. The term is often applied to Muslims who go to great lengths to apply excommunication (*takfīr*, q.v.) to other Muslims. See also *ghulūw.*

ghulūw – exaggeration, extremism. The term is often used with regard to excommunication of other Muslims (*takfīr*, q.v.). See also *ghulāt.*

ḥadīth (pl. *aḥādīth*, but given as *ḥadīth*s in this study) – a story consisting of a chain of transmitters (*isnād*) and some content (*matn*) containing information about or from the first generations of Muslims, particularly the Prophet Muhammad. *Ḥadīth*s have played a major role in the formation of Islamic law (*sharī'a*, q.v.) and in the doctrines and publications of Salafis (q.v.).

ḥākimiyya – sovereignty. According to many Islamists, sovereignty of a country and its laws should be God's alone. The term was popularised by Sayyid Qutb (1906–1966) and adopted by Jihadi-Salafis.

ḥalāl – allowed, permitted. The opposite of *ḥarām* (q.v.). The term is applied to all kinds of issues that are considered admissible according to Islamic law (*sharīʿa*, q.v.). See also *istiḥlāl*.

ḥarām – forbidden. The opposite of *ḥalāl* (q.v.). The term is applied to all kinds of issues that are considered forbidden according to Islamic law (*sharīʿa*, q.v.).

hijra – emigration. Most often used in Islamic history to refer to the emigration of the Prophet Muhammad from Mecca to Medina in 622 A.D., but also applied to modern-day religiously motivated emigration, such as the perceived duty to move from the *dār al-ḥarb* (q.v.) to the *dār al-Islām* (q.v.).

***ḥizb* (pl. *aḥzāb*)** – (political) party or group.

***ḥukm* (pl. *aḥkām*)** – (Islamic legal) ruling.

iʿānat al-kuffār – the act of helping non-Muslims (*kuffār* (sing. *kāfir*, q.v.)), particularly against other Muslims in times of war. It is seen by most modern Salafi (q.v.) scholars as part of loyalty and disavowal (*al-walāʾ wa-l-barāʾ*, q.v.). According to some scholars, including al-Maqdisi, *iʿānat al-kuffār* is strictly forbidden. See also *al-istiʿāna bi-l-kuffār*.

ʿibāda – worship. On the basis of Q. 9: 31, several scholars, including al-Maqdisi, include the following or application of man-made laws (*qawānīn waḍʿiyya*, q.v.), as opposed to Islamic ones, in their definition of worship too.

ijtihād – independent reasoning on the basis of the scriptural sources of Islam without necessarily remaining within the limits of one Islamic legal school of thought (*madhhab*, q.v.). The opposite of blind emulation (*taqlīd*, q.v.).

ʿilm – (Islamic) knowledge.

īmān – faith. The opposite of unbelief (*kufr*, q.v.).

imāra – the emirate or leadership of a group, army unit or political entity. See also *amīr*.

irjāʾ – postponement. The term is linked to the Murjiʾa (q.v.), an early-Islamic trend advocating the postponement of judgement over a person's sins and leaving it to God.

irtidād – apostasy. This makes one an apostate (*murtadd*, q.v.) and an unbeliever (*kāfir*, q.v.). See also *ridda*.

al-istiʿāna bi-l-kuffār – the act of asking non-Muslims (*kuffār* (sing. *kāfir*, q.v.)) for help, especially against other Muslims in times of war. It is seen by most modern Salafi (q.v.) scholars as part of loyalty and disavowal (*al-walāʾ wa-l-barāʾ*, q.v.). According to some scholars, including al-Maqdisi, *al-istiʿāna bi-l-kuffār* is strictly forbidden. See also *iʿānat al-kuffār*.

istiḥlāl – making or considering something that is forbidden (*ḥarām*, q.v.) permissible (*ḥalāl*, q.v.). With regard to the question of unbelief (*kufr*, q.v.), having the belief that something wrong is actually right is one of the conditions that turns minor unbelief (*kufr aṣghar*) into major unbelief (*kufr akbar*), thereby expelling its culprit from Islam. See also *iʿtiqād*, *jaḥd*.

iʿtiqād – conviction. With regard to the question of unbelief (*kufr*, q.v.), the conviction that one is committing a sin without refraining from it is one of the conditions that turns minor unbelief (*kufr aṣghar*) into major unbelief (*kufr akbar*), thereby expelling its culprit from Islam. See also *istiḥlāl*, *jaḥd*.

jaḥd/juḥūd – negation. With regard to the question of unbelief (*kufr*, q.v.), the negation of the supposed truth of Islam and its rulings is one of the conditions that turn minor unbelief (*kufr aṣghar*) into major unbelief (*kufr akbar*), thereby expelling its culprit from Islam. See also *istiḥlāl*, *iʿtiqād*.

jāhiliyya – the pre-Islamic age that Muslims identify as a period of ignorance. The term was also used by Sayyid Qutb (1906–1966) to refer to the supposed state of ignorance Muslim countries live in nowadays, and has also been adopted by Jihadi-Salafis as such.

***kabīra* (*kabāʾir*)** – a major sin. It can be equated with minor unbelief (*kufr aṣghar*, q.v.) and should not be confused with major unbelief (*kufr akbar*).

***kāfir* (pl. *kuffār*/*kāfirūn*)** – unbeliever, a non-Muslim. An apostate of Islam (*murtadd*, q.v.) becomes a *kāfir* once he/she has abandoned Islam. See also *mushrik*.

Khawārij (sing. Khārijī) – seceders. The term refers to an early-Islamic group that seceded from the majority of Muslims and advocated the excommunication (*takfīr*, q.v.) of other Muslims for acts of minor unbelief (*kufr aṣghar*, q.v.). The label is often used by quietist Salafis (q.v.) to de-legitimise Jihadi-Salafis. In that sense, the term 'Khawārij' is the opposite of 'Murjiʾa' (q.v.). See also *irjāʾ*.

khurūj – revolt against the ruler. This is strongly rejected by quietist Salafis (q.v.) but often advocated by Jihadi-Salafis.

kufr – unbelief. The opposite of faith (*īmān*, q.v.). Salafis (q.v.) divide *kufr* into major unbelief (*kufr akbar*), which expels its culprit from

Islam, and minor unbelief (*kufr aṣghar*), which does not, unless it is accompanied by *iʿtiqād* (q.v.), *istiḥlāl* (q.v.) or *jaḥd* (q.v.).

madhhab **(pl.** ***madhāhib*****)** – Islamic legal school. In Sunni Islam, there are four schools of law: the Hanbali, Hanafi, Shafiʿi and Maliki legal schools. Each is usually treated as legitimate in the eyes of the others, but Salafis (q.v.) reject the blind emulation (*taqlīd*, q.v.) of any one school of law and instead advocate independent reasoning on the basis of the scriptural sources of Islam (*ijtihād*, q.v.).

maḥabba – affection. This term is often equated with *walāʾ* (q.v.). See also *muẓāhara*.

majlis al-shūrā – consultation council. See also *shūrā*.

manhaj – method. The term refers to the method of applying the creed (*ʿaqīda*, q.v.) that Salafis (q.v.) follow in their treatment of the sources, worship and dealings with society. It is a very important concept since the *manhaj* is mostly responsible for setting Salafis apart from other Sunni Muslims, who may have the same ideas but do not apply them similarly.

maʿṣiya – disobedience.

maṣlaḥa **(pl.** ***maṣāliḥ*****)** – (general) interest. In this study, the term is used in contexts where certain things may be legitimate but not in the interest of Islam and Muslims.

mujaddid **(pl.** ***mujaddidūn*****)** – renewer. According to tradition, every hundred years will see a new and important renewer in Islam.

mujāhid **(pl.** ***mujāhidūn*****)** – jihad fighter.

murājaʿa – revisionism. Al-Maqdisi has been accused of this by some of his critics.

Murji'a – an early-Islamic trend advocating the postponement (*irjāʾ*, q.v.) of judgement over a person's sins and leaving it to God. Quietist Salafis (q.v.) unwilling to apply excommunication (*takfīr*, q.v.) to rulers of Muslim countries are often accused of using *irjāʾ* by Jihadi-Salafis, including al-Maqdisi. See also Khawārij.

murtadd **(pl.** ***murtaddūn*****)** – apostate. Al-Maqdisi and other Jihadi-Salafis accuse the rulers of Muslim countries of being apostates for their adherence to other, non-Islamic laws. See also *irtidād*, *kāfir*, *kufr*, *mushrik*, *ridda*, *shirk*.

al-mushābaha li-l-kuffār – looking like unbelievers (*kuffār* (sing. *kāfir*, q.v.)). This is frowned upon by Salafis (q.v.) and is – rightly or wrongly – often conflated with loyalty and disavowal (*al-walāʾ wa-l-barāʾ*, q.v.). See also *tashabbuh al-kuffār*.

mushrik **(pl.** ***mushrikūn*****)** – polytheist. Al-Maqdisi and other Jihadi-Salafis accuse the rulers of Muslim countries of being polytheists for their adherence to other, non-Islamic laws. See also *irtidād*, *kāfir*, *kufr*, *murtadd*, *ridda*, *shirk*.

mustaḥabb – commendable. This term is applied to aspects of Islam that are not compulsory (*wājib*, q.v.) and that, subsequently, are believed not to be punished by God when abandoned but the performance of which is said to be rewarded.

muwaḥḥid **(pl.** ***muwaḥḥidūn*****)** – an upholder of the unity of God (*tawḥīd*, q.v.). Salafis (q.v.) sometimes call themselves this because of their allegedly strong preference for and adherence to *tawḥīd*.

muwālāt – a form of loyalty (*walā'*, q.v.), which, when directed towards non-Muslims (*kuffār* (sing. *kāfir*, q.v.)), is considered a form of minor unbelief (*kufr aṣghar*, q.v.). See also *tawallī*.

muẓāhara – assistance, often equated with loyalty (*walā'*, q.v.) and considered forbidden (*ḥarām*, q.v.) when given to unbelievers (*kuffār* (sing. *kāfir*, q.v.)). See also *maḥabba*.

naṣīḥa **(pl.** ***naṣā'iḥ*****)** – advice. Quietist Salafis (q.v.) often find this the preferred way of expressing criticism of rulers. See also *walī l-amr*.

al-nāsikh wa-l-mansūkh – the abrogating and the abrogated. One of several methods of Qur'ānic exegesis to reconcile seemingly contradictory verses in which the later verses abrogate the earlier ones.

qawānīn waḍ'iyya **(sing.** ***qānūn waḍ'ī*****)** – positive law, but in this context translated as man-made laws. Salafis (q.v.) oppose man-made laws and favour Islamic law (*sharī'a*, q.v.), although they do so in highly different ways.

qitāl – fighting. Al-Maqdisi distinguishes *qitāl al-tamkīn* (fighting to consolidate one's power in a certain territory) from *qitāl al-nikāya* (fighting to hurt the enemy and his interests). He considers both legitimate in principle but has a strong preference for the former.

qiyās – analogical reasoning. One of the methods used in exegesis to derive new rules from existing ones. Salafis (q.v.) do not reject this outright but have a strong preference for relying on the literal texts themselves.

Rāfiḍa/Rawāfiḍ – rejecters, deserters. A derogatory term for Shiites, used by many Salafis (q.v.).

ra'y – personal opinion. A means for scholars of Islamic jurisprudence (*fuqahā'*, q.v.) to create new rulings (*aḥkām* (sing. *ḥukm*, q.v.)) on the basis of existing texts using one's own or others' opinions. Salafis (q.v.) reject this but distinguish this from independent reasoning (*ijtihād*, q.v.), which they see as a legitimate way of deriving rulings from the text.

ridda – apostasy. This makes one an apostate (*murtadd*, q.v.) and an unbeliever (*kāfir*, q.v.). See also *irtidād*.

ṣaḥwa – revival. In this study, the term refers to the Saudi movement that was inspired by Wahhabism and Muslim Brotherhood ideas and grew in importance from the 1960s onwards. It played a major role in the opposition to the Saudi regime in the 1990s.

salaf – see *al-salaf al-ṣāliḥ*.

al-salaf al-ṣāliḥ – the pious predecessors. Refers to the first three generations of Muslims who, according to a *ḥadīth* (q.v.), are the best in Islamic history. Salafis (q.v.) try to emulate these generations as much and in as many spheres of life as possible.

Salafis – see Salafism.

Salafism – the trend in Islam whose adherents try to emulate the first three generations of Muslims (*al-salaf al-ṣāliḥ*, q.v.) as much and in as many spheres of life as possible.

shahāda – the Islamic confession of faith. It reads: 'There is no god but God and Muhammad is the messenger of God.' It is the most basic creed (*ʿaqīda*, q.v.) in Islam and is the first of Islam's five pillars or basic duties.

sharīʿa – Islamic law. The term refers to the path Muslims should follow, which is supposedly embodied by the numerous writings on Islamic legal issues. Because Salafis (q.v.) believe that religious innovations (*bidaʿ*, sing. *bidʿa*, q.v.) have crept into this system of laws throughout the centuries, they reject the *sharīʿa* as it is understood by many other Muslims, i.e., the systems of the different legal schools (*madhāhib*, sing. *madhhab*, q.v.) developed by the *fuqahāʾ* (q.v.) throughout the course of Islamic history. Their own alternative remains rather vague, however.

sharīf **(pl.** ***shurafāʾ/ashrāf*****)** – a descendant of the Prophet Muhammad. The Jordanian king claims to be a *sharīf*, a title that is respected by many Muslims but has little other significance.

shaykh – patriarch, leader. Title for a religious scholar or for someone respected for other reasons.

shirk – polytheism. Jihadi-Salafis accuse rulers of polytheism (*shirk*, q.v.) because of their reliance on man-made laws (*qawānīn waḍʿiyya*, q.v.) at the expense of Islamic law (*sharīʿa*, q.v.). Because they equate laws with idols (*aṣnām*, q.v.; *ṭawāghīt*, sing. *ṭāghūt*, q.v.) and adhering to these laws with worship (*ʿibāda*, q.v.) on the basis of Q. 9: 31, Jihadi-Salafis accuse people who consciously follow 'un-Islamic' laws out of conviction (*iʿtiqād*, q.v.) of being polytheists (*mushrikūn*, q.v.).

shūrā – consultation. Islamists who want to incorporate democracy into their ideas sometimes use this term as a supposedly Islamic form of democracy. Al-Maqdisi rejects this.

tabarru' – see *barā'*.

tabdīl – exchange. In this study, the term refers to the complete exchange of Islamic law (*sharīʿa*, q.v.) with another system of laws or a non-Islamic constitution. According to some Salafis (q.v.), including al-Maqdisi, this act of exchange is such a clear example of unbelief (*kufr*, q.v.) that no further proof of someone's true intentions is necessary.

ṭāghūt **(pl.** ***ṭawāghīt*****)** – idols. Al-Maqdisi and other Jihadi-Salafis see the rulers of Muslim countries and their man-made laws (*qawānīn waḍʿiyya*) as idols for the obedience they enjoy from people, which should only be directed at God. See also *aṣnām*.

taḥkīm – legislation. See also *tashrīʿ*.

al-ṭā'ifa al-manṣūra – the victorious group. This term refers to the Muslims who are, on the basis of a *ḥadīth* (q.v.), believed to be the only victorious group on Judgement Day. Salafis (q.v.) believe they are part of this group. See also *ahl al-Sunna wa-l-jamāʿa*, *al-firqa al-nājiya*.

tajdīd – renewal. See also *mujaddid*.

takfīr – excommunication of other Muslims, declaring other Muslims to be unbelievers (*kuffār* (sing. *kāfir*, q.v.)), Al-Maqdisi advocates this when dealing with legislative issues and thus favours *takfīr* of the rulers of Muslim countries, but is careful in his application of the concept beyond the legislative sphere.

ṭālib ʿilm – a student of (religious) knowledge, a knowledge seeker. A term that many Salafis (q.v.) apply to themselves, thereby indicating that they see themselves as seekers of the correct knowledge of Islam. See also *ʿilm*.

taqlīd – blind emulation of a particular school of law (*madhhab*, q.v.). See also *ijtihād*.

tashabbuh al-kuffār – looking like unbelievers (*kuffār* (sing. *kāfir*, q.v.)). This is frowned upon by Salafis (q.v.) and is – rightly or wrongly – often conflated with loyalty and disavowal (*al-walā' wa-l-barā'*, q.v.). See also *al-mushābaha li-l-kuffār*.

tashrīʿ – legislation. See also *taḥkīm*.

tatarrus – term that refers to a human shield (*turs*) used by the Muslims' enemies that does not prohibit the jihad fighters (*mujāhidūn*, q.v.)

from attacking them, even if the innocents used as a human shield are killed.

tawallī – a form of loyalty (*walāʾ*, q.v.), which, when directed towards non-Muslims (*kuffār* (sing. *kāfir*, q.v.)), is considered a form of major unbelief (*kufr akbar*, q.v.). See also *muwālāt*.

tawḥīd – the unity of God. This is a strong focal point in Salafism (q.v.) and in Islam as a whole. Salafis (q.v.) divide *tawḥīd* into three different types: *tawḥīd al-rubūbiyya* (the unity of lordship), *tawḥīd al-asmāʾ wa-l-ṣifāt* (the unity of names and attributes) and *tawḥīd al-ulūhiyya* (the unity of divinity). The first refers to basic ideas of monotheism such as that there is only one God and Creator. The second refers to God's unique nature and incomparability. The third form refers to the idea that only God may be worshipped.

taʾwīl – interpretation.

***ʿulamāʾ* (sing. *ʿālim*)** – scholars, particularly religious scholars.

umma – the worldwide community of Muslims.

wājib – compulsory. Acts that are *wājib al-dīn* are compulsory. Neglecting them is not a form of major unbelief (*kufr akbar*, q.v.) but only a form of minor unbelief (*kufr aṣghar*).

walāʾ – see *al-walāʾ wa-l-barāʾ*.

al-walāʾ wa-l-barāʾ – loyalty and disavowal. *Walāʾ* refers to the friendship, loyalty and dedication Muslims should show to their co-religionists, whereas *barāʾ* denotes the distance, disavowal, hatred and enmity Muslims should show towards non-Muslims (*kuffār* (sing. *kāfir*, q.v.)). While many scholars interpret this concept solely in a social and apolitical way, others treat it also as a concept relevant to situations of military conflict, during which Muslims should always side with their fellow-believers against non-Muslims. See also *ʿadāwa*, *baghḍāʾ*, *maḥabba*, *al-mushābaha li-l-kuffār*, *muwālāt*, *muẓāhara*, *tashabbuh al-kuffār*, *tawallī*.

***walī l-amr* (pl. *wulāt al-amr*)** – the ruler. Quietist Salafis (q.v.) believe this ruler should be obeyed and, in case of criticism, should be given advice (*naṣīḥa*, q.v.). Political Salafis, however, believe protests and/or political participation are allowed, and Jihadi-Salafis believe the *walī al-amr* may be fought if he is an apostate (*murtadd*, q.v.).

yāsiq/yāsa – the Mongol system of laws. This system was criticised by Taqi l-Din Ahmad b. Taymiyya (1263–1328) for its mixture of Islamic and non-Islamic elements. Modern-day Jihadi-Salafis, including al-Maqdisi, sometimes compare the laws of Muslim countries today with the *yāsiq*.

Note on Transliteration

Throughout this study, I have transliterated Arabic words using the transliteration system of the *International Journal of Middle East Studies* (IJMES). I have, however, also transliterated some more common terms that IJMES does not transliterate (e.g., Qurʾan/Qurʾān). Moreover, I have transliterated names and titles of books in the footnotes but not in the text itself. Some words, such as *ḥadīth*, have not been given their accurate plural forms (*aḥādīth*) but a slightly simplified English plural (*ḥadīth*s).

Introduction

In the decade that has passed since the terrorist attacks of 11 September 2001, many once-obscure people have become celebrities of a sort. Names such as 'Osama bin Laden' and 'Ayman al-Zawahiri' have become well known, even to people with only a passing interest in the Middle East, terrorism and Islamism. One name that is clearly not part of this group belongs to the person whose ideas and influence form the subject of this book: Abu Muhammad al-Maqdisi. Although this Jordanian radical Islamic ideologue has received some media attention because of the spectacular acts of terrorism by Abu Musʿab al-Zarqawi, a former leader of al-Qaʿida in Iraq and once a student of al-Maqdisi's, he remains virtually unknown to the general public, even in the Middle East. It therefore came as a surprise to many when, in 2006, the Combating Terrorism Center at West Point, New York, published a study of radical Islam that concluded that, contrary to popular perception, the most influential scholar in the world of militant Islamism today was not former al-Qaʿida leader Osama bin Laden or his successor Ayman al-Zawahiri, but precisely this little-known man called Abu Muhammad al-Maqdisi.[1]

It is clear that al-Maqdisi has indeed been an influential ideologue among like-minded Muslims across the world and that his influence goes far beyond simply having been the teacher of al-Zarqawi. His Arabic website (www.tawhed.ws) offers the largest library of jihadi literature on the Internet and his writings have been translated into about a dozen

[1] William McCants (ed.), *The Militant Ideology Atlas*, Executive Report, West Point, NY: Combating Terrorism Center, 2006, 8–9.

other languages, most of which are available on his English website (www.tawhed.net). Al-Maqdisi is seen as an important ideologue by Islamist movements from Algeria to Indonesia, his works are praised and quoted by radical Muslim scholars across the Muslim world and he has been a prominent scholarly adviser to Jihadi-Salafi groups in the Gaza Strip and the North Caucasus since 2008.[2]

Despite the geographical diversity of these groups and scholars, however, they seem to have at least one thing in common, namely that all of them belong to a branch of Sunni Islam called Salafism. Since Salafi ideology is the basis of al-Maqdisi's writings and central to explaining his influence on others, we must first deal with this topic in some detail before turning to a historical overview of the development of radical Islam in the Arab world and an explanation of the theoretical framework and the methodology of this study and the sources used. This introduction concludes by presenting an overview of the rest of the book.

The Salafi Ideological Basis

Just like al-Maqdisi's name, 'Salafism' was not a household word before 11 September 2001. Although several publications partly dealing with (aspects of) Salafism as it has developed since the 1970s had appeared before '9/11'[3], this was not reflected in common knowledge about the subject. This changed dramatically after the terrorist attacks on that day, when a large number of people became interested in the Salafi ideas associated with al-Qaʿida, the organisation behind the attacks. Although the number of books and articles dealing with al-Qaʿida and global radical Islam increased greatly after 2001, the rising interest in Salafism was only partly matched in scholarly publications focussing on the ideological tenets of this branch of Islam. Several publications have explored the link between Salafism and al-Qaʿida[4], have treated the

[2] For an overview of the groups and scholars influenced by al-Maqdisī, see Joas Wagemakers, 'A Quietist Jihadi-Salafi: The Ideology and Influence of Abu Muhammad al-Maqdisi', unpublished PhD thesis, Radboud University, Nijmegen, 2010, 1–2.

[3] Quintan Wiktorowicz, 'The Salafi Movement in Jordan', *International Journal of Middle East Studies*, vol. 32, no. 2, 2000, 219–40.

[4] *Id.*, 'The New Global Threat: Transnational Salafis and Jihad', *Middle East Policy*, vol. 8, no. 4, December 2001, 18–38; Quintan Wiktorowicz and John Kaltner, 'Killing in the Name of Islam: Al-Qaeda's Justification for September 11', *Middle East Policy*, vol. 10, no. 2, 2003, 76–92.

former as a de-territorialised and a-cultural phenomenon[5] or have dealt with contemporary Salafism in individual countries such as Iraq[6] and Yemen[7]. It was not until quite recently, however, that in-depth studies dealing with Salafism as a whole and its ideology in particular started appearing.[8] Apart from the importance of Salafi ideas for this study, the relative lack of in-depth treatments of the ideological underpinnings of Salafism is therefore another reason to deal with this subject at some length. Moreover, it also introduces some of the main concepts and terminology used throughout this study.

Defining Salafism

I use the term 'Salafism' to refer to those Muslims who try to emulate the 'pious predecessors' (*al-salaf al-ṣāliḥ*, hence the name Salafism) as closely and in as many spheres of life as possible and construct their beliefs, their behaviour and their reading of the sources of Islam to further that goal. Based on several traditions of the Prophet Muhammad (*ḥadīth*s), these predecessors are usually limited to the first three generations of Islam and are considered to be – in the words of the Prophet – 'the best of my community' (*khayr ummatī*).[9] They are believed to embody the purest and most authentic form of Islam. Salafis subsequently see themselves as the group that follows the only 'true' form of Islam and therefore believe they are the *ṭā'ifa manṣūra* (the victorious group) or the *firqa nājiya*

5 Olivier Roy, *Globalized Islam: The Search for a New Umma*, New York: Columbia University Press, 2004.

6 Mohammed M. Hafez, *Suicide Bombers in Iraq: The Strategy and Ideology of Martyrdom*, Washington, D.C.: United States Institute of Peace Press, 2007, 63–87.

7 Laurent Bonnefoy, 'Salafism in Yemen: A "Saudisation"?' in: Madawi al-Rasheed (ed.), *Kingdom without Borders: Saudi Arabia's Political, Religious and Media Frontiers*, London: Hurst & Co., 2008, 245–62; François Burgat and Muhammad Sbitli, 'Les Salafis au Yémen ou . . . la modernisation malgré tout', *Chroniques yéménites*, no. 10, 2002; Bernard Haykel, 'The Salafis in Yemen at a Crossroads: An Obituary of Shaykh Muqbil al-Wadiʿi of Dammaj (d. 1422/2001)', *Jemen Report*, no. 2, 2002, 28–37.

8 Roel Meijer (ed.), *Global Salafism: Islam's New Religious Movement*, London: Hurst & Co., 2009; Bernard Rougier (ed.), *Qu'est-ce que le salafisme?* Paris: Presses Universitaires de France, 2008; Quintan Wiktorowicz, 'The Salafi Movement: Violence and Fragmentation of Community', in: Miriam Cooke and Bruce B. Lawrence (eds.), *Muslim Networks from Hajj to Hiphop*, Chapel Hill & London: University of North Carolina Press, 2005, 208–34.

9 For these traditions, see *Ṣaḥīḥ al-Bukhārī*, book 57 ('Kitāb Faḍā'il Aṣḥāb al-Nabī . . . '), chapter 1 ('Faḍā'il Aṣḥāb al-Nabī . . . '), nos. 2–3; *Ṣaḥīḥ Muslim*, book 44 ('Kitāb Faḍā'il al-Ṣaḥāba . . . '), chapter 52 ('Faḍl al-Ṣaḥāba, thumma lladhīna Yalūnahum, thumma lladhīna Yalūnahum'), nos. 2533–6.

(saved sect), the group of Muslims that – according to several *ḥadīth*s – will remain steadfast in their pursuit of the truth and will consequently be saved from hellfire.[10]

The concept most central to those I (and others) refer to as Salafis is *tawḥīd* (the unity of God). Apart from simply seeing this as monotheism as it is generally understood (the belief in only one god), Salafis distinguish three different kinds of *tawḥīd*: *tawḥīd al-rubūbiyya* (the unity of Lordship, referring to the belief that there is only one Lord and Creator), *tawḥīd al-asmāʾ wa-l-ṣifāt* (the unity of names and attributes, indicating that God is one and utterly unique in all his characteristics) and *tawḥīd al-ulūhiyya* (the unity of divinity, referring to the idea that only God is divine and therefore the only being worthy of worship). Because Salafis have such a strict understanding of what constitutes *tawḥīd* and because this concept can be seen as the basis of Islam, practices such as the veneration of so-called saints among Muslims are denounced as examples of violating the unity of God and are thus seen as expressions of polytheism (*shirk*) and unbelief (*kufr*). According to Salafis, the person guilty of such a sin is a polytheist (*mushrik*) and an unbeliever (*kāfir*) who becomes the subject of excommunication (*takfīr*) since he or she can no longer be called a Muslim. Salafis also object to any popular or cultural traditions added to the doctrines or practices of Islam, which – in their view – tarnish the purity of the religion as embodied by the lives of the pious predecessors. Such practices are referred to as 'religious innovations' (*bidʿa*, pl. *bidaʿ*) by Salafis, who try to shun them as much as possible.[11]

Salafis as I describe them also express what they believe to be their strict emulation of the *salaf* in not following the different schools of Islamic law (*sharīʿa*). In Sunni Islam, there are four such legal schools (*madhāhib*, sing. *madhhab*): the Hanafi, Shafiʿi, Maliki and Hanbali schools, each named after the person on the basis of whose ideas these schools developed. It has traditionally been common practice for Sunni Muslims to follow the rulings of one of these *madhāhib* (*taqlīd*), often depending on the geographical region one is from, with each of the four schools recognising each other as orthodox and legitimate. Salafis reject *taqlīd*, however,

[10] Bernard Haykel, 'On the Nature of Salafi Thought and Action', in: Roel Meijer (ed.), *Global Salafism: Islam's New Religious Movement*, London: Hurst & Co., 2009, 33–4; Quintan Wiktorowicz, 'Anatomy of the Salafi Movement', *Studies in Conflict and Terrorism*, vol. 29, no. 3, 2006, 207; *id.*, *The Management of Islamic Activism: Salafis, the Muslim Brotherhood, and State Power in Jordan*, Albany, NY: State University of New York Press, 2001, 111–12, 120.

[11] Haykel, 'Nature', 39; Wiktorowicz, *Management*, 113–17.

since they believe one should only follow the original two sources of Islam, the Qur'ān and the example of the Prophet Muhammad (Sunna) as embodied by the various *ḥadīth*s. If these do not provide clear-cut answers to their questions, Salafis advocate independent interpretation of these two sources (*ijtihād*), freed from the boundaries that the various schools impose.[12]

The Roots of Salafism

Although Salafism in its present form came into existence in the latter half of the twentieth century, its roots go back hundreds of years. The desire to emulate the pious predecessors – particularly the Prophet himself and the first four 'rightly guided caliphs' (the so-called *rāshidūn*) – can be said to have always been part of Sunni Islam in general, not just its Salafi current. It is the strictness and methodology with which Salafis try to live up to the standard set by the *salaf* and their willingness to gear their teachings and beliefs towards that goal, however, that distinguishes them from other Sunni Muslims. Because of their emphasis on precisely emulating the first generations of Islam, Salafis attach great importance to finding, studying and following *ḥadīth*s about the predecessors. This search for as many details about the *salaf* as possible in order to apply them in one's own life so as to live in a strictly Islamic way is rooted in the eighth-century movement known as the *ahl al-ḥadīth*. This group of scholars from Medina had a strong preference for using only the Qur'ān and the Sunna in their reasonings.[13] This trend to rely on *ḥadīth*s to complement the Qur'ān at the expense of non-scriptural sources of the *sharīʿa* such as analogical reasoning (*qiyās*) or scholars' own legal opinions (*ra'y*) eventually became important to all schools of Islamic law, especially the Hanbali one, which followed the principles espoused by the scholar Ibn Hanbal (780–855).[14] Through Hanbali scholars such as Ibn Taymiyya (1263–1328), his student Ibn Qayyim al-Jawziyya (1292–1350) and Ibn ʿAbd al-Wahhab (1703–92), the principles behind the *ahl al-ḥadīth* – emulating the pious predecessors as closely as possible – strongly influenced the modern-day movement we now call Salafism.

[12] Haykel, 'Nature', 42; Wiktorowicz, *Management*, 119–20.
[13] Haykel, 'Nature', 38.
[14] Joseph Schacht, *An Introduction to Islamic Law*, Oxford: Oxford University Press, 1982, 63, but see also Harald Motzki, *The Origins of Islamic Jurisprudence: Meccan Fiqh before the Classical Schools* (transl. Marion H. Katz), Leiden: Brill, 2002, 18–49, esp. 18–22, and 287–97.

Despite the fact that the tenets of Hanbalism and the teachings of Ibn ʿAbd al-Wahhab (often referred to as 'Wahhabism') have been major sources of influence on Salafism, they should not be equated with it. There is a tendency among some to lump especially the terms 'Wahhabism' and 'Salafism' together. Although there is indeed reason to do so – many of the beliefs, doctrines and sources used are the same – there are differences. The term 'Salafism' refers to the broad movement of Muslims who meticulously try to live according to the example of the *salaf* as they see fit, whereas 'Wahhabism' – a term rejected by its adherents – refers to the specific type of Salafism propagated by the eighteenth-century reformer Muhammad b. ʿAbd al-Wahhab from the central Arabian region of Najd. One could thus say that Wahhabism is the Najdi branch of Salafism. There are, in fact, many Muslims whom one might call Salafis but not Wahhabis. Adherents to the belief that the *salaf* should be emulated as closely and in as many spheres of life as possible have been found in areas outside Najd for centuries[15] and they have sometimes differed ideologically with the latter, for instance on Wahhabis' overly strict enforcement of their beliefs, their lack of tolerance towards others and their limited use of *ijtihād*.[16]

Just as contemporary Salafism should not be equated entirely with Wahhabism, it should also not be confused with the late nineteenth- and early twentieth-century movement often referred to as Salafism.[17] This modernist trend, propagated by thinkers such as Jamal al-Din al-Afghani (1838/39–97), Muhammad ʿAbduh (1849–1905) and Rashid Rida (1865–1935) did indeed try to move Islam back into the direction of the *salaf* but with a completely different objective. Whereas contemporary Salafis try to emulate the predecessors to purify Islam and revert to its supposedly original and true form, Al-Afghani, ʿAbduh, Rida and others did so in order to rid Islam of the centuries of legal and historical

15 Barbara Daly Metcalf, *Islamic Revival in British India: Deoband, 1860–1900*, Oxford: Oxford University Press, 2002 [1982], 268–96.

16 Hala Fattah, '"Wahhabi" Influences, Salafi Responses: Shaikh Mahmud Shukri and the Iraqi Salafi Movement, 1745–1930', *Journal of Islamic Studies*, vol. 14, no. 2, 2003, 127–48; Stéphane Lacroix, 'L'apport de Muhammad Nasir al-Din al-Albani au salafisme contemporain', in: Bernard Rougier (ed.), *Qu'est-ce que le salafisme?* Paris: Presses Universitaires de France, 2008, 46–7.

17 Recent research has shown that the term 'Salafism' in the modernist sense was not an accurate term to describe its adherents and did not represent a clear trend. See Henri Lauzière, 'The Construction of *Salafiyya*: Reconsidering Salafism from the Perspective of Conceptual History', *International Journal of Middle East Studies*, vol. 42, no. 3, 2010, 369–89.

baggage that had, in their view, turned it into a rigid religion unfit for modern times. By going back to the earliest period of their religion, they wanted to strip Islam of this 'burden' so it could be rebuilt again from the bottom up in a way that was assertively Islamic but compatible with the challenges of their time. Although these reformists shared a preference for certain concepts with their present-day namesakes, such as an emphasis on *tawḥīd* and a rejection of *taqlīd*, in the end theirs was a thoroughly modernist discourse, as opposed to the purifying tone of contemporary Salafis.[18] In some cases, such as among nineteenth-century Salafi scholars in Iraq and Syria, Muslims espoused both a purifying and a modernising form of Salafism: on the one hand they strove to strip Islam of what they considered to be sinful deviations and religious innovations, but they also did so partly in order to better prepare the religion for the challenges presented by modern life. This partial embrace of modernity, albeit one couched in a purifying religious discourse, is a crucial difference with the contemporary Salafism that is central to this study.[19]

Labelling Salafism

This discussion suggests that labelling Salafism is somewhat problematic and that the name 'Salafism' is not universally applied to the same group of people. This is indeed the case, and not just among scholars of Salafism. The people referred to in this study as Salafis also reject this label sometimes. Believing that labelling believers in different ways only leads to unwelcome divisions within Islam, some Muslims I call Salafis have argued that they should really be seen as followers of *al-salaf al-ṣāliḥ*, the *ahl al-Sunna wa-l-jamāʿa* (the people of the Sunna and the community), or simply as Muslims. The first of these three options more or less boils down to the same as the term 'Salafis', the second is too subjective to be

[18] For a good overview of Al-Afghanī's, ʿAbduh's and Riḍā's ideas, see Albert Hourani, *Arabic Thought in the Liberal Age, 1798–1939*, Cambridge: Cambridge University Press, 1983 [1962], 103–60, 222–44.

[19] For such Salafī trends in Iraq, see, for instance, Itzchak Weismann, 'Genealogies of Fundamentalism: Salafi Discourse in Nineteenth-Century Baghdad', *British Journal of Middle Eastern Studies*, vol. 36, no. 2, 2009, 267–280; for Syria, see David Dean Commins, *Islamic Reform: Politics and Social Change in Late Ottoman Syria*, New York & Oxford: Oxford University Press, 1990; Mun'im Sirry, 'Jamāl al-Dīn al-Qāsimī and the Salafi Approach to Sufism', *Die Welt des Islams*, vol. 51, no. 1, 2011, 75–108; Itzchak Weismann, 'Between Ṣūfī Reformism and Modernist Rationalism – A Reappraisal of the Origins of the Salafiyya from the Damascene Angle', *Die Welt des Islams*, vol. 41, no. 2, 2001, pp. 206–237; *id.*, *Taste of Modernity: Sufism, Salafiyya, and Arabism in Late Ottoman Damascus*, Leiden: Brill, 2001, pp. 263–304.

useful for an academic study and the third is far too broad to be of any use. It is therefore important to note that my use of the term 'Salafism' and its derivatives is not based on what the people I refer to as 'Salafis' call themselves. Instead, it is partly based on common practice among Western scholars of the subject, but also on my own observation that some Muslims share the strict attempt to emulate the *salaf* in various ways, legitimising the use of a label derived from that word. My use of the term 'Salafism' should therefore be seen as a label that *I* use, not as one that is necessarily endorsed by the people it refers to.

The people I label 'Salafis' all share the basic ideas I have outlined here. There are, however, significant differences between Salafis. Two different terms are particularly relevant in this respect: *ʿaqīda* (creed) and *manhaj* (method). The term *ʿaqīda* refers to the beliefs and doctrines that Salafis subscribe to and has been described earlier in its most basic form. Because of Salafis' desire to purify Islam of religious innovations and other 'un-Islamic' influences, defining exactly what their creed entails is very important to them, hence the many documents outlining the exact beliefs of Salafis.[20] *Manhaj*, on the other hand, refers to the method of applying this creed. The Saudi Salafi scholar Salih b. Fawzan al-Fawzan has distinguished three different forms of this concept. The first of these is Salafis' method of dealing with the sources of Islam. The second is the method of worship (*ʿibāda*) and the third is the *manhaj* of dealing with society.[21]

The first form of *manhaj* is probably universally agreed upon by Salafis since they all believe in a strictly literal reading of the sources, even if that means texts cannot be reconciled with one another, and eagerly search for textual – as opposed to rationally argued – proof for their beliefs.[22] The second and third forms, however, are controversial. Although Salafis agree that the worshipping of saints is a form of *shirk*, they do not have the same ideas on what constitutes worship. As we will see later, several scholars – including al-Maqdisi – believe that following laws can also be seen as a form of worship, a point that is contested by others. The third form of *manhaj* mentioned by al-Fawzan is probably the most controversial

[20] See, for example, Muḥammad Ṣāliḥ al-ʿUthaymīn, *The Muslims* [sic] *Belief*, www.allaahuakbar.in/scholars/uthaymeen/muslims_belief.htm, n.d.; Abū Baṣīr al-Ṭarṭūsī, *Hādhihi ʿAqīdatunā wa-Hādhā lladhī Nadʿū ilayhi*, www.tawhed.ws/r?i=xdvnxy3h, 2002.

[21] Ṣāliḥ b. Fawzān al-Fawzān, *Why Manhaj?* www.allaahuakbar.in/aqeedah/manhaj/index.htm, n.d.

[22] Wiktorowicz, 'Anatomy', 210–12; *id.*, *Management*, 114–15.

one, however, as it deals with contentious social and political issues such as parliamentary participation and the use of violence.

Based on the division between *ʿaqīda* and *manhaj*, Wiktorowicz, in a seminal article, has distinguished three types of Salafis: quietists (or purists, as he calls them), politicos and jihadis.[23] According to Wiktorowicz, they all agree on issues relating to *ʿaqīda* but differ when it comes to *manhaj*, which he more or less equates with the third form of *manhaj* distinguished earlier, namely the method of dealing with society. Quietists focus on the propagation of their message (*daʿwa*) through lessons, sermons and other missionary activities and stay away from politics and violence, which they leave to the ruler (*walī l-amr*). This group includes major Salafi scholars such as the Syrian scholar Muhammad Nasir al-Din al-Albani (d. 1999) and the Saudis ʿAbd al-ʿAziz b. Baz (d. 1999) and Muhammad Salih al-ʿUthaymin (d. 2001).[24] Politicos, on the other hand, do engage in political debate, or even participate in elections and parliaments, and include Saudi scholars such as Salman al-ʿAwda, Safar al-Hawali[25] and the Egyptian Abu ʿAbdallah ʿAbd al-Rahman b. ʿAbd al-Khaliq. Jihadi-Salafis are perhaps the least-defined group in the literature on Salafism in general and are usually seen simply as violent Salafis or the ones who support jihad. This is wrong, however, since – as we will see later on – *all* Salafis view jihad as a legitimate Islamic concept and support it (at least in principle) in cases where non-Muslim enemies invade Muslim countries, even though they may have practical objections to actually waging war in such cases. The people I refer to as Jihadi-Salafis go much further than just supporting such a 'classical jihad', and believe that religiously motivated war may also be waged to solve political problems within Muslim societies themselves, most particularly to overthrow the supposedly unbelieving rulers of Islamic countries. Thus, Jihadi-Salafis, in my use of the term, are those Salafis who believe that jihad should not just be waged against invading or aggressive non-Muslim enemies but should also be used in a revolutionary way against the 'apostate' rulers in their own midst.

Although Wiktorowicz's article has done much to clarify the differences among Salafis, his division of them is somewhat too schematic. His assertion, for example, that all Salafis agree on the creed is true when it

23 *Id.*, 'Anatomy', 225–8.

24 Haykel, 'Nature', 49; Peter Mandaville, *Global Political Islam*, London & New York: Routledge, 2007, 248.

25 See Mamoun Fandy, *Saudi Arabia and the Politics of Dissent*, New York: Palgrave, 1999, 61–113, for an in-depth treatment of these men.

comes to its basic tenets as just described but not when dealing with its details. Questions about issues such as what constitutes faith and, especially, when a Muslim can be said to have lost his or her faith and can be declared an 'infidel' are controversial among Salafis and are answered in different ways, as we will see later on. Furthermore, Wiktorowicz's treatment of the term *manhaj* suggests that Salafis are either quietists, politicos or jihadis. In this study, however, I argue that this need not be the case since Salafis may well transcend the borders of one particular type of *manhaj* and emphasise, for instance, both *daʿwa* and jihad in their writings as useful ways of expressing contention and dealing with society and politics.

One such example of a Salafi whose ideology challenges the division made by Wiktorowicz is al-Maqdisi. I contend that al-Maqdisi, even though he is clearly a Jihadi-Salafi, uses arguments, concepts and terms that show he is very close to the quietist creed. Moreover, his emphasis on the use of *daʿwa* shows that he also partly adopts the method of quietist Salafis. Therefore, one might say that al-Maqdisi is, in fact, a 'quietist Jihadi-Salafi'. In this study, I argue that al-Maqdisi's closeness to quietist Salafis in both *ʿaqīda* and *manhaj* is a major factor in explaining his influence among certain Salafis and his lack thereof among others.

The Development of Radical Islam

The outline given here has described in some detail what Salafism entails and has pointed out that al-Maqdisi belongs to its jihadi branch. Jihadi-Salafism, however, did not come into existence in an ideological vacuum, as the information given here might suggest. Before it became what it is nowadays, it went through many stages of development and was often influenced by events and groups not directly linked to Salafi beliefs. The following paragraphs deal with the development of radical forms of Islam in the Arab world and how this culminated into Jihadi-Salafism as we know it today. Just like the description of Salafism, this must be dealt with in some detail since it introduces many of the events relevant for the rest of this book and provides a historical basis from which subsequent chapters continue.

The Muslim Brotherhood and Its Heirs

The roots of today's radical Islamic organisations in the Arab world can be traced to the founding of a movement that is still widespread and very active in several countries: the Muslim Brotherhood. Founded by an Egyptian called Hasan al-Banna (1906–49) in 1928, the movement quickly spread from its humble beginnings in Ismaʿiliyya to the rest of Egypt and, later, to other countries. Al-Banna, a student of the aforementioned Rashid Rida, wanted the Brotherhood to be an activist and assertive movement focussed on instilling a strong Muslim identity in his fellow countrymen and -women. The founding and development of the movement should be seen in the context of colonialism in general and the British occupation of Egypt in particular. In fact, the strong British presence in Ismaʿiliyya – a city close to the strategically and economically important Suez Canal – made a deep impression on al-Banna.[26]

The Brotherhood was engaged in different activities, including education and political activism but also, sometimes, violence against the Egyptian government. The precise direction the movement should take was contested under al-Banna's rule[27] but conflicts over this issue could mostly be contained. When al-Banna was assassinated in 1949, however, the disputes over what policies to pursue became apparent. Partly fuelled by tensions and disagreements over the new leadership of the Brotherhood, the movement disintegrated steadily as its members first co-operated with the so-called 'Free Officers' led by Muhammad Najib (Neguib) and Jamal ʿAbd al-Nasir (Nasser), who staged a revolution in 1952, but were later put in prison by Nasser after they were accused of trying to assassinate him.[28] The splits within the Brotherhood, exacerbated by the Egyptian regime's crackdown on the movement, produced two distinct branches. The first was a politically moderate and non-violent branch that considered the state legitimate and eventually started participating in parliamentary elections. This trend dominated the Brotherhood and eventually came to encompass the entire movement.[29] Since the 1990s, this moderate trend has developed even further into a movement referred to as the Wasaṭiyya (centrism), which no longer strives explicitly for the implementation of Islamic law, as the Brotherhood does, but uses

[26] The two best studies in English on the early history of the Brotherhood are Brynjar Lia, *The Society of the Muslim Brothers in Egypt: The Rise of an Islamic Mass Movement, 1928–1942*, Reading, UK: Ithaca/Garnet, 1998; Richard P. Mitchell, *The Society of the Muslim Brothers*, Oxford: Oxford University Press, 1969.

[27] Mitchell, *Society*, 52–5.

[28] *Ibid.*, 116–62.

[29] For a recent study on this subject, see Chris Harnisch and Quinn Mecham, 'Democratic Ideology in Islamist Opposition? The Muslim Brotherhood's "Civil State"', *Middle Eastern Studies*, vol. 45, no. 2, March 2009, 189–205.

religion more as a moral framework through which one can engage in politics.[30]

The second and – for this study – most important branch produced by the Brotherhood was a radical one that did not accept the legitimacy of the state and advocated the violent overthrow of its regime. This way of thinking was expressed most explicitly within the movement by one of its leading ideologues, Sayyid Qutb (1906–66). Imprisoned by the Nasser regime and executed in 1966, Qutb contended that Egyptian society lived in a state of pre-Islamic ignorance (*jāhiliyya*) that should be countered by an effort to re-establish the sovereignty of God (*ḥākimiyya*) through the use of jihad.[31] Qutb's ideas failed to have much long-term impact on the Brotherhood itself but influenced other, more radical Egyptian groups all the more. Organisations that developed in the 1970s and 1980s, such as the Islamic Jihad (responsible for the assassination of the Egyptian President Anwar al-Sadat in 1981)[32], al-Jamaʿa al-Islamiyya[33] and Jamaʿat al-Muslimin (better known as al-Takfir wa-l-Hijra)[34], were all in varying degrees influenced by radical ideas such as Qutb's.

30 See, for example, Joshua Stacher, 'Post-Islamist Rumblings in Egypt: The Emergence of the Wasat Party', *Middle East Journal*, vol. 56, no. 3, 2002, 415–32. A similar trend can be seen within the Jordanian Muslim Brotherhood. See Mohammad Suliman Abu Rumman, *The Muslim Brotherhood in the 2007 Jordanian Parliamentary Elections: A Passing 'Political Setback' or Diminished Popularity?* Amman: Friedrich-Ebert-Stiftung, 2007.

31 Sayed Khatab, '*Hakimiyyah* and *Jahiliyyah* in the Thought of Sayyid Qutb', *Middle Eastern Studies*, vol. 38, no. 3, 2002, 145–70; William E. Shepard, 'Sayyid Qutb's Doctrine of *Jāhiliyya*', *International Journal of Middle East Studies*, vol. 35, no. 4, 2003, 521–45. See also Sayyid Quṭb, *Milestones*, New Delhi: Islamic Book Service, 2005 [2001]. See also the original Arabic version (*Maʿālim fī l-Ṭarīq*) at www.tawhed.ws/a?a=r5kf57rg.

32 Johannes J. G. Jansen, *The Neglected Duty: The Creed of Sadat's Assassins and Islamic Resurgence in the Middle East*, New York & London: Macmillan, 1986; Gilles Kepel, *Muslim Extremism in Egypt: The Prophet and the Pharaoh* (transl. John Rothschild), Berkeley & Los Angeles: University of California Press, 2003 [1985].

33 Omar Ashour, 'Lions Tamed? An Inquiry into the Causes of De-Radicalization of Armed Islamist Movements: The Case of the Egyptian Islamic Group', *Middle East Journal*, vol. 61, no. 4, 2007, 596–625; Roel Meijer, 'Commanding Right and Forbidding Wrong as a Principle of Social Action: The Case of the Egyptian al-Jamaʿa al-Islamiyya', in: Roel Meijer (ed.), *Global Salafism: Islam's New Religious Movement*, London: Hurst & Co., 2009, 189–220.

34 See especially Saad Eddin Ibrahim's publications, including 'Anatomy of Egypt's Militant Islamic Groups: Methodological Note and Preliminary Findings', *International Journal of Middle East Studies*, vol. 12, 1980, 423–53; *id.*, 'Egypt's Islamic Activism in the 1980s', *Arab Studies Quarterly*, vol. 10, no. 2, April 1988, 632–57.

The Spread of Wahhabism

At the same time as the developments just described took place, another important trend could be discerned. Under pressure from the crackdown by Nasser's regime in Egypt and similarly repressive policies in other Arab states, many Muslim Brothers fled their home countries and settled in Saudi Arabia in the 1960s and 1970s. Saudi Arabia, a country governed on the basis of the strict and highly conservative Wahhabi ideology, welcomed the Muslim Brothers. The latter, through the influential positions they attained and their international networks, gave a much-needed boost to the efforts by Saudi Arabia to spread Wahhabism across the Muslim world. Through Saudi organisations such as the Muslim World League, founded in the early 1960s to counter the revolutionary socialist rhetoric of Nasser's regime, Muslim Brothers helped Saudi Arabia spread its Wahhabi message while rebuilding their own careers at the same time.[35]

Just as the revolutionary rhetoric coming from Egypt spurred Saudi Arabia to propagate Wahhabism as a counter message, the rhetoric emanating from the Islamic Revolution in Iran in 1979 further emphasised the need for Saudi Arabia to increase its efforts to provide Muslims with a conservative alternative to these radical ideas. Helped by the enormous wealth generated by soaring oil prices as a result of the 1973 oil crisis, Saudi Arabia therefore became increasingly active in spreading Wahhabism across the Muslim world.[36] Moreover, the booming oil-industry in the Gulf attracted many workers from across the Arab world. These men often became more conservative through their intensive contacts particularly with Saudi Arabia and took their new-found ideas with them when returning to their home countries. Thus, both through intense efforts to spread a Wahhabi message as well as through migrant-workers' experiences in the Gulf and Saudi Arabia in particular, a more conservative Salafi form of Islam spread across the Arab (and Muslim) world. This abetted an ongoing trend of increased religiosity in the Arab world as a result of the lost Arab-Israeli war in 1967, which severely discredited

[35] Gilles Kepel, *The War for Muslim Minds: Islam and the West* (transl. Pascale Ghazaleh), Cambridge, MA, & London: Belknap/Harvard University Press, 2004, 170–7, but see also Madawi al-Rasheed, *Contesting the Saudi State: Islamic Voices from a New Generation*, Cambridge: Cambridge University Press, 2007, 73–4.

[36] Saeed Shehabi, 'The Role of Religious Ideology in the Expansionist Policies of Saudi Arabia', in: Madawi al-Rasheed (ed.), *Kingdom without Borders: Saudi Arabia's Political, Religious and Media Frontiers*, London: Hurst & Co., 2008, 183–97.

Nasser's socialist message, and thereby helped create a favourable climate for Islamic movements.[37]

The 'Afghan Arab' Phenomenon

The Arab world in the 1960s, and particularly the 1970s and 1980s, thus saw two broad trends relevant for this study: a spread of radical ideas such as those of Qutb, especially in Egypt but also in other countries[38], and an increasing Salafi conservatism as a result of Saudi Wahhabi propaganda and Arabs working in the Gulf countries. In the midst of all this, the Soviet Union, in order to aid the fledgling Afghan communist regime as part of its Cold War efforts to expand its sphere of influence, invaded Afghanistan in 1979. At that point, the interests of several different actors dovetailed in such a way that a new phenomenon came about: the 'Afghan Arabs'. When Afghanistan was invaded, many newly committed Muslims in the Arab world saw it as their religious duty to help liberate Muslim Afghanistan from the communist Soviets. Since many Arab regimes had looked upon the greater religiosity of their populations – particularly when expressed through radicalism – with suspicion, they were eager to get rid of these men by sending them off to wage jihad against the Soviets in Afghanistan. As these efforts proved a good opportunity for Saudi Arabia to show its piety by propagating jihad and for the United States to fight its Cold War Soviet enemy by proxy, both countries supported the Afghan Arabs financially.[39]

Instrumental in the Arab efforts to liberate Afghanistan was a Palestinian Muslim Brother called ʿAbdallah ʿAzzam (1941–89). Having worked in Saudi Arabia as a lecturer at King ʿAbd al-ʿAziz University in Jeddah, where he taught the young Osama bin Laden, he became impressed by stories of Arab jihad fighters (*mujāhidūn*) from Afghanistan and decided to move to Peshawar in Pakistan. There, he set up the so-called Services Bureau (Maktab al-Khidmāt, MAK) to facilitate and organise the Arabs coming to fight the Soviets in Afghanistan. Through

[37] Gilles Kepel, *Jihad: The Trail of Political Islam* (transl. Anthony F. Roberts), Cambridge, MA: Belknap/Harvard University Press, 2002 [2000], 61–75.

[38] *Ibid.*, 66–7. For the example of Algeria, see for instance Kate Zebiri, 'Islamic Revival in Algeria: An Overview', *The Muslim World*, vol. 83, nos. 3–4, July-October 1993, 205–6.

[39] Anwar ul-Haq Ahady, 'Saudi Arabia, Iran and the Conflict in Afghanistan', in: William Malley (ed.), *Fundamentalism Reborn? Afghanistan and the Taliban*, New York: New York University Press, 117–9; Barnett Rubin, 'Arab Islamists in Afghanistan', in: John L. Esposito (ed.), *Political Islam: Revolution, Radicalism, or Reform?*, Boulder, CO, & London: Lynne Rienner Publishers, 1997, 184–9.

MAK, an international network of Arab fighters was built that included Osama bin Laden and Ayman al-Zawahiri and would later serve as the basis of what has become known as al-Qaʿida.[40]

It should be pointed out that the Afghan Arabs were not a homogeneous group of fighters. Some, like Bin Laden, had a Wahhabi (and thus Salafi) background, while others, including ʿAzzam himself, were part of the non-Salafi Muslim Brotherhood. As will become clear in Chapters 2 and 3, there are significant differences in how Islamic ideologues view jihad, and these differences were also present among *mujāhidūn* in Afghanistan. They concentrated on questions such as whether the *mujāhidūn* should focus on Afghanistan or also direct their efforts towards fighting their own regimes back home. Within these disputes, Osama bin Laden, whose great wealth propelled him to an important position among Afghan Arabs, increasingly tended to side with the latter position, propounded by Ayman al-Zawahiri amongst others, at the expense of his support for ʿAzzam, who held the former view. Bin Laden's and al-Zawahiri's trend was further strengthened when ʿAzzam was assassinated in 1989, shortly after the Soviet forces withdrew from Afghanistan.[41]

After the Soviet withdrawal in 1989, the conflict in Afghanistan did not stop, but continued for some years between various Afghan factions, sometimes with the help of Arabs. Around this time, and in the next few years, many Afghan Arabs decided to go home again. Despite (or probably because of) the fact that their countries had often not only allowed but even encouraged them to go to Afghanistan, they were not welcomed back. Although the experiences of the Afghan Arabs returning to their home countries cannot be generalised, it is clear that many of them failed to reintegrate into society and joined militant Jihadi-Salafi groups.[42] As we will see later, this experience proved to be of great importance in determining al-Maqdisi's influence.

40 Jason Burke, *Al-Qaeda: The True Story of Radical Islam*, London & New York: I.B. Tauris, 2003, 72–5; Bernard Rougier, 'Le Jihad en Afghanistan et l'émergence du salafisme-jihadisme', in: Bernard Rougier (ed.), *Qu'est-ce que le salafisme?*, Paris: Presses Universitaires de France, 2008, 67-8.

41 Rohan Gunaratna, *Inside al Qaeda: Global Network of Terror*, New York: Berkley, 2003, 29–36; Rougier, 'Jihad', 77–80. See also *id.*, *Everyday Jihad: The Rise of Militant Islam among Palestinians in Lebanon* (transl. Pascale Ghazaleh), Cambridge, MA, & London: Harvard University Press, 2007, 76–84.

42 Mohammed M. Hafez, 'Jihad After Iraq: Lessons from the Arab Afghans Phenomenon', *CTC Sentinel*, vol. 1, no. 4, March 2008, 1–4.

The Gulf War and Beyond

Apart from the important phenomenon of the returning Afghan Arabs, the late 1980s and early 1990s were an eventful time across the globe. The Berlin Wall fell and the Soviet Union collapsed, effectively ending the Cold War. In the Arab world, the Palestinian uprising against Israeli occupation – the intifada – started in 1987, while the Iran-Iraq war that had been waged throughout the 1980s came to a halt in 1988. Although most Arab countries had supported Iraq in this war, that country had been dealt some heavy blows, including financially. Since neighbouring Kuwait was flooding the market with cheap oil, thereby rendering Iraq unable to get back on its feet financially through its own oil profits, the Iraqi dictator Saddam Husayn decided to invade the country. This started another military conflict in the Persian Gulf, with an international coalition made up of Arab and Western armies succeeding in liberating Kuwait. Before that, however, Saudi Arabia decided to invite 500,000 U.S. soldiers to protect itself against any possible attempt by Iraq to invade that country too.

Both the relatively easy way in which the international coalition led by the United States, which only a few years before had supported Iraq in its war with Iran, pushed back Saddam Husayn's army, as well as the Saudi decision to allow half a million U.S. soldiers on its soil, led to a profound shock in the Arab world. International military intervention in a region that witnessed colonialism not so long ago, as well as the important role the United States – widely seen as complicit in Israel's treatment of the Palestinians – played in all of this, caused anger and resentment among many Arabs, including Islamists.[43] The reactions of Islamist movements in the Arab world to the Gulf War and the events surrounding it were diverse and often had to take into account that support for Saddam Husayn – widespread among the people in general – might lead to a decline in funding from countries such as Kuwait and Saudi Arabia.[44] In the latter country itself, however, the Gulf War and particularly the presence of U.S. soldiers on Saudi soil, sparked protests and the beginning of a strong opposition movement that – in its more radical forms – went

[43] James Piscatori, 'Religion and Realpolitik: Islamic Responses to the Gulf War', in: James Piscatori (ed.), *Islamic Fundamentalisms and the Gulf Crisis*, Chicago: The American Academy of Arts and Sciences, 1991, 3–18.

[44] For a good overview of Islamist reactions to the Gulf War, see James Piscatori (ed.), *Islamic Fundamentalisms and the Gulf Crisis*, Chicago: The American Academy of Arts and Sciences, 1991.

so far as to deny the legitimacy of the Saudi regime, as we will see in Chapters 4 and 5.

Although the impact of the Gulf War was probably less strong in other Arab countries than in Saudi Arabia, it stimulated further resentment against the West and certain Arab regimes. The extent to which this has influenced the development of radical Islam in the Arab world is unclear. It may well, however, have abetted the greater religiosity and Salafi conservatism as a result of the decline of Nasser's Arab socialism after 1967 and the spread of Wahhabism, as well as the increased radicalisation through the publications of Qutb and the return of the Afghan Arabs mentioned earlier. The latter factors certainly played a role in creating or developing Jihadi-Salafi movements (i.e., groups that combined Salafi ideas with jihad against their own regimes) in countries such as Jordan (see Chapter 8), Morocco[45], Egypt and Algeria. Through a combination of radical ideology and government repression, movements such as the Egyptian Jamaʿa Islamiyya and the Algerian Groupe Islamique Armée and the Groupe Salafiste pour la Prédication et le Combat became involved in a military conflict with their governments, leading to widespread arrests and thousands of casualties.[46]

The heavy fighting between the Arab states and the Jihadi-Salafi movements thus resulted in many members of the latter either ending up in prison or being killed. There was a third group of militants, however, who left their home countries – some for the second time – for Afghanistan. This country had become an attractive alternative to the repression at home since the strict regime of the Taliban began its rule there in 1996. One of the militants who moved to Afghanistan again was Osama bin Laden. He had gone back to his home country Saudi Arabia after the Soviet Union withdrew from Afghanistan but left again in 1992 to participate in the Islamic revolution in Sudan. When U.S. and Saudi pressure on Sudan mounted to expel Bin Laden, who had in the meantime become a

[45] See, for example, Abdessamad Dialmy, 'Le Terrorisme Islamiste au Maroc', *Social Compass*, vol. 52, no. 1, 2005, 67–82.

[46] For the Egyptian Jamaʿa Islamiyya's fight with the government, see Mohammed M. Hafez and Quintan Wiktorowicz, 'Violence as Contention in the Egyptian Islamic Movement', in: Quintan Wiktorowicz (ed.), *Islamic Activism: A Social Movement Theory Approach*, Bloomington & Indianapolis, Ind.: Indiana University Press, 2004, 77–80. On the various movements in Algeria and their bloody battle with the state, see Mohammed M. Hafez, 'From Marginalization to Massacres: A Political Process Explanation of GIA Violence in Algeria', in: Quintan Wiktorowicz (ed.), *Islamic Activism: A Social Movement Theory Approach*, Bloomington & Indianapolis, Ind.: Indiana University Press, 2004, 37–60.

terrorism suspect and had had his Saudi passport revoked in 1994 for his criticism of his home country, the Sudanese regime asked him to leave. He then left for Afghanistan again with his entourage and eventually set up the global jihad organisation we now know as al-Qaʿida on the basis of the MAK he had abandoned earlier.[47]

After the terrorist attacks of 11 September 2001, for which al-Qaʿida was responsible, the United States launched a war against the Taliban regime in Afghanistan, which refused to hand over Bin Laden. This conflict initiated what would become known as the American-led 'war on terror' and was followed by a military attack against Iraq in 2003 on the basis of that country's alleged possession of weapons of mass destruction and its supposed ties to al-Qaʿida. These wars and the widespread and increased resentment against the U.S. they brought about again led many Arabs to move to Afghanistan and this time also Iraq to fight the invading American and other Western armies, just as others had done in the 1980s. Several of the groups these men set up, as well as certain existing organisations, eventually 'joined' al-Qaʿida by presenting themselves as local affiliates of the mother organisation in Afghanistan/Pakistan, taking on names such as 'al-Qaʿida in the Land of the Two Rivers', 'al-Qaʿida on the Arabian Peninsula' and 'al-Qaʿida in the Islamic Maghrib'. These organisations seem to represent the latest stage in the development of Jihadi-Salafism in the Arab world.[48]

Jihadi-Salafi Ideologues

Jihadi-Salafism, as it developed in the Arab world over the past decades, was thus directly or indirectly influenced by the revolutions in Egypt and Iran in 1952 and 1979 respectively, the wars in Afghanistan and the Persian Gulf, as well as by ideological trends such as the spreading of Wahhabism and the ideas of Qutb. Apart from the latter, it is not clear what role individual ideologues have played in the development of Jihadi-Salafism. Since this highly ideological movement constantly seeks guidance and justification in the writings of its scholars, it is interesting to see what influence some of these people have had.

47 Mariam Abou Zahab and Olivier Roy, *Islamist Networks: The Afghan-Pakistan Connection* (transl. John King), New York: Columbia University Press, 2004, 13–18, 48–53.

48 There are also organisations that are clearly Jihādī-Salafī in nature but do not necessarily claim the name of al-Qāʿida, such as the Jihādī-Salafīs in Lebanon. See Rougier, *Everyday*; *id.*, 'Fatah al-Islam: Un Réseau Jihadiste au Cœur des Contradictions Libanaises', in: Bernard Rougier (ed.), *Qu'est-ce que le salafisme?* Paris: Presses Universitaires de France, 2008, 179–210.

Apart from the enormous media attention that some militant leaders have been given, several more serious publications have appeared about them too, such as about Abu Musʿab al-Zarqawi[49] and, of course, Osama bin Laden[50]. Among Jihadi-Salafi *ideologues*, however, only the ideas of al-Qaʿida strategist Abu Musʿab al-Suri[51] and the first leader of al-Qaʿida on the Arabian Peninsula, Yusuf al-ʿUyayri[52], have been dealt with in detail. Writings dealing with al-Maqdisi beliefs, in spite of his influence, only treat specific aspects of his ideology[53] or his alleged revisionism in later years.[54] Publications dealing with his ideology as a whole are rare and do not focus on his influence and how this should be explained.[55] Several authors have dealt with al-Maqdisi's influence on the Islamist

49 Fu'ād Ḥusayn, *Al-Zarqāwī: Al-Jīl al-Thānī li-l-Qāʿida*, Beirut: Dār al-Khayyāl, 2005; Loretta Napoleoni, *Insurgent Iraq: Al Zarqawi and the New Generation*, New York: Seven Stories Press, 2005.

50 Peter L. Bergen, *Holy War Inc.: Inside The Secret World of Osama bin Laden*, New York: Free Press, 2002; *id.*, *The Osama bin Laden I Know: An Oral History of Al-Qaeda's Leader*, New York: Free Press, 2006.

51 See the publications by Brynjar Lia on al-Sūrī, including *Architect of Global Jihad: The Life of al-Qaida Strategist Abu Musʿab Al-Suri*, London: Hurst & Co., 2007; *id.*, '"Destructive Doctrinairians": Abu Musʿab al-Suri's Critique of the Salafis in the Jihadi Current', in: Roel Meijer (ed.), *Global Salafism: Islam's New Religious Movement*, London: Hurst & Co., 2009, 281–300.

52 See Roel Meijer's publications, including 'Yūsuf al-ʿUyairī and the Making of a Revolutionary Salafi Praxis', *Die Welt des Islams*, vol. 47, 2007, nos. 3–4, 422–59; *id.*, 'Yusuf al-Uyairi and the Transnationalisation of Saudi Jihadism', in: Madawi al-Rasheed (ed.), *Kingdom without Borders: Saudi Arabia's Political, Religious and Media Frontiers*, London: Hurst & Co., 2008, 221–43.

53 Joas Wagemakers, 'Defining the Enemy: Abū Muḥammad al-Maqdisī's Radical Reading of Sūrat al-Mumtaḥana', *Die Welt des Islams*, vol. 48, nos. 3–4, 2008, 348–71; *id.*, 'The Transformation of a Radical Concept: *Al-Wala' wa-l-Bara'* in the Ideology of Abu Muhammad al-Maqdisi', in: Roel Meijer (ed.), *Global Salafism: Islam's New Religious Movement*, London: Hurst & Co., 2009, 81–106.

54 Nelly Lahoud, 'In Search of Philosopher-Jihadis: Abu Muhammad al-Maqdisi's Jihadi Philosophy', *Totalitarian Movements and Political Religions*, vol. 10, no. 2, 2009, 205–20; *id.*, *The Jihadis' Path to Self-Destruction*, London: Hurst & Co., 2011, 241–5; Joas Wagemakers, 'Reclaiming Scholarly Authority: Abu Muhammad al-Maqdisi's Critique of Jihadi Practices', *Studies in Conflict and Terrorism*, vol. 34, no. 7, 2011, 523–39.

55 Dirk Baehr, *Kontinuität und Wandel in der Ideologie des Jihadi-Salafismus: Eine ideentheoretische Analyse der Schriften von Abu Musʿab al-Suri, Abu Mohammed al-Maqdisi und Abu Bakr Naji*, Bonn: Bouvier, 2009, 117–36; Daurius Figueira, *Salafi Jihadi Discourse of Sunni Islam in the 21st Century: The Discourse of Abu Muhammad al-Maqdisi and Anwar al-Awlaki*, Bloomington, Ind.: iUniverse, Inc., 2011, pp. 1–76; Aḥmad Ḥusnī, 'Qirā'a fī Kitāb *Imtāʿ al-Naẓar fī Kashf Shubhāt Murji'at al-ʿAṣr*', *Al-Misbār*, no. 5, May 2007, 167–73; Ṭāhir al-Sharqāwī, 'Abū Muḥammad al-Maqdisī... Thunā'iyyat al-Muqaddas wa-l-ʿUnf', *Al-Misbār*, no. 5, May 2007, 131–43; Joas Wagemakers, 'A "Purist Jihadi-Salafi": The Ideology of Abu Muhammad al-Maqdisi', *British Journal of Middle Eastern Studies*, vol. 36, no. 2, August 2009, 283–99.

opposition in Saudi Arabia but only in a very narrow way and, since it was not the focus of their research, just very superficially.[56] In short, despite his widely acknowledged importance, there is a huge gap in the current academic literature on al-Maqdisi's influence on Jihadi-Salafis and how this can be explained. This book tries to fill this gap by focussing precisely on these issues.

Theoretical Framework, Methodology and Sources

Framing

The past few years have seen an increasing number of publications devoted to Islamic movements analysed with the use of Social Movement Theory (SMT). More a collection of theoretical concepts than a clear-cut theory per se, SMT has existed for decades and has, in various forms, been used to analyse numerous American and European social movements as well as those in the Arab world. One aspect of SMT that is particularly useful and relevant for this study, since it deals with ideas and how people are influenced by them, is 'framing'. The term is derived from 'frames', a concept that refers to the 'schemata of interpretation' that allow 'its users to locate, perceive, identify, and label a seemingly infinite number of concrete occurrences defined in its terms'.[57] In other words, frames are prisms through which people view, explain and interpret themselves and the rest of the world and that colour and influence their perceptions.

The concept of 'framing' was incorporated into SMT by scholars such as Snow and Benford, who have pointed out that social movements and other contentious actors often portray events and people in a certain way so as to draw people's attention, arouse their interest and – ideally – get them involved in action for a certain cause. Successful efforts by movements or other contentious actors to make their own frames resonate with any particular audience are referred to as 'frame resonance' or 'frame alignment'.[58] This is obviously an important factor in order for people to join a movement or follow a certain person.

[56] Thomas Hegghammer and Stéphane Lacroix, 'Rejectionist Islamism in Saudi Arabia: The Story of Juhayman al-ʿUtaybi Revisited', *International Journal of Middle East Studies*, vol. 39, no. 1, 2007, 115–16; al-Rasheed, *Contesting*, 121–5.

[57] Erving Goffman, *Frame Analysis: An Essay on the Organization of Experience*, New York: Harper & Row, 1974, 21.

[58] See David A. Snow et al., 'Frame Alignment Processes, Micromobilization, and Movement Participation', *American Sociological Review*, vol. 51, August 1986, 464–81; David

Frames should preferably be broad so as to appeal to as large a group as possible, but also incorporate concepts that resonate with people's beliefs. Framers therefore often make use of aspects of people's culture to achieve frame resonance. One author, in an oft-cited article, even refers to culture as a '"tool kit" of symbols, stories, rituals, and world views' from which framers can take various aspects to make their ideas resonate.[59] Consequently, aspects of culture, religion or other values that people hold dear are often used in framing by movements and other actors. In the case of Islamist groups and ideologues, framers obviously make use of Islam a great deal. Such frames have included the Palestinian Hamas's view (adopted from the Muslim Brotherhood from which it sprang) that the conflict with Israel can only be dealt with through Islam ('Islam is the solution') or that the Palestinians were actually fighting not just a state but a worldwide Jewish conspiracy.[60] Other examples include military conflicts in Muslim countries such as Iraq or Afghanistan, which are framed by some Islamic ideologues as not just political issues but actually attacks on Islam itself.[61]

Despite the fact that framing is all about ideas, it should not be equated or confused with ideology. Whereas the term 'ideology' – whose definition is certainly not agreed upon – refers to a more or less complex system of ideas and concepts that are at least to a certain extent interconnected, frames are much simpler, as the examples given earlier show. Moreover, frames are flexible and adaptable and can be highly successful in some situations but fail utterly in others. The example of Islam being framed as 'under attack' mentioned earlier, for example, undoubtedly draws part of its popularity from the fact that several Muslim countries are involved in military conflicts with non-Muslim states. One can imagine that the same frame would be far less resonant in the absence of such conflicts and the

A. Snow and Robert D. Benford, 'Ideology, Frame Resonance, and Participant Mobilization', in: Bert Klandermans, Hanspeter Kriesi and Sidney Tarrow (eds.), *International Social Movement Research, Vol. I: From Structure to Action – Comparing Social Movement Research Across Cultures*, Greenwich, CT, & London: JAI Press, 1988, 197–217.

59 Ann Swidler, 'Culture in Action: Symbols and Strategies', *American Sociological Review*, vol. 51, April 1986, 273.

60 Glenn E. Robinson, 'Hamas as Social Movement', in: Quintan Wiktorowicz (ed.), Islamic Activism: *A Social Movement Theory Approach*, Bloomington & Indianapolis, Ind.: Indiana University Press, 2004, 130–2.

61 Joas Wagemakers, 'Framing the "Threat to Islam": *Al-Wala' wa-l-Bara'* in Salafi Discourse', *Arab Studies Quarterly*, vol. 30, no. 4, 2008, 1–22.

daily media attention for them.[62] It is this reciprocal relationship between ideas on the one hand and the political and socio-economic context in which they are spread on the other that makes the framing perspective so useful. Besides paying attention to contextual factors, this study therefore draws on the insights and concepts derived from framing to help explain al-Maqdisi's (lack of) influence among certain people. In this context, it is important to point out that framing will not be used here, as it sometimes is by other scholars, to analyse the mobilisational success of frames. In that sense, one could argue that al-Maqdisi has utterly failed to mobilise anything more than a tiny fraction of believers, considering the small minority of Jihadi-Salafis among more than a billion Muslims worldwide. My objective is rather to concentrate on those Muslims who do espouse Jihadi-Salafi or broadly similar ideas, and analyse why they were (not) influenced by al-Maqdisi and his writings.

Methodology

This book addresses the question: Why has al-Maqdisi been so influential on the Jihadi-Salafi movement? To be able to answer this question, however, we must first find out what al-Maqdisi's influence has been. To learn more about this, I first made use of search engines on Jihadi-Salafi websites such as www.tawhed.ws to find out what authors cite al-Maqdisi's works or name him as an important scholar. I subsequently analysed the content and origin of these citations. Presuming that not all people who have been influenced by al-Maqdisi have actually mentioned him or his works by name, I also employed another method that entailed finding out what (if anything) makes al-Maqdisi's writings unique. I subsequently tried to find the concepts, ideas or arguments first or only formulated in al-Maqdisi's works in the writings of other scholars. Although this method is not 100 percent secure, I have found scholars whose books do not mention al-Maqdisi or his writings by name but have nevertheless most probably been influenced by him.

It is very well possible that al-Maqdisi's influence is greater than the research based on the methodology described here shows. This has to do partly with the obvious impossibility of talking to each and every person who might possibly have read al-Maqdisi's books, but it also has to do with the fact that people may be influenced by aspects of his writings that are not uniquely his. If, in such a case, they do not mention him or

[62] See, for example, Brynjar Lia, 'Al-Qaida's Appeal: Understanding its Unique Selling Points', *Perspectives on Terrorism*, vol. 2, no. 8, 2008, 3–10, esp. 2–3.

his writings by name, it is impossible for a researcher to conclude on the basis of these texts alone whether any influence of al-Maqdisi's has taken place. Although suspicions in this direction may be confirmed by further research in the form of interviews, the subject of this study – a branch of Islam whose most important adherents are often dead, imprisoned or in highly inaccessible places – makes that unlikely, too.

After having established what al-Maqdisi's influence has been, we can try to answer the question as to why al-Maqdisi has been influential. The method employed here was to start with an extensive reading of the literature on framing so as to establish what constitutes a good and successful frame, when frame alignment can be expected and what techniques framers use to achieve this. I then moved on to al-Maqdisi's writings to try and find these characteristics and features there. After I identified the factors in his writings that, according to framing theory, would be decisive in determining the frame's and the framer's influence, I checked the validity of these claims with – where and when possible – (former) followers of al-Maqdisi, his direct students, former fellow inmates, his friends, acquaintances and opponents as well as al-Maqdisi himself to find out whether these factors were indeed the causal factors of his influence that framing theory suggests.

Sources

Apart from the extensive secondary literature, magazine and newspaper articles on radical Islam in the Arab world, the sources used in this study consist of the writings of al-Maqdisi himself, as found on his website, as well as the writings of many other (Jihadi-) Salafis that have either been influenced by him or are important for other reasons. Most of these sources are in Arabic, but some are also in English and include books, articles, communiqués, letters, sermons and fatwas. All Internet sources used in this book were still available in July 2011, unless indicated otherwise.[63]

A second source used for this study consists of some forty semi-structured personal interviews with Arab journalists covering radical Islam, opponents as well as (former) followers of al-Maqdisi, his direct students, his former cellmates, friends, acquaintances and al-Maqdisi

[63] Some sources have multiple titles, which may be confusing sometimes. The URLs given provide direct access to the correct source, however. References to page numbers are always to the Word- or PDF-versions of a document, not to their HTML-formats, unless that was the only format available.

himself. These interviews were conducted in Jordan, Saudi Arabia, England and Lebanon, as well as by phone or e-mail in the period 2008–9. Some of these interviewees have been interviewed many times before by researchers – although not with regard to al-Maqdisi specifically – while others have (as far as I know) never been interviewed for this purpose before. Considering the fact that the ideological backgrounds of the interviewees range from radical Islamist to anti-Islamist, from deeply religious to highly secular and from academic to uneducated, it is interesting to see that each of them has, from his own perspective, contributed to a coherent and consistent image of al-Maqdisi and his influence, as we will see.

Overview

In Part I, I will first give an overview of his life and his development as a scholar in Chapter 1. This shows that the notion of a 'quietist Jihadi-Salafi' can clearly be discerned from the people and writings that influenced him. Chapters 2 and 3 deal with al-Maqdisi's ideology and its application in today's Muslim world, respectively, both viewed in the context of the larger spectrum of radical Islamic ideologues. As we will see in later chapters, al-Maqdisi's writings have changed throughout the years in their choice of topics, but he has remained remarkably consistent in his beliefs, and the ideology described in Chapters 2 and 3 has been the core of his doctrine for over a quarter century. These two chapters also show that al-Maqdisi, while certainly not the only Jihadi-Salafi ideologue, should be seen as a radical thinker but one who differs from others in his closeness to the quietist Salafi *ʿaqīda* and *manhaj*, justifying the label 'quietist Jihadi-Salafi'.

As mentioned, it would be impossible for any researcher to try to find each and every person who has been influenced by al-Maqdisi, analyse what this influence has been and why it has taken place. The barriers of language, time and money are too great for any researcher to overcome. This study therefore concentrates on those areas where al-Maqdisi's influence has been most pronounced, namely the Islamic opposition in Saudi Arabia, the development of the concept of *al-walāʾ wa-l-barāʾ* (loyalty and disavowal) and the Jihadi-Salafi movement in Jordan. As mentioned, al-Maqdisi's influence has been greater only in these areas. There is little reason, however, to assume that in all those other places, al-Maqdisi has been much more than simply one of a number of scholars considered very important. In the areas treated in the more or less chronologically arranged Chapters 4 to 9, on the other hand, al-Maqdisi has had a significant impact.

Part II deals with al-Maqdisi's influence on the Islamic opposition in Saudi Arabia in the period 1989 to 2005. This period, beginning with his book *Al-Kawashif al-Jaliyya fi Kufr al-Dawla al-Saʿudiyya* in 1989 and ending with the fall of the Saudi branch of al-Qaʿida in 2005, saw a rising influence of al-Maqdisi's writings after the Gulf War in 1990. In Chapter 4, I show that al-Maqdisi's writings had a limited impact on the ideological underpinnings of the protests caused by this war but, as we will see in Chapter 5, were highly influential on al-Qaʿida on the Arabian Peninsula in 2003–5. I argue that this can be explained by al-Maqdisi's timely contribution to the shocks caused by the Gulf War, but mostly by his excellent framing that – though clearly jihadi in nature – seemed tailor-made for a Saudi audience raised on the quietist writings of the Wahhabi tradition.

Part III traces al-Maqdisi's influence on the concept of *al-walāʾ wa-l-barāʾ* from 1984 onwards, the year when his important book *Millat Ibrahim* was written. Chapter 6 shows what al-Maqdisi's exact contribution has been to the idea that it is inadmissible to ask non-Muslims for help (*al-istiʿāna bi-l-kuffār*), particularly at a time of war, an important aspect of *al-walāʾ wa-l-barāʾ*. Chapter 7 makes clear how al-Maqdisi has made an original contribution to *al-walāʾ wa-l-barāʾ* by interpreting the concept in a legislative way. I argue that his (lack of) influence on others in this respect can be explained by pointing to al-Maqdisi's cleverly framed arguments, which are often very close to those of quietist Salafis (Chapter 6), and his difficult framing efforts as a result of having an audience that seems to have no need for his legislative version of *al-walāʾ wa-l-barāʾ* (Chapter 7).

Part IV deals with al-Maqdisi's influence on the Jordanian Jihadi-Salafi community from the time he moved to that country in 1992 until 2009. His impact on this community can be found in his personal role as an important shaykh (Chapter 8) and his specific writings against the Jordanian regime, quietist Salafis and those al-Maqdisi claims go to extremes in applying *takfīr* (Chapter 9). This can be explained, I argue, by looking respectively at his ability to provide an ideological foundation for a budding Jihadi-Salafi community in disarray in the early 1990s and his strong position in so-called framing disputes with the state and quietist Salafis. At the same time, however, his inability to present his criticism of extremists in such a way as to achieve widespread resonance among them caused some to abandon his ideas.

The notion of al-Maqdisi's being a 'quietist Jihadi-Salafi' is the thread running through all these chapters as the main explanation for his influence and his lack thereof. This is dealt with throughout the quarter century between 1984 and 2009. Since this study focuses on al-Maqdisi's influence as an ideologue rather than on his life, the former year was chosen because that is when al-Maqdisi wrote his first important book, *Millat Ibrahim*. The latter year was chosen because he was imprisoned in 2010 and has produced few writings since then.

PART I

AL-MAQDISI'S LIFE AND HIS PLACE IN THE JIHADI IDEOLOGICAL SPECTRUM, 1959–2009

1

Wavering between Quietism and Jihadism

> He is Abu Muhammad ʿAsim b. Muhammad b. Tahir al-Barqawi, known as al-Maqdisi, of ʿUtaybi descent, from the village of Barqa in the district of Nablus.[1]

As straightforward as these words may sound, they bring up a lot of questions. If al-Maqdisi was born in Barqa (also pronounced as Burqa), a small village on the West Bank, why does he call himself 'al-Maqdisi' (the Jerusalemite)? Moreover, if he is Palestinian – whether from Barqa or from Jerusalem – how can he claim to be ʿUtaybi (i.e., of the central Arabian ʿUtayba tribe)? In fact, why does he mention this at all? Such questions show that the quote opening this chapter is not as simple as it seems. In fact, al-Maqdisi's name is exemplary of his life in general in the sense that much of it is unknown in the existing information about him. As we will see in Chapter 5, however, seemingly trivial things such as al-Maqdisi's name and descent proved to be quite important to certain people.

This chapter starts with al-Maqdisi's childhood years in the West Bank and Kuwait, before moving on to the important period of his life spent studying in Saudi Arabia and writing and teaching in Pakistan/Afghanistan, where he came into contact with people who would later play major roles in al-Qaʿida. Finally, we will focus on the period since 1992, when al-Maqdisi moved to Jordan, where he still lives

[1] These were the first words of al-Maqdisī's biography on his website (www.tawhed.ws/a?a=2qrikosd) until January or February 2009. Soon after that, his biography was expanded to include more details.

(in prison since September 2010) and became embroiled in a troubled relationship with Abu Musʿab al-Zarqawi, and started becoming the major radical ideologue he is today. This chapter concentrates on the first fifty years of al-Maqdisi's life (1959–2009) and shows that his quietist Jihadi-Salafism is a position that he slowly but surely acquired through multiple and rather diverse Islamic sources.

Al-Maqdisi's Childhood Years

Abu Muhammad al-Maqdisi was born in 1959 as ʿIsam al-Barqawi. He later took on the linguistically related name ʿAsim instead of ʿIsam[2] because the former was also the name of several companions of the Prophet Muhammad and the latter may be used for both men and women.[3] His *nisba*[4] ('al-Maqdisi'), however, has proved most puzzling to many, particularly in combination with his claim that he is also ʿUtaybi. The answer lies in the fact that the ʿUtayba tribe has two main branches, Barqa and Ruqa. The latter has a sub-branch called Hafi, to which al-Maqdisi belongs. He therefore is a descendent of the Ruqa branch of the ʿUtayba tribe, not its Barqa branch. Al-Maqdisi's surname 'al-Barqawi' is not of tribal but of geographical origin; it was derived from the village where he was born. The name 'al-Maqdisi', finally, has nothing to do with his own origins but is simply a reference to the most important city nearest to where al-Maqdisi was born. Therefore, if one were to include all the parts of al-Maqdisi's name, it would be Abu Muhammad ʿIsam/ʿAsim b. Tahir b. Muhammad al-Barqawi al-Maqdisi al-Hafi al-Ruqi al-ʿUtaybi.[5]

Several families, including some of al-Maqdisi's ancestors, moved from Najd in Saudi Arabia to Barqa, just as the Sayf tribe from Yemen did. Because of the Arabian origin of these tribes, it has been suggested that Barqa is actually a Hanbali village in the midst of the overwhelmingly Shafiʿi Palestinian region.[6] Even if this is true, it did not affect al-Maqdisi, who remembers very little about his early childhood in Barqa. Growing

[2] See Abū Muḥammad al-Maqdisī, *Liqā' min Khalf Quḍbān al-Murtaddīn 'Sana 1418'*, www.tawhed.ws/r?i=j44n2568, 1997, 2.

[3] Abū Muḥammad al-Maqdisī, e-mail message to the author, 3 October 2009.

[4] The term *nisba* in Arabic names refers to the connection between a person and his or her region, city or tribe of origin, school of law or school of thought. In al-Maqdisī's case, his name refers to Jerusalem.

[5] Interviews with Abū Muḥammad al-Maqdisī, Amman, 13 January 2009; Mishārī al-Dhāyidī, Riyadh, 8 November 2008; ʿAbd al-Raḥmān b. ʿAbd al-ʿAzīz al-Hadlaq, Riyadh, 26 November 2008. See also *Al-Sharq al-Awsaṭ*, 7 July 2005.

[6] Interview with Fahad al-Shāfī, Riyadh, 11 November 2009.

up as the eldest child of a farmer with only one sister, his small family was initially quite poor and lived in a house with al-Maqdisi's grandfather. Their situation improved, however, because al-Maqdisi's father worked his way up financially to become a nurse in a hospital and the family were able to afford their own house. Only a few years after al-Maqdisi was born, the family moved to Kuwait to find work there.[7]

Growing up in Kuwait

Al-Maqdisi's family was part of a large group of Palestinians moving to Kuwait. As a result of the 1948 war in Palestine, many Palestinians fled, were driven out or emigrated from their homeland and went into exile. Several hundreds of them, mostly highly educated professionals, ended up in Kuwait. Because their arrival coincided with the discovery of oil in Kuwait, they came to play a significant role in the Kuwaiti bureaucracy needed to cope with the country's newly founded industry. A second wave of Palestinians came in the 1950s and early 1960s, consisting mostly of uneducated labourers and farmers. Palestinian immigration further increased when the country waived any visa requirements for Jordanians (including people from the West Bank, which was part of Jordan from 1948–67) in the late 1950s.[8] The swelling numbers of Palestinian immigrants in Kuwait and the social change that took place as a result of their arrival eventually led to greater restrictions on immigration in the late 1960s, however. Still, in 1970 there were more than 140,000 Palestinians in Kuwait.[9] Twenty years later, when the decision by the Palestine Liberation Organisation (PLO) to support Saddam Husayn during the Gulf War led to the mass expulsion of the Palestinians from Kuwait, their number had grown to 400,000, of whom 350,000 were Jordanians (including West Bankers).[10]

7 Interview with al-Maqdisī, Amman, 13 January 2009. The exact age at which al-Maqdisī moved to Kuwait is not entirely clear, but it is certainly when he was only a small child. See Jamāl Khāshuqjī and Yāsir Abū Hilāla, 'Al-Munaẓẓir al-Fikrī li-Munaffidhī nfijār al-Riyāḍ: Al-'Unf Farīḍa, al-Dīmūqrāṭiyya Shirk!', *Al-Wasaṭ*, no. 235, 29 July–4 August 1996, 14.

8 Shafeeq Ghabra, 'Palestinians in Kuwait: The Family and the Politics of Survival', *Journal of Palestine Studies*, vol. 17, no. 2, 1988, 63; Ann M. Lesch, 'Palestinians in Kuwait', *Journal of Palestine Studies*, vol. 20, no. 4, 1991, 42–3; Yann Le Troquer and Rozenn Hommery al-Oudat, 'From Kuwait to Jordan: The Palestinians' Third Exodus', *Journal of Palestine Studies*, vol. 28, no. 3, 1999, 37–8.

9 Troquer and Hommery al-Oudat, 'Kuwait', 38.

10 Lamia Radi, 'Les Palestiniens du Koweit en Jordanie', *Monde Arabe Maghreb Machrek*, no. 144, April-June 1994, 55.

The arrival of the Barqawi family in Kuwait was part of the second wave of Palestinian immigrants. Al-Maqdisi's father eventually got a job at the Ministry of Health and the family were relatively well-off.[11] Significantly, al-Maqdisi's parents were not very religious people. His mother, according to al-Maqdisi himself, only prayed very rarely, and his father never prayed at all. It was therefore not his parents who inspired him to become more religious but his friends from the neighbourhood and school, with whom he went to the mosque to pray and listen to the Friday sermon. Al-Maqdisi himself states that this period, when he was a young teenager, was the start of his becoming religious.[12]

Because of his growing religiosity, al-Maqdisi wanted to study Islam at the Islamic University of Medina, a renowned institute of Islamic learning. His parents, however, wanted him to study engineering or medicine. In the end, al-Maqdisi decided to leave Kuwait and go to the former Yugoslavia. An originally Syrian scholar who was a great source of influence on al-Maqdisi in his teenage years in Kuwait, Muhammad Surur, had some Muslim friends at the University of Sarajevo, and al-Maqdisi, together with two friends who graduated with him from secondary school, decided they would continue their studies there. They soon found out, however, that the classes would not be in English but in Serbian. Although the three boys did study that language for several months, they quickly realised that it was too difficult for them. Moreover, al-Maqdisi claims that the fact that women and girls were present and mingled with the men and boys at the university in Sarajevo was not to his liking at the time. He subsequently decided to go to the University of Mosul in Iraq to study biology.[13]

Although the language obviously proved to be no problem in Mosul, certain things had not changed. Al-Maqdisi was still not studying religion and he was again at a university where men and women sat together in classrooms. Moreover, the political climate in Iraq in the early 1980s was not very welcoming. In 1980, the war between Iraq and Iran started, and when al-Maqdisi tried to get more acquainted with Islamist movements and ideology, he was once arrested for two days for 'having Islamic books'[14]. When he returned to Kuwait for a holiday and like-minded friends confronted him with their belief that it was forbidden to attend

[11] Khāshuqjī and Abū Hilāla, 'Al-Munaẓẓir', 14.
[12] Interview with al-Maqdisī, Amman, 13 January 2009.
[13] *Ibid.*
[14] Khāshuqjī and Abū Hilāla, 'Al-Munaẓẓir', 14.

a university where men and women mingled freely, he therefore decided to quit his study and finally pursue his long-cherished dream: studying religion in Saudi Arabia.[15]

Becoming a Quietist Jihadi-Salafi

The Palestinian community of Kuwait in the 1960s, 1970s and 1980s, in which al-Maqdisi grew up and to which he returned after abandoning his studies in Iraq, was a highly politicised one, as may be expected of people who partly arrived as a result of the conflict with Israel and were heavily influenced by the Kuwaiti branch of the PLO.[16] The fact that most of them were not allowed to integrate into society and become Kuwaiti citizens probably also played a role in maintaining their strong Palestinian identity. Research among Palestinian children in Kuwait in the 1970s has shown that most of them saw themselves first and foremost as Palestinians – even if they had never actually been in Palestine – as well as that many had strong anti-Jewish feelings and a very pronounced love of their homeland.[17] This patriotism and sense of being Palestinian could be found among the dominant Palestinian factions such as Fatah, but also among members of the Palestinian branch of the Muslim Brotherhood in Kuwait.[18]

Sowing the Seeds of Salafism

Amidst the Kuwaiti Palestinians who had a strong love of their homeland, al-Maqdisi appears to have been somewhat of an exception. He never seems to have had a strong Palestinian identity – anathema to the strictly religious (as opposed to nationalist) ideas of Salafism – and openly admits that the Palestinian question plays only a marginal role in his writings at best.[19] The mosque he attended when he was 16 or 17 years old was run by a group of people that included an Egyptian preacher called Hasan Ayyub and a man named Gharib Tawba, who were both in their 40s and members of the Muslim Brotherhood. Consequently, the sermons of Ayyub were often about the alleged faults of Muslim rulers and politics in

15 Interview with al-Maqdisī, Amman, 13 January 2009.

16 Mouin Rabbani, 'The Making of a Palestinian Islamist Leader: An Interview with Khalid Mishal: Part I', *Journal of Palestine Studies*, vol. 37, no. 3, 2008, 62–3.

17 Tawfic E. Farah, 'Political Socialization of Palestinian Children in Kuwait', *Journal of Palestine Studies*, vol. 6, no. 4, July 1977, 90–102.

18 Rabbani, 'Making', 63–6.

19 Interview with Abū Muḥammad al-Maqdisī, al-Ruṣayfa, 17 January 2009.

the Arab world. Al-Maqdisi liked this political message of an Islam critical of the rulers, and slowly but surely came to believe that the regimes in the Muslim world were illegitimate and even 'infidel' on the basis of what he saw as their less than perfectly Islamic rule and conduct. He was never really satisfied with Ayyub's Brotherhood-flavoured message, however, and eventually gravitated towards the supposedly more purist message of Salafism.[20] He found some of the answers he was looking for in the teachings of the aforementioned Muhammad Surur.[21]

Surur, whose full name is Muhammad Surur Zayn al-ʿAbidin, was one of the Muslim Brothers from Syria who fled the regime there in 1965 and went to Saudi Arabia, where he adopted a more Salafi approach and was instrumental in promoting a politicised version of Wahhabism in the kingdom.[22] He left the country for Kuwait in 1973 and stayed there for ten years, when he moved to London and later to Jordan. While maintaining the politicised discourse of the Muslim Brotherhood, Surur was influenced by Salafi scholars such as Ibn ʿAbd al-Wahhab and used some of their writings to criticise political rulers. He subsequently rejected the unquestioning loyalty of some Wahhabi scholars to the Saudi state but, significantly, also condemned attempts to overthrow regimes as he believed this would lead to civil strife (*fitna*).[23]

It was precisely Surur's combination of criticism of the political rulers, which would later feature so prominently in al-Maqdisi's own writings, and his use of some important Salafi sources that attracted al-Maqdisi. He was, however, looking for more than just a Salafi-*inspired* ideologue. Although al-Maqdisi now admits that Surur was the best he could find at the time, he later rejected the man's teachings.[24] He was thus not completely satisfied, and continued studying and reading, looking for more Salafi answers than Surur's to the questions he had. In his search, he became acquainted with the radical but essentially non-Salafi writings of Sayyid Qutb. Al-Maqdisi admired Qutb's *takfīr* of the rulers and his call to fight jihad against them, but at the same time acknowledged

20 For more on Salafism in Kuwait, see Carine Lahoud, 'Koweït: salafismes et rapports au pouvoir', in: Bernard Rougier (ed.), *Qu'est-ce que le salafisme?*, Paris: Presses Universitaires de France, 2008, 123–35.

21 Interview with al-Maqdisī, Amman, 13 January 2009.

22 Kepel, *War*, 176–7.

23 Al-Rasheed, *Contesting*, 73–7.

24 Abū Muḥammad al-Maqdisī, e-mail message to the author, 18 May 2009.

that Qutb made mistakes.[25] He believes, however, that many Salafis discard Qutb's ideas simply because he was not a Salafi but fail to understand how valuable those ideas are. While al-Maqdisi shares some of the Salafi criticism of Qutb, such as that his arguments and reasoning as well as his clothes and appearance are not strictly Salafi, his own writings have come to the same conclusion as Qutb's – the rulers are infidels and their laws are un-Islamic – but they have been re-reasoned in a Salafi way.[26]

Al-Maqdisi was also influenced by the ideas of Juhayman al-ʿUtaybi's followers. Juhayman (d. 1980), the Saudi leader of the group of rebels that occupied the Grand Mosque of Mecca for two weeks in 1979, had developed a radical Salafi discourse that was, however, quite disorganised and explicitly did not apply *takfīr* to the rulers of Saudi Arabia[27], with which al-Maqdisi disagreed.[28] Other scholars with whom al-Maqdisi was acquainted in the late 1970s and early 1980s included Yusuf ʿId, Sami Dallal and the originally Egyptian political Salafi scholar Abu ʿAbdallah ʿAbd al-Rahman b. ʿAbd al-Khaliq. Importantly, he had also become acquainted with the teachings of major Salafi scholars such as Muhammad Nasir al-Din al-Albani (d. 1999) and ʿAbd al-ʿAziz b. Baz (d. 1999) and found their books enlightening and extremely useful. Because of their politically quietist approach to religion, however, al-Maqdisi states that they did not succeed in providing him with the combination of full-blown Salafism and *takfīr* of the rulers that he was looking for. It thus seems that all these names show that al-Maqdisi was trying to obtain knowledge from various Islamist and Salafi-oriented sources but failed to find exactly what he was looking for. His search would end when he finally reached Saudi Arabia and stayed there for a year, a period he describes as 'the most important period in my intellectual life' (*ahamm fatra fī ḥayātī l-ʿilmī*), when he became – in his own words – 'a *real* Salafi'.[29]

25 *Id.*, *Majmūʿ Fatāwā l-Shaykh Abū* [sic] *Muḥammad al-Maqdisī*, n.p.: Muʾassasat Arḍ al-Ribāṭ al-Iʿlāmiyya, 2007, 105–6; *id.*, *Mīzān al-Iʿtidāl fī Taqyīm Kitāb ʻAl-Mawrid al-Zulālʼ*, www.tawhed.ws/r?i=aerucf47, 2001 [1987].

26 Interviews with al-Maqdisī, Amman, 13 January 2009; al-Ruṣayfa, 17 January 2009.

27 Juhaymān b. Sayf al-ʿUtaybī, *Risālat al-Imāra wa-l-Bayʿa wa-l-Ṭāʿa wa-Ḥukm Talbīs al-Ḥukkām ʿalā Ṭalabat al-ʿIlm wa-l-ʿĀmma*, www.tawhed.ws/r?i=fcchouzr, n.d., 9, 12, 26.

28 Interview with al-Maqdisī, al-Ruṣayfa, 17 January 2009; Abū Muḥammad al-Maqdisī, *Al-Kawāshif al-Jaliyya fī Kufr al-Dawla al-Saʿūdiyya*, www.tawhed.ws/t, 2000/1 [1989], 188.

29 Interviews with al-Maqdisī, Amman, 13 January 2009; al-Ruṣayfa, 17 January 2009.

Studying in Saudi Arabia

When al-Maqdisi quit his studies in Iraq, he decided to write letters to the major shaykhs in Saudi Arabia, asking them if he might be allowed to study at the Islamic University of Medina instead of war-torn Mosul where, al-Maqdisi wrote, he had to study with women.[30] Although he was never officially accepted as a student, al-Maqdisi did eventually travel to Saudi Arabia for the *ʿumra* and the *ḥajj*, the annual minor and major pilgrimage to Mecca, where he overstayed his visa to be able to study. After being told by Ibn Baz, probably the most important scholar in the country at the time and later the mufti of the kingdom, that he could make use of the university's facilities without actually being an official student, al-Maqdisi began studying as much as he could. One particular and – in hindsight – life-changing moment came when he went to the library of the Prophet's mosque in Medina, where he became acquainted with the long tradition of Wahhabism through *Al-Durar al-Saniyya*, a multi-volume collection of major Wahhabi writings. He passionately told me about how this was an eye-opener to him:

> In the small library, there was an old book. [...] It was called *Al-Durar al-Saniyya fi l-Ajwibat al-Najdiyya*. And I saw this old book for the very first time then. I was still a youngster. I took the book and I opened it...I read and I read and I read! It was my first time and I read a very large part of the book! It offered tools! It connected the fatwas of the Najdi imams with the period that we live in![31]

This experience, and the other Wahhabi writings he encountered during this visit to the library and on other occasions, finally gave al-Maqdisi what he was looking for. It provided him with the fully Salafi arguments, concepts (such as *al-walāʾ wa-l-barāʾ*) and ideas that he wanted but, unlike the writings of al-Albani and Ibn Baz, these applied *takfīr* more easily. It was this combination of unadulterated Salafism on the one hand and the tools for excommunication of the rulers on the other that he had sought from others but had never found. Since both quietist Salafis and al-Maqdisi drew heavily from the writings of these 'imams of the Najdi propagation' (*aʾimmat al-daʿwa al-Najdiyya*), as the major eighteenth- and nineteenth-century Wahhabi scholars are referred to, al-Maqdisi's arguments and reasoning – though ultimately leading to a radical conclusion – came very close to those of quietist Salafis.[32]

[30] Abū Muḥammad al-Maqdisī, *Sayfān wa-Nakhla*, www.tawhed.ws/r?i=16100901, 2009.
[31] Interview with al-Maqdisī, Amman, 13 January 2009.
[32] *Ibid.*

Al-Maqdisi used his year in Saudi Arabia to collect all kinds of writings that interested him, and the concepts and ideas found therein almost immediately made their way into his own writings. One of his first books[33], written in 1983 when he had already returned from Saudi Arabia, was still mostly a collection of sayings of various non-Wahhabi scholars. Although he used the book to write about concepts that would later become central to his ideology, such as *shirk*, *kufr*, *takfīr*, idols (*ṭawāghīt*) and man-made laws (*qawānīn waḍʿiyya*), he quoted the Wahhabi scholar Hamd b. ʿAtiq (d. 1883), who would later become a significant source of influence on him (see Chapter 6), but only once.[34] The writings that followed, however, clearly reflected his year in Saudi Arabia. Books such as *Millat Ibrahim* (1984), *Iʿdad al-Qada al-Fawaris bi-Hajr Fasad al-Madaris* (1986/7), *Kashf al-Niqab ʿan Shariʿat al-Ghab* (1988) and *Al-Kawashif al-Jaliyya fi Kufr al-Dawla al-Saʿudiyya* (1989) were heavily influenced by Wahhabi writings, and particularly the concept of *al-walāʾ wa-l-barāʾ*.

It is not entirely clear how al-Maqdisi spent his time in Saudi Arabia when he was not studying. He himself says he visited many different places[35] and he is said to have returned to the country several times and made contacts with and paid visits to the former sympathisers of Juhayman al-ʿUtaybi, even as late as the late 1980s[36], sometimes to discuss his work or study with them.[37] As we will see in Chapter 4, al-Maqdisi's highly critical writings on Saudi Arabia were probably not known to the authorities until the early 1990s or, in any case, were not considered dangerous enough to bar him from entering the country. The statements of several people that they saw al-Maqdisi during the *ḥajj* in the late 1980s are therefore entirely plausible. The fact that these people recognised him as a scholar or even sat down to listen to him in the Grand Mosque in Mecca suggests that he had already acquired some stature as an ideologue among them.[38]

33 An even earlier work can be found in Abū Muḥammad al-Maqdisī, *Risālatān fī Bidaʿ al-Masājid*, www.tawhed.ws/t, 2009 [1986/7], 52–64, but this was too early to reflect any strong Wahhābī influence.

34 *Id.*, *Irshād al-Mubtadī ilā Qawāʿid al-Saʿdī*, www.tawhed.ws/t, 2009 [1983], 45.

35 Al-Maqdisī, e-mail message to the author, 18 May 2009.

36 Hegghammer and Lacroix, 'Rejectionist', 115–16.

37 Manṣūr al-Nuqaydān, e-mail message to the author, 6 December 2008; interview with al-Dhāyidī, Riyadh, 8 November 2009.

38 Interviews with al-Shāfī, Riyadh, 11 November 2008; Yūsuf al-Daynī, Jeddah, 13 November 2008; *Al-Sharq al-Awsaṭ*, 14 January 2004.

From Kuwait to Peshawar and Back

In the early 1980s, al-Maqdisi finished his year in Saudi Arabia, and moved back to Kuwait. There, equipped with potentially radical but entirely Salafi writings that he had collected in Saudi Arabia, he wrote what is perhaps his most important book: *Millat Ibrahim*. In it, he re-reasoned arguments such as Qutb's from a Salafi perspective and with heavy use of the concept of *al-walāʾ wa-l-barāʾ*. This way, the book became a Salafi indictment of Muslim states that fail to rule by Islamic law, as we will see later on. Now having already written an important book, he subsequently went to Peshawar in Pakistan, as other men from all over the Arab world did in the 1980s, to help fight the Soviet Union, which had invaded Afghanistan in 1979.[39]

Although he is said to have participated in military training near the Afghanistan/Pakistan border, he did not actually engage in any combat[40], contrary to what some have claimed.[41] Al-Maqdisi himself says about this period that he found out in Afghanistan that he was 'illiterate' in the use of weapons and that he decided to focus on what he had always done, namely *daʿwa*.[42] He thus spent his time in Peshawar as a shaykh, not as a fighter, and as such engaged in teaching and spreading his writings. His book *Millat Ibrahim* was printed in Peshawar, where he also wrote a book that accused Saudi Arabia of being an infidel state, *Al-Kawashif al-Jaliyya fi Kufr al-Dawla al-Saʿudiyya*, and which was also printed in Peshawar.[43] He is said to have enjoyed some influence in Peshawar since his books were widespread there and he was quite well-known among the Arab *mujāhidūn*. His ideas were not uncontroversial among jihad fighters in Peshawar, however. Saudi and many other *mujāhidūn* had come there to fight the Soviets, not to hear that their own state was un-Islamic, and al-Maqdisi's *takfīr* of the kingdom was therefore certainly not universally accepted.[44] Al-Maqdisi also claims he differed with ʿAbdallah ʿAzzam, the leader of the Afghan Arabs, on what strategy to pursue in Afghanistan. Although they did not have any conflicts, al-Maqdisi says, '[I] was not among his followers'.[45]

39 Interview with al-Maqdisī, Amman, 13 January 2009.
40 *Al-Waṭan*, 5 July 2005; interview with Ḥasan Abū Haniyya, Amman, 9 August 2008.
41 Khāshuqjī and Abū Hilāla, 'Al-Munaẓẓir', 11.
42 Interview with al-Maqdisī, al-Ruṣayfa, 17 January 2009.
43 Interview with al-Maqdisī, Amman, 13 January 2009.
44 Telephone interview with Jamāl Khāshuqjī, 27 November 2008.
45 Khāshuqjī and Abū Hilāla, 'Al-Munaẓẓir', 13.

ʿAzzam, like al-Maqdisi himself, was more of a scholar than a fighter, and in that sense he seems typical of the sort of people al-Maqdisi forged ties with during his stay in Peshawar: fellow ideologues, not organisational or military activists. This included his relations with the leadership of what would later become al-Qaʿida. Thus, al-Maqdisi states that 'despite having participated in teaching in the camps of al-Qaʿida in Afghanistan as well as teaching in its *sharʿī* (Islamic legal) institute in Peshawar', 'I never had the honour of meeting [Osama bin Laden]', a man he admiringly refers to as 'the imam of the jihad fighters'. Yet Bin Laden's successor as leader of al-Qaʿida, Ayman al-Zawahiri, who is much more of an ideologue than his predecessor ever was, has closer ties to al-Maqdisi. The two are said to have met in Peshawar, and al-Maqdisi refers to al-Zawahiri as 'a friend of mine'.[46] As we will see in Chapter 7, the same applies to the Syrian al-Qaʿida strategist Abu Musʿab al-Suri, who al-Maqdisi claims to have met when working as a religious instructor in the camps of Khost in Afghanistan and who may even have been influenced by his teachings and who has certainly cited his works on several occasions.

Because al-Maqdisi did not stay in Afghanistan/Pakistan for very long, he never really seems to have become very well acquainted with the core of al-Qaʿida's leaders, and his relations with them therefore seem to be distant and based primarily on ideological kinship. This is even more true of a group of scholars who are not part of al-Qaʿida's core ideological or strategic leadership but who are nevertheless instrumental in shaping the broader radical Islamic movement around the organisation. Such scholars include the Jordanian-British Abu Qatada al-Filastini, the Kuwaiti Hamid b. ʿAbdallah al-ʿAli, the Syrian-British Abu Basir al-Tartusi, with whom he has engaged in extensive ideological discussions[47], and the Egyptian-British Hani al-Sibaʿi, who has defended him against his ideological detractors.[48]

46 Abū Muḥammad al-Maqdisī, *Ḥiwār al-Shaykh Abī Muḥammad al-Maqdisī maʿa Majallat 'al-ʿAṣr'*, www.tawhed.ws/r?i=j37307wg, n.d. [2002/3], 6–7.

47 See Joas Wagemakers, 'An Inquiry into Ignorance: A Jihādī-Salafī Debate on *Jahl* as an Obstacle to *Takfīr*', in: Nicolet Boekhoff-van der Voort, Kees Versteegh and Joas Wagemakers (eds.), *The Transmission and Dynamics of the Textual Sources of Islam: Essays in Honour of Harald Motzki*, Leiden: Brill, 2011, 301–27.

48 Abū Muḥammad al-Maqdisī and Hānī al-Sibāʿī, *Al-Rasāʾil al-Mutabādila bayna l-Shaykh Abī Muḥammad al-Maqdisī wa-l-Duktūr Hānī al-Sibāʿī Ḥafiẓahu llāh*, www.tawhed.ws/r?i=040309ga, 2009.

Al-Maqdisi thus seems to have forged few ties with al-Qaʿida activists (fighters, organisers, etc.), and mostly appears to have established lasting – but distant – relationships with other ideologues. In fact, the only major exception to this seems to be his relationship with the Jordanian leader of what later became al-Qaʿida in Iraq, Abu Musʿab al-Zarqawi. Unlike al-Maqdisi, al-Zarqawi – who was born in 1966 as Ahmad Fadil Nazzal al-Khalayila – did fight in Afghanistan. In the early 1990s, the two are said to have met in Peshawar at the home of Abu l-Walid al-Ansari[49], a jihadi ideologue himself, although it is unclear how their relationship in Afghanistan/Pakistan developed from there. While it is likely that al-Zarqawi, being a zealous and uneducated youngster from the poverty-stricken industrial city of al-Zarqa', was inclined to learn from the older and more learned al-Maqdisi, no reliable account of this period exists as of yet. Whatever the case may have been, however, al-Maqdisi's lack of ties to many prominent fighters and his general focus on *daʿwa* as opposed to military matters would come to haunt him, as we will see in Chapter 9.

After spending time in Peshawar spreading his books, al-Maqdisi returned to Kuwait, where he continued his writing. During this period, he supported himself by working in a book printing shop, where he would eventually become manager.[50] Interestingly, at that time he was on good terms with a Jordanian quietist Salafi scholar named ʿAli b. Hasan al-Halabi. During one of my interviews with him, al-Maqdisi even showed me a book that he had been given by al-Halabi and in which the latter had written: 'This is a gift for my brother ʿIsam al-Barqawi, may God protect him.'[51] This is significant since al-Maqdisi would later heavily criticise al-Halabi for the latter's unwillingness to apply *takfīr* to the rulers. Al-Halabi acknowledges that he used to be on good terms with al-Maqdisi, but that 'when the truth of the man was revealed I never met him again'.[52] The fact that al-Maqdisi could be on such good terms with a quietist Salafi possibly shows that he did not just resemble quietists in his writings but also in his personal relations.

49 Abū l-Walīd al-Anṣārī, 'Al-Zarqāwī al-Shaykh al-Jalīl alladhī ʿaraftu', *Ṣadā l-Jihād*, vol. 2, no. 17, Jumādā l-Ukhrā 1428/June-July 2007, 26; Abū Muḥammad al-Maqdisī, *Al-Zarqāwī: Āmāl wa-Ālām (Munāṣara wa-Munāṣaḥa)*, www.tawhed.ws/r?i=dtwiam56, 2004, 1.

50 Al-Maqdisī, e-mail message to the author, 18 May 2009.

51 Interview with al-Maqdisī, al-Ruṣayfa, 17 January 2009.

52 Interview with ʿAlī b. Ḥasan al-Ḥalabī, Amman, 19 January 2009.

Al-Maqdisi later changed jobs and went into the trading business because it allowed him to work flexible hours.[53] Combining his work with his growing influence as a scholar, he could have gone on living like this for quite some time, were it not for the invasion of Kuwait by the Iraqi army in 1990. As a result of Yasir 'Arafat's decision to back Iraqi dictator Saddam Husayn against the international coalition amassing against him, virtually all Palestinians were expelled from Iraq. This meant that they had to go back to their home countries, which for al-Maqdisi, as for most other Palestinians in Kuwait, was Jordan, where he would meet al-Zarqawi again.

Al-Maqdisi's Troubled Relationship with al-Zarqawi

Jordan is a country that, having been created by Britain less than a century ago and receiving most of the Palestinian refugees from the Arab-Israeli wars, has always struggled with its identity. Since a sizeable portion of its population (perhaps even the majority) is of Palestinian descent, the question of 'who is a Jordanian?' is not easily answered. On top of this, the hundreds of thousands of Palestinians that arrived in Jordan from Kuwait over a period of a few years from 1990 onwards proved to be a heavy burden on Jordanian society. Many of them had never been to Jordan in their lives, but because they had been born in the Jordanian-controlled West Bank between 1948 and 1967, they were officially Jordanian citizens. As we will see in more detail in Chapter 8, the Palestinians also came at a moment when the country was going through an eventful era, with the Gulf War, an economic crisis and the peace process with Israel all taking place at the same time. While many Palestinians ended up in poor refugee camps at the outskirts of cities such as al-Zarqa' and proved to be an economic burden on top of the crisis the country was going through at that time, many also greatly contributed to the struggling economy by setting up shops and firms.[54]

Al-Maqdisi's Arrival in Jordan

The Palestinians arriving from Kuwait could basically be divided into two groups. The first was the group of relatively well-off, middle-class Palestinians who were not only responsible for setting up the new businesses just mentioned but also for spreading more liberal values. Their lifestyles

53 Al-Maqdisī, e-mail message to the author, 18 May 2009.
54 Radi, 'Palestinienes', 59–61; Le Troquer and Hommery al-Oudat, 'Kuwait', 40–4.

sometimes caused a shock among some traditionally more conservative Jordanians, and in certain cases exacerbated the already tense relations between Palestinians and Jordanians in the kingdom. The second group consisted of more Salafi-oriented Palestinians, some of whom had spent time in Afghanistan and Pakistan. Al-Maqdisi was obviously part of the latter group, and as such he came to Jordan in 1992.[55]

From the beginning of al-Maqdisi's stay in Jordan, he seems to have been involved in attempts to spread his writings and was assisted in his efforts by Abu Musʿab al-Zarqawi. The latter had returned from Afghanistan in the same period as al-Maqdisi and had apparently found out his address through the aforementioned Abu l-Walid al-Ansari.[56] Together, they gathered a group of young men around them with whom they tried to spread al-Maqdisi's writings. This group, later known in the media as Bayʿat al-Imam (Fealty to the Imam), has been described by several authors as a violent, or even a terrorist, organisation, thereby suggesting that military activities were their primary aim.[57] Although the group did indeed engage in one armed attack, it mostly focussed on *daʿwa*, and al-Zarqawi, notwithstanding his violent reputation in later years, is said to have been quite devoted to al-Maqdisi during this period.[58] Nevertheless, the group did get involved in armed activity against Israel. Their attack was foiled by the Jordanian security service, however, landing al-Maqdisi, al-Zarqawi and about a dozen other men in prison with a fifteen years' sentence.[59]

The Prison Years, 1994–1999

The group, once in prison, tried to continue its activities as much as possible by proclaiming their message and recruiting new followers among fellow-prisoners and even targeting guards with their ideas, as we will see in Chapter 9. Although the efforts by al-Maqdisi and the other members of his group to spread their views certainly did not pay off with everyone, they did lead to an increase in the number of their followers.[60]

[55] International Crisis Group, *Jordan's 9/11: Dealing with* Jihadi *Islamism*, ICG Middle East Report no. 47, Amman and Brussels, 23 November 2005, 4.

[56] Al-Maqdisī, *Al-Zarqāwī*, 1.

[57] Jean-Charles Brisard, *Zarqawi: The New Face of Al-Qaeda*, New York: Other Press, 2005, 31–8; Napoleoni, *Insurgent*, 62–4.

[58] Ḥusayn, *Al-Zarqāwī*, 85–99.

[59] For more detailed accounts of this period regarding al-Maqdisī's influence, see Chapters 8 and 9.

[60] International Crisis Group, *Jordan's*, 9.

There were differences between the approaches the various 'members' of al-Maqdisi's group took, however, which became exemplified in the ways al-Maqdisi and the young al-Zarqawi dealt with others: while the former, despite his explicit message, spread his ideas in a friendly and kind manner, al-Zarqawi was much harsher, blunter and more direct to those he considered his enemies. His behaviour, unlike al-Maqdisi's, sometimes expressed itself in verbal or even physical abuse towards the prison guards.[61]

Confrontational behaviour, especially if it took on the forms that al-Zarqawi used, was not tolerated by the authorities in prison, and it would therefore often result in the prisoners' suffering physical abuse, torture and long periods in solitary confinement.[62] Al-Maqdisi himself is also said to have been tortured during this period.[63] In spite of this, however, he did consider his time in prison as very profitable, and it was probably the most important intellectual period of his life after his stay in Saudi Arabia, since he got the opportunity to write some of his most important books and studies. He also devoted special attention to specific questions that fellow inmates had about politics, the rulers and coping with life as prisoners, and even had the time to write about issues outside his normal range of interests, such as Christianity.

Still, although al-Maqdisi could devote much time to writing, tensions rose within the group, particularly between its two most important 'members': al-Maqdisi and al-Zarqawi. The former had been the leader of the group before their prison sentence and early on during their stay in gaol, but after a while, al-Zarqawi took over the leadership. It is not entirely certain why this happened. It might have been because al-Maqdisi wanted the time to write and took the decision himself to withdraw from the leadership to let al-Zarqawi take over, as al-Maqdisi himself maintains.[64] While this may be true, another important factor was that many prisoners preferred al-Zarqawi's stronger and more confrontational approach to al-Maqdisi's more gentle nature, which put the latter in the position of spiritual leader. Al-Zarqawi's toughness in the face of torture and other maltreatment, his discipline towards others but also himself, as well as

61 Napoleoni, *Insurgent*, 68–70.

62 Ḥusayn, *Al-Zarqāwī*, 14–17; Napoleoni, *Insurgent*, 75–76; al-Maqdisī, *Liqā' min Khalf Quḍbān al-Murtaddīn 'Sana 1418'*, 5, 9.

63 Interviews with Abū Haniyya, Amman, 9 August 2008; Fu'ād Ḥusayn, Amman, 5 August 2008.

64 Al-Maqdisī, *Liqā' min Khalaf Qaḍbān al-Murtaddīn 'Sana 1418'*, 1–2.

his stronger leadership qualities, were apparently more attractive to their fellow prisoners than al-Maqdisi's indirect and friendly approach.[65]

On the question of leadership inside prison, al-Maqdisi himself tries to downplay the significance of the matter, and states:

> I myself chose to leave the leadership and pass it on to Abu Musʿab [al-Zarqawi]. The matter is not like some foolish writers (*baʿd al-kuttāb al-sukhafāʾ*) have portrayed it, that there was a quarrel or a dispute (*khuṣūma am nizāʿ*) about the leadership! As if it was the leadership of a state! It was the limited leadership of a prison (*imārat sijn qāṣira maḥdūda*).[66]

These words may be true, but the change in the group's leadership reflected the new ways in which both al-Maqdisi and al-Zarqawi were perceived by their fellow prisoners, and it was here – in gaol – that the later tensions between the two men have their roots. As we will see in Chapter 9, the leadership issue was not just indicative of al-Maqdisi's and al-Zarqawi's different personalities but also of growing rifts between their ideological outlook and the way they were seen by their respective supporters.

In spite of al-Zarqawi's growing power inside the various prisons that he and the rest of the group were in, outside the prison walls al-Maqdisi became increasingly influential. Because visiting rules for prisoners, even political ones, were rather lax, al-Maqdisi's writings could be smuggled out of prison, sometimes page by page, via family members or even co-operative guards, allowing them to be spread around the country.[67] This way, al-Maqdisi became well-known among like-minded Jordanians because of his writings, even during the time he spent in gaol. When al-Maqdisi was moved to the prison in al-Salt, for instance, radical youngsters from that city flocked to visit the famous shaykh that had come to their town.[68]

The situation of al-Maqdisi's fame growing outside prison while al-Zarqawi's star rose on the inside continued until 1999 when the new Jordanian king, ʿAbdallah II, who had just succeeded his recently deceased father, decided to pardon a number of political prisoners, including al-Maqdisi and al-Zarqawi as well as most of the rest of their group. The

[65] Ḥusayn, *Al-Zarqāwī*, 14; Napoleoni, *Insurgent*, 66–76; Mary Anne Weaver, 'Inventing al-Zarqawi', *The Atlantic Monthly*, July/August 2006, 94; interviews with ʿAbdallāh Abū Rummān, Amman, 15 January 2009; Yūsuf Rabāba, Amman, 12 January 2009.

[66] Al-Maqdisī, *Al-Zarqāwī*, 1–2.

[67] Weaver, 'Inventing', 94; interviews with Abū Haniyya, Amman, 9 August 2008; al-Maqdisī, Amman, 13 January 2009; Marwān Shaḥāda, Amman, 13 January 2009.

[68] Interview with ʿAbdallāh Abū Rummān, Amman, 15 January 2009.

various differences that had been brewing between the different members of al-Maqdisi's group were expressed most clearly by the actions many of them took when released: while al-Zarqawi (as well as others) quickly moved to Afghanistan and later Iraq, becoming perhaps the most wanted terrorist in the world second only to Osama bin Laden, al-Maqdisi stayed in Jordan, where he tried to pick up his normal life again.

In and Out of Prison

Although al-Maqdisi tried to return to the life he had led before he went to prison, he was quickly arrested again. In late 1999, a planned terrorist attack on four different sites (a hotel in Amman, a Jordanian-Israeli border crossing and two Christian holy sites, all frequented by American and Israeli tourists) was foiled by the Jordanian authorities. In this so-called 'Millennium Plot', which was supposed to take place on 1 January 2000 (hence the name), twenty-eight men were charged with planning these attacks. Al-Maqdisi was also arrested since he was believed to have been involved in the attacks as well.[69] In an interview during his stay in prison as a result of his arrest, al-Maqdisi stated that he knew some of the men charged with involvement in the plot but that he was only arrested because some of his books had been found in the homes of the culprits. He claimed, however, that the real reasons behind the arrests were to 'satisfy America, which controls the global system, and to make enemies out of the Muslim *mujāhidūn*, who they describe [by using the label of] terrorism everywhere' and also 'to defame the *daʿwa* and the jihad and to defame the reputation (*sumʿa*) of the *mujāhidūn*.'[70]

Al-Maqdisi was eventually found innocent of the charges and kept a rather low profile for the next few years. The years around the turn of the millennium, however, coincided with some very important events related to radical Islam. Al-Qaʿida arose in Afghanistan in the late 1990s, some of its spectacular attacks in Nairobi and Dar es-Salaam (1998), Yemen (2000) and the United States (2001) took place and the United States subsequently launched its 'war on terrorism', leading to the invasion of Afghanistan in 2001 and Iraq in 2003. In this period, with fighters travelling to different countries to wage war against the United States, al-Maqdisi turned to a different genre in his writings, namely that of giving advice to young radicals whom he believed had gone too far in

69 International Crisis Group, *Jordan's*, 10.

70 Abū Muḥammad al-Maqdisī, *Liqāʾ min Khalf Quḍbān Sijn Suwāqa 'Sana 1420'*, www.tawhed.ws/r?i=dgxh8xf7, 1999, 1–2.

their quest for jihad. Although this criticism of extreme forms of jihad (and particularly *takfīr*) was not new in his writings, it did become much more pronounced after 2001 and particularly after al-Zarqawi became infamous for his massive suicide bombings in Iraq.[71]

The period between al-Maqdisi's critical writings on jihadis and his release from prison was actually quite short, because he was quickly arrested again. This time, al-Maqdisi was said to have been involved in a conspiracy to attack U.S. soldiers in the northern Jordanian city of Mafraq and was arrested and interrogated in November 2002.[72] Al-Maqdisi himself claims that he was only engaged in *daʿwa* activities in Mafraq and that when he learned about the plans to stage this attack he actually advised against it because he believed the men planning it were too inexperienced.[73] This does indeed seem to have been the case since al-Maqdisi was acquitted of the charges after being held in pre-trial detention until December 2004, although he was not released until June 2005.[74] All of this did not mean, however, that al-Maqdisi had turned against jihad. In fact, about a month before his arrest in the Mafraq case, he praised two men who had attacked Americans in Kuwait and used the tract he wrote about them to denounce the Kuwaiti parliament, government and laws.[75]

Despite al-Maqdisi's continued support for various forms of jihad in principle, he did become increasingly worried about events in Iraq and other countries during this period. He wrote several tracts about it, which were much more widely read than before since al-Maqdisi had launched a website, probably around the year 2002, on which he put not only other people's work but also all of his own writings. Therefore, when he wrote several tracts critical of jihadi practices in general and his former pupil al-Zarqawi's actions in Iraq in particular, the differences between the two men that were rooted in their prison period spilled into the open and became the focus of intense media attention. This started when al-Maqdisi

[71] See, for instance, Abū Muḥammad al-Maqdisī, *Risālat Munāṣaḥa wa-Tadhkīr ilā Baʿḍ al-Ikhwa*, www.tawhed.ws/r?i=ggno87z3, 1992/3. His most important work in this respect remains *Al-Risāla al-Thalāthīniyya fī l-Taḥdhīr min al-Ghulūw fī l-Takfīr*, www.tawhed.ws/t, 1998/9.

[72] *Al-Sharq al-Awsaṭ*, 14 January 2004.

[73] Al-Maqdisī, e-mail message to the author, 18 May 2009.

[74] Human Rights Watch, *Arbitrary Arrest and Detention of ʿIsam al-ʿUtaibi (Abu Muhammad al-Maqdisi)*, www.hrw.org/en/news/2007/12/03/arbitrary-arrest-and-detention-isam-al-utaibi-abu-muhammad-al-maqdisi, 3 December 2007, 1.

[75] Abū Muḥammad al-Maqdisī, *Barāʾat al-Muwaḥḥidīn min ʿUhūd al-Ṭawāghīt wa-Amānihim li-l-Muḥāribīn*, www.tawhed.ws/r?i=70q3bqpe, 2002.

wrote a book called *Waqfat maʿa Thamarat al-Jihad* in 2004, in which he scolded many *mujāhidūn* for their lack of knowledge about Islam and their surroundings, their extreme paranoia or dangerous negligence and their sometimes reckless use of violence. He further criticised his former student al-Zarqawi in particular in a tract written specifically about him. In this document, al-Maqdisi advises al-Zarqawi to stop the widespread use of suicide bombings, indiscriminate violence and *takfīr* of entire groups of people because it is wrong to do so and hurts the image of Islam.[76]

Shortly after he wrote these documents critical of certain jihadi practices, al-Maqdisi was released on 28 June 2005 on the apparently explicit condition that he not make any statements to the media.[77] He did give several interviews to Jordanian newspapers, however, in which he reiterated his criticism of al-Zarqawi.[78] This was confirmed when al-Maqdisi gave an interview to the well-known Arabic satellite channel Al-Jazeera, in which he was allowed to go into more detail about this issue and could explain more thoroughly that it was not his intention to slander al-Zarqawi and that he did not reject jihad as such but that he simply disagreed with some of its extremist expressions.[79]

This criticism of al-Zarqawi by al-Maqdisi is the subject of several academic publications.[80] Al-Maqdisi himself later told me that his critical writings and interviews were expressions of his genuine worry that jihad, a concept embedded in Islamic law and supported by al-Maqdisi under certain conditions, was being tarnished by reckless activities by young fighters. This was not, however, how al-Zarqawi interpreted his former mentor's critique. In a rebuttal of al-Maqdisi's 'advice', al-Zarqawi states that he was surprised to read these comments and gives a detailed refutation of al-Maqdisi's criticism. This includes the claim that he consults with scholars in Iraq about the legitimacy of his attacks, and is therefore not reckless. He also defends his use of suicide bombings and attacks against Shiites. Moreover, al-Zarqawi wonders why al-Maqdisi chose to

76 *Id.*, *Al-Zarqāwī*.
77 *Al-Sharq al-Awsaṭ*, 4 July 2005.
78 *Al-Ghad*, 5 July 2005; *Al-ʿArab al-Yawm*, 5 July 2005.
79 *Abū Muḥammad al-Maqdisī. Al-Salafiyya al-Jihādiyya*, www.aljazeera.net/channel/archive/archive?ArchiveId=129776, 6 July 2005.
80 Steven Brooke, 'The Preacher and the Jihadi', in: Hillel Fradkin, Husain Haqqani and Eric Brown (eds.), *Current Trends in Islamist Ideology*, vol. III, Washington D.C.: Hudson Institute, 2006, 60–3; Nibras Kazimi, 'A Virulent Ideology in Mutation: Zarqawi Upstages Maqdisi', in: Hillel Fradkin, Husain Haqqani and Eric Brown (eds.), *Current Trends in Islamist Ideology*, vol. II, Washington D.C.: Hudson Institute, 2005, 65–9.

make these comments in the media when he had already expressed them in his writings, and wants to know why he made them now.[81]

Al-Zarqawi writes that the war in Iraq is heavily testing the resolve of the *mujāhidūn* and this is probably why he wondered about al-Maqdisi's motives to express his criticism at that moment. One might also wonder whether al-Maqdisi's release from prison had anything to do with this. It could be argued that al-Maqdisi was acquitted because of these critical writings so that he might use his freedom to act as a moderating force against people such as al-Zarqawi. This is, however, unlikely for two reasons. Firstly, although al-Maqdisi was critical of certain practices among some *mujāhidūn*, his writings also clearly showed that he did support jihad and the use of violence against the Americans and the rulers of the Muslim world in general. The Jordanian authorities were unlikely to release a man who held these views, only to let him express them, unless there was another, more compelling reason. Secondly, in spite of al-Maqdisi's criticism of reckless jihadis and some of al-Zarqawi's actions, his media statements eventually landed him in prison again on 6 July 2005, a week after he had been released, since he had not been allowed to contact the media and had clearly violated that prohibition. One could argue, of course, that al-Maqdisi may have made a deal with the Jordanian authorities to denounce terrorism and was released for that reason but that he simply did not (entirely) keep his promises. Since neither party is very likely to admit that this was the case, it will probably remain unclear.

Whatever the true reason behind al-Maqdisi's re-arrest, he remained in prison without officially being charged of anything until March 2008. The reason he was released then was again unclear, but most probably had to do with his deteriorating health and the pressure that was being applied on the Jordanian authorities to release him since he had not been charged with anything.[82] His health problems had come about as a result

[81] Abū Muṣʿab al-Zarqāwī, *Bayān wa-Tawḍīḥ limā Athārahu l-Shaykh al-Maqdisī fī Liqāʾihi maʿa Qanāt al-Jazīra*, n.p., n.d. I would like to thank Paul Schrijver for providing me with this document.

[82] Human Rights Watch, *Human Rights Watch Letter to Jordanian Prime Minister Dahabi on Detention of ʿIsam al-ʿUtaibi (Abu Muhammad al-Maqdisi)*, www.hrw.org/en/news/2007/12/03/human-rights-watch-letter-jordanian-prime-minister-dahabi-detention-isam-al-utaibi-a, 3 December 2007. See also *id.*, *Jordan: Rampant Beatings in Prisons Go Unpunished*, www.hrw.org/en/news/2007/08/29/jordan-rampant-beatings-prisons-go-unpunished, 30 August 2007; *id.*, *Jordan: Clarifications on World Report Chapter 2008*, www.hrw.org/en/news/2008/02/18/jordan-clarifications-world-report-chapter-2008, 18 February 2008; Amnesty International, *'Your Confessions Are Ready for You to*

of his hunger strike, which he had started because he had not been allowed to attend his father's funeral earlier.[83] That was about the only thing that was heard of him in the almost three years that he spent in prison again. Virtually no writings of his were released in this period, and when he was eventually released, only Middle Eastern media seemed to pay attention to it.[84]

Al-Maqdisi may have wanted to return to a quiet life, concentrating on his writings and staying away from media attention. For about six months, no new writings of his appeared on his website, and until his re-arrest in September 2010 and his subsequent sentence to five years' imprisonment on the charge of recruiting terrorists in July 2011[85], he supported himself by running a shop in which his sons work, selling things like fragrant herbs and honey.[86] Immediately after his release in 2008, however, some journalists wondered if al-Maqdisi would use his freedom to continue his 'revisions', a reference to al-Maqdisi's earlier writings that were critical of certain jihadi practices and were seen by some as a moderation of views he had held before. Although this claim is not correct, since al-Maqdisi has been critical of certain forms of jihad and especially *takfīr* since the early 1990s[87], his own protestations against this 'accusation'[88] did not silence his critics. In fact, 2008 and 2009 saw unprecedented criticism of al-Maqdisi by certain Jihadi-Salafis in Jordan and also on the Internet. This criticism did not just focus on his alleged revisionism but also on al-Maqdisi's supposedly faulty ideology and – especially – his lack of any credentials as a jihad fighter.[89]

I contend that al-Maqdisi's strong preference for *daʿwa* over jihad – even though he considers the latter to be legitimate – can, like other

Sign': Detention and Torture of Political Suspects, www.amnesty.org/en/library/info/MDE16/005/2006/en, 23 July 2006.

83 *Reuters*, 17 June 2007.

84 *Al-ʿArab al-Yawm*, 13 March 2008; *Al-Ḥayāt*, 13 March 2008; *Middle East Times*, 18 March 2008; Ṭāmir al-Ṣamādī, 'Iṭlāq Sarāḥ al-Maqdisī baʿda Iḍrābihi ʿan al-Ṭaʿām wa-Tardī Awḍāʿahu al-Ṣiḥḥiyya', *Al-Sabīl*, no. 737, 18–24 March 2008, 2; *Al-Sharq al-Awsaṭ*, 13 March 2008.

85 *Al-Quds al-ʿArabī*, 28 July 2011; *Associated Press*, 28 July 2011.

86 Al-Maqdisī, e-mail message to the author, 18 May 2009.

87 See Joas Wagemakers, 'Abu Muhammad al-Maqdisi: A Counter-Terrorism Asset?', *CTC Sentinel*, vol. 1, no. 6, May 2008, 8–9; *id.*, 'Reclaiming', 526–9.

88 Abū Muḥammad al-Maqdisī, *Al-Thabāt al-Thabāt fī Zaman al-Tarājuʿāt*, www.tawhed.ws/r?i=khlovemo, 2008; *id.*, *As'ila ḥawla ftirāʾāt Mansūba li-l-Shaykh Abī Muḥammad al-Maqdisī*, www.tawhed.ws/r?i=gerbashi, 2008.

89 See Joas Wagemakers, 'Invoking Zarqawi: Abu Muhammad al-Maqdisi's Jihad Deficit', *CTC Sentinel*, vol. 2, no. 6, June 2009, 14–17; *id.*, 'Reclaiming', 529–33.

aspects of his ideology, be explained by pointing to al-Maqdisi's quietist Jihadi-Salafi background. His closeness to quietist Salafism, rooted in his experiences during his youth, his studies and his religious preferences, means that the quietist *manhaj* of dealing with society through *daʿwa* is not downplayed by him but valued as a useful tool to bring about change, even though he believes jihad can also be used for this. A seemingly similar argument has been used before by Brooke to explain the differences between al-Maqdisi and al-Zarqawi, but Brooke makes the mistake of linking this to a difference of opinion about *takfīr* and fails to take al-Maqdisi's ideological background into account.[90] In what follows, I argue that al-Maqdisi's quietist Jihadi-Salafism is a major factor in explaining both his influence and the criticism levelled against him. Before dealing with this, however, we must first turn to al-Maqdisi's ideological place in the jihadi spectrum.

[90] Brooke, 'Preacher', 57–60.

2

Al-Maqdisi's Quietist Jihadi-Salafi *'Aqīda*

This study shows what Abu Muhammad al-Maqdisi's influence has been and how it can be explained. To assess al-Maqdisi's influence and why he has been so influential, it is obviously necessary to determine what al-Maqdisi's ideology is. Although this study focuses on one Jihadi-Salafi ideologue in particular, it is important not to deal with al-Maqdisi's ideas in isolation but in the context of Islamic thought on the issue that distinguishes Jihadi-Salafis from others: their specific views on jihad. This chapter therefore concentrates on al-Maqdisi's radical views on jihad and how he differs from more traditional beliefs and the ideas of other ideologues on this issue. This is not to suggest that the following is an exhaustive account of the ideas on jihad as expressed throughout history. That would go beyond the scope of this study. My objective here is rather to explain and contextualise al-Maqdisi's views on jihad by looking at its origins in early Islam and how it was subsequently (re)formulated by certain prominent ideologues and scholars. Therefore, although there are more sides to jihad than those mentioned here, such as the spoils of war[1] or martyrdom[2], only those aspects relevant for a discussion of al-Maqdisi's views will be dealt with.

[1] Majid Khadduri, *War and Peace in the Law of Islam*, Baltimore: Johns Hopkins University Press, 2008 [1955], 118–32; *id.*, *The Islamic Law of Nations: Shaybānī's Siyar*, Baltimore: Johns Hopkins University Press, 1966, 106–29; Isam Kamel Salem, *Islam und Völkerrecht: Das Völkerrecht in der islamischen Weltanschauung*, Berlin: Express Edition, 1984, 129–36.

[2] Rudolph Peters, *Jihad in Classical and Modern Islam: A Reader*, Princeton: Markus Wiener Publishers, 1996, 21–4; David Cook, *Martyrdom in Islam*, Cambridge: Cambridge University Press, 2007.

It is important to point out that, in spite of being a Jihadi-Salafi, al-Maqdisi has not actually written a great deal about jihad per se. Although it is clear what his views are on this subject, most of his writings related to jihad focus on the specific question of who should be fought and why, not on what jihad is or how to wage it. This chapter and the next do focus on these issues, however, since they are important in order to fully understand al-Maqdisi's views and influence. In what follows, I concentrate on issues related to creed in this chapter, and on questions having to do with the methodology of applying these ideas in Chapter 3. This distinction is a relevant one in this respect since ideologues agreeing on a certain problem from the perspective of creed may not agree on the method used to solve it, as we will see. Through the use of the term *ʿaqīda*, this chapter concentrates on the Islamic origins of jihad, how some important Muslim scholars have reinterpreted jihad and what al-Maqdisi's position is in this debate. It deals first with classical jihad, the least controversial form of fighting most often found in the sources, largely based on secondary literature. The chapter then concentrates on the question of how and why jihad has been turned against Muslim rulers, as argued by various scholars including al-Maqdisi, also mostly based on secondary sources. Finally, the chapter focuses on how the global jihad advocated by al-Qaʿida came about and what al-Maqdisi's views are on this. By placing al-Maqdisi in these wider debates on jihad, it will become clear that his gradual development towards quietist Jihadi-Salafism as described in Chapter 1 can also be discerned in his ideology.

Classical Jihad

The word 'jihad' often conjures up images of violence, terrorism and suicide bombings, at least among Western audiences. This is hardly surprising, since Islamic movements engaged in those practices often refer to their struggle as a jihad. The concept of jihad is much more nuanced than the rhetoric and actions of terrorists would have us believe, however. Derived from the verb *jāhada* (to strive, to exert oneself), the verbal noun 'jihad' can have various meanings, depending on the context, including military ones. This section focuses on how this military form of 'striving' is found in the Qur'ān and the *sharīʿa* and what al-Maqdisi's views are on this type of fighting, referred to here as classical jihad.

Jihad in the Qur'ān

According to Islamic tradition, the strictly monotheistic message of the Prophet Muhammad (570–632), which he preached in Mecca from about

610 onwards, caused some to follow him, while others viewed it as a threat to their own religious customs and even their business interests, which were sometimes tied to their polytheistic cult.[3] As a result, the Meccans treated the increasing number of Muslims harshly, eventually causing Muhammad and his followers to move to Yathrib (later known as Medina) to escape the persecution of the Meccans in 622. After this *hijra* (emigration), Muhammad became the leader of the community of Muslims in Medina and was frequently engaged in raids and battles with the Meccans, eventually leading to his conquest of Mecca and his increasing power and authority on the Arabian Peninsula until his death in 632.[4]

The changing fortunes in Muhammad's life – from persecuted preacher to victorious leader – can be seen in the Qurʾānic text as the Prophet is said to have proclaimed it. In the Meccan verses of the Qurʾān, fighting (*qitāl*) is not mentioned, nor would the Muslims have been able to fight, given their weakness *vis-à-vis* their opponents. Q. 25: 52, for example, encourages believers to 'obey not the unbelievers, but struggle [or strive] with them thereby [the Qurʾān] mightily (*jāhidhum bihi jihādan kabīran*)'.[5] Passages such as this one indicate that jihad only refers to non-violent 'striving' in the Meccan verses. Similarly, another Meccan verse (16: 125) states 'call thou to the way of thy lord (*udʿu ilā sabīl rabbika*) with wisdom and good admonition, and dispute with them (*jādilhum*) in the better way'. These words seem to confirm the message conveyed in the former verse, namely that contentious relations with Meccan non-Muslims should be solved by calling people to Islam (*daʿwa*, from which the word *udʿu* cited above is derived), and not to take up weapons.[6]

[3] Marshall G. S. Hodgson, *The Venture of Islam: Conscience and History in a World Civilization*, 3 vols., Chicago and London: University of Chicago Press, 1974, vol. I, 154–72; Hugh Kennedy, *The Prophet and the Age of the Caliphates: The Islamic Near East from the Sixth to the Eleventh Century*, London and New York: Longman, 1986, 25–8, 31–3.

[4] Reuven Firestone, *Jihad: The Origin of Holy War in Islam*, New York and Oxford: Oxford University Press, 1999, 106–25; Hans Kruse, *Islamische Völkerrechtslehre*, Bochum: Studienverlag Brockmeyer, 1979, 46–8; Alfred Morabia, *Le Gihad dans l'Islam médiéval*, Paris: Albin Michel, 1993, 52–68.

[5] All Qurʾānic verses were taken from A. J. Arberry, *The Koran Interpreted*, New York: Touchstone, 1955.

[6] Michael Bonner, *Jihad in Islamic History: Doctrines and Practice*, Princeton and Oxford: Princeton University Press, 2006, 21–2; David Cook, *Understanding Jihad*, Berkeley, Los Angeles & London: University of California Press, 2005, 32–3; Firestone, *Jihad*, 51–3; Abdulaziz A. Sachedina, 'The Development of *Jihad* in Islamic Revelation and History', in: James Turner Johnson and John Kelsay (eds.), *Cross, Crescent, and Sword: The Justification of War in Western and Islamic Tradition*, New York: Greenwood

In the verses said to have been revealed in Medina, however, there are many references to military struggle with non-Muslims, such as Q. 22: 39, which states that 'leave is given to those who fight (*li-lladhīna yuqātilūna*) because they were wronged', or 'fight in the way of God (*qātilū fī sabīl Allāh*) with those who fight with you, but aggress not: God loves not the aggressors' (Q. 2: 190). Some verses seem to have an offensive approach and command the Muslims to attack. These include Q. 8: 39 ('fight them (*qātilūhum*) till there is no persecution (*fitna*) and the religion (*dīn*) is God's entirely')[7] and the verse stating: 'fight those who believe not in God and the Last Day and do not forbid what God and His Messenger have forbidden' (9: 29).[8] Viewed within the broader context of the Mecca-Medina relations and the insecure position in which the Muslim community still found itself *vis-à-vis* the polytheistic Meccans, however, even these verses can be interpreted as defensive.[9]

This shows that the Qur'ān interpreted in light of Muhammad's life gives different meanings of jihad and is inconclusive about how believers should deal with non-Muslims. To solve this problem and other issues related to seemingly contradictory verses, Muslim scholars developed several tools to reconcile them, including the (not universally accepted) theory of *al-nāsikh wa-l-mansūkh* (the abrogating and the abrogated), which states that when verses contradict each other, the later ones abrogate the earlier verses.[10] This led such scholars to reach the conclusion that the so-called 'sword verse' (Q. 9: 5) constituted the culmination of jihad: 'Slay the idolaters wherever you find them and take them, and confine them, and lie in wait for them at every place of ambush.'[11]

The development of *al-nāsikh wa-l-mansūkh* was preceded by the Muslim conquests of lands beyond the Arabian Peninsula. This expanded territory was later referred to as the *dār al-Islām* (the abode of Islam), the area where Muslims were in control. Its opposite, the *dār al-ḥarb*

Press, 1990, 38–9. See also Q. 15: 94; 29: 46. See also Ella Landau-Tasseron, 'Jihād', in: J. Dammen McAuliffe (ed.), *Encyclopaedia of the Qur'ān*, 6 vols., Leiden: Brill, 2003, vol. III, 36–8.

7 See also Q. 2: 193, which is almost literally the same.

8 Firestone, *Jihad*, 53–64.

9 Harald Motzki, 'Ist die Gewaltanwendung von Muslimen gegen Nichtmuslime religiös bedingt? Eine Studie der klassischen ǧihād-Konzeptionen', in: Benjamin Jokisch, Ulrich Rebstock and Lawrence I. Conrad (eds.), *Fremde, Feinde und Kurioses: Innen- und Außenansichten unseres muslimischen Nachbarn*, Berlin & New York: Walter de Gruyter, 2009, 417–52, esp. 424–35.

10 Landau-Tasseron, 'Jihād', 39.

11 Firestone, *Jihad*, 47–125, esp. 47–91. See also Bonner, *Jihad*, 23–7.

(the abode of war), was the territory that Muslims were – at least in theory – at war with. Although it is not clear how the early Muslims viewed the different verses of the Qurʾān dealing with fighting, it seems that later Muslim scholars may have used some (seemingly most offensive) Medinan verses to legitimise these conquests in retrospect.[12]

Jihad in Islamic Law

The military and sometimes offensive forms of jihad described here came to dominate the books of Islamic law, but were not always applied and practised as such throughout Islamic history. Military expansion slowed down and, perhaps more importantly, Sufism and moralist forms of Islam were on the ascent, leading to an increasing trend to interpret jihad as a spiritual struggle against one's own sins, based on non-violent Qurʾānic verses such as those mentioned earlier and similar *ḥadīth*s of Muhammad.[13] Although this notion of a spiritual jihad has survived to this day, Muslim scholars were once again confronted with the need to wage a military jihad when the *dār al-Islām* was invaded by the Crusaders in the Middle East and by the Reconquista in Spain, both from the eleventh century onwards. These non-Muslim invasions led to an increase of writings on military forms of jihad and a further development of the concept.[14]

Unlike in earlier military encounters between Islamic and Christian armies, the Crusades and the Reconquista made Muslims the defending side. This situation recurred several times in the centuries to come, perhaps most significantly through colonialism in the nineteenth and twentieth centuries. Perhaps as a reaction to the new reality of non-Muslims invading Muslim territory and Muslims living under Christian rule, scholars of Islamic law emphasised the idea of jihad as *farḍ ʿalā l-ʿayn* (an individual duty incumbent upon all Muslims) over *farḍ ʿalā l-kifāya* (a collective duty that can be performed by a limited number of fighters). The latter of these two terms, which both existed even before the Crusades, applied when Muslims had to expand the *dār al-Islām*, which occurred less and less, indicating that if a sufficient number of Muslims were engaged in it, others were exempt from fighting. If Muslims were attacked, however, the situation was more threatening, and fighting became an individual duty for all Muslims.[15] This latter

[12] Sachedina, 'Development', 37.
[13] Richard Bonney, *Jihād from Qurʾān to bin Laden*, New York: Palgrave MacMillan, 2004, 91–107; Morabia, *Gihad*, 324–30.
[14] Cook, *Understanding*, 51–2, 57–63.
[15] Kruse, *Islamischer*, 49–51; Peters, *Jihad*, 3–4. See also Bonner, *Jihad*, 106–16.

dimension of jihad – defensive war against a non-Muslim invader – was used by the Ottoman Empire at the beginning of World War I to legitimise its defence against the allied forces[16], and was also employed by Muslims in the nineteenth- and twentieth-century struggles for national liberation against colonial occupation. These anti-colonial struggles and the need for peaceful relations with non-Muslim countries caused modern Muslim scholars such as the Indian Sayyid Ahmad Khan (1817–98) and the aforementioned Egyptians Muhammad ʿAbduh and Rashid Rida to reframe jihad as pertaining only to defensive struggles directed at aggressors.[17] This way, the classical doctrine of jihad was reformulated in a way similar to Western concepts of 'just war' as developed by Christian thinkers such as Augustine and Thomas Aquinas.[18] Indeed, several studies have compared jihad with Western 'just war'[19] or international law, both from Muslim[20] and non-Muslim points of view[21].

The defensive military struggle as formulated in Islamic law and by modern scholars is also the context in which the efforts of the Palestinian Muslim Brother ʿAbdallah ʿAzzam to lead the Afghan jihad against the Soviet Union should be seen. Though 'Azzam is sometimes referred to as the mentor of Bin Laden, his ideas on jihad were quite different from Bin Laden's global jihad[22], as we will see. In one of his books, ʿAzzam makes the case for jihad against the Soviets by pointing out that all four Sunni schools of Islamic law agree that a defensive jihad is a personal

16 R. Tschudi, 'Die Fetwa's des Schejch-ül-Islâm über die Erklärung des heiligen Krieges, nach dem Tanîn, Nummer 2119 vom 15. November 1914', *Der Islam*, vol. 5, 1914, 391–3.

17 Rudolph Peters, *Islam and Colonialism*, The Hague: Mouton, 1979, 39–104, 125–30; Bonney, *Jihād*, 29–30.

18 Peters, *Islam*, 121–30.

19 See for instance John Kelsay, *Arguing the Just War in Islam*, Cambridge, MA, & London: Harvard University Press, 2007, but see also Ella Landau-Tasseron, 'Is *Jihād* Comparable to Just War? A Review Article', *Jerusalem Studies in Arabic and Islam*, vol. 34, 2008, 535–50.

20 Muhammad Hamidullah, *The Muslim Conduct of State*, Lahore: Sh. Muhammad Ashraf, 1996 [1935].

21 Ann Elizabeth Mayer, 'War and Peace in the Islamic Tradition and International Law', in: John Kelsay and James Turner Johnson (eds.), *Just War and Jihad: Historical and Theoretical Perspectives on War and Peace in Western and Islamic Traditions*, New York: Greenwood Press, 1991, 195–226; Peters, *Islam*, 135–50.

22 Thomas Hegghammer, 'Abdallah Azzam, the Imam of Jihad', in: Gilles Kepel and Jean-Pierre Milelli (eds.), *Al Qaeda in its own Words* (transl. Pascale Ghazaleh), Cambridge, MA, & London: Harvard University Press, 2008 [2005], 101.

duty and thus compulsory for every able-bodied Muslim.[23] He points out that the classical scholars of all stripes agree with this view[24] and how the rules drawn up by these scholars are applied in the Afghan war.[25] ʿAzzam's reliance on so many classical scholars, the support his views receive from Saudi, Yemeni and Syrian scholars[26] and his treatment of relevant Islamic legal issues, such as whether *mujāhidūn* need to ask their parents, spouses or creditors for permission during a defensive war[27] underlines the fact that his views on jihad are congruent with the prescriptions of the *sharīʿa*. ʿAzzam's importance with regard to jihad therefore lies not in any new ideas but in his ability to use his writings and personal charisma to mobilise Arabs for the Afghan cause, based on a version of jihad that had existed long before.

Al-Maqdisi and Classical Jihad

In applying the foregoing to al-Maqdisi's ideas, it should be stressed that the notion of jihad as a defensive military struggle is rather uncontroversial among Salafi scholars in general, including quietists. The fact that the latter are referred to in this study as 'quietists' and not as 'Jihadi-Salafis' does not mean that they reject jihad in principle. The war in Afghanistan in the 1980s is a case in point. A quietist scholar such as al-Albani is said to have been instrumental in encouraging Muslims to join the war against the Soviet Union in Afghanistan.[28] The same was true for major Saudi quietist scholars such as Ibn Baz and Muhammad b. Salih al-ʿUthaymin (d. 2001), who also agreed that the Afghan war constituted a genuine jihad.[29] Al-Maqdisi – despite being a Jihadi-Salafi – agrees with them. His stay in Afghanistan during the war in the 1980s clearly showed his support for the efforts of the *mujāhidūn* there, and in one of his books, he explicitly acknowledges the legitimacy of the Afghan jihad.[30] Similarly, after the U.S. government launched its 'war on terrorism' in response to

[23] ʿAbdallāh ʿAzzām, *Al-Difāʿ ʿan Arāḍī l-Muslimīn Ahamm Furūḍ al-Aʿyān*, www.tawhed.ws/r?i=x483iubf, n.d., 9–12.
[24] *Ibid.*, 12–16.
[25] *Ibid.*, 27–42.
[26] *Ibid.*, 2.
[27] *Ibid.*, 21–2.
[28] Interview with Usāma Shaḥāda, Amman, 12 January 2009.
[29] Rougier, 'Jihad', 71.
[30] Abū Muḥammad al-Maqdisī, *Millat Ibrāhīm wa-Daʿwat al-Anbiyāʾ wa-l-Mursalīn wa-Asālīb al-Ṭughāt fī Tamyīʿihā wa-Ṣarf al-Duʿāt ʿanhā*, www.tawhed.ws/t, 1984, 68.

'9/11', he called on Muslims to help their brethren in Afghanistan against the invading American army and its allies.[31]

Al-Maqdisi's agreement with classical jihad as described in Islamic law and expressed in defensive warfare does not mean that he often propagates this type of jihad. This may be related to his – and other Salafis' – different conception of the *sharīʿa*, on which classical jihad is based. In his view, the *sharīʿa* accumulated all kinds of rulings, regulations and laws throughout the centuries that cannot be traced back directly to the Qurʾān and the Sunna but have been added to the body of Islamic law by *fuqahāʾ* (Muslim legal scholars). Al-Maqdisi believes this sometimes results in *bidaʿ* that cause deviance and should therefore be rejected.[32] He believes that all additional rules should be within the confines of what the sources say about any given subject and should always have scriptural evidence in order for Muslims not to be led astray.[33] This means that al-Maqdisi's concept of the *sharīʿa* is at odds with the centuries-old Islamic legal tradition we have looked at so far, causing him to reject the latter in favour of his own, rather unclear version. Another reason for al-Maqdisi's lack of focus on classical jihad is that he considers jihad against the Muslim world's own rulers more important, as we will see later. He mostly treats jihad as a tool to oppose *kufr* and *shirk* in order to advance the cause of Islam embodied in *tawḥīd*, and therefore does not limit jihad to just fighting but also sees *daʿwa* as a form of struggle ('jihad of the tongue') through which this goal can be achieved[34], a position for which he is also criticised, as we will see in Chapter 9. The term 'jihad' in this study refers only to armed struggle, however.

From the preceding, it becomes clear that al-Maqdisi's idea of jihad is a multi-faceted one, encompassing both violent (fighting) and non-violent (*daʿwa*) forms. Al-Maqdisi's way of confronting the *dār al-ḥarb*, or *dār al-kufr* (the abode of unbelief) as he calls it, is complicated by his idea that the entire world is actually part of the abode of unbelief. He only separates the world into the original abode of unbelief (*dār al-kufr al-aṣliyya*), where most people are non-Muslims, and the recent abode of unbelief (*dār al-kufr al-ḥāditha*), where most inhabitants follow Islam.[35]

[31] *Id.*, *Wujūb Nuṣrat al-Muslimīn fī Afghānistān*, www.tawhed.ws/t, 2001, 22–3.

[32] Abū Muḥammad al-Maqdisī, *Al-Qawl al-Nafīs fī l-Taḥdhīr min Khadīʿat Iblīs*, www.tawhed.ws/t, n.d., 1–2.

[33] *Ibid.*, 7–9, 13–27.

[34] Interview with al-Maqdisī, al-Ruṣayfa, 17 January 2009; Abū Muḥammad al-Maqdisī, *Waqfāt maʿa Thamarāt al-Jihād*, www.tawhed.ws/t, 2004, 114.

[35] Al-Maqdisī, *Risālat Munāṣaḥa*, 1; *id.*, *Waqfāt*, 124; *id.*, *Al-Zarqāwī*, 9.

This effectively makes the entire world the object of al-Maqdisi's jihad. How he arrived at this position is rooted in another branch of the history of jihad, which we will deal with now.

Turning Jihad against Muslim Rulers

The outwardly directed military struggle in relation to non-Muslims as seen earlier is historically probably the dominant form of jihad, but Islamic law recognises that apart from conflicts between the *dār al-Islām* and the *dār al-ḥarb*, there may also be problems *within* the abode of Islam that require the use of armed force against other Muslims. This type of jihad, as described by Islamic law, can be seen as an effort to consolidate, rather than expand, the *dār al-Islām*, and may be applied by the leader of the Muslims (the imam) against apostates, deserters, highway robbers and, importantly, dissenters or rebels (*bughāt*). The *fuqahā'* did not entirely agree on the correct punishment of rebels, but jihad was seen as an option that could be used against them.[36] According to Islamic law, rebellion against the imam is never justified except if the imam does not 'fulfil the basic obligations of a member of the Muslim community', such as performing prayers.[37] The following section can be said to deal with this exception and focuses on how jihad against Muslim rulers was justified by certain Muslim scholars, what the Salafi debate is on *takfīr* of these rulers and what al-Maqdisi's position is on this issue.

Justifying Jihad against Muslim Rulers

Although the threat represented by *bughāt* was clearly different from attacks emanating from the *dār al-ḥarb*, the types of military jihad described in this chapter so far have at least one thing in common: they are all based on the idea that the imam, as the leader of the worldwide Muslim community (*umma*), is the one who ultimately calls for and commands the jihad. Even the rebellion caused by *bughāt* was to be met with a jihad launched by the imam. Islamic law, in other words, does not seem to recognise the legitimacy (or perhaps even the possibility) of ordinary Muslims taking matters into their own hands and calling for

36 Khadduri, *War*, 76–80; *id.*, *Islamic*, 230–53; Joel L. Kraemer, 'Apostates, Rebels and Brigands', *Israel Oriental Studies*, vol. 10, 1983, 58–9.

37 John Kelsay, *Islam and War: A Study in Comparative Ethics*, Louisville, KY: Westminster/John Knox Press, 1993, 88.

a jihad themselves, independent of the imam. One person who did see this possibility and was instrumental and highly influential in changing jihad into a concept that could also be turned *against* the ruler was the mediaeval scholar Ibn Taymiyya.

Taqi l-Din Ahmad b. Taymiyya (1263–1328), a Syrian Hanbali scholar who lived at the time of the destructive Mongol invasions of the Middle East, was known as a polemical, fiercely independent and strict scholar who did not mince words, even when speaking to those in power. He was, therefore, a controversial figure in his day and age whose sanity has even been questioned[38] and who found himself imprisoned because of his beliefs several times.[39] Although Ibn Taymiyya was influential in several areas, only one of them concerns us here, namely his justification of jihad against Muslim rulers. As mentioned, the *fuqahāʾ* traditionally believed that *bughāt* were not allowed to revolt against Muslim rulers, except when the latter were not proper Muslims. Ibn Taymiyya seems to have agreed with this principle, and the belief that life under a tyrannical ruler was better than civil strife has often been ascribed to him as well. Still, it was the exception to the rule that was used by Ibn Taymiyya to declare the governing Mongols, who converted to Islam after coming to power in parts of the Muslim world, a legitimate object of jihad. Ibn Taymiyya stated that despite their conversion, the Mongols did not rule on the basis of Islam but according to their own system of laws, known as *yāsiq* or *yāsa*. Because Ibn Taymiyya believed ruling on the basis of the *sharīʿa* to be a fundamental part of being a Muslim, the Mongols' unwillingness to do so meant that they were, in effect, non-Muslims, and Ibn Taymiyya therefore called for jihad against them.[40]

Ibn Taymiyya's reasoning against the Mongol rulers of his time and in favour of jihad against them makes clear that *takfīr* of Muslim rulers is an important if not essential part in legitimising rebellion. Muslim scholars have generally been highly reluctant, however, to apply *takfīr* to other Muslims because this would place the latter outside the bounds of Islam

[38] See Donald P. Little, 'Did Ibn Taymiyya have a Screw Loose?', *Studia Islamica*, no. 41, 1975, 93–111.

[39] For more on Ibn Taymiyya's life, see Henri Laoust, *La Biographie d'Ibn Taimīya d'après Ibn Kathīr*, Damascus: Institut Français de Damas, 1943.

[40] Bonner, *Jihad*, 143–4; Bonney, *Jihād*, 115–16, 121, 424–5; Emmanuel Sivan, *Radical Islam: Medieval Theology and Modern Politics*, New Haven & London: Yale University Press, 1985, 96–100. See also Laoust, *Biographie*, 121–32. Interestingly, Ibn Taymiyya also accused the Mongols of being *bughāt* because he believed that they had challenged and overthrown the existing Islamic order. See *ibid.*, 130–1.

and make them subject to the death penalty.[41] Although, as we will see, the question of what exactly constitutes *kufr*[42] and when one may be called an apostate or an unbeliever is not agreed upon[43], it is clear that, under the influence of especially Ibn Taymiyya, modern radical scholars have made extensive use of the concept of *takfīr* to condemn the rulers of their countries on religious grounds. First and foremost among these is the Egyptian literary scholar Sayyid Qutb. As is the case with Salafis, *tawḥīd* played a major role in Qutb's thinking. He believed that, since God is the only deity, his oneness should be found in every sphere of life, including in legislation and in the rule of a country. Qutb therefore stated that laws and government of a state should reflect the *ḥākimiyya* of God[44], a term he had adopted from the works of the Pakistani ideologue Abu l-Aʿla Mawdudi (1903–79)[45], who had developed a theory of what an Islamic state should look like.[46] Qutb believed that no country in the world was ruled entirely according to the *sharīʿa*, and they thereby failed to give God sole sovereignty in the legislative sphere. As such, even Muslim countries could not be called Islamic states but should be referred to as *jāhilī* states, entities existing in a situation of ignorance similar to that of pre-Islamic times.[47] The issue of legislation was so important to Qutb because he framed the following of laws as a form of worship. Based on Q. 9: 31, which states that '[Jews and Christians] have taken their rabbis and their monks as lords (*arbāban*) apart from God', Qutb concluded that following (religious) leaders in legislation amounts to taking them as lords (and, implicitly, gods) and thus equals worshipping them as if they were divine. Following non-Islamic laws therefore constitutes the worshipping of other gods, which is contrary to the fundamental principle of Islamic

[41] Bernard Lewis, 'Some Observations on the Significance of Heresy in the History of Islam', *Studia Islamica*, no. 1, 1953, 52–62.

[42] For more on the origins of the term *kufr*, see Toshihiko Izutsu, *Ethico-Religious Concepts in the Qur'ān*, Montreal: McGill-Queen's University Press, 2002 [1959], 119–249, esp. 119–77.

[43] Rudolph Peters and Gert J. J. de Vries, 'Apostasy in Islam', *Die Welt des Islams*, vol. 17, no. 1, 1977, 1–25.

[44] Yvonne Y. Haddad, 'Sayyid Qutb: Ideologue of Islamic Revival', in: John L. Esposito (ed.), *Voices of Resurgent Islam*, New York & Oxford: Oxford University Press, 1983, 89.

[45] Ahmad S. Moussalli, *Radical Islamic Fundamentalism: The Ideological and Political Discourse of Sayyid Qutb*, Beirut: American University of Beirut, 1992, 151. See also Khatab, '*Hakimiyyah*', 145–70.

[46] Charles J. Adams, 'Mawdudi and the Islamic State', in: John L. Esposito (ed.), *Voices of Resurgent Islam*, New York & Oxford: Oxford University Press, 1983, 99–133.

[47] Quṭb, *Milestones*, 82–3. See also Shepard, 'Sayyid', 523.

monotheism as expressed in *tawḥīd*. According to this reasoning, the leaders of Muslim countries, all of whom supposedly follow un-Islamic laws, are infidels[48] who should be fought through the use of jihad.[49]

In spite of the similarity between the arguments of Qutb and Ibn Taymiyya, it is not entirely clear to what extent the former was influenced by the latter. Qutb, notwithstanding the influence of intellectuals such as Mawdudi, seems to have been a rather original thinker. This was perhaps less so with the main ideologue behind the murder of the Egyptian President Anwar al-Sadat in 1981, Muhammad ʿAbd al-Salam Faraj (1954–82), who was heavily influenced by Ibn Taymiyya. In a booklet in which he frames jihad as 'the absent duty' (*al-farīḍa al-ghāʾiba*) that is incumbent on Muslims but has been neglected so far, Faraj draws an explicit parallel between Ibn Taymiyya's situation under Mongol rule and Egypt in the 1970s. He concludes that the rulers of Egypt are the same or even worse than the Mongols in Ibn Taymiyya's time and therefore should be condemned as apostates and infidels[50] and fought by means of jihad.[51]

It is doubtful whether twentieth-century scholars such as Qutb and Faraj are truly heirs of the mediaeval Ibn Taymiyya since the latter's oeuvre was much wider and more nuanced than he is given credit for by radicals. It is therefore not surprising that Egyptian scholars tried to refute the ideas of both Qutb and Faraj, claiming the assassins of Sadat had misunderstood Ibn Taymiyya.[52] Nevertheless, his fatwas against the Mongol rulers do seem to constitute his most lasting legacy, particularly among radical Muslims. In fact, the report referred to at the very beginning of this book, which states that al-Maqdisi is the most influential jihadi thinker alive, also mentions that Ibn Taymiyya is the most influential mediaeval scholar and Qutb the most-cited modern thinker among radical Muslims.[53] Through their writings, an influential theory came

[48] Quṭb, *Milestones*, 86.

[49] *Ibid.*, 53–76; Yvonne Y. Haddad, 'The Qur'anic Justification for an Islamic Revolution: The View of Sayyid Qutb', *Middle East Journal*, vol. 37, no. 1, 1983, 27–8.

[50] Muḥammad ʿAbd al-Salām Faraj, *Al-Farīḍa al-Ghāʾiba*, www.tawhed.ws/a?a=a5ieej5j, n.d., 4–10. See also Jansen, *Neglected*, esp. 166–79.

[51] Faraj, *Al-Farīḍa*, 14–32.

[52] Rachel Scott, 'An "Official" Islamic Response to the Egyptian al-Jihād Movement', *Journal of Political Ideologies*, vol. 8, no. 1, 2003, 50–58; Sivan, *Radical*, 103–4. See also Malika Zeghal, 'Religion and Politics in Egypt: The Ulema of al-Azhar, Radical Islam, and the State (1952–94)', *International Journal of Middle East Studies*, vol. 31, no. 3, 1999, 371–99.

[53] McCants (ed.), *Militant*, Executive Report, 7–8, 13, 15.

into existence that stated that Muslim rulers whose conduct – particularly with regard to legislation – was not in accordance with the *sharīʿa* ceased to be Muslims and were therefore legitimate targets of jihad. This theory became part of the ideas espoused by ideologues I refer to as Jihadi-Salafis – including al-Maqdisi – and as such has become what I believe is the defining difference over jihad between them and quietist Salafis: the latter support jihad in the classical sense in at least one of its meanings, namely as fighting to defend the *dār al-Islām* from invasions by countries of the *dār al-ḥarb*, while Jihadi-Salafis are those Salafis who believe jihad may indeed be waged for that reason but also against Muslim rulers within the *dār al-Islām*.

The Debate over Takfīr *of Muslim Rulers*

Although jihad against Muslim rulers sets Jihadi-Salafis apart from their quietist counterparts, the differences among both Salafi and non-Salafi scholars about the underlying justification of this jihad – *takfīr* of the rulers – are less clear-cut. As mentioned, the issue of what acts by Muslim rulers can be classified as *kufr* and thus justify *takfīr* is not agreed upon and, moreover, is more complicated than the ideas of Qutb and Faraj suggest. In the debate on this issue, the key question is obviously: what constitutes *kufr*? Salafi scholars throughout Islamic history have given some detailed answers to this question, distinguishing different sinful acts. Some of these, such as worshipping idols or making blasphemous remarks about the Prophet, are considered to be so clearly in violation of what Islam stands for that they immediately turn a Muslim guilty of such acts into a *kāfir*. Such sins are referred to as greater or major unbelief (*kufr akbar*), or simply as *kufr*. A person guilty of this need not even be tested on his or her beliefs, whether or not he or she was misinformed about such grave sins or perhaps made a mistake in interpreting scripture. *Kufr akbar* is considered to be so clearly sinful that no further proof of a person's unbelief is necessary to apply *takfīr*.[54] This is different, however, with lesser or minor unbelief (*kufr aṣghar*), which refers to major sins (*kabāʾir*, sing. *kabīra*), such as drinking wine or eating pork, that are not sinful enough to expel a person guilty of them from Islam and therefore justify

[54] There are many articles by quietist Salafis dealing with this topic. See, for example, Abū Iyād, *Kufr Can Occur without Istihlaal or Juhood*, www.salafipublications.com, n.d.; *id.*, *Kufr Can Occur without Believing in Kufr or Desiring it*, www.salafipublications.com, n.d.; *Imaam Ibn Baaz on Imaan, Kufr, Irjaa and the Murjiʾah*, www.salafipublications.com, n.d., 2; *Nine Rules Concerning Kufr and Takfir*, www.salafipublications.com, n.d., 2.

takfīr. This changes, however, if a person not only commits a major sin but also makes clear that he or she – despite knowing it is forbidden in Islam – considers it permissible (*istiḥlāl*), believes it to be right (*iʿtiqād*) or uses such a sin to negate (part of) Islam (*jaḥd* or *juḥūd*). In such a case, major sins that would normally be lesser unbelief then become greater unbelief, allowing *takfīr* against the person guilty of this.[55]

The division of sins described here is a very Salafi one and is not universally accepted, but it does provide a good starting point for an overview of the debate on this issue, in which – historically – roughly four different positions can be distinguished. The first position was held by an early Islamic trend called the Murjiʾa, whose adherents believed that judgement over people's sins should be subject to postponement (*irjāʾ*, from which the name Murjiʾa is derived) and left to God alone. They believed that actions by Muslims, no matter how grave they were, should not be condemned as *kufr* since only belief in the heart is what really matters, and God alone can judge that. In relation to the distinction between *kufr akbar* and *kufr aṣghar*, the Murjiʾa therefore believed that even sins that could be put in the first category were no reason for *takfīr* since even then ordinary human beings would not be able to establish the true beliefs of the culprit.[56]

The second and third positions in this debate are held by quietist Salafi scholars who, when deciding whether *takfīr* may be used against Muslim rulers applying *qawānīn waḍʿiyya*, often quote Q. 5: 44–7. These verses refer to 'Whoso judges not according to what God has sent down (*man lam yaḥkum bi-mā anzala llāh*)' as 'unbelievers' (*al-kāfirūn*), 'evildoers' (*al-ẓālimūn*) and 'the ungodly' (*al-fāsiqūn*). In deciding whether rulers, because of their alleged application of 'man-made laws', fall into the category of *kuffār/kāfirūn*, *ẓālimūn* or *fāsiqūn* – only the first of which legitimises *takfīr* – quietist Salafi *ʿulamāʾ* (scholars) hold the second and third positions in this debate. Those scholars holding the second position disagree with any 'un-Islamic' laws that Muslim rulers may occasionally

55 *Sayings of the Ulamaa' Regarding Ruling by Other than what Allaah has Revealed and the Two Types of Kufr*, www.salafipublications.com, n.d.; Muḥammad b. Ṣāliḥ al-ʿUthaymīn, *Shaikh Ibn ʿUthaymeen on al-Hukmu bi-ghayri maa Anzallallaah*, www.salafipublications.com, n.d.; ʿAbd al-Salām al-Burjis, *A Treatise on Ruling by other than what Allaah has Revealed*, www.salafipublications.com, n.d. See also Wagemakers, 'Transformation', 97–9.

56 For a good overview of the Murjiʾa, see Wilferd Madelung, 'Murdjiʾa', in: C. E. Bosworth, E. van Donzel, W. P. Heinrichs and Ch. Pellat (eds.), *Encyclopaedia of Islam: New Edition*, 12 vols., Leiden: Brill, 1993, vol. VII, 605–7.

apply, but they consider them to be 'only' manifestations of lesser unbelief since no clear indication of *istiḥlāl*, *iʿtiqād* or *jaḥd* on the part of the rulers can be seen.[57] This also applies when rulers do not just use 'man-made laws' occasionally or even frequently but exchange the whole body of Islamic laws for a secular one (*tabdīl*). Even in such a case, quietist scholars holding the second position believe that clear proof of a ruler's unbelief (in the form of *istiḥlāl*, *iʿtiqād* or *jaḥd*) is necessary to justify *takfīr* against them.[58] Since Muslim rulers are unlikely to give them this proof by, for example, explicitly and verbally negating Islamic law, this group of quietist Salafi scholars, which includes the aforementioned al-Albani and Ibn Baz, makes it virtually impossible to apply *takfīr* against them.

Quietist Salafi scholars holding the third position in this debate are very close to the ones mentioned earlier. They also disagree with any incidentally or even frequently applied man-made laws and also believe them to be acts of *kufr aṣghar* as long as they are not accompanied by any proof of unbelief in the rulers' hearts as manifested in *istiḥlāl*, *iʿtiqād* or *jaḥd*. They differ, however, in their judgement of the systematic application of man-made laws in the form of a secular constitution or another system that replaces the laws of Islam. While the Salafi scholars holding the second position believe that even in such a case, proof of the rulers' unbelief is necessary to excommunicate them, the ones holding the third position state that this is not needed since the rulers' complete adoption of another system of law in itself is proof of the unbelief in their heart underlying their actions. Thus, prominent quietist Salafi scholars such as the aforementioned al-Fawzan and Ibn al-ʿUthaymin as well as the former Saudi mufti Muhammad b. Ibrahim Al al-Shaykh (d. 1969) see the systematic application of man-made laws as *kufr akbar*.[59]

57 Muḥammad Nāṣir al-Dīn al-Albānī, *Concerning Those who do not Rule by what Allaah SWT has Revealed*, www.salafipublications.com, n.d.; *Imaam al-Albani and his Argument against Ahl ut-Takfir*, www.salafipublications.com, n.d.; Muḥammad b. Ṣāliḥ al-ʿUthaymīn, *Shaikh Ibn Uthaimeen on Ibn Baz and Albani's Position on Ruling by Other than what Allaah has Revealed*, www.salafipublications.com, n.d.

58 ʿAbd al-ʿAzīz b. Bāz, *Imaam Ibn Baaz on Tabdeel and Kufr Doona Kufr*, www.salafipublications.com, n.d.; *The Creed of Imaam al-Albaanee on Takfir and Apostasy*, www.salafipublications.com, 2000, 8, footnote 9.

59 Ṣāliḥ b. Fawzān al-Fawzān, *Shaikh Salih al-Fawzan Explains his Words in Kitaab ut-Tawheed on Ruling by other than what Allaah has Revealed*, www.salafipublications.com, n.d.; Muḥammad b. Ibrāhīm Āl al-Shaykh, *Risālat Taḥkīm al-Qawānīn*, www.tawhed.ws/a?a=ug3vtxq5, n.d.; al-ʿUthaymīn, *Shaikh*; *Creed*, 8, footnote 9. See also *Shaykh Abdul-Azeez ar-Raajihee on Secular Laws, Changing the Whole of the Deen,*

The fourth position in this debate is held by an early Islamic trend called the Khawārij, who seceded (*kharaja*, hence the name) from the Muslim community over a conflict between two caliphs, ʿAli b. Abi Talib and Muʿawiya b. Abi Sufyan, in 657. The Khawārij represent the complete opposite of the Murjiʾa in that the former did not just consider the sins described earlier as *kufr akbar* as reason for *takfīr*, but also the major sins included in the *kufr aṣghar* category, regardless of any further proof of a person's unbelief. Thus, whereas the Murjiʾa assumed that even Muslims guilty of *kufr akbar* were still believers in their heart, the Khawārij dismissed even those involved in *kufr aṣghar* as 'infidels'.[60]

Within this debate on unbelief, al-Maqdisi – despite being a Jihadi-Salafi – holds the third position, which several quietists also adhere to. While there are other aspects of quietist Salafism that he disagrees with, and he also rejects the unwillingness of the other scholars in this category to rebel against the ruler in order to change 'man-made laws' into Islamic ones, which is a question of *manhaj* dealt with in Chapter 3, he does share their views on what constitutes *kufr*. Unlike other Jihadi-Salafis who are more extreme on this issue, do not deal with it at all or rely on the works of Ibn Taymiyya or a modern non-Salafi such as Qutb, al-Maqdisi closely resembles quietist Salafism in his conclusions, arguments and terminology on this topic. This further underlines his position as a quietist Jihadi-Salafi, as a closer look at his own justification of jihad against Muslim rulers shows.

Al-Maqdisi's Views on Jihad against Muslim Rulers

Al-Maqdisi's starting point in justifying jihad against Muslim rulers is to explain his ideas on *takfīr* and *kufr* and relate them to the central concept of *tawḥīd*. He stresses the necessity of the oneness of God 'in all its types' including 'ruling' (*al-ḥukm*) and 'legislation' (*al-tashrīʿ*) and states that Muslims should not just apply the rulings of the Qurʾān and the Sunna but should be in total submission (*al-taslīm al-muṭlaq*) to them.[61] Like Qutb, al-Maqdisi makes the connection between 'un-Islamic' legislation on the one hand and the violation of *tawḥīd* through the worship of other gods on the other. He similarly quotes Q. 9: 31, in which Jews and

and the Accusation of Irjaaʾ against Ahl us-Sunnah, www.salafipublications.com, n.d., 1.

60 Elie Adib Salem, *Political Theory and Institutions of the Khawārij*, Baltimore: Johns Hopkins University Press, 1956, 31–7.

61 Abū Muḥammad al-Maqdisī, *Kashf al-Niqāb ʿan Sharīʿat al-Ghāb*, www.tawhed.ws/t, 1988, 10–11.

Christians are accused of taking their rabbis and monks as 'lords' for following their rules, as the basis of his argument:

They did not prostrate before their rabbis or bow down to them . . . but their obeying them in making the forbidden permissible (*fī taḥlīl al-ḥarām*) and making the permissible forbidden (*taḥrīm al-ḥalāl*) and agreeing with them on that is considered by God to be taking lords for them . . . because obedience in legislation (*al-ṭāʿa fī l- tashrīʿ*) is worship (*ʿibāda*), which is not permitted to be directed at anyone but God.[62]

Al-Maqdisi's condemnation of un-Islamic legislation is applied practically to several countries of which he has intimate knowledge, such as Kuwait. The influence that both the mediaeval Salafi scholar Ibn Taymiyya and the modern literary critic Qutb had on al-Maqdisi, already apparent in his focus on legislation and his comparing it with worship of other gods, is even clearer in his treatment of the laws in Kuwait, a country he lived in at the time when he wrote about it. Because he considers man-made laws and their legislators to be other gods, al-Maqdisi actually refers to them as *ṭawāghīt*. He states that 'it is demanded of every Muslim – in every time and place – if he is to be a Muslim who upholds the *tawḥīd* (*Musliman muwaḥḥidan*), that he realises the true meaning of "there is no god but God"'. This is to be done by 'unbelief in every idol (*al-kufr bi-kull ṭāghūt*) and faith in God and submission to him alone', referring to this – on the basis of Q. 2: 256 – as 'the most firm handle' (*al-ʿurwa al-wuthqā*) that believers can hold on to.[63] He continues by stating that the 'most disgusting idol of the age in this country of ours (*ashnaʿ ṭawāghīt al-ʿaṣr fī baladinā hādhā*) and in many of the countries of the Muslims is this [Kuwaiti] constitution and its man-made laws (*hādhā l-dustūr wa-qawānīnuhu l-waḍʿiyya*)'.[64] Al-Maqdisi then proceeds to frame this belief as the ultimate consequence of the Islamic confession of faith, thereby making such ideas of relevance to every Muslim:

Know that your Islam and your *tawḥīd* will not be perfected and the meaning of 'there is no god but God' will not be realised and that you will not find your way to Paradise until you disbelieve and disavow every idol, the most important of which is this: the modern idol that most people follow, pay and worship with the worship of legislation.[65]

62 *Id.*, *Al-Dīmuqrāṭiyya Dīn*, www.tawhed.ws/t, n.d., 5.
63 *Id.*, *Kashf al-Niqāb*, 16.
64 *Ibid.*, 18.
65 *Ibid.*, 19.

These words show that al-Maqdisi frames man-made laws as idols and thus sees them as challenges to *tawḥīd* and, subsequently, Islam itself. Furthermore, this statement entails that simply pronouncing the Islamic confession of faith and fulfilling one's basic duties as a Muslim is apparently not enough to be a good believer; one must also apply the Islamic rejection of idols to legislation.[66] Within this context, he draws a comparison between the Kuwaiti constitution and the *yāsiq*, echoing the accusations Ibn Taymiyya levelled at the rulers of his time. Al-Maqdisi claims that, just as the *yāsiq* was a combination of different systems of law, so today's legislative systems in the Muslim world, and Kuwait in particular, are not purely Islamic but bear the traces of European influence. This 'plurality of sources of legislation' (*taʿaddud maṣādir al-tashrīʿ*), according to al-Maqdisi, also means 'the plurality of lords and gods served besides God' (*taʿaddud al-arbāb wa-l-āliha al-maʿbūda min dūni llāh*) and thus constitutes *shirk* and *kufr*.[67] The difference is, al-Maqdisi claims, that in the Mongols' time, people rose up and rebelled against them, while nowadays most people do not even realise that there is anything wrong with them.[68]

To counter people's ignorance of Kuwait's 'man-made laws', al-Maqdisi proceeds to do what Faraj refrained from doing in his comparison between the *yāsiq* and Egyptian laws, namely to give a meticulous analysis of what is so bad about them. Al-Maqdisi quotes Article 6 of the Kuwaiti constitution, for example, which states that the country has a 'democratic system of rule' (*niẓām al-ḥukm al-dīmuqrāṭī*). This in itself shows, al-Maqdisi states, that the people are the source of legislation instead of God.[69] Similarly, he points to the freedom of religion and equality guaranteed by the Kuwaiti constitution, juxtaposing this with the saying of the Prophet that 'he who changes his religion, kill him' (*man baddala dīnahu fa-qtulūhu*) and verses from the Qurʾān (such as 5: 100) that seemingly support inequality by distinguishing between 'the corrupt' and 'the good'.[70]

This passage, although it shows why al-Maqdisi disagrees with man-made laws, does not explain how he justifies calling *qawānīn waḍʿiyya*

[66] See also *id.*, *Kashf Shubhāt al-Mujādilīn ʿan ʿAsākir al-Shirk wa-Anṣār al-Qawānīn*, www.tawhed.ws/t, 1999 [1995], 17–29.
[67] *Id.*, *Kashf al-Niqāb*, 28.
[68] *Ibid.*, 20–2.
[69] *Ibid.*, 35–7.
[70] *Ibid.*, 38–41.

manifestations of *kufr* (*akbar*) instead of simply lesser unbelief. As mentioned, al-Maqdisi is very close to quietist Salafi scholars in his treatment of unbelief. Like them, he deems acts and sayings that blatantly violate the most important underpinnings of Islam – such as insulting the Prophet – to be acts of greater unbelief that expel a person from Islam, regardless of whether *istiḥlāl*, *iʿtiqād* or *jaḥd* is involved.[71] Also similar to quietist Salafis, he does not consider incidentally applied man-made rulings and laws to be manifestations of *kufr akbar*, unless they are accompanied by *istiḥlāl*, *iʿtiqād* or *jaḥd*.[72] This applies when such a sin is frequently repeated, even hundreds of times.[73] The situation changes, however, as soon as rulers start applying whole new systems of laws as the basis of their legislation instead of Islamic ones. This, according to al-Maqdisi, clearly shows that they are unbelievers in their hearts, and such a sin is therefore *kufr akbar*, for which no further proof of unbelief is necessary.[74] Such a situation, according to al-Maqdisi, is similar to the one the aforementioned verse Q. 5: 44 deals with. This verse, dealing with Jews who followed their own system of laws, also does not mention any explicit *istiḥlāl*, *iʿtiqād* or *jaḥd* but nevertheless brands them as unbelievers.[75] Al-Maqdisi therefore treats rulers who have substituted an Islamic system of laws with a secular or otherwise non-Islamic one as people of an entirely different religion.[76]

Al-Maqdisi's views on this issue as described here are in perfect harmony with those of the scholars holding the third position distinguished previously. This shows that, in spite of the seemingly enormous ideological gap between Jihadi-Salafis and quietist ones because of their differences over jihad, al-Maqdisi's ideas and arguments regarding *kufr* are actually very close to those of quietist Salafis in general, and are virtually indistinguishable from some of them in particular. This will become even clearer in Chapters 6 and 7, in which we look at *al-walāʾ wa-l-barāʾ*, a concept used by both quietist Salafis and their Jihadi counterparts. There is, however, a practical matter that does distinguish al-Maqdisi from

71 *Id.*, *Imtāʿ al-Naẓar fī Kashf Shubhāt Murjiʾat al-ʿAṣr*, www.tawhed.ws/t, 1999/2000 [1991/2], 17, 23, 83; *id.*, *Tabṣīr al-ʿUqalāʾ bi-Talbīsāt Ahl al-Tajahhum wa-l-Irjāʾ*, www.tawhed.ws/t, 1996, 48.

72 *Id.*, *Imtāʿ*, 49, 83; *id.*, *Tabṣīr*, 44–6.

73 *Id.*, *Imtāʿ*, 46; *id.*, *Tabṣīr*, 129.

74 *Id.*, *Imtāʿ*, 46, 49, 51–2, 57–60, 88; *id.*, *Mukhtaṣar 'Kashf al-Niqāb ʿan Sharīʿat al-Ghāb': Al-Dustūr al-Urdunnī*, www.tawhed.ws/t, 1996, 19; *id.*, *Tabṣīr*, 44–6.

75 *Id.*, *Tabṣīr*, 109–11.

76 See also Wagemakers, 'Transformation', in: Meijer (ed.), *Global*, 99–101.

scholars such as al-Fawzan, Ibn Ibrahim and others. Although they all believe that *tabdīl* of an Islamic system of laws is a form of *kufr akbar*, the latter are highly reluctant to reach the conclusion that a country has substituted Islam for something else in its legislation. Al-Maqdisi, however, believes that all Muslim countries practise *tabdīl* in their laws and that the question of lesser unbelief in legislation is, in fact, a purely theoretical one.[77]

Al-Maqdisi's belief that all Muslim countries are guilty of substituting Islamic law with another system of legislation also explains – to return to the question with which we ended the section of this chapter on classical jihad – why he sees the entire world as *dār al-kufr*. If one views the world as divided between non-Muslim countries such as France and the United States on the one hand and Muslim countries whose leaders have thrown out Islamic law and replaced it with secular legislation on the other, as al-Maqdisi does, one could indeed make the case that there is no such thing as *dār al-īmān* or *dār al-Islām*. It should be pointed out, however, that al-Maqdisi's belief that the entire world is *dār al-kufr* does not mean that he applies *takfīr* to each and every Muslim. In fact, al-Maqdisi goes into great detail to show that general *takfīr* of entire groups of people or even nations is wrong and sinful. He meticulously points out that *takfīr* is subject to certain conditions and must not be used casually[78], and singles out dozens of situations in which people apply *takfīr* but must not, or should at least be very careful. These include the impermissibility of calling someone a *kāfir* if he or she is unwilling to join a particular group or organisation[79], but also the warning that, although *takfīr* should be applied to the rulers and their legislation since they are infidel in nature, the people who follow and obey them need not be.[80]

On account of al-Maqdisi's argument that all Muslim states in the world are based on un-Islamic systems and are thus worthy of *takfīr*, he believes that jihad against these regimes is legitimate. In fact, al-Maqdisi prefers jihad to be aimed at the rulers of the Muslim world and not at non-Muslim invaders, although he is certainly not against that. This preference of his was probably also the reason for his aforementioned difference of opinion with ʿAzzam, a staunch defender of classical jihad, as we have seen, when they met each other in Afghanistan. Two reasons

77 Al-Maqdisī, *Imtāʿ*, 49–50; *id.*, *Tabṣīr*, 129–31.

78 *Id.*, *Hādhihi ʿAqīdatunā*, www.tawhed.ws/t, 1997, 26–30; *id.*, *Al-Risāla al-Thalāthīniyya*, 12–85; *id.*, *Risāla li-l-Shaykh Abī Baṣīr*, www.tawhed.ws/r?i=qmof80po, n.d., 1–6.

79 *Id.*, *Al-Risāla al-Thalāthīniyya*, 154–62, see also 148–53.

80 *Ibid.*, 290–356.

for al-Maqdisi's preference for jihad against Muslim rulers can be discerned in his writings. Firstly, al-Maqdisi believes that the apostasy (*kufr al-ridda*) of the rulers is worse than the 'original unbelief' (*al-kufr al-aṣlī*) of, for example, Jews in Israel. Secondly, al-Maqdisi quotes a verse from the Qur'ān (9: 123) that states that the nearest enemy, here equated with the Muslims' own regimes, should be attacked first.[81] The fact that al-Maqdisi deems jihad against Muslim rulers more important than the fight against Israel and America underscores how serious the issue of legislation is to him. In fact, he accuses Muslim regimes of actively attacking *tawḥīd* and Islam. The rulers and their laws, al-Maqdisi maintains, are responsible for 'killing the religion (*qatl al-dīn*), causing the creed to die (*imātat al-ʿaqīda*) and destroying it (*hadmihā*)'.[82] Likewise, the rulers' substitution of Islamic law is not just about 'leaving the *tawḥīd* and avoiding it' (*tark al-tawḥīd wa-l-iʿrāḍ ʿanhu*) but leads to 'destroying it and waging war on it' (*hadmahu wa-ḥarbahu*).[83] Seen within this context, it is perhaps not surprising that, in relation to the aformentioned debate on whether jihad should be offensive or defensive, al-Maqdisi sees his favoured jihad as a purely defensive fight. Since he claims that the entire world is *dār al-kufr*, occupied either by infidels or apostate rulers, any jihad in his view is defensive.[84] Moreover, al-Maqdisi also claims that, precisely because he considers his preferred jihad to be defensive, it is an individual duty incumbent on all Muslims, not just on a limited number.[85]

By reasoning as described here, al-Maqdisi thus on the one hand deviates greatly from Islamic tradition by excommunicating Muslim rulers for their legislation and focussing his preferred jihad on their regimes. On the other hand, however, al-Maqdisi clearly adheres very closely to Salafi tradition and – presumably consciously – frames his own rather unorthodox views as firmly rooted in the centuries' old development of jihad through his use of terms such as *dār al-kufr*, defensive jihad and *farḍ ʿalā l-ʿayn*. Al-Maqdisi has held on to this view in spite of a growing trend among Jihadi-Salafis since the late 1990s to favour global jihad, the third and final form of militant jihad distinguished in this study, to which we must also briefly pay attention.

81 *Id.*, *Hādhihi*, 35; *id.*, *Liqā' min Khalf Quḍbān al-Murtaddīn 'Sana 1418'*, 11; *id.*, *Millat*, 67–8; *id.*, *Tabṣīr*, 102, 147–8.
82 *Id.*, *Kashf al-Niqāb*, 50.
83 *Id.*, *Imtāʿ*, 88.
84 *Id.*, *Waqfāt*, 83.
85 *Ibid.*, 98.

Global Jihad

Apart from the classical form of jihad, which eventually culminated in defensive warfare of the *dār al-Islām* as espoused by men such as ʿAzzam, and the jihad against the ruling regimes preferred by al-Maqdisi, a third form can be distinguished that is ideologically related to the second. This form of jihad, referred to here as global jihad, gained adherents after the fight by various Jihadi-Salafi movements against their own regimes, particularly in Egypt and Algeria, had not been successful. Many of their members had either been killed or locked up, presenting them with the choice of quitting or moving in a different direction. While some chose the first option, others decided to rethink their priorities, as this section shows.

Fighting the 'Far Enemy'

While many Jihadi-Salafis who suffered the repression of their states still believed the primary battleground was in their own home countries, it gradually dawned on them that they would not succeed because of the overwhelming military power of the ruling regimes there and, significantly, the support the latter got from the West. This realisation led to the formulation of a new theory, which stated that Muslim regimes would never fall as long as their Western backers kept up their support. This led some Jihadi-Salafis to direct their attention to those backers instead of their own regimes, hoping that by fighting a global jihad against the United States and its allies they could weaken Western support for their own regimes, in turn making the latter more vulnerable to jihad.[86] The U.S. and its allies are sometimes referred to in this scenario as 'the head of the snake' (*raʾs al-afʿā*), the idea being that if you cut off the head of the snake, the rest of its body (the Muslim regimes they support) will shrivel up.[87]

Instrumental in formulating this new theory of fighting the 'far enemy' (the U.S. and its allies) instead of the 'near enemy' (Muslim regimes) was Ayman al-Zawahiri, who would later become the leader of al-Qaʿida after Bin Laden's death in 2011. Together with Bin Laden and several others, he set up a new trend aimed at fighting the powers allegedly behind the Muslim regimes. This trend manifested itself in 1996, when Bin Laden

[86] Fawaz A. Gerges, *The Far Enemy: Why Jihad Went Global*, Cambridge: Cambridge University Press, 2005, 24–32.

[87] Ḥusayn, *Al-Zarqāwī*, 202–13.

issued a declaration of jihad against the United States for its presence on the Arabian Peninsula. The declaration was special because it showed that Bin Laden's criticism was really directed at Saudi Arabia[88], but his message of war was aimed at the United States. since that country was seen as the reason why Saudis were unable to change their country for the better. To be sure, Bin Laden was also critical of America and Israel from the start, independently of what these countries had to do with Saudi Arabia.[89] His focus, however, seems to have been with the latter, particularly in the mid-1990s.[90] The trend led to the so-called 'World Islamic Front', which gradually came to be equated with the name al-Qaʿida, announcing its jihad against 'Jews and Crusaders' in a declaration signed by four other radical global jihadis, including al-Zawahiri[91], and culminated in the terrorist attacks of 11 September 2001.

The global jihad and '9/11' were not accepted by all Jihadi-Salafis. The attacks themselves and the subsequent U.S.-led 'war on terrorism' did not lead to the massive closing of ranks among jihadis that al-Qaʿida had apparently hoped for. Moreover, some believed that the organisation had clearly got itself involved in a situation that it could not handle, and was held responsible for bringing about an American reprisal on Afghanistan.[92] Particularly critical of al-Qaʿida and its use of terrorism was the Egyptian al-Jamaʿa al-Islamiyya, a group that had been responsible for violent attacks for years but had, in the 1990s, made a remarkable U-turn in its ideological outlook by revising its views, disavowing violence and integrating itself into the Egyptian political and social system.[93] Besides deconstructing al-Qaʿida's arguments for taking their jihad to America, the group also criticised Bin Laden's organisation for such things as widening the gap between the Muslim world and the West and stirring up anti-Islamic feelings.[94]

Al-Maqdisi on Global Jihad

In the midst of this debate over global jihad, al-Maqdisi has been rather quiet. Since he believes that the primary targets of jihad should be Muslim

88 Bruce Lawrence (ed.), *Messages to the World: The Statements of Osama bin Laden*, London & New York: Verso, 2005, 28–9.
89 *Ibid.*, 3–14.
90 *Ibid.*, 15–19, 31–43.
91 *Ibid.*, 58–62.
92 Gerges, *Far*, 192–9.
93 Ashour, 'Lions', 596–625.
94 Gerges, *Far*, 200–10.

regimes, it is perhaps not surprising that he has not made any contribution to the idea that jihad should be taken to a global level. The few statements al-Maqdisi has made on this issue, however, show that he supports the attacks of 11 September 2001. He openly says so in an interview, stating: 'Yes, I supported ["9/11"] and I was happy with them as every Muslim who knows the crimes of the Americans and their Jewish brothers against his *umma* was happy with them.' Al-Maqdisi also praises Bin Laden, calling him 'the imam of the *mujāhidūn* in this age'. He is similarly positive about al-Zawahiri, referring to him as 'one of the most important [men] of the Salafi-Jihadi trend (*min ru'ūs al-tayyār al-jihādī al-salafī*) in our time [who] is doubtlessly greatly beneficial (*lā shakk anna lahu faḍl ʿaẓīm*) to this trend with his writings, his jihad, his steadfastness and his standing side by side with shaykh Osama bin Laden'.[95] Al-Maqdisi further states that 'we are in need of men like ["9/11" hijackers] Muhammad ʿAta, Ziyad al-Jarrah, Marwan al-Shahi, Ahmad al-Ghamidi and their brothers'.[96]

Apart from these statements, al-Maqdisi has not paid much attention to the idea of a global jihad and instead has continued to propagate his own views on jihad and *takfīr*. He did write a book entitled *Mashruʿ al-Sharq al-Awsat al-Kabir* ('the Greater Middle East Project'), a reference to the American policy for the Middle East and Central Asia unfolded by then President George W. Bush of which the war in Afghanistan was part. This book, however, dealt more with American foreign policy in general and Western and Israeli democracy than with the 'war on terrorism' or the attacks that preceded it.[97] Al-Maqdisi also wrote a book shortly after the attacks, but this focussed not so much on legitimising the idea of a global jihad as it did on the duties of Muslims during the war in Afghanistan and the broader 'war on terrorism'.[98] Al-Maqdisi did have much to say about the way jihad was being fought prior to but also after '9/11', however, and openly questioned whether waging jihad – though legitimate – was always such a good idea. These are issues of *manhaj*, however, to which we must now pay specific attention.

95 Al-Maqdisī, *Ḥiwār*, 6.
96 *Id.*, *Waqfāt*, 30.
97 *Id.*, *Mashrūʿ al-Sharq al-Awsaṭ al-Kabīr*, www.tawhed.ws/t, 2004.
98 *Id.*, *Wujūb*.

3

Al-Maqdisi's Quietist Jihadi-Salafi *Manhaj*

When comparing al-Maqdisi's ideas on what jihad is and against whom it should be waged with those of quietist Salafis, we find that there is a great deal of resemblance between them. So much so that the ideas on al-Maqdisi's underlying justification of jihad against the rulers – *kufr* and *takfīr* – are virtually the same as those of some quietists. That is *ʿaqīda*, however. The *manhaj* of applying critical views of rulers in practice is a different matter and one in which al-Maqdisi more clearly distinguishes himself from quietists, although less so than might be expected from a Jihadi-Salafi.

This chapter looks at how Salafi scholars, in particular al-Maqdisi, have translated their *ʿaqīda vis-à-vis* Muslim rulers into practice. We will first look at the choice between *daʿwa* and jihad. While the latter is obviously associated with Jihadi-Salafis, this does not necessarily mean that they are always in favour of waging jihad, as al-Maqdisi shows. Then we will move on to jihad strategy or, in other words, how a jihad should be waged, and what al-Maqdisi has to say about this. Finally, this chapter deals with the question of who may be targeted during an actual jihad. In all three sections of the chapter, it becomes clear that al-Maqdisi is indeed a Jihadi-Salafi who supports jihad against Muslim rulers and in other contexts in principle, but who is nevertheless close to quietists in his support for *daʿwa* and his fear for extremism and excesses during actual fighting.

Daʿwa or Jihad?

As we saw in the Introduction, *manhaj* is a concept referring to the method of applying the *ʿaqīda* in different contexts. While the term is broader than simply the application of the creed in politics and society, this is the dimension that this section focusses on by describing what *manhaj* quietist Salafis and al-Maqdisi choose. This can be portrayed as a simple choice between *da'wa* and jihad but, as the question mark in the subheading of this section indicates, it is slightly more complicated than that.

Quietists' Manhaj

The sometimes critical views of quietist Salafis towards Muslim rulers are, as the 'quietist' label I use for them indicates, not translated into organised political action. The reasons for this differ. In the case of many Saudi Wahhabi scholars, their quietist attitude can be said to be the result of the increasing realisation that their preservation as the country's ideological backbone can only be sustained if they are subservient to the political rulers, who are the only ones able to guarantee and protect their role in Saudi society. This realisation dates back to at least the nineteenth century, when the failure of some scholars to side with the ruler helped bring about disunity and strife, eventually leading to the temporary collapse of Saudi rule. Needless to say, the growing subservience of the scholars since the nineteenth century was stimulated and enforced by the political rulers.[1] Other scholars, such as al-Albani, simply believe that political action leads people away from adhering to the tenets of Islam and should therefore be avoided in order to focus on religious study.[2] Still others believe that politics must be shunned because it does not always take the interests of the *umma* into account but is more about power and influence.[3] Whatever the reason, these scholars believe that criticism of rulers or any other issue in Muslim society should not be expressed in the form of political action or violence. Their alternative is peacefully calling on people to mend their ways and return to Islam as it should be in their eyes. These efforts to use *da'wa* for such purposes express themselves specifically with regard to the rulers in the form of advice

[1] Guido Steinberg, *Religion und Staat in Saudi Arabien: Die wahhabitischen Gelehrten, 1902–1953*, Würzburg: Ergon, 2002, 427–69; *id.*, 'The Wahhabi Ulama and the Saudi State: 1745 to the Present', in: Paul Aarts and Gerd Nonneman (eds.), *Saudi Arabia in the Balance: Political Economy, Society, Foreign Affairs*, London: Hurst & Co., 2005, 18–30.

[2] Stéphane Lacroix, 'Between Revolution and Apoliticism: Nasir al-Din al-Albani and his Impact on the Shaping of Contemporary Salafism', in: Roel Meijer (ed.), *Global Salafism: Islam's New Religious Movement*, London: Hurst & Co., 2009, 69.

[3] Interview with al-Ḥalabī, Amman, 19 January 2009.

(*naṣīḥa*), preferably in private. Apart from having ideological objections to political action or jihad against the rulers, these scholars also argue that uprisings against sinful rulers will only bring more evil and lead to *fitna*.[4] Moreover, these scholars also believe that if punishment for the transgressions of any Muslim is to be used, this is the prerogative of the authorities, not individual Muslims or groups.[5]

A somewhat similar position – criticism of rulers combined with non-violent expressions of it – is held by the Syrian Salafi-inspired scholar Muhammad Surur mentioned previously. Surur rejects the extreme loyalty to the rulers of certain scholars in Saudi Arabia, whom he labels 'the party of the rulers' (*ḥizb al-wulāt*), which includes some of those mentioned in this discussion. Yet he does not accept the idea of fighting regimes through jihad either, as the 'party of the exaggerators' (*ḥizb al-ghulāt*) advocates, since – like the Salafi scholars mentioned earlier – he believes this will cause chaos and strife. He considers himself as positioned between these two groups: critical of the rulers but not advocating fighting them. An admirer of the late mufti Muhammad b. Ibrahim Al al-Shaykh because of his independence of the Saudi state, Surur believes that scholars must be independent but critical of the state to fulfil their true potential.[6]

Al-Maqdisi's Two-Pronged Approach

Al-Maqdisi, though in agreement with most or even all of the quietists' theoretical ideas on *kufr* and *takfīr*, has a different view when it comes to *manhaj*. It has already become clear that al-Maqdisi's strong emphasis on legislation makes any avoidance of political issues unlikely. On top of that, he also rejects the idea that jihad leads to chaos, or *fitna*. In fact, al-Maqdisi completely reframes the situation as portrayed by quietists. He refers to the attack on and occupation of the Grand Mosque of Mecca by Juhayman al-ʿUtaybi in 1979, for example, as a *fitna* because of the rebels' armed action inside the sanctuary and their shedding the blood of innocent Muslims there. He scolds the Saudi state, however, for causing an even worse *fitna* by not living up to its Islamic credentials

4 ʿAbd al-ʿAzīz b. Bāz, *Imaam Ibn Baz on the Manhaj of Correcting the Rulers*, www.salafipublications.com, n.d.; Muḥammad b. Ṣāliḥ al-ʿUthaymīn, *Imaam Ibn Uthaymeen on the Manhaj of Correcting Rulers*, www.salafipublications.com, n.d.

5 Ṣāliḥ b. Fawzān al-Fawzān, *Shaikh Salih al-Fawzaan on those who Ought to Pronounce Takfir and Establish the Hadd Punishment*, www.salafipublications.com, n.d.

6 Al-Rasheed, *Contesting*, 74–7.

because – among other things – it fails to apply Islamic law properly.[7] Since al-Maqdisi believes that applying non-Islamic laws is a violation of the unity of God, he dismisses the calls of those who are unwilling to confront the rulers with their allegedly un-Islamic rule by stating that 'perhaps the majority [of those unwilling to resist the rulers] would use the excuse of the general interest (*maṣlaḥa*) of the *daʿwa* and [the avoidance of] *fitna*. But what *fitna* is greater than concealing the *tawḥīd* and deceiving the people about their religion?'[8] Considering this, it is not surprising that al-Maqdisi not only rejects the idea that people like himself cause *fitna* but actually accuses those scholars unwilling to confront the rulers as 'the scholars of strife' (*ʿulamāʾ al-fitna*).[9]

Al-Maqdisi's reframing of the debate on the correct *manhaj* results in the quietists being branded as the ones promoting *fitna*, instead of the other way around. This might suggest that al-Maqdisi also rejects the preferred method of the quietists – *daʿwa* – altogether. A more detailed look at al-Maqdisi's writings, however, reveals that, despite the real and important differences between him and quietists, he is also closer to them in *manhaj* than one might think. This is expressed most clearly in al-Maqdisi's insistence that, in spite of the legitimacy and desirability of jihad, *daʿwa* is still necessary, as we will see in Chapters 8 and 9. Although al-Maqdisi does not share quietists' pro-regime sentiments that may cause them to focus solely on *daʿwa*, his view that *daʿwa* should not be dismissed in favour of jihad does partly adopt quietist Salafis' preferred method. To be sure, al-Maqdisi never rejects jihad and actively continues to promote it even when stressing the value of *daʿwa*, but his insistence on preserving and promoting the call to Islam shows that he is not just close to quietists in *ʿaqīda*-related questions on *kufr* and *takfīr* but also shares some of their *manhaj*. Al-Maqdisi does have something to say about situations in which actual fighting takes place, however.

Jihad Strategy

As became clear in Chapter 2, the caliph, who, as imam of the *umma*, would at least in theory be in command of the armies, was central in fighting to expand the Muslim empires.[10] He also enjoyed great influence

[7] Al-Maqdisī, *Al-Kawāshif*, 179–82.
[8] *Id.*, *Millat*, 23.
[9] *Id.*, *Wujūb*, 28, 31, 37.
[10] Khadduri, *War*, 87–8.

in other matters related to jihad, such as the spoils of war, which he could – within the confines of the rules on this issue as stipulated by Islamic law – divide and distribute among the Muslims as he saw fit.[11] The fact that the imam was formally in control and that there were actual armies fighting on behalf of an existing territorial unit shows that jihad from the seventh or eighth century until the early twentieth century was – at least in theory – an organised and state-centred effort, even if it was quite different in practice.[12] This section deals with how two major Jihadi-Salafi strategists and al-Maqdisi use or abandon this tradition in their own views on jihad strategy.

Jihadi-Salafi Views on Jihad Strategy

Jihad as led by an imam on behalf of an Islamic empire was, of course, quite different from the jihad waged by modern-day Islamic movements, who are often persecuted by the authorities in their home countries and collectively have no state of their own. Being hampered in one's organisation because of law enforcement and anti-terrorism measures, as well as the absence of a territorial base, are thus problems that modern jihadi ideologues have to deal with. Present-day jihadi strategists therefore try to find ways of adjusting jihad to current circumstances and look for the most effective strategy to hurt their enemies while taking these constraints into account. Perhaps the most important of these strategists is a Syrian supporter of the global jihad as espoused by al-Qaʿida, Mustafa b. ʿAbd al-Qadir Sitt Maryam Nasr, better known as Abu Musʿab al Suri (b. 1958), who was arrested by Pakistani police in 2005.[13] In a massive study in which he calls for 'global Islamic resistance' (*al-muqāwama al-Islāmiyya al-ʿālamiyya*), al-Suri gives an extensive overview of the experiences of various jihad organisations in different countries[14] and their mixed results[15]. Considering the differences in strategy and tactics employed by jihad movements and organisations, he presents what he calls 'the constitution of the global Islamic resistance call' (*dustūr daʿwat al-muqāwama al-Islāmiyya al-ʿālamiyya*), meant to provide a basic overview of the

[11] *Ibid.*, 118–33; *id.*, *Islamic*, 106–29.

[12] Albrecht Noth, 'Von der medinensischen "Umma" zu einer muslimischen Ökumene', in: Albrecht Noth and Jürgen Paul (eds.), *Der islamische Orient: Grundzüge seiner Geschichte*, Würzburg: Ergon, 1998, 104.

[13] Lia, *Architect*, 1.

[14] Abū Muṣʿab al-Sūrī, *Daʿwat al-Muqāwama al-Islāmiyya al-ʿĀlamiyya*, 2 vols., www.tawhed.ws/a?a=hqkfgsb2, 2004, vol. I, 683–818.

[15] *Ibid.*, 819–59.

situation in which *mujāhidūn* find themselves in today's world and how jihad should be seen in it. This constitution contains ideas that are radically different from the legal rulings on an organised and state-based approach that dominated jihad theory in earlier centuries. Article 1 of this constitution, for instance, states that 'the call for global Islamic resistance' – a concept that in itself is somewhat different from the more territorial jihad as defined by Islamic law – 'is not a party or an organisation, nor a limited group but an open call. [...] It is possible for any organisation, group or individual convinced of its method, its goals and its way (*bi-manhajihā wa-ahdāfihā wa-ṭarīqihā*) to join it, directly or indirectly.'[16] Similarly at odds with traditional views of jihad is Article 9, in which al-Suri contends that the rulers of the Muslim world are 'apostate infidels' (*kuffāran murtaddīn*) because – among other reasons – 'they rule the countries of the Muslims on the basis of something other than what God has revealed'. It is therefore not surprising that al-Suri maintains in Article 10 that 'the global Islamic resistance call renders null and void the legitimacy of any pact, assurance of protection, agreement or covenant of protection (*'ahd aw amān aw mu'āhada aw dhimma*) presented by the rulers of the Muslim countries to the infidels'.[17]

Based on such unorthodox ideas, al-Suri distinguishes three different strategies employed by *mujāhidūn* since the 1960s: the school of activist organisations (*madrasat al-tanẓīmāt al-ḥarakiyya*), which he associates with the jihadi groups in Egypt and other countries that tried to topple regimes and establish Islamic states; the school of open fronts and overt confrontations (*madrasat al-jabhāt al-maftūḥa wa-l-muwājahāt al-makshūfa*), a reference to combat experiences that took place on battlefields such as those in Afghanistan; and the school of individual jihad and the terrorism of small cells (*madrasat al-jihād al-fardī wa-irhāb al-khalāyā l-ṣaghīra*), expressed in relatively small attacks by individuals as well as in operations executed by cells independently of a central organisation. Judging these three strategies on the different results they have yielded, al-Suri considers the first to have been a complete failure, while he deems the latter two at least partial successes.[18] He therefore advocates a strategy of global jihad that relies on individual and small cell operations and makes use of the jihad of open fronts when possible.[19] As such, the jihadi

[16] *Ibid.*, vol. II, 923.
[17] *Ibid.*, 925.
[18] *Ibid.*, 1353–64.
[19] *Ibid.*, 1364–88.

strategy that al-Suri promotes is thus not centrally organised nor led by any state. The idea behind this strategy is to confuse and exhaust the enemy by frequent and recurring attacks, simultaneously agitating other Muslims, causing them to join the jihad and thereby slowly but surely making the *mujāhidūn* victorious.[20] While this scenario may be highly successful in wreaking havoc in both Muslim countries and in the West, the relatively unorganised and global nature of this strategy as well as the response of the governments attacked means that this jihad will likely not lead to the consolidation of jihadi gains in the form of an Islamic state.

Standing in stark contrast to al-Suri's writings on jihadi strategy is a book on jihad by another prominent radical ideologue, the Egyptian ʿAbd al-Qadir b. ʿAbd al-ʿAziz (b. 1950), also known as Sayyid Imam and Dr. Fadl. One of the main ideologues and the first leader of the Egyptian Islamic Jihad Organisation, Ibn ʿAbd al-ʿAziz has been in Egyptian custody since 2004 and has recently become a controversial figure among fellow Jihadi-Salafis for his apparent revisions of his earlier points of view.[21] Since he was one of the most prominent ideologues advocating jihad against Muslim regimes, his ideas on the correct way to fight jihad are naturally different from those of global jihadis such as al-Suri. This is clearest in Ibn ʿAbd al-ʿAziz's description of what he believes to be the correct organisation of fighting. Unlike in al-Suri's decentralised jihad, Ibn ʿAbd al-ʿAziz places great emphasis on the leadership (*al-imāra*) during fighting by mentioning numerous Prophetic traditions stating that leadership during jihad is a necessity.[22] He spends more than 250 pages describing the duties of a leader (*amīr*), traditionally appointed by the imam as a commander of the army, which include general tasks such as leading the fighters in prayer or personally inspecting their weapons but also taking the lead role in their training.[23]

Ibn ʿAbd al-ʿAziz's emphasis on leadership, his description of the *amīr*'s duties based on extensive use of the scriptural sources and his use of the language of classical jihad give the impression that he is writing about

[20] *Ibid.*, 1376.

[21] See Amel Lamnaouer and Romain Caillet, 'De l'usage du jihad: la fin d'une ère en Égypte? Les revisions idéologiques de Sayyid Imam', in: Hadjar Aouardji and Hélène Legeay (eds.), *L'Égypte dans l'année 2007*, Cairo: CEDEJ, 2008, 85–115; Lawrence Wright, 'The Rebellion Within: An Al Qaeda Mastermind Questions Terrorism', *The New Yorker* (www.newyorker.com/reporting/2008/06/02/080602fa_fact_wright), 2 June 2008.

[22] ʿAbd al-Qādir b. ʿAbd al-ʿAzīz, *Risālat al-ʿUmda fī Iʿdād al-ʿUdda li-l-Jihād fī Sabīl Allāh*, 2 vols., www.tawhed.ws/a?a=85ud42ss, n.d., vol. I, 50–1.

[23] *Ibid.*, 108–382.

warfare as described by Islamic jurists and as led by an imam. Ibn ʿAbd al-ʿAziz believes, however, that jihad may be fought in the absence of an imam or when the ruling imam is guilty of unbelief. Since he considers the rulers of the Muslim world to be infidels and therefore unsuitable to lead a jihad, Ibn ʿAbd al-ʿAziz states that – instead of having the imam appoint an *amīr* – believers must choose one of their own, just like the first generation of Muslims did when their leader was slain.[24] It thus seems as if the author tries to use the rulings on leadership during fighting as derived from Islamic legal thought on classical jihad to frame his own unorthodox ideas of fighting 'the near enemy' as a modern-day adaptation of a centuries' old tradition. As a consequence, the writings on this issue by Ibn ʿAbd al-ʿAziz, like the classical jurists' works, show a preference for a more organised and centrally led jihad than those by al-Suri. On the issue of consolidating the gains of jihad through the establishment of an Islamic state or at least some kind of territorial base, Ibn ʿAbd al-ʿAziz remains silent, however.[25] It is precisely this issue that al-Maqdisi, who is not nearly as detailed and thorough on jihadi strategy as either al-Suri or Ibn ʿAbd al-ʿAziz, is most concerned with.

Al-Maqdisi's Jihad Strategy

Al-Maqdisi clearly does not seem to agree with the decentralised global jihad strategy that al-Suri advocates. He laments the badly planned and wrongly executed attacks by youngsters he meets and hears about, who seem to be full of enthusiasm but lacking in expertise and experience, sometimes leading to their arrest and imprisonment, from which they are not released until they have told the secret service everything it needs to know.[26] Al-Maqdisi further refers to youngsters who, instead of being negligent and careless, become overly paranoid in their lifestyle so as not to get caught by the police. He mentions youngsters he has visited who insisted on turning up the volume of the radio when speaking, even about trivial matters, so as not to be overheard by the secret service. Others wrote down their plans of attack in such great detail, al-Maqdisi states, that a police raid on their house not only led to their immediate

[24] *Ibid.*, 54–8.
[25] A middle position (exhausting enemies by individual attacks but also with a strong emphasis on organisation) seems to be taken by Abū Bakr Nājī. See Abū Bakr Nājī, *Idārat al-Tawaḥḥush: Akhṭar Marḥala Satamurru bi-hā l-Umma*, www.tawhed.ws/a?a=chr3ofzr, n.d., 15–22. See also Brynjar Lia, 'Doctrines for Jihadi Terrorist Training', *Terrorism and Political Violence*, vol. 20, no. 4, 2008, 518–42.
[26] Al-Maqdisī, *Waqfāt*, 32–5, 105–10, 130–1.

arrest but also ended their plans and the entire jihad cell they belonged to, simply because it was impossible to deny their intentions, which had been described so meticulously.[27] Al-Maqdisi also criticises actions that may be legitimate but are not very wise, such as filming attacks and showing them on the Internet. These acts, particularly beheadings and other executions, damage the image of Islam and do not help jihad in any way, al-Maqdisi maintains. Instead, *mujāhidūn* should take the circumstances in which they operate into account and base their actions on that.[28]

As we will see in Chapter 9, al-Maqdisi has been heavily criticised for the book in which he scolded young jihad fighters because some believed he was attacking jihad itself or revising some of his earlier views. Such criticism misses the point of the book, however, as al-Maqdisi's tone throughout the entire text is not one of moderation but of concern for a jihad that he holds dear and has helped inspire but now sees tarnished by actions that he sometimes sees as illegitimate, at other times simply as very unwise. This is also the reason he states that 'it is not allowed to be silent about these mistakes'[29] and that 'we suffer (*innanā nata'allamu*) nowadays when we witness the dwarfing (*taqzīm*), the shrinking (*taḥjīm*) and, in fact, the distortion (*maskh*) of the jihad'[30]. For the same reason, he also advises youngsters on how to improve their jihad by pointing to the well-planned attacks of 11 September 2001[31] and, especially, the example of the Prophet Muhammad. Al-Maqdisi claims that Muhammad was very skilled at deceiving his enemies, and planned his attacks well[32], and ascribes this to the Prophet's ability and willingness to take the context in which he operated into account, from which today's fighters can learn.[33]

Al-Maqdisi's complaints about the actions of *mujāhidūn* mentioned so far do not necessarily contradict al-Suri's ideas. Although the latter calls for individual attacks and operations by small, independent cells, that does not mean that they should not be planned and executed properly. One could therefore assume that al-Suri would probably agree with al-Maqdisi's criticism. Still, al-Maqdisi goes further in his insistence that jihad should be organised and planned. He points out that individual

27 *Ibid.*, 38–40.
28 *Ibid.*, 91–4.
29 *Ibid.*, 35.
30 *Ibid.*, 106.
31 *Ibid.*, 30.
32 *Ibid.*, 36–8.
33 *Ibid.*, 54, 64–6. See also Ibn 'Abd al-'Azīz, *Risālat*, 23, 220–386.

operations are unlikely to damage the enemy very much and will probably not lead to any significant change. Though he considers such actions legitimate, he advises youngsters to cooperate in groups.[34] Also, he is said to have had the intention of establishing a board of Sunni scholars that could issue fatwas and spread a message of jihad among youngsters, and he has actually succeeded in doing so.[35]

These statements, emphasising the need for collective and centralised instead of individual efforts, underline al-Maqdisi's belief that jihad, with regard to the results it yields, can take two forms nowadays. The first is *qitāl al-nikāya* and refers to fighting to hurt the enemy or his interests; the second is called *qitāl al-tamkīn* and denotes the battle to consolidate one's presence in a certain territory. Al-Maqdisi believes that the first is good and legitimate and obviously needed when fighting an enemy. He also maintains, however, that while this type of fighting happens in abundance, *qitāl al-tamkīn* is sorely lacking among today's *mujāhidūn*. He complains that jihad has proved very good at striking various enemies but that Muslims have sometimes wasted their chances of following through on them by grabbing and consolidating power through the establishment of a sort of safe haven for *mujāhidūn*, for example in the form of an Islamic state. This way, al-Maqdisi claims, the fighters just keep fighting without ever achieving anything in the long term. Even highly successful operations such as the assassination of Egyptian President Anwar al-Sadat or the one on '9/11', he believes, were in the end still forms of *qitāl al-nikāya*. Al-Maqdisi therefore urges *mujāhidūn* not to abandon efforts at *qitāl al-tamkīn* in favour of legitimate but ultimately useless attacks.[36]

Al-Maqdisi's preferred strategy for jihad thus makes clear that he agrees with the legitimacy of individual attacks, as al-Suri does, but prefers collective efforts and, moreover and unlike both al-Suri and Ibn ʿAbd al-ʿAziz, emphasises the need for a state or area in which Muslims can consolidate the gains of jihad. This means, ironically, that his favoured form of jihad somewhat resembles the traditional organised and state-centred one found in classical writings on jihad, albeit from a very different perspective. A final question remains, however, namely who the concrete targets of al-Maqdisi's jihad should be.

34 Al-Maqdisī, *Waqfāt*, 31–2.

35 *Al-ʿArab al-Yawm*, 5 July 2005. See www.tawhed.ws/FAQ/. For more on this group, see Joas Wagemakers, 'Protecting Jihad: The Sharia Council of the Minbar al-Tawhid wa-l-Jihad', *Middle East Policy*, vol. 18, no. 2, 2011, 148–62.

36 Al-Maqdisī, *Waqfāt*, 48–56.

Targets of Jihad

In dealing with the question of who constitutes a legitimate target of jihad – equated here only with people, not material objects – the most important Islamic source dealing with this is the Sunna. Prophetic traditions treating this issue are scattered throughout the different *ḥadīth*-collections. At least two of them mention that Muhammad explicitly forbade killing women and children in general during a raid.[37] Based on such and other rulings dealing with related issues, Islamic jurists agreed that women and children, but also other people not considered combatants such as monks and the elderly, were not to be attacked.[38] The question of whether these persons actually participated in fighting the Muslims or in helping the enemies of the Muslims is very important. Although the *fuqahā'* do not agree on certain details such as whether non-combatant males may be killed, or the exact status of monks in this respect, most seem to agree that persons who refrain from or are unable to participate in combat or helping enemy combatants (sometimes apart from non-combatant adult males) may not be killed.[39]

The question of the legitimate targets of jihad becomes particularly important with regard to the oft-used tactic of suicide bombings, when violence is almost necessarily indiscriminate and therefore highly likely to hurt some of the people that may not be attacked according to Islamic law. Needless to say, there were no suicide bombings in the days of the Prophet or in the centuries that followed. With regard to the important issue here – indiscriminate violence – there are, however, some indications as to how Muslims should behave during warfare. Several traditions exist in which Muhammad allowed women and children to be killed as collateral damage during a night raid, in which the fighters may not have been able to distinguish between combatants and non-combatants.[40] From such traditions, most Islamic jurists concluded that in cases when it is

[37] See *Ṣaḥīḥ Muslim*, book 32 (book 19 in other collections) ('Kitāb al-Jihād wa-l-Siyar'), chapter 8 ('Bāb Taḥrīm Qatl al-Nisā' wa-l-Ṣibyān fī l-Ḥarb'), nos. 4319–20 (1744 in other collections). See also Peters, *Jihad*, 13.

[38] Khadduri, *War*, 103–4.

[39] Cook, *Understanding*, 58–63; Kelsay, *Islam*, 59–67; Ella Landau-Tasseron, '*Non-Combatants' in Muslim Legal Thought*, Research Monographs on the Muslim World, Center on Islam, Democracy and the Future of the Muslim World, Washington, D.C.: Hudson Institute, Series 1, no. 1, 2008; Peters, *Jihad*, 33–6, 49.

[40] See *Ṣaḥīḥ Muslim*, book 32 (book 19 in some collections) ('Kitāb al-Jihād wa-l-Siyar'), chapter 9 ('Bāb Jawāz Qatl al-Nisā' wa-l-Ṣibyān fī l-Bayāt min ghayr Ta'ammud'), nos. 4321–3 (1745 in some collections). See also Peters, *Jihad*, 13.

difficult to distinguish between combatants and non-combatants, imprecise attacks with, for instance, mangonels (devices operated by a spring used to hurl great rocks or other heavy material) on enemy targets are allowed, even if it kills the people one may generally not attack. Conditions for allowing this varied among the scholars, but they included the necessity of targeting the enemy, not the non-combatants[41], and serving the greater interest of the Muslim community[42]. Interestingly, this ruling is upheld by some jurists even if the enemy uses Muslims as a human shield, thereby causing believers to become collateral damage.[43] This section deals with how several modern scholars as well as al-Maqdisi fit into this debate on indiscriminate violence.

Modern Scholars on Indiscriminate Violence

The idea that killing citizens is allowed either as collateral damage or because they can be seen as combatants for aiding the enemy has also found its way into the writings of modern scholars commenting on present-day conflicts. In relation to the idea of collateral damage, the Egyptian shaykh al-Azhar, for example, has argued with regard to Palestinian suicide bombings against Israeli civilians that these are allowed, provided they target soldiers. If civilians die in such operations, they may be seen as unintended victims of legitimate attacks.[44] Similarly, Faris al-Zahrani, better known as Abu Jandal al-Azdi (b. 1976 or 1977), a prominent ideologue of al-Qaʿida on the Arabian Peninsula (QAP), defends killing civilians by quoting scholars who argue that it is allowed as collateral damage if one does not intend to hit them or if it serves the general war against the unbelievers.[45]

The reasoning on collateral damage is taken to perhaps its ultimate consequences by the Saudi scholar Nasir b. Hamd al-Fahd (b. 1968) in his treatise on the permissibility of using weapons of mass destruction. Since these weapons can kill thousands in a single strike and are designed specifically for such massive destruction, attacks using them are the epitome of indiscriminate violence. Al-Fahd argues that Muslims are allowed to employ these during fighting, however, if the jihad necessitates their use. In such a case, if women and children are accidentally hit in an attack

41 Khadduri, *Islamic*, 102; *id.*, *War*, 107.
42 *Id.*, *War*, 107.
43 Cook, *Jihad*, 55–6; Khadduri, *Islamic*, 102; *id.*, *War*, 107.
44 Kelsay, *Arguing*, 141.
45 Abū Jandal al-Azdī, *Nuṣūṣ al-Fuqahāʾ ḥawla Aḥkām al-Ighāra wa-l-Tatarrus*, www.tawhed.ws/r?i=nw8coox6, 2003, 6–25.

on the enemy, it is permitted as collateral damage. To support his case, al-Fahd points to the traditions allowing indiscriminate attacks and the use of mangonels mentioned earlier.[46]

Modern scholars have also tried to expand the concept of combatants and the persons who help them by including people in that category who are not usually seen as such. As we saw before, the question of whether someone is a combatant is an important one because it allows such people to be targeted by jihad. If modern scholars therefore want to legitimise violence against civilians, they need to find some way of framing them as combatants even if they are not. A case in point is the Egyptian scholar Yusuf al-Qaradawi (b. 1926), who is often considered the most influential Sunni scholar alive today. Al-Qaradawi states that, because both men and women in Israel must perform military service at a certain age, Israeli society is, in fact, a militarised one. This means that every Israeli is at least a potential soldier, making all Israelis combatants and therefore legitimate targets of jihad.[47] In his reasoning, al-Qaradawi stretches the concept of combatant to include people who are not soldiers but may be ones in future. In spite of this extraordinary argument, in other cases al-Qaradawi nevertheless seems to adhere closely to the traditional idea that only combatants may be killed. He declared attacks on civilians in Iraq impermissible[48], for example, and roundly condemned the attacks on '9/11' for failing to distinguish between combatants and non-combatants. Such a reasoning might be considered inconsistent but, as Kelsay points out, if one accepts al-Qaradawi's reasoning that all Israelis are soldiers, he is actually quite consistent in his belief that attacks may not target civilians.[49]

A person who stretches the definition of a combatant even further than al-Qaradawi is Bin Laden, who argues not only that the Pentagon, attacked on '9/11', was a military target but also that the people inside the other target on that day, the World Trade Center, were financial backers of the United States and therefore complicit in the latter's alleged crimes against Muslims.[50] Bin Laden also claims that American civilians

[46] Nāṣir b. Ḥamd al-Fahd, *Risāla fī Ḥukm Istikhdām Asliḥat al-Damār al-Shāmil ḍidda l-Kuffār*, www.tawhed.ws/r?i=2gi7siuw, 2003, 9–11, 12–13.

[47] Kelsay, *Arguing*, 141.

[48] 'Al-Qaraḍāwī Yuḥarrimu 'Amaliyyāt Khaṭf al-Madaniyyīn', www.qaradawi.net/site/topics/article.asp?cu_no=2&item_no=3423&version=1&template_id=231&parent_id=17, 2004.

[49] Kelsay, *Arguing*, 142–3.

[50] Lawrence (ed.), *Messages*, 119.

in general, because they live in a democratic country, are responsible for choosing their leaders and therefore support their government's policy, making them involved in the combat that the United States engages in.[51] In an interview, Bin Laden indicates that several scholars have shown that such attacks are legitimate, including the Saudi scholars Humud b. 'Uqala' al-Shu'aybi (1927–2002), Sulayman b. Nasir al-'Ulwan (date of birth unknown) and the first leader and ideologue of QAP, Yusuf al-'Uyayri (d. 2003).[52] These scholars do indeed point to the supposed status of combatant of all Americans[53] and Israelis[54] due to their democratically elected government and their military service duties, respectively.

Several modern, often radical scholars have thus justified indiscriminate violence against non-Muslim women and children (and even Muslims if they are used as human shields) based on the idea that they should be seen as unintended victims of legitimate attacks. They have also simultaneously tried to stretch the meaning of what a combatant is so as to include people who are sometimes – as in the case of ordinary Americans – only remotely linked to the actual soldiers fighting Muslims. The same two arguments of collateral damage and a reframing of combatants appear in al-Maqdisi's writings, though – because of his preferred jihad against Muslim regimes – with a different twist.

Al-Maqdisi on Indiscriminate Violence

As mentioned before, al-Maqdisi has not written much about global jihad, and the same is true about its targets and the use of indiscriminate violence. Still, in reaction to '9/11' and some of the expressions of jihad that al-Maqdisi observed from the 1990s onwards, he did write enough to give his readers an idea about his thoughts on the issue of indiscriminate violence. He is more emphatic than most scholars mentioned earlier, for example, in stating that killing non-combatant women, children and other people generally exempt from the fighting can only be done unintentionally, and that the general rule is that they may not be targeted. He points out, for example, that *mujāhidūn* should be urged to attack military

51 *Ibid.*, 164–5.

52 *Ibid.*, 116–17.

53 Ḥumūd b. 'Uqalā' al-Shu'aybī, *Ḥukm mā Jarā fī Amrīkā min Aḥdāth*, www.tawhed.ws/r?i=horoxyam, 2001, 1, 6–7; Yūsuf al-'Uyayrī, *Ḥaqīqat al-Ḥarb al-Ṣalībiyya al-Jadīda*, www.tawhed.ws/a?a=cfmaghvc, 2001, 31–3.

54 Sulaymān b. Nāṣir al-'Ulwān, *Ḥukm Qatl Aṭfāl wa-Nisā' al-Kuffār fī l-'Amaliyyāt al-Istishhādiyya*, www.tawhed.ws/r?i=enpuzc42, 2001, 4–5.

targets, 'even if they are from among the occupying Jews in Palestine'.[55] He also states with regard to killing Muslims as collateral damage:

> You must know my brothers that the blood of a Muslim is dear (*ghālin*) and its sanctity great (*ḥurmatahu ʿaẓīma*) and [that] the violation of Muslim blood (*istibāḥat dimāʾ al-Muslimīn*) is a great danger (*khaṭar ʿaẓīm*) and that abstaining from killing a thousand infidels (*tark qatl alf kāfir*) – as our scholars have determined – is of less value than deliberately shedding a cupping-glass of Muslim blood (*safk miḥjama min dam Muslim ʿamdan*).[56]

Coming from a man who believes that killing non-Muslims is often a good thing, this is obviously a strong statement. In spite of this, however, al-Maqdisi shows that he does recognise the possibility of legitimately killing women, children and even Muslims. Like other radical scholars, he states that if Muslims try to target their enemies, indiscriminate violence may be used, even if it leads to the killing of women, children and other Muslims. He also confirms that the presence of Muslims among the enemy is no reason to cancel an attack on the latter, as long as the Muslims are not targeted.[57]

Even when arguing that non-combatants may sometimes be killed, however, he apparently still feels compelled to emphasise that children especially may not be targeted and that one should try to avoid places where they gather, such as 'a kindergarten, their schools and their parties'.[58] This tendency to call for relative restraint is even clearer in his treatment of suicide bombings. While he believes these are legitimate methods to target the enemy, he maintains they are only to be used in exceptional circumstances, and laments the fact that they are sometimes used to kill only one or two non-Muslims, which can also be done with a gun.[59] He also scolds *mujāhidūn* for their tendency to revert to such spectacular attacks, and even says that 'many youngsters have fallen in love with explosive operations (*qad aṣbaḥa kathīr min al-shabāb mughram bi-ʿamaliyyāt al-tafjīr*) [...] as if jihad is no good without explosives (*wa-kaʾanna l-jihād lā yaṣlaḥu illā bi-l-mutafajjirāt*)!!'[60] With regard to considering the killing of other Muslims as collateral damage in suicide attacks, al-Maqdisi claims that some *mujāhidūn* use the statements by

55 Al-Maqdisī, *Wujūb*, 31.
56 *Id.*, *Waqfāt*, 5.
57 *Id.*, *Wujūb*, 29–32.
58 *Ibid.*, 31.
59 *Id.*, *Waqfāt*, 2, 114, 123–4; *id.*, *Al-Zarqāwī*, 10; *Al-Jazira*, 6 July 2005.
60 *Id.*, *Waqfāt*, 2.

the Prophet allowing such victims, if there is no other possibility, as an excuse to kill fellow believers much more randomly. This, he believes, is not only a misinterpretation of Muhammad's words but also leads to the killing of dozens of innocent Muslims.[61]

Al-Maqdisi is not only concerned with the general illegitimacy of killing Muslims, however. He also wonders openly why fighters target buses, churches and Shiite mosques, since such attacks do not further the cause of Islam in any way, he claims. He further states that such operations only tarnish the image of Islam and help its enemies.[62] Al-Maqdisi's reasoning against targeting Shiites deserves special mention. Apart from some isolated references to Shiites as Rawāfiḍ (refusers or deserters)[63], a derogatory term, and an introduction to someone else's book about this branch of Islam[64], al-Maqdisi has not written anything about them. It is therefore not surprising that his argument for not targeting Shiites is somewhat shallow. Al-Maqdisi states:

> Ordinary Shiites are like ordinary Sunnis. I am not saying 100 per cent but you will find among them [people] who know nothing except prayer and fasting and do not know the details of the [Jaʿfari Shiite] school of law that our brothers talk about [as expressed] in the distortion (*taḥrīf*) of the Qur'ān and other forms of unbelief (*al-mukaffirāt*) that some Sunni scholars excommunicate the Rāfiḍa Shiites for.[65]

The fact that Jihadi-Salafis often differ in their interpretations from other Muslims, scholars and Islamic law shows that their views can frequently be challenged, as this chapter and the previous one have shown. Al-Maqdisi's argument against attacking Shiites, however, is unlikely to be accepted even among fellow Jihadi-Salafis. While they may agree not to attack them, the idea that most Shiites are simply like most Sunnis, unaware of the specific beliefs that separate them from their Sunni brethren, simply seems to be wrong. In fact, al-Zarqawi, at whom much of this criticism was directed, specifically mentions this in a rebuttal of al-Maqdisi's critique, stating that ordinary Shiites do know about

[61] *Ibid.*, 3–4.
[62] *Ibid.*, 7–8; *id.*, *Al-Zarqāwī*, 9–12; Wā'il al-Batīrī, 'Abū Muḥammad al-Maqdisī: Tabarra'tu Mirāran wa-Takrāran mimmā Yartakibuhu l-baʿḍ min ʿAmaliyyāt ghayr Munḍabiṭa bi-Ḥudūd al-Sharʿ Yadhhabu Ḍaḥiyyatahā Ālāf al-Abriyā' min dūna Fā'ida', *Al-Sabīl*, no. 896, 4 June 2009, 5.
[63] See, for example, al-Maqdisī, *Al-Kawāshif*, 8.
[64] Abū Anas al-Shāmī, *Al-Shīʿa*, www.tawhed.ws/a?a=qecrkm8c, 2009, 1–11.
[65] *Al-Jazīra*, 6 July 2005. See also al-Batīrī, 'Abū', 5; al-Maqdisī, *Al-Zarqāwī*, 12.

specifically Shiite beliefs, such as their reverence for Muhammad's grandson Husayn and their imams.[66]

Apart from al-Maqdisi's arguments for seeing victims of indiscriminate violence in certain circumstances as collateral damage, and his reasoning against such thinking in other situations, he also tries to expand the concept of combatant, as other scholars have done. He states, for example, that if women and children help non-Muslims in their fight against Muslims in any way, including with vague notions such as giving one's opinion (*al-ra'y*), they can be included in the category of combatants and may therefore legitimately be fought.[67] He even states explicitly:

> Everyone who knows the religion of God and [knows] something about the reality of America, its policies, its support for Israel and its assistance to the Jews against the Muslims, its assistance to the idols of the Arabs and others against the *mujāhidūn* by seizure, killing and submission, its enmity and war against Islam and the Muslims, its imprisonment of the scholars of the Muslims and the *mujāhidūn* [. . .] knows with certainty (*ʿilm al-yaqīn*) that it is effectively a state at war (*dawlat ḥarb*) and that its people are a people at war (*shaʿb muḥārib*).[68]

Al-Maqdisi thus tries to stretch the need for women, children and others to be engaged in fighting as a condition for their being called combatants. In this sense, he is not very different from other scholars mentioned earlier. As has become clear in the preceding sections, however, al-Maqdisi's jihad is not primarily aimed at America or Israel but at the rulers of the Muslim world. In spite of the difference in target, he implicitly tries to apply a method of expanding the definition of combatants similar to the one used for Americans and Israelis. Al-Maqdisi's targets of jihad are the rulers of the Muslim world because of their alleged man-made legislation. As mentioned, al-Maqdisi refers to these people as *ṭawāghīt*. These rulers (kings, presidents and prime ministers) are not the only ones guilty of unbelief, however, since their regimes rest on the people that work for them. These people are usually referred to in al-Maqdisi's works as *anṣār al-ṭawāghīt* (the helpers of the idols). The question is, of course: who are these helpers? Do they include army generals, civil servants working for ministers and perhaps even postmen working for the state's postal services? Al-Maqdisi has tried to answer this question specifically and in a way that again expands his concept of the enemy and the people who

66 Al-Zarqāwī, *Bayān*.
67 Al-Maqdisī, *Wujūb*, 32–3.
68 *Ibid.*, 23.

help them by including persons in the category of *anṣār al-ṭawāghīt* that would usually never be seen as combatants.

In describing who these *anṣār* are, Al-Maqdisi states that people should choose God and stay away from 'every corrupt post (*kull waẓīfa fāsida*) that involves helping the servants of the *yāsiq* (*iʿānat li-ʿabīd al-yāsiq*) in favour of their injustice (*ẓulmihim*) or confirmation or help (*iqrār aw nuṣra*) of their laws'.[69] This statement makes legislation a central issue by referring to the *yāsiq*, the Mongol system of law with which al-Maqdisi compares modern Muslim states' laws. It also seems to suggest that the people included in the category of *anṣār* are at least those who are somehow upholding the regime and their laws and are actively working for the system's survival. This is indeed the way al-Maqdisi intends it to be interpreted as the people he explicitly includes in his definition of the *anṣār al-ṭawāghīt* fit this description. These include the army, the police and the national and/or royal guards since they protect the regime and uphold the laws that al-Maqdisi refuses to accept. Since these laws are affronts to *tawḥīd* and Islam, according to al-Maqdisi, he considers the army, the police and the national and/or royal guard to be 'in the forefront of those who wage war on God and his religion' (*muqaddimat al-muḥāribīn li-llāh wa-li-dīnihi*).[70] For waging war against 'true Muslims', al-Maqdisi also considers people working for the security services to be included since they 'spy on the believers (*ahl al-īmān*) and pass on their information to their friends among the servants of the *yāsiq*'.[71] While these people may be seen as persons traditionally included in the category of combatants because of their military or security-related jobs, the same cannot be said of the civil servants who levy taxes, enforce fines and work at customs and similar, related offices. Since these people actively help enforce the regime's rules financially, however, al-Maqdisi also deems their jobs acts of *kufr*.[72] The final persons al-Maqdisi identifies as part of the group that helps the *ṭawāghīt* include servants, ambassadors and messengers working for 'the servants of the *yāsiq*'[73], persons working in the justice system as district attorneys or lawyers for their explicit upholding of the man-made laws and members of parliament and ministers.[74]

Al-Maqdisi considers the people mentioned to be helpers of the regimes and their laws who are complicit in the regimes' supposed fight against

69 *Id.*, *Kashf al-Niqāb*, 113.
70 *Ibid.*, 116.
71 *Ibid.*, 122–3. The quote is on 122.
72 *Ibid.*, 125–6.
73 *Ibid.*, 127.
74 *Ibid.*, 128–33.

Islam and are therefore, in a way, similar to people aiding combatants waging war on Muslims. By including these people in the circle of enemies that may be fought through jihad, al-Maqdisi thus widens the group of enemies just as Bin Laden's treatment of every American as a combatant does. While al-Maqdisi is quite specific about who is included in this group and who is not, the term 'helpers of the idols' is easily misinterpreted to include persons who are only vaguely tied to the regime but may nevertheless find themselves the object of *takfīr* if radical Muslims believe they are complicit in the regime's alleged crimes. Al-Maqdisi seems to realise this possibility and therefore states that the professions he includes in the group of helpers entail protection of man-made laws and helping the regime against the Muslims who uphold *tawḥīd* (*muwaḥḥidūn*). This is different, al-Maqdisi maintains, from other government jobs such as conductor on a train or bus.[75] Posts such as this or mere administrative government jobs should not be the subject of *takfīr*, al-Maqdisi believes, although he claims to stay away from them himself.[76] Similarly, while working as a judge or a lawyer shows that one supports and tries to uphold a *kufr* law, citizens demanding their rights on the basis of and seeking help through that law are not *kuffār*. One must take into account that people are weak, al-Maqdisi believes, and have to resort to man-made systems of law since they have no other possibility. He does call on people not to do this, however.[77]

In the method of application of his creed, al-Maqdisi thus tries to expand the circle of those who may be fought by including people upholding, protecting or legislating on behalf of the regime as *anṣār al-ṭawāghīt*. At the same time, al-Maqdisi is careful not to let this group expand too much, and points to those that should be excluded from it. This relative moderation, just like his emphasis on not using unbridled violence, abets his ideas on *takfīr* dealt with in Chapter 2 as well as his emphasis on *daʿwa*, which both show that al-Maqdisi is often closer to quietist Salafis than one might think. How al-Maqdisi's beliefs and identity as a 'quietist Jihadi-Salafi' affected his framing efforts of several specific issues is dealt with in the next six chapters.

[75] *Ibid.*, 134–6.
[76] *Id.*, *Al-Risāla al-Thalāthīniyya*, 318–21, 336–42.
[77] *Ibid.*, 322–35.

PART II

AL-MAQDISI'S INFLUENCE ON THE SAUDI ISLAMIC OPPOSITION, 1989–2005

4

Saudi Arabia's Post–Gulf War Opposition

As we saw in Chapter 1, al-Maqdisi was heavily influenced by the time he spent in Saudi Arabia and the Wahhabi writings he found there. He has nevertheless been a staunch critic of Saudi Arabia and Wahhabi scholars who are loyal to its regime. This not only shows that Wahhabi writings can be used in both pro- and anti-Saudi ways, but it also makes clear how al-Maqdisi uses the Wahhabi tradition, which is mostly adopted by quietist Salafis, for jihadi purposes, thereby further underlining his position as a quietist Jihadi-Salafi.

In this chapter, we will look first at the history of Wahhabi opposition to the Saudi system from within the country itself, especially the wave of opposition to the regime after the Gulf War of 1990. The chapter then focuses on al-Maqdisi's ideas on Saudi Arabia, what impact they have had on the post–Gulf War opposition until 1995 and how this influence can be explained. The year 1995 was chosen because this is when the phase of post–Gulf War opposition more or less came to an end.

Wahhabism and the Saudi System

The past two decades have seen the publication of a relatively large number of studies on the history of Wahhabism, ranging from the apologetic[1] to the highly critical[2] and everything in between[3], as well as the history

1 Natana J. DeLong-Bas, *Wahhabi Islam: From Revival and Reform to Global Jihad*, Oxford: Oxford University Press, 2004.

2 Hamid Algar, *Wahhabism: A Critical Essay*, Oneonta, NY: Islamic Publications International, 2002.

3 Mohammed Ayoob and Hasan Kosebalaban (eds.), *Religion and Politics in Saudi Arabia: Wahhabism and the State*, Boulder, CO, & London: Lynne Rienner Publishers, 2009;

of Saudi Arabia in general[4]. From these and other studies, we learn that the Saudi state began with the territorial ambitions of Muhammad b. Saʿud (d. 1765), the ruler of al-Dirʿiyya, a settlement in the central Arabian region called Najd. His pact in 1744 with fellow Najdi Muhammad b. ʿAbd al-Wahhab (1703–92), the strict Salafi reformist scholar whose ideas would become known as 'Wahhabism' and gave Ibn Saʿud religious legitimacy, became the basis for three Saudi states. The alliance conquered large parts of the Arabian Peninsula and set up an emirate with al-Dirʿiyya as it capital. The families of the two men – the Al Saʿud and the Al al-Shaykh – have formed the two pillars of the state ever since, from the first Saudi realm (1744–1818), through its successor (1824–91) to the current state of Saudi Arabia (1932–).[5]

The pact between the Al Saʿud and the Al al-Shaykh proved to be an enduring alliance. The former became what is now known as the Saudi royal family, which formed the political pillar of all three Saudi states and whose members became the country's kings and most important ministers. The descendants of Ibn ʿAbd al-Wahhab, on the other hand, were eventually given key positions at religious and educational facilities and institutions and, as a result, held great sway over societal and doctrinal issues. The religious legitimacy provided by the Al al-Shaykh to the Al Saʿud was reciprocated by the protection of the *ʿulamāʾ* provided by the rulers. This way, Saudi Arabia's rulers had enough room to apply their preferred policies, while simultaneously keeping up their image as a pious Islamic state because of its religious foundation and its status as protector of the holy places in Mecca and Medina. This image of piety that the state assumed has become institutionalised throughout the years, so that the seemingly separate identities of being a Muslim and a citizen are inextricably mixed in Saudi Arabia. This fusion between statehood and religion,

David Commins, *The Wahhabi Mission and Saudi Arabia*, London & New York: I.B. Tauris, 2006; Michael Cook, 'On the Origins of Wahhābism', *Journal of the Royal Asiatic Society*, vol. 2, no. 2, 1992, 191–202; Steinberg, *Religion*.

4 David E. Long, *The Kingdom of Saudi Arabia*, Gainsville: University Press of Florida, 1997; Tim Niblock, *Saudi Arabia: Power, Legitimacy and Survival*, London & New York: Routledge, 2006; Madawi al-Rasheed, *A History of Saudi Arabia*, Cambridge: Cambridge University Press, 2002; Alexei Vassiliev, *The History of Saudi Arabia*, London: Saqi Books, 2000 [1998].

5 Two recent works giving a detailed account of the role religious scholars have played in Saudi Arabia's history are Muhammad Al Atawneh, *Wahhābi Islam Facing the Challenges of Modernity: Dār al-Iftā in the Modern Saudi State*, Leiden: Brill, 2010; Nabil Mouline, *Les clercs de l'islam: Autorité religieuse et pouvoir politique en Arabie Saoudite, XVIIIe – XXIe siècle*, Paris: Presses Universitaires de France, 2011.

as well as the country's self-imposed duty to spread the message of Islam, are actively promoted by both the royal family and in education.[6]

Wahhabi Resistance to the Saudi Regime

The strict Wahhabi image that Saudi Arabia uses to present itself often excludes groups of Muslims considered deviant, such as Sufis and Shiites. This exclusive nature of Wahhabism may seem preferable for a country that sees itself as the 'state of the unity of God' (*dawlat al-tawḥīd*), but it also acts as a double-edged sword. Although it provides the country with an important religious status, it also sets a very high standard that its rulers must necessarily live up to in their policies. During several episodes in Saudi Arabia's history, certain elements from within the country challenged the rulers on religious grounds in ways that were rooted in Wahhabi tradition itself.

The first major challenge to Saudi rule on Wahhabi grounds came from the so-called Ikhwan (brothers). This band of fighters was used by the first king of the current Saudi state, ʿAbd al-ʿAziz b. ʿAbd al-Rahman Al Saʿud (also known as Ibn Saʿud, 1880–1953), to conquer parts of the Arabian Peninsula. The king had also established ties with the British, wanted cordial relations with neighbouring countries and took a more or less conciliatory approach towards minorities such as Shiites. This meant that he wanted to limit the conquering zeal of the Ikhwan somewhat. The latter, however, did not agree, and challenged the king over this issue, who eventually confronted the Ikhwan militarily and defeated them at the Battle of Sibilla in 1929.[7]

The second, partly Wahhabi-inspired challenge to Saudi rule came in 1979, when a group of rebels under the direction of Juhayman al-ʿUtaybi (d. 1980) occupied the Grand Mosque of Mecca on the eve of the new Muslim century. They claimed that one of them, Muhammad

[6] Eleanor Abdella Doumato, 'Manning the Barricades: Islam According to Saudi Arabia's School Texts', *Middle East Journal*, vol. 57, no. 2, 2003, 230–47; Joseph Nevo, 'Religion and National Identity in Saudi Arabia', *Middle Eastern Studies*, vol. 34, no. 3, July 1998, 34–53; Madawi al-Rasheed, 'God, the King and the Nation: Political Rhetoric in Saudi Arabia in the 1990s', *Middle East Journal*, vol. 50, no. 3, 1996, 359–71, esp. 365–71.

[7] John S. Habib, *Ibn Saud's Warriors of Islam: The Ikhwan of Najd and Their Role in the Creation of the Saudi Kingdom, 1910–1930*, Leiden: Brill, 1978, 121–55; Joseph Kostiner, 'On Instruments and Their Designers: The Ikhwan of Najd and the Emergence of the Saudi State', *Middle Eastern Studies*, vol. 21, no. 3, July 1985, 313–18; Guido Steinberg, 'Wahhabi *ʿulama* and the state in Saudi Arabia, 1927', in: Camron Michael Amin, Benjamin C. Fortna and Elizabeth Frierson (eds.), *The Modern Middle East: A Sourcebook for History*, Oxford: Oxford University Press, 2006, 57–61.

b. ʿAbdallah al-Qahtani, was the promised Mahdi ('the guided one', a Messianic figure). Al-ʿUtaybi's writings, however, showed that – at least for him personally – Messianic zeal played perhaps only a secondary role.[8] He claimed to be a descendant of one of the Ikhwan that King ʿAbd al-ʿAziz had defeated, and used religious arguments to point out that the ruling Saudi regime was illegitimate, though not infidel. Although he makes his case against the Saudi rulers in a rather unorganised way, it is clear that al-ʿUtaybi partly relies on certain Wahhabi writings and was actually part of a broader pietistic Wahhabi-inspired movement that became politicised in the 1970s.[9] The group of rebels was defeated after a two-week standoff and dozens of them were executed. Like-minded activists continued their activities abroad, however, and also influenced al-Maqdisi, as we saw in Chapter 1.

The third, and perhaps most important partly Wahhabi-inspired challenge to the Saudi regime came in the form of a trend that originated in the 1960s. As we saw in the Introduction, numerous Muslim Brothers from around the Arab world moved to Saudi Arabia to escape persecution in their home countries from the 1960s to the 1980s. They integrated into the country's educational facilities and as such gained major influence within the new universities of Saudi Arabia.[10] As Madawi al-Rasheed points out, official, state-sponsored Wahhabism was (and is) mostly concerned with ritual issues in people's daily lives and generally leaves moral and political issues to the rulers. The immigrant Muslim Brothers and like-minded Saudis, however, combined Wahhabism with the Brotherhood's political activism and thereby helped bring about the *ṣaḥwa*: a resurgence of a more politically sensitive and critical Wahhabism in the 1970s and 1980s.[11] A major difference between the *ṣaḥwa* and the two previous Wahhabi-inspired rebellions was that the two earlier challenges could be seen as radical outgrowths of the Saudi-Wahhabi system itself, while the *ṣaḥwa* clearly represented a mixture of Wahhabism with a political activism alien to the Wahhabi tradition.[12]

The development of the *ṣaḥwa* was facilitated by the Saudi regime after 1979 because it was eager to portray itself as pious after its status had been challenged by Juhayman al-ʿUtaybi's occupation of the Grand

[8] Al-ʿUtaybī, *Risālat*.

[9] Hegghammer and Lacroix, 'Rejectionist', 103–22.

[10] Stéphane Lacroix, *Les islamistes saoudiens: une insurrection manquée*, Paris: Presses Universitaires de France, 2010, 48–64; al-Rasheed, *Contesting*, 59–101, esp. 65–72.

[11] Al-Rasheed, *Contesting*, 59–72. See also Kepel, *War*, 170–80.

[12] Lacroix, *Islamistes*, 65.

Mosque. This expressed itself in (amongst other things) more funding for religious institutions, a greater role for the *ʿulamāʾ*, an increase in the number of mosques and the king's adoption of the title 'Custodian of the Two Holy Places' (*khādim al-ḥaramayn*). In this climate of increased official religiosity, the *ṣaḥwa* could flourish.[13] Although 'members' of the *ṣaḥwa* were quite politicised and critical of official Wahhabism[14], they did not openly challenge the regime. This stopped, however, shortly after the Iraqi dictator Saddam Husayn invaded Kuwait and threatened Saudi Arabia.

The Gulf War

The *ṣaḥwa* and the Al Saʿud collided drastically in 1990 when the Saudi government decided to allow 500,000 American soldiers within its borders to protect it from a possible attack by the Iraqi army. Although the decision is said to have been a controversial one among the ruling Saudi princes, King Fahd (r. 1982–2005) eventually went ahead with it and also managed to convince the official *ʿulamāʾ* to approve of inviting these non-Muslim soldiers in such large numbers.[15]

Despite the support of the official *ʿulamāʾ*, the invitation of the American soldiers caused a shock among the *ṣaḥwa* scholars, who saw the United States as an enemy, and a staunch supporter of Israel's. After it became known, the invitation of the soldiers sparked a protest movement that was broader than just the *ṣaḥwa* and far from homogeneous. It included liberal Saudis who, sensing that the regime was at a weak point in its popularity and authority, asked for reforms in the sphere of human rights, legislation and democratisation.[16] Another group was the so-called Advice and Reform Committee (ARC), led by Osama bin Laden, which seems to have consisted mostly of people who had

[13] Toby Craig Jones, 'Religious Revivalism and its Challenge to the Saudi Regime', in: Mohammed Ayoob and Hasan Kosebalaban (eds.), *Religion and Politics in Saudi Arabia: Wahhabism and the State*, Boulder, CO, & London: Lynne Rienner, 2009, 110–12; Gwenn Okruhlik, 'Making Conversation Permissible: Islamism and Reform in Saudi Arabia', in: Quintan Wiktorowicz (ed.), *Islamic Activism: A Social Movement Theory Approach*, Bloomington & Indianapolis, Ind.: Indiana University Press, 2004, 254–5.

[14] See, for example, Safar b. ʿAbd al-Raḥmān al-Ḥawālī, *Ẓāhirat al-Irjāʾ fī l-Fikr al-Islāmī*, 2 vols., www.tawhed.ws/a?a=q3vtcgx3, 1985/6. See also Kepel, *War*, 174–6; Lacroix, *Islamistes*, 177–9.

[15] Mordechai Abir, *Saudi Arabia: Government, Society and the Gulf Crisis*, London & New York: Routledge, 1993, 174, 178–9.

[16] Richard Dekmejian, 'The Liberal Impulse in Saudi Arabia', *Middle East Journal*, vol. 57, no. 3, 2003, 403.

fought the Soviet Union in Afghanistan and who held more radical ideas than the *ṣaḥwa*. Although such people came to play a more prominent role in the Saudi opposition in later years (see Chapter 5), their influence during the period dealt with here seems to have been rather minor, and I will therefore concentrate on the *ṣaḥwa* in this chapter.[17]

The *ṣaḥwa* (as well as some older sympathisers, who sometimes had personal reasons to support the movement)[18], became the backbone of the protests against the state after the Gulf War. The two men most closely associated with this phenomenon – to the extent that they are referred to as the '*ṣaḥwa* shaykhs' (*shuyūkh al-ṣaḥwa*) – are Salman al-ʿAwda and Safar al-Hawali. These two men, both educated and politicised in the 1970s and 1980s, led protests, held critical sermons (spread through audio cassettes) and wrote books about international politics, from which it became clear that they were not going to accept Saudi foreign policy as easily as the official *ʿulamāʾ* had done.[19]

Although the protest movement led by al-ʿAwda and al-Hawali was sparked by the decision to allow the American soldiers into the country and centred around this topic, it was not limited to this particular issue but had a wider agenda demanding political and social reform. As such, participants within the movement presented the Saudi king with a 'Letter of Demands' (*khiṭāb al-maṭālib*) in 1991. It contained both secular demands, dealing with democratisation and equality, as well as religious ones, concerning the interests of the *umma* and the application of the *sharīʿa*. Although the letter did refer to the need to avoid alliances that 'violate' the *sharīʿa* – an obvious reference to Saudi ties with America – the other demands made clear that the movement had roots that went deeper than this incident.[20] In 1992, it was followed by a longer document entitled 'The Memorandum of Advice' (*mudhakkirat al-naṣīḥa*), which carried a similar message but was much more detailed about topics such as the judiciary and the proper role of scholars.[21]

17 Fandy, *Saudi*, 177–94.

18 Lacroix, *Islamistes*, 201–6.

19 Fandy, *Saudi*, 61–113; Okruhlik, 'Making', 255–7; Joshua Teitelbaum, *Holier than Thou: Saudi Arabia's Islamic Opposition*, Washington, D.C.: The Washington Institute for Near East Policy, 2000, 25–32.

20 For English translations of the Letter of Demands, see R. Hrair Dekmejian, 'The Rise of Political Islamism in Saudi Arabia', *Middle East Journal*, vol. 48, no. 4, 1994, 630–1; Daryl Champion, *The Paradoxical Kingdom: Saudi Arabia and the Momentum of Reform*, New York: Columbia University Press, 2003, 222–3.

21 *Mudhakkirat al-Naṣīḥa*, www.alhramain.com/text/payan/alnseha/1.htm (accessed 6 May 2008), 1992.

The Letter of Demands and the Memorandum of Advice make clear that many of the *ṣaḥwa*'s wishes were, in fact, more political than strictly religious in the sense that they do not primarily rely on the Qur'ān, the Sunna and other religious sources. Demands for an independent and empowered consultative council (*majlis al-shūrā*), equality, an end to corruption, a more equal distribution of wealth and a stronger army could all just as easily have been made by secular reformers, particularly since most were framed in exclusively political terms.[22] The Memorandum of Advice put more stress on religious legitimacy, such as the request to increase the role of the *'ulamā'* and the wish to see the media employed for the purpose of *da'wa*, but this document also focussed on issues such as the army, foreign relations and human rights.[23] The political nature of the *ṣaḥwa* was underlined by the speeches and writings of al-ʿAwda and al-Hawali, who argued much more – but certainly not exclusively – in terms of international politics and American-led conspiracies against Saudi Arabia than by using strictly religious language.[24]

In 1993, an organisation was founded called the Committee for the Defence of Legitimate Rights (CDLR, al-Lajna li-Difāʿ al-Ḥuqūq al-Sharʿiyya), which basically strove for organised political reform along the lines of the Letter of Demands and the Memorandum of Advice. The Saudi state, meanwhile, was shocked by the reformist initiatives, and initially decided to give in to the protests by announcing reforms. As the demands grew louder, bolder and even became organised through the CDLR, however, the Saudi government became increasingly willing to repress dissenters in various ways.[25] These included attacking their message with official fatwas and counter documents, and some of the petitioners, including al-ʿAwda and al-Hawali in 1994, were imprisoned, while others, among them prominent CDLR member Saʿd al-Faqih and its spokesman Muhammad al-Masʿari, fled the country and settled in London in 1994.[26] There, the movement eventually split and lost much of its influence. Although the use of faxes and the Internet allowed the exiled opposition to continue its activities in a sometimes very effective

[22] Dekmejian, 'Rise', 630–1; Lacroix, *Islamistes*, 214–19.

[23] *Mudhakkirat*; Lacroix, *Islamistes*, 219–23.

[24] Fandy, *Saudi*, 63–84, 94–112; Teitelbaum, *Holier*, 29–30. See, for example, Safar b. ʿAbd al-Raḥmān al-Ḥawālī, *Kashf al-Ghumma 'an 'Ulamā' al-Umma*, http://saaid.net/book/open.php?cat=84&book=540, 1991.

[25] For an in-depth analysis of how the Saudi state countered the *ṣaḥwa*, see Lacroix, *Islamistes*, 238–59.

[26] Al-Rasheed, *History*, 172–6.

way[27], halfway through the 1990s the Saudi regime seemed to have succeeded in thwarting most of the *ṣaḥwa*'s opposition.

Al-Maqdisi's Framing of Saudi Arabia

The *ṣaḥwa*'s critical ideas expressed after the Gulf War clearly went beyond the decision to invite the American soldiers. They were part of a broader and politicised Wahhabi reformist critique of Saudi Arabia's policies and its system and should be viewed within the context of general discontent about the country. Al-Maqdisi's ideas on Saudi Arabia, on the other hand, though similar to the *ṣaḥwa*'s critique in several ways, were different in three respects, two of which are important for this chapter: though clearly employing a politicised discourse, al-Maqdisi framed the regime and his critique of it in a more religious way than the *ṣaḥwa* activists and shaykhs did; and al-Maqdisi's discourse drew much more radical conclusions with regard to the supposed sinfulness of the Saudi system.

Judging Saudi Arabia on Its Religious Credentials

The inherent but latent tension between Saudi Arabia's reputation as the supposed 'state of *tawḥīd*' and the more complex reality of interests and international relations the country found itself in surfaced when the regime was confronted by the Ikhwan, Juhayman al-ʿUtaybi and the *ṣaḥwa*. Similarly, al-Maqdisi frames Saudi Arabia as a country that does not live up to its own Salafi-Wahhabi ideology. His first major book, *Millat Ibrahim*, occasionally mentions Saudi Arabia as an example of a state that claims to be pious but in reality is not.[28] His most comprehensive and sustained effort against the Saudi state can be found in a different book, however, called *Al-Kawashif al-Jaliyya fi Kufr al-Dawla al-Saʿudiyya*, which came out in 1989 and in which he criticises Saudi Arabia on religious grounds.[29]

Roughly speaking, al-Maqdisi criticises Saudi Arabia for three things. The first is its legislation. As we saw in Chapter 2, Islamic legislation is extremely important to al-Maqdisi, and he applies this attitude in great

[27] Mamoun Fandy, 'CyberResistance: Saudi Opposition between Globalization and Localization', *Comparative Studies in Society and History*, vol. 41, no. 1, January 1999, 124–47, esp. 134–46; Joshua Teitelbaum, 'Duelling for *Daʿwa*: State vs. Society on the Saudi Internet', *Middle East Journal*, vol. 56, no. 2, 2002, 222–39, esp. 226–7.

[28] Al-Maqdisī, *Millat*, 16, 69.

[29] *Id.*, *Al-Kawāshif*. See also al-Rasheed, *Contesting*, 121–3.

detail to Saudi laws. He claims that the kingdom, despite its reputation for piety, does not actually govern according to the laws of Islam but applies 'man-made laws'.[30] He accuses the Saudi government of applying un-Islamic legislation under the guise of different names, so as to give the impression that all its laws are truly Islamic and that other, non-Islamic rules are not actually laws. '[Saudi Arabia] does not apply the word "laws" to [its laws]. On the contrary', al-Maqdisi writes. 'It calls them "systems" (*anẓima*), "protocols" (*marāsim*), "instructions" (*taʿlīmāt*), "orders" (*awāmir*), "decrees" (*lawāʾiḥ*) or "policies" (*siyāsāt*).' He proves this by quoting a book on Saudi law that states that '"the words 'law' (*qānūn*), 'legislation' (*tashrīʿ*) and '*sharīʿa*' are only applied in Saudi Arabia to the rulings that appear in Islamic law (*al-sharīʿa al-Islāmiyya*). Those man-made rulings that exceed [the *sharīʿa*] are considered 'systems', 'instructions' or 'orders'."'[31]

Al-Maqdisi mentions examples of Saudi laws that supposedly contradict the *sharīʿa*. He states that increased trade with other countries, for instance, has resulted in trade laws that are not of Islamic origin but of Arab or even European origin.[32] He also writes that books published in Saudi Arabia need to be approved by the state, which, he sarcastically points out, results in a situation where one is 'not allowed' to publish truly Islamic books in the *dawlat al-tawḥīd*.[33] He further remarks that one has to look carefully to see whether these are really Saudi laws and not Kuwaiti laws, which – as we have seen – al-Maqdisi has also condemned.[34]

Significant in all of al-Maqdisi's work, but especially in *Millat Ibrahim* and *Al-Kawashif al-Jaliyya*, is that he makes extensive use of Wahhabi sources. Eighteenth- and nineteenth-century scholars such as Muhammad b. ʿAbd al-Wahhab, Sulayman b. ʿAbdallah Al al-Shaykh and Hamd b. ʿAtiq are quoted extensively. One could therefore say that *Al-Kawashif al-Jaliyya*, the sources of which he collected in Saudi Arabia when he stayed there[35], is a Wahhabi-flavoured *j'accuse* against the Wahhabi state itself. One of the ways al-Maqdisi does this is by showing that Saudi Arabia's laws do not conform to the norms of Islam according to the fatwas by a former mufti of the kingdom itself, Muhammad b. Ibrahim Al

30 Al-Maqdisī, *Al-Kawāshif*, 4.
31 *Ibid.*, 15.
32 *Ibid.*, 16.
33 *Ibid.*, 21.
34 *Ibid.*, 18.
35 Interview with al-Maqdisī, Amman, 13 January 2009.

al-Shaykh (d. 1969). He lists law after law that Saudi Arabia introduced but that was rejected as contrary to Islamic law by Ibn Ibrahim, who nevertheless remained loyal to the *walī l-amr*. According to al-Maqdisi, Ibn Ibrahim tried to keep the kingdom from deviating from the *sharīʿa* but to no avail since the rulers adopted the laws anyway. He mentions examples, including trade laws[36] and regulations related to smoking[37], that were condemned by Ibn Ibrahim, and as such al-Maqdisi frames the Saudi state as so unwilling to live up to its religious underpinnings that it does not even listen to its own mufti.

The second point of criticism al-Maqdisi writes about has to do with Saudi ties to foreign organisations and institutions that govern on the basis of man-made laws. Equating these laws with objects of worship or *ṭawāghīt*, he states that Saudi Arabia should not have ties with organisations that blatantly violate God's *tawḥīd* by accepting other gods in the form of man-made laws. Examples he mentions are the International Court of Justice and the United Nations (UN). Since these are based on documents such as the UN Charter, which Saudi Arabia necessarily subscribes to because of its membership of the UN, it actively endorses an organisation that is based on man-made laws.[38] Although one may get the impression that al-Maqdisi's opposition to the UN has more to do with politics than with his religious conviction – he claims, for instance, that the UN 'yields to Jewish influence' and protects the interests of big states[39] – he mostly frames his opposition in a religious way. Al-Maqdisi claims, for example, that issues such as equality of religions and the sexes, opposition to offensive warfare and peaceful relations between Muslims and non-Muslims are seen as positive and desirable by the UN but are completely contrary to Islam.[40] He also condemns Saudi ties with Arab organisations such as the Gulf Cooperation Council and the Arab League because he believes these are also based on non-*sharʿī* laws.[41]

The third point of criticism of Saudi Arabia, and the most political one al-Maqdisi tries to make, is the inadmissibility of strong Saudi-U.S. ties. It is with regard to this topic that al-Maqdisi is closest to the writings of al-ʿAwda and al-Hawali, although they and other *ṣaḥwa* proponents also mentioned the importance of the *sharīʿa*, of course. Al-Maqdisi first

36 Al-Maqdisī, *Al-Kawāshif*, 33–6.
37 *Ibid.*, 40–1.
38 *Ibid.*, 59–81.
39 *Ibid.*, 64.
40 *Ibid.*, 67–9.
41 *Ibid.*, 105–39.

shows how deep and close the relationship is between the United States and Saudi Arabia, and then goes on to give a detailed overview of Saudi defence expenditure, which clearly leads to the conclusion that, although the kingdom has spent billions of dollars on weaponry, it still has a weak and incompetent army.[42]

The reasons for the Saudi army's incompetence in spite of its huge investments lie, according to al-Maqdisi, in the fact that most of the money is spent on American advisors, soldiers, trainers and planners. He maintains that these men and women, as well as the compounds and cities they live in, are employed to 'achieve the goals and policies of the United States of America', not Saudi interests.[43] Al-Maqdisi states that it can therefore be said that America is the real power on the Arabian Peninsula and that the 30,000 U.S. soldiers now on Saudi soil might perhaps even increase to 100,000 in the future. In light of this, as well as the alleged American attempts to keep oil prices low at the expense of Saudi profits and the continued U.S. support for Israel, al-Maqdisi wonders how any Arab country could possibly have such strong ties with the United States.[44] He underlines this point by giving many specific examples of weapon systems Saudi Arabia bought from the United States, supposedly placing itself more and more under American influence.[45] This argument, as well as the previous ones used, lead al-Maqdisi to pass a harsher judgement on the kingdom than many of the *ṣaḥwa* activists did.

Saudi Arabia as a Kufr *State*

The writings by *ṣaḥwa* activists presented to the Saudi king as well as the books by al-ʿAwda and al-Hawali, were highly critical of the state and its policies but never openly questioned the legitimacy of its rulers. Al-Maqdisi, by contrast, does so all the time. As we have seen in Chapter 2, al-Maqdisi believes that all Muslim countries in the world are systematically governed by un-Islamic laws and are therefore guilty of *kufr akbar*, and their rulers should accordingly be labelled *kuffār*. By extensively quoting the Saudi mufti Muhammad b. Ibrahim, who makes it perfectly clear that some of the country's laws are irreconcilable with the *sharīʿa* and even explicitly states that this is *kufr*, which results in expulsion from Islam[46], al-Maqdisi frames Saudi Arabia as a state of unbelief because of

[42] *Ibid.*, 87–91.
[43] *Ibid.*, 92.
[44] *Ibid.*, 95–6.
[45] *Ibid.*, 96–103.
[46] See, for example, *ibid.*, 45.

its own laws and those of organisations of which the country is a member. In fact, the title of al-Maqdisi's book on the kingdom conveys a similar message, pointing to the 'unbelief of the Saudi state'. Since Saudi Arabia was founded as an Islamic state and Islam forms the very basis of the country, this is as harsh an attack on the rulers' legitimacy as one can possibly imagine.

In framing the rulers of Saudi Arabia as infidels, al-Maqdisi even goes further than a previous Wahhabi-inspired rebel who challenged the Al Saʿud's legitimacy, Juhayman al-ʿUtaybi. As we saw in Chapter 1, the latter explicitly did not apply *takfīr* to the rulers because he did not consider them infidels.[47] Al-Maqdisi, however, regrets that al-ʿUtaybi did not go that far, and states that Juhayman 'was ignorant of their unbelief and apostasy'.[48] He also believes that the Saudi rulers' unbelief can be seen in the fact that 'today, the [British] flag of the cross flutters in the streets of Jeddah, Riyadh and other [cities] next to the flag of *tawḥīd*!!!!' He adds, in what may be meant as a slightly conspiratorial tinge to his arguments, that King Fahd openly 'wears the cross of the Christians (*ṣalīb al-naṣārā*) and the sign of Freemasonry (*shiʿār al-māsūniyya*)'.[49] Al-Maqdisi's conclusion based on all of this is that 'there is no difference between this state and other Arab *ṭāghūt* systems (*al-anẓima al-ṭāghūtiyya al-ʿArabiyya al-ukhrā*)'.[50]

Just as al-Maqdisi's analysis of the problems in Saudi Arabia is quite harsh and uncompromising, so is his analysis of what to do about it. He advises 'true' believers to move away from the state's sinful behaviour through *hijra* and, more importantly, to wage jihad against the state. Having established that Saudi Arabia, through its supposed use of other gods in the form of man-made laws, is in clear violation of *tawḥīd*, he writes that the state should be fought 'until the religion is God's entirely' (Q. 8: 39). He adds that the *ʿulamāʾ* have stipulated that if a ruler 'shows clear unbelief (*al-kufr al-bawāḥ*), it is necessary to stand up against him (*al-qiyām ʿalayhi*), remove him (*ʿazlahu*) and replace him (*tabdīlahu wa-taghyīrahu*) to set up the divine law of God (*sharʿ Allāh*) and a full realisation of his *tawḥīd* (*taḥqīq tawḥīdihi kāmilan*)'. According to al-Maqdisi, this 'realisation of God's *tawḥīd*' is the goal of fighting the Saudi state.[51]

47 Al-ʿUtaybī, *Risālat*, 9–12.
48 Al-Maqdisī, *Al-Kawāshif*, 188.
49 *Ibid.*, 11.
50 *Ibid.*, 13.
51 *Ibid.*, 143–4.

Al-Maqdisi's Influence on Saudi Arabia's Post–Gulf War Opposition

The impact of al-Maqdisi's writings mentioned earlier on the *ṣaḥwa* surfaced after the Gulf War but had its roots in the 1980s, when al-Maqdisi spent time in Afghanistan and Pakistan, where he wrote his book on Saudi Arabia. Although, as we saw in Chapter 1, *Al-Kawashif al-Jaliyya* was not universally accepted among the fighters in Afghanistan and Pakistan, his teaching there caused his writings to spread among them, and several people who were there at the time have stated that his writings were well-known in the Afghan-Pakistani border area.[52] Moreover, the Saudi government preferred to keep its own men in Afghanistan and Pakistan separate from others, and a specific guest house was set up to achieve this. The man behind this effort was Jamil al-Rahman, the Afghan leader of a faction called Jamaʿat al-Daʿwa ila l-Qurʾan wa-l-Hadith, whose Saudi-sponsored activities attracted the more Salafi-oriented Arabs coming to Afghanistan.[53] Although there was also Saudi cooperation with other groups and Saudis did not exclusively join al-Rahman's group[54], these efforts to control the direction of those coming from the kingdom must have led to a greater Wahhabi-flavoured cohesion among them. In addition to this, the group is also said to have developed a preference for the practice of *takfīr*, which put it at odds with its Saudi sponsor and eventually led to efforts to stop the kingdom's money from going there.[55] Considering this mixture of Wahhabism and *takfīr* of Muslim rulers, it is not surprising that al-Maqdisi's books are said to have been especially influential among this group of Afghan Arabs.[56]

Spreading al-Maqdisi's Writings

Al-Maqdisi's writings (primarily *Al-Kawashif al-Jaliyya*, but also *Millat Ibrahim* and at least one smaller treatise[57]) were smuggled into the

52 Interviews with al-Dhāyidī, Riyadh, 8 November 2008; al-Shāfī, Riyadh, 11 November 2008. Telephone interview with Khāshuqjī, 27 November 2008.

53 Noorhaidi Hasan, 'The Salafi Madrasas of Indonesia', in: Farish A. Noor, Yoginder Sikand and Martin van Bruinessen (eds.), *The Madrasa in Asia: Political Activism and Transnational Linkages*, Amsterdam: Amsterdam University Press, 2008, 268; Thomas Hegghammer, *Jihad in Saudi Arabia: Violence and Pan-Islamism since 1979*, Cambridge: Cambridge University Press, 2010, 46.

54 Olivier Roy, *The Failure of Political Islam* (transl. Carol Volk), London: I. B. Tauris, 1994 [1992], 117–20.

55 Rubin, 'Arab', 196–7.

56 Al-Nuqaydān, e-mail message to the author, 6 December 2008.

57 Interview with al-Dhāyidī, Riyadh, 8 November 2008.

kingdom in the late 1980s and early 1990s by Saudis returning from Afghanistan and Pakistan (perhaps primarily those who were part of al-Rahman's group), as well as from Kuwait.[58] Although this was done with the books of other ideologues too, according to one well-informed Saudi government official, al-Maqdisi's *Al-Kawashif al-Jaliyya* was the most important of them.[59] These books were often taken back to the kingdom because people liked them, but others brought al-Maqdisi's writings to show their shaykhs in Saudi Arabia what kind of 'deviant' books circulated in Afghanistan and Pakistan. Several copies are also said to have been intercepted at the airport in Riyadh, indicating that the Saudi authorities may have had at least some idea of the fact that anti-Saudi writings were circulating in Afghanistan and Pakistan.[60] During my fieldwork in Saudi Arabia, several former followers of al-Maqdisi's ideas indicated that, once these books were inside the country, they spread them by hand by faxing them to others or photocopying them for friends.[61] In the days before the Internet, this was probably the most effective way to spread clandestine literature, and, not surprisingly, this was also how some of the *ṣaḥwa* literature was spread in the early 1990s.[62]

Although it is not entirely clear what al-Maqdisi's activities were in Saudi Arabia in the 1980s besides studying in Medina, it is certain that his personal presence contributed little if anything to his influence in the country simply because he spent so little time there. Even some of his former followers who actually met him in Saudi Arabia only did so for a very short while during the smaller pilgrimage (*ʿumra*), when al-Maqdisi taught some youngsters.[63] Other information about al-Maqdisi's activities in the kingdom gives no indication that his presence in Saudi Arabia has in any way influenced his following there, and it is therefore

58 Interviews with al-Daynī, Jeddah, 13 November 2008; al-Dhāyidī, Riyadh, 8 November 2008; Muḥammad al-Dawsarī, Riyadh, 25 November 2008; al-Hadlaq, Riyadh, 26 November 2008; al-Shāfī, Riyadh, 11 November 2008. Al-Nuqaydān, e-mail message to the author, 6 December 2008.

59 Interview with al-Hadlaq, Riyadh, 26 November 2008.

60 Al-Nuqaydān, e-mail message to the author, 6 December 2008. Interview with Saʿūd al-Sarḥān, London, 2 July 2008. See also Abū Qatāda al-Filasṭīnī, *Bayna Manhajayn '9'*, www.tawhed.ws/r?i=u33n7szs, n.d., 2–3.

61 Interviews with al-Daynī, Jeddah, 13 November 2008; al-Dhāyidī, Riyadh, 8 November 2008; ʿAbd al-ʿAzīz b. Fayṣal al-Rājiḥī, Riyadh, 18 November 2008; al-Shāfī, Riyadh, 11 November 2008.

62 Uriya Shavit, 'Al-Qaeda's Saudi Origins: Islamist Ideology', *Middle East Quarterly*, vol. 13, no. 4, 2006, 4.

63 Interviews with al-Daynī, Jeddah, 13 November 2008; al-Hadlaq, Riyadh, 26 November 2008; al-Shāfī, Riyadh, 11 November 2008.

safe to assume that his impact on the Saudi Wahhabi opposition after the Gulf War – apart from factors beyond his person – is due to his writings.

The Scope of al-Maqdisi's Influence

The exact scope of al-Maqdisi's influence on the post–Gulf War *ṣaḥwa* opposition until 1995 is difficult to gauge. One might assume that a book such as *Al-Kawashif al-Jaliyya*, which deals extensively with the controversial relations with America and (correctly) predicted that the number of U.S. soldiers in Saudi Arabia might increase, would be hugely influential among the *ṣaḥwa*. It appears, however, that this was not the case. The Letter of Demands and the Memorandum of Advice show no clearly discernible traces of al-Maqdisi's ideas, and neither do the writings of the most important leaders of the *ṣaḥwa*, al-ʿAwda and al-Hawali. They never cite his writings nor do they name al-Maqdisi as an important scholar whose books people should read. This does not necessarily mean, however, that they were not influenced by al-Maqdisi's work. Al-Hawali, for instance, recommended one of al-Maqdisi's books[64] to his students, according to one of them.[65] Others have indicated that they believed al-ʿAwda, and particularly al-Hawali, had read, agreed with or had even been influenced by al-Maqdisi's works but would not say so in public.[66]

Beyond anecdotal examples such as the ones mentioned here, it is difficult to prove that al-Maqdisi had any influence on the Wahhabi opposition of the relevant period. In fact, during interviews with ideologically diverse people who are very knowledgeable about the post–Gulf War protests, I was repeatedly told that al-Maqdisi had very little impact on the *ṣaḥwa*.[67] One interviewee, a prominent member of the CDLR at the time, even stated that he had never read *Al-Kawashif al-Jaliyya*.[68] There is, however, one exception to this general rule. In 1995, the spokesman of the CDLR, Muhammad al-Masʿari, published a rewritten and, according to its author, improved version of al-Maqdisi's book.[69] Al-Masʿari's work, though stylistically different and better organised than al-Maqdisi's

64 Al-Maqdisī, *Imtāʿ*.

65 Interview with al-Daynī, Jeddah, 13 November 2008.

66 Interviews with al-Dawsarī, Riyadh, 25 November 2008; al-Shāfī, Riyadh, 11 November 2008; ʿAbdallāh al-ʿUtaybī, London, 1 August 2008. See also Lacroix, *Islamistes*, 205.

67 Interviews with Saʿd al-Faqīh, London, 11 March 2008; Muḥammad al-Masʿarī, London, 10 March 2008; al-Sarḥān, London, 2 July 2008.

68 Interview with al-Faqīh, London, 11 March 2008.

69 Muḥammad b. ʿAbdallāh al-Masʿarī, *Al-Adilla al-Qaṭʿiyya ʿalā ʿadam Sharʿiyyat al-Duwayla al-Saʿūdiyya*, London: Committee for the Defence of Legitimate Rights (CDLR), 2002 [6th ed.], 7–8.

book, is very close to *Al-Kawashif al-Jaliyya* in content. Like the latter, it describes Saudi history and the kingdom's policies, deals with Saudi Arabia's supposedly man-made laws and its international relations and spends quite some time dealing with Saudi ties with the United States and the UN. Some of the chapter headings are even almost the same as al-Maqdisi's. Although al-Masʿari, who is a supporter of the Islamist but essentially non-violent Hizb al-Tahrir, draws conclusions similar to al-Maqdisi's – he calls the first king of the current Saudi state 'the previous *ṭāghūt* of the [Arabian] Peninsula', for instance[70] – his book is nevertheless written from a somewhat different point of view than the one it was based on, as we will see later.

Considering the few people who explicitly cite al-Maqdisi or his works, as well as the consistent image that arose from my interviews indicating that he had not been influential on the *ṣaḥwa*, we must conclude – simply for lack of evidence showing otherwise – that al-Maqdisi's importance during this period – if any – lay elsewhere. This importance can be found in the spreading of his writings throughout Saudi Arabia, which may not have led to much (discernible) influence among the *ṣaḥwa*, but will probably have acquainted them and other like-minded or more radical people with his books. This is particularly important in light of Saudi policy against the mostly *ṣaḥwa*-led opposition after the Gulf War.

In the aftermath of the Gulf War, the Saudi government saw the *ṣaḥwa* – and not the more radical trends represented, for example, by Bin Laden's Advice and Reform Committee – as its enemy. Several authors have pointed out, however, that more radical ideas were slowly spreading beneath the surface.[71] Hegghammer has emphasised that this trend should not be overestimated and did not (yet) constitute a secretive al-Qaʿida-type terrorist organisation.[72] The potential for radical anti-Saudi ideas, however, was certainly there. Ironically, these tendencies were facilitated by the Saudi government, which concentrated on cracking down on the *ṣaḥwa* and tended to ignore the spread of more radical ideas, including those of al-Maqdisi.[73] This, as one Saudi official who works

70 *Ibid.*, 24.

71 Abdullah F. Ansary, 'Combating Extremism: A Brief Overview of Saudi Arabia's Approach', *Middle East Policy*, vol. 15, no. 2, 2008, 112; Bruce Riedel and Bilal Y. Saab, 'Al Qaeda's Third Front: Saudi Arabia', *Washington Quarterly*, vol. 31, no. 2, 2008, 34.

72 Thomas Hegghammer, 'Islamist Violence and Regime Stability in Saudi Arabia', *International Affairs*, vol. 84, no. 4, 2008, 707.

73 Interview with al-Daynī, Jeddah, 13 November 2008. Al-Nuqaydān; e-mail message to the author, 6 December 2008.

for the Interior Ministry and wished to remain anonymous admits, was a grave mistake since it allowed a more dangerous ideology to spread without much opposition. The familiarity with al-Maqdisi's writings among certain Saudis that resulted from this proved important when the *ṣaḥwa* had been defeated through imprisonment, forced exile and co-optation but a more radical opposition emerged in the form of al-Qaʿida on the Arabian Peninsula, dealt with in detail in the next chapter. First, however, we must explain al-Maqdisi's (lack of) influence on the Saudi Wahhabi opposition in the aftermath of the Gulf War.

Explaining al-Maqdisi's Influence

The impact al-Maqdisi had on the post–Gulf War *ṣaḥwa* was, as far as we can tell, limited. His book *Al-Kawashif al-Jaliyya* was nevertheless important in the period 1990–5 because it spread among scholars and activists critical of the Saudi state at a time when the latter were mostly focussed on dealing with the *ṣaḥwa*. How can these two slightly conflicting phenomena be explained? The literature on framing offers tools to explain this (lack of) influence in the form of the so-called 'core framing tasks' as well as 'cognitive liberation'.

Core Framing Tasks

Snow and Benford have shown that for a frame to be adopted by the public, which al-Maqdisi apparently mostly failed to achieve with regard to the *ṣaḥwa*, it has to resonate with their ideas and beliefs. To be able to do this, a frame has three core tasks: diagnostic, prognostic and motivational framing.[74] The first deals with describing what the problem is and who is to blame for it; the second has to do with suggesting a solution to the problem; and the third constitutes a call for action.[75] The idea behind this is that if a frame performs these three tasks in a way that resonates with the public, it will likely be successful. If it does not, however, it is unlikely

[74] Snow and Benford, 'Ideology', 199–204; Robert D. Benford and David A. Snow, 'Framing Processes and Social Movements: An Overview and Assessment', *Annual Review of Sociology*, vol. 26, 2000, 615–18.

[75] See also Bert Klandermans, 'Mobilization and Participation: Social-Psychological Expansions of Resource Mobilization Theory', *American Sociological Review*, October 1984, vol. 49, 583–600; *id.*, 'The Formation and Mobilization of Consensus', in: Bert Klandermans, Hanspeter Kriesi and Sidney Tarrow (eds.), *International Social Movement Research, Vol. I: From Structure to Action – Comparing Social Movement Research Across Cultures*, Greenwich, CT, & London: JAI Press, 1988, 175–96.

to resonate fully with the target audience and therefore will probably not lead to contentious action.

If we apply this idea to the diagnostic framing of the problem in Saudi Arabia by both the *ṣaḥwa* and al-Maqdisi, we can see that the two are quite different. As described earlier, the *ṣaḥwa* had plenty of criticism for the Saudi state, but much of this was of a political nature, focussing on the country's ties with America and issues such as equality and increased representation of the people in ruling the country. Although it did have a religious agenda, the *ṣaḥwa* seemed mostly concerned with political issues and did not openly question the regime's legitimacy. By contrast, al-Maqdisi mostly challenged the regime on its religious credentials and did not accept it at all. He even went so far as to label Saudi Arabia a *kufr* state. Whereas the problem according to the *ṣaḥwa* can be said to have lain in some aspects of Saudi policy, for al-Maqdisi the problem was the Saudi regime itself.

When looking at the prognostic and motivational aspects of the frames of both the *ṣaḥwa* and al-Maqdisi, a similar conclusion can be drawn. The *ṣaḥwa* was essentially part of a movement striving for reform, not revolution, and tried to work within the confines of the Saudi system, not on top of its ruins. It therefore sought its solutions in reforming aspects of Saudi policies, hence the Letter of Demands and the Memorandum of Advice, and called on its supporters to engage in non-violent protest actions. Al-Maqdisi, however, saw jihad against the Saudi regime as the most important solution to the problem he perceived in the kingdom, and his writings regularly mention it as the best action people can take.[76]

It thus seems that al-Maqdisi's framing of the situation was quite different from that of the *ṣaḥwa*, in spite of their partly shared critique of the Saudi state. It is interesting to note that even the one adherent to the *ṣaḥwa* who was noticeably influenced by al-Maqdisi during this period – al-Masʿari – is not very positive about him. Although he praises al-Maqdisi for his willingness to take on the Saudi state and for dealing with the Saudi-U.S. ties, he also criticises him for being far too rooted in the quietist Wahhabi tradition to be taken completely seriously. He scoffs at al-Maqdisi's writing about 'all these issues of smoking and such rubbish', which 'shows the weak Wahhabi mentality', and concludes that 'what al-Maqdisi is offering is deficient to say the least. He really

[76] See, for instance, al-Maqdisī, *Al-Kawāshif*, 114.

needs a quantum leap in Islamic thought that fits into the twenty-first century.'[77]

It could be argued that the fault lines between the ideas of the *ṣaḥwa* and al-Maqdisi were not as strict as this argument suggests. Indeed, the *ṣaḥwa* itself was not a monolith, and there was a time when Osama bin Laden spoke highly of al-ʿAwda and al-Hawali, suggesting that their different frames of the situation converged at one point.[78] Moreover, at least some adherents to the *ṣaḥwa* are said to have secretly held more radical views than the ones they expressed in public. Several people have stated, for example, that al-Hawali admitted in private that Saudi Arabia was a *kufr* state but would not say so in public for fear of his position.[79] Similarly, al-Faqih admitted that the people behind the CDLR consciously chose 'human rights' as one of the overarching themes for their activities because it was acceptable in both Islam and the West and allowed them – in his words – to 'ride the waves' of popular sentiment, possibly as a cover for their more radical views.[80] In this context, it is also interesting to note that al-Masʿari's radical views of the Saudi state mentioned here were not published until 1995, when he had reached London and was no longer confined by Saudi pressure on him.[81]

All of this could indicate that the *ṣaḥwa* actually agreed much more with al-Maqdisi than its framing of the situation in public suggested. This does not, however, reconcile the *ṣaḥwa*'s politicised Muslim Brotherhood-type Wahhabism with al-Maqdisi's quietist Jihadi-Salafism, and it also does not explain why my fieldwork among some of the people involved at the time consistently showed al-Maqdisi to have been of little influence on the *ṣaḥwa*. In the early 1990s – before the Saudi government repressed the *ṣaḥwa* by various means – it seems that al-Maqdisi's descriptions of the kingdom and his call for jihad against it really were a bridge too far for most *ṣaḥwa* activists. Their ambiguous attitude *vis-à-vis* al-Maqdisi's ideas, however, explains why people who may not have entirely agreed

77 Interview with al-Masʿarī, London, 10 March 2008.

78 See, for example, Lawrence (ed.), *Messages*, 8.

79 Interviews with al-Masʿarī, London, 10 March 2008; al-ʿUtaybī, London, 1 August 2008.

80 Interview with al-Faqīh, London, 11 March 2008.

81 The same applied to another document allegedly written by Saʿd al-Faqīh, Abū Qatāda al-Filasṭīnī and Muḥammad al-Masʿarī called *Al-Niẓām al-Saʿūdī fī Mīzān al-Islām*, www.tawhed.ws/r?i=geijr8cj, 1996. This book is also much harsher in its criticism than the previous *ṣaḥwa* texts.

with him nevertheless showed an interest in his ideas when they were spread in the 1990s.

Cognitive Liberation

The term 'cognitive liberation' was coined by Doug McAdam in his landmark study on the civil rights movement in the United States. In his book, McAdam states that social movements need good resources to organise and mobilise people and also need the structural openings or political opportunities that allow them to do so. Apart from resources and opportunities, however, McAdam argues that movements also need a situation in which the public realise that the moment to take contentious action has arrived. The term 'cognitive liberation' refers to this realisation. The shifting political opportunities provide the public with 'cognitive cues' that trigger this process, McAdam states, while existing movements and organisations mobilise their resources to capitalise on this change in attitude in order to take contentious action.[82]

McAdam has named several political and cultural opportunities that can provide the public with cognitive cues that lead to cognitive liberation. These include ideological or cultural contradictions, which 'dramatize a glaring contradiction between a highly resonant cultural value and conventional social practices'; suddenly imposed grievances, a term denoting dramatic events that 'increase public awareness of and opposition to previously accepted social conditions'; and dramatisations of system vulnerability, referring to events that expose a regime's weakness.[83] The process of cognitive liberation that these events may bring about was not labelled as such before McAdam but was described similarly. Fox Piven and Cloward, for instance, write about this process as involving three aspects: (parts of) the system or regime of a country lose their legitimacy in the eyes of the public; people who until then may have seen their situation as inevitable begin to see openings for change; and those who normally remain passive now start believing they have the power to alter their situation.[84]

[82] Doug McAdam, *Political Process and the Development of Black Insurgency, 1930–1970*, Chicago & London: University of Chicago Press, 1999 [1982], 34–5, 48–51, 105–6.

[83] *Id.*, 'Culture and Social Movements', in: Enrique Laraña, Hank Johnston and Joseph R. Gusfield (eds.), *New Social Movements: From Ideology to Identity*, Philadelphia: Temple University Press, 1994, 39–41.

[84] Francis Fox Piven and Richard A. Cloward, *Poor People's Movements: Why They Succeed, How They Fail*, New York: Pantheon Books, 1977, 3–4.

Cognitive liberation has also become part of the literature on framing. Like the latter, it is an attempt to reincorporate beliefs, psychology and 'grievance interpretation' into social movement theory.[85] This becomes particularly clear in the work of Sharon Erickson Nepstad, who states that the three core framing tasks distinguished above 'can facilitate progression through the three stages of cognitive liberation'.[86] In one of her articles she states that this facilitation – in the absence of a social movement – can also be done by an external actor.[87] This conclusion has been criticised, however, by Futrell, who claims that people do not necessarily need a social movement or an external actor to help them become 'cognitively liberated' but can also reach that stage themselves through interpretive processes of the situation they are in.[88]

If we apply the above to the subject of this chapter, it is obvious that the Saudi invitation of 500,000 U.S. soldiers was the dramatic change in opportunity or, in other words, the 'cognitive cue' that made people realise something was wrong. The subsequent events that took place in the kingdom conform quite accurately with the theoretical framework of McAdam and Fox Piven and Cloward. There were indeed glaring contradictions between the Saudi state's official social policy of encouraging citizens to stay away from non-Muslims as much as possible on the one hand and its invitation of half a million 'infidels' from – of all places – the United States on the other.[89] This may not have cost the regime its legitimacy altogether but it was a blow to its credibility.[90] Similarly, the invitation was indeed a 'suddenly imposed grievance' that made many Saudis refuse to accept their situation any longer, as was evident in the treatises presented to the king. Although offering petitions to Saudi rulers may not sound controversial, at the time it was, and it therefore caused a shock among the rulers, who claimed that advice was welcome but only in private, not in public.[91] Finally, the reliance on American soldiers

85 Snow et al., 'Frame', 465–6.

86 Sharon Erickson Nepstad, 'The Process of Cognitive Liberation: Cultural Synapses, Links, and Frame Contradictions in the U.S.-Central America Peace Movement', *Sociological Enquiry*, vol. 67, no. 4, November 1997, 471–3. The quote is on 472.

87 *Ibid.*, 472–85.

88 Robert Futrell, 'Framing Processes, Cognitive Liberation, and NIMBY Protest in the U.S. Chemical-Weapons Disposal Conflict', *Sociological Enquiry*, vol. 73, no. 3, August 2003, 362–3.

89 See, for example, al-Rasheed, *Contesting*, 34–7.

90 Interview with al-Masʿarī, London, 10 March 2008.

91 Interview with al-Faqīh, London, 11 March 2008.

did indeed show the Saudi regime's vulnerability – perceived as such by activists[92] – which encouraged people to challenge the state.[93]

It was in this climate of cognitive liberation that the *ṣaḥwa* shaykhs preached against the regime's policies, the Letter of Demands and the Memorandum of Advice were published, the CDLR was founded and – most importantly for this study – al-Maqdisi's *Al-Kawashif al-Jaliyya* was smuggled into the country and spread around. With regard to the question as to what actor capitalised on the cognitive cue – a social movement, the people themselves or an external actor – one could argue that all three did. It was the social movement that came into existence after the Gulf War that was responsible for various types of contentious action. This social movement was based, however, on pre-existing networks of scholars and academics with a rather coherent socio-political and religious base[94], meaning that there were critical trends prior to the formation of a social movement. Moreover, protests such as those accompanying the arrest in 1989 of another *ṣaḥwa* scholar, ʿA'id al-Qarni, showed that there was at least some support from the people for criticism of the regime that might reach cognitive liberation by itself.[95]

Gwenn Okruhlik has argued that writings such as the Memorandum of Advice helped create cognitive liberation after the Gulf War.[96] Similarly, al-Maqdisi's *Al-Kawashif al-Jaliyya* also contributed to this process but as an external actor (i.e., separate from any movement or group) and, as we have seen earlier, less influentially than the *ṣaḥwa* writings. Combining this theoretical dimension with the scope of al-Maqdisi's impact on the Saudi opposition from 1990–5, one could sum up his influence during this period as a (small) external ideological contribution to the more widespread attempts to capitalise on the cognitive cue that the invitation of the U.S. soldiers had brought about.

Several opposition groups vied for the public's attention after the Gulf War, and the *ṣaḥwa* was clearly the most successful. Although, as we have seen, al-Maqdisi's conclusions went too far for the *ṣaḥwa*, the decreased legitimacy of the state, its greater vulnerability and its widely despised invitation of the U.S. soldiers created a cognitive liberation conducive to anti-Saudi views, including al-Maqdisi's. *Al-Kawashif al-Jaliyya*, in other

92 Interviews with al-Faqīh, London, 11 March 2008; al-Masʿarī, 10 March 2008.
93 Telephone interview with Khāshuqjī, 27 November 2008. Dekmejian, 'Liberal', 403.
94 Dekmejian, 'Rise', 635–6.
95 Anonymous [Saʿd al-Faqīh], *The Rise and Evolution of the Modern Islamic Reform Movement in Saudi Arabia*, n.p., n.d. This document was provided to me by its author.
96 Okruhlik, 'Making', 261.

words, could tap right into the popular mood among certain groups of Saudis, despite the unwillingness of most to take their contention as far as al-Maqdisi wanted.[97] His influence during this period should therefore be attributed more to the timing and general anti-Saudi content of his writings than to his specific conclusions. This changed, however, with the advent of al-Qaʿida on the Arabian Peninsula, to which we must now turn.

97 Apart from activists and former followers of al-Maqdisī's who confirmed this to me, this was also confirmed by a Saudi government official who wished to remain anonymous, as well as by a staunch Saudi ideological opponent of al-Maqdisī's. Interview with al-Rājiḥī, Riyadh, 18 November 2008.

5

Al-Qaʿida on the Arabian Peninsula

After the launch of the U.S.-led 'war on terrorism', and particularly the invasion of Afghanistan as a response to '9/11' in 2001, al-Qaʿida's ability to move and strike was severely hampered. This loss of territorial and operational freedom was compensated for, however, by new groups that were founded or reorganised under the label of al-Qaʿida across the Arab world.[1] One of those was al-Qaʿida on the Arabian Peninsula (al-Qāʿida fī Jazīrat al-ʿArab). This chapter concentrates on how this particular group, which launched a series of attacks on mostly Western targets in Saudi Arabia from 2003 onwards, came about, what al-Maqdisi's influence on them has been and why he was so influential. The focus is on the years 1995–2005, since in 1995 the *ṣaḥwa*-led opposition after the Gulf War can be said to have ended and a new and violent phase of contention started, while al-Qaʿida on the Arabian Peninsula (QAP) more or less ceased to exist as a Saudi organisation in 2005.

As we saw in the previous chapter, al-Maqdisi made extensive use of the Wahhabi religious tradition, mostly used by quietist Salafis, to make his case against the Saudi regime, thereby further underlining his position as a quietist Jihadi-Salafi. This becomes even clearer with QAP: while al-Maqdisi's framing of the problems in Saudi Arabia failed to attract many followers of the non-violent, political and relatively moderate *ṣaḥwa*, his radical solutions combined with his close adherence to the (quietist) Salafi-Wahhabi tradition and Saudi historical imagination are precisely what explains his ideological influence on QAP, as we will see.

[1] Thomas Hegghammer, 'Global Jihadism after the Iraq War', *Middle East Journal*, vol. 60, no. 1, 2006, 14–15.

The Rise of al-Qaʿida on the Arabian Peninsula (QAP)

The *ṣaḥwa* activism described in the previous chapter came as a shock to the Saudi regime, and it took until 1995 to effectively suppress this phenomenon, which had never been violent. This changed dramatically when the Wahhabi-inspired activism in Saudi Arabia took a much more militant turn in late 1995, when on 13 November a car bomb exploded at a U.S. training mission of the Saudi National Guard building in Riyadh, killing five Americans and two Indians and injuring dozens. Although several groups claimed responsibility for the bombing, only four men, later identified as ʿAbd al-ʿAziz al-Muʿaththam, Khalid al-Saʿid, Riyad al-Hajiri and Muslih al-Shamrani, were held responsible for the bombing and were later executed for this act.[2] Three of the perpetrators (all in their twenties at the time) told interrogators (and a TV audience) that they had fought in Afghanistan and, significantly, had been influenced by Muhammad al-Masʿari, Osama bin Laden and Abu Muhammad al-Maqdisi.[3] Although these confessions could be the product of coercion, a closer look at these men and their ideological background reveals that this is unlikely.

Bayt Shubrā

One of the culprits of the bombing, al-Muʿaththam, apparently not only claimed to have been influenced by al-Maqdisi but also that he had visited him in Jordan because he was interested in *takfīr* of Muslim regimes, particularly Saudi Arabia's.[4] It is clear from al-Maqdisi's writings that he was indeed asked about such issues by 'the people of the Peninsula (*ahl al-jazīra*)'.[5] In a later interview, al-Maqdisi confirmed that he had met several times with al-Muʿaththam, who had come to him for religious rulings and advice.[6] Considering al-Maqdisi's views on the Saudi regime, it is not surprising that he condemned the execution of its perpetrators, and scolded the kingdom's rulers for their supposedly false propaganda and spoke highly of al-Muʿaththam.[7]

2 Fandy, *Saudi*, 1–2; Teitelbaum, *Holier*, 73–6.
3 Burke, *Al-Qaeda*, 154–5; Fandy, *Saudi*, 2–3; Teitelbaum, *Holier*, 76–7.
4 Teitelbaum, *Holier*, 76.
5 Abū Muḥammad al-Maqdisī, *Al-Maṣābīḥ al-Munīra fī l-Radd ʿalā As'ilat Ahl al-Jazīra*, www.tawhed.ws/t, n.d.
6 Khāshuqjī and Abū Hilāla, 'Al-Munaẓẓir', 14.
7 Abū Muḥammad al-Maqdisī, *Wa-hal Afsada l-Dīn illā l-Mulūk wa-Aḥbār Sū' wa-Ruhbānahā*, www.tawhed.ws/r?i=4knoq5e8, n.d.; *id.*, *Tabṣīr*, 5–7.

The visits paid to al-Maqdisi by al-Muʿaththam were not isolated incidents. In the late 1980s and early 1990s – probably under the influence of the greater religiosity displayed by the Saudi regime to counter challenges such as those of Juhayman al-ʿUtaybi – some Saudis became increasingly pious and, in certain cases, dismayed about what they saw as the sinfulness of society and the state. This was expressed in, among other things, small groups or communities of mostly young people who tried to withdraw from society to study Islam in small circles at people's homes. One of those groups settled in the Shubrā neighbourhood of Riyadh in a house referred to as Bayt Shubrā (the house of Shubrā). Because of their criticism of the state and their pietistic attitudes, the visitors to Bayt Shubrā rejected both state-supported scholars on the one hand and the political *ṣaḥwa* on the other, but were naturally attracted to the writings of Juhayman al-ʿUtaybi, al-Maqdisi and those of certain nineteenth-century Wahhabi scholars.[8]

From interviews with former visitors to Bayt Shubrā, it became clear that most activities taking place there concentrated on studying Islamic creed, the Qurʾān and the Sunna, including with a Mauritanian teacher called Muhammad al-Hasan Walad al-Didu al-Shinqiti. The visitors – who were all young adults of a middle class background with generally low educational levels – considered themselves adherents to the *ahl al-ḥadīth* tradition. Although the group was made up of persons with diverse ideological backgrounds, they seem to have had in common a distinct inclination towards strict Salafism (particularly of a Wahhabi flavour) and – for most – a growing antipathy towards the Saudi state. It is obvious that they found plenty of both in the writings of al-Maqdisi available to them (primarily *Millat Ibrahim* and *Al-Kawashif al-Jaliyya*) and they zealously photocopied and read these books.[9]

The reason Bayt Shubrā is important for this chapter is that al-Muʿaththam and two other Riyadh bombers visited that house in the early 1990s and were influenced ideologically there, including by al-Maqdisi's writings, which presented a sharp critique of (Saudi) politics from a Salafi point of view. This not only shows that the testimonies of the Riyadh bombers indicating their attraction to al-Maqdisi's books

[8] Hegghammer and Lacroix, 'Rejectionist', 116.

[9] Interviews with al-Dawsarī, Riyadh, 25 November 2008; al-Dhāyidī, Riyadh, 8 November 2008; al-Sarḥān, London, 2 July 2008; al-ʿUtaybī, London, 1 August 2008. Al-Nuqaydān, e-mail message to the author, 6 December 2008.

were probably authentic, but also that they were part of a broader group of people who were extremely critical of the Saudi state and were, in some cases, not afraid to act upon that criticism with violence. This does not mean, however, that all visitors to Bayt Shubrā were violent. Most of them were never involved in armed attacks, and some of them have since become prominent liberal journalists[10], while others have pursued careers as professionals. As Hegghammer and Lacroix have pointed out, however, the visitors to Bayt Shubrā – though initially a-political – grew increasingly politicised in the early 1990s, when so much criticism of the regime was expressed.[11] Moreover, several regular or occasional visitors to Bayt Shubrā, including Ibrahim al-Rayyis, Saʿud al-ʿUtaybi and ʿAbd al-ʿAziz al-Muqrin, later joined QAP.[12]

From the Riyadh Bombing to the QAP Campaign

The clear link between some visitors to Bayt Shubrā in the early 1990s on the one hand and violent attacks and even QAP on the other raises the question of whether there may be a connection between the contention expressed immediately after the Gulf War and the rise of al-Qaʿida in Saudi Arabia in the early 2000s. Several authors have approached this question through the prism of Social Movement Theory, stating that the post–Gulf War opposition constituted a social movement that protested against government policy in various ways.[13] Meijer has argued that the post–Gulf War protests and the later campaign by QAP from 2003 onwards constituted two phases within one 'cycle of contention', i.e., two rounds of protest in a larger conflict led by a single social movement. Both rounds started with mobilisation and, through various means applied by the state, ended with demobilisation.[14] Meijer's work states that QAP was originally part of the *ṣaḥwa* but later parted ways with this movement

[10] Stéphane Lacroix, 'Between Islamists and Liberals: Saudi Arabia's new Islamo-Liberal Reformists', *Middle East Journal*, vol. 58, no. 3, 2004, 352–4; *id.*, 'Islamo-Liberal Politics in Saudi Arabia', in: Paul Aarts and Gerd Nonneman (eds.), *Saudi Arabia in the Balance: Political Economy, Society, Foreign Affairs*, London: Hurst & Co., 2005, 43–4.

[11] Hegghammer and Lacroix, 'Rejectionist', 117.

[12] *Ibid.*, 117, 122, note 87; interviews with al-Dawsarī, Riyadh, 25 November 2008; al-Sarḥān, London, 2 July 2008; al-ʿUtaybi, London, 1 August 2008.

[13] Meijer, 'Yusuf al-Uyairi and the Transnationalisation of Saudi Jihadism', 221–43; Okruhlik, 'Making', 250–69.

[14] Roel Meijer, 'The "Cycle of Contention" and the Limits of Terrorism in Saudi Arabia', in: Paul Aarts and Gerd Nonneman (eds.), *Saudi Arabia in the Balance: Political Economy, Society, Foreign Affairs*, London: Hurst & Co., 2005, 271–89.

and attempted to gain the upper hand at its expense.[15] Hegghammer, the foremost expert on QAP, has questioned this argument, however, and argues that Meijer's approach does not explain the eight-year gap between the suppression of the *ṣaḥwa* in 1995 and the QAP-instigated violence that erupted in 2003. Hegghammer therefore contends that Saudi Islamism should be broken down into smaller parts, each to be analysed separately.[16]

Hegghammer is correct to point out that Saudi Islamism is heterogeneous – which Meijer does not deny – and that Meijer's explanation of why mobilisation only reoccurred in 2003 is rather short. It is undeniable, however, that there were also ideological similarities between the *ṣaḥwa* and QAP. Apart from the fact that both were critical of the Saudi state, the first leader of QAP, Yusuf al-ʿUyayri, scolded the *ṣaḥwa* shaykh Salman al-ʿAwda, who had moderated his views when he was released from prison, for having abandoned his more confrontational approach.[17] This shows that al-ʿUyayri was at least somewhat supportive of the *ṣaḥwa*'s earlier position. Similarly, Bin Laden himself spoke highly of Salman al-ʿAwda and Safar al-Hawali, as well as other shaykhs associated with the *ṣaḥwa*.[18] In spite of these examples, Hegghammer is nevertheless right in stating that the *ṣaḥwa* was clearly a reformist group and therefore different from the violent QAP, which also becomes clear in their different reception of al-Maqdisi's writings, as we will see later.

Meijer's argument that 'the repression and control of the non-violent opposition [in 1991–5] opened the way for a violent phase of the cycle of contention'[19] seems correct. Hegghammer acknowledges that the Riyadh bombing in 1995 was probably, as Meijer states, connected to the crackdown on the *ṣaḥwa* as well as to the execution of ʿAbdallah al-Hudayf, a man who had attacked a Saudi policeman earlier that year and was a

[15] *Id.*, 'Yusuf al-Uyairi and the Transnationalisation of Saudi Jihadism', 225.

[16] Hegghammer, 'Islamist, 702–3; *id.*, 'Violence politique en Arabie Saoudite: Grandeur en décadence d'"Al-Qaida dans la péninsule arabique"', in: Bernard Rougier (ed.), *Qu'est-ce que le salafisme?* Paris: Presses Universitaires de France, 2008, 107–8.

[17] Meijer, 'Yusuf al-Uyairi and the Transnationalisation of Saudi Jihadism', 232–4. For an extensive treatment of al-ʿUyayrī's ideology, see Roel Meijer, 'Che Guevara van de Jihad: Yusuf al-Ayiri', *ZemZem: Tijdschrift over het Midden-Oosten, Noord-Afrika en Islam*, vol. 3, no. 1, 2007, 126–31; *id.*, 'Re-reading al-Qaeda: Writings of Yusuf al-Ayiri', *ISIM Review*, no. 18, 2006, 16–17; *id.*, 'Yūsuf al-ʿUyairī and the Making of a Revolutionary Salafi Praxis', 422–59.

[18] Fandy, *Saudi*, 186–7; Lawrence (ed.), *Messages*, 13–14.

[19] Meijer, '"Cycle"', 276.

friend of the bombers.[20] It is not entirely clear, however, whether the QAP campaign of attacks that started in 2003 is also part of the same trend. It appears that, ideological similarities with al-Qa'ida notwithstanding, the Riyadh bombing was an isolated incident and its perpetrators acted on their own, independently of Bin Laden's orders. Several attacks followed in the period 1995–2003, the most famous of which is the bombing of the U.S. Air Force compound at Khobar Towers at al-Zahran in 1996, killing 19 American soldiers and injuring hundreds. This was probably the work of the Shiite Saudi Hizbullah[21], however, and thus should not be seen as part of the same trend since it came from an entirely different and unrelated group. The other attacks that occurred until 2003 were scattered and relatively small and clearly distinct from the campaign that QAP launched.

The rise of QAP has been described in several studies, most meticulously by Hegghammer. The latter contends that QAP was much more a pan-Islamic group than a socio-revolutionary organisation – that is, driven by international causes concerning the Muslim world rather than the desire to overthrow the Saudi government.[22] He therefore traces the history of QAP to the late 1990s, when several areas of the Muslim world, such as Chechnya and Kosovo (1999) as well as the Palestinian territories (2000), became embroiled in conflict, thereby reinvigorating a pan-Islamic spirit in Saudi Arabia. Combined with the introduction of the Internet in the kingdom in 1999, which facilitated the spread of jihadi literature, as well as the emergence of a radical network led by Afghanistan veteran Yusuf al-'Uyayri in 2000 that was willing to work in the service of Bin Laden, the groundwork was laid for the launching of al-Qa'ida operations.[23] Several authors have pointed out that Bin Laden's decision to launch a campaign of attacks inside Saudi Arabia was closely connected with certain international developments. The terrorist attacks of '9/11' and the subsequent U.S.-led war in Afghanistan deprived al-Qa'ida

20 Thomas Hegghammer, 'Jihad, Yes, But Not Revolution: Explaining the Extraversion of Islamist Violence in Saudi Arabia', *British Journal of Middle Eastern Studies*, vol. 36, no. 3, 2009, 401.

21 *Id.*, 'Deconstructing the Myth about al-Qa'ida and Khobar', *CTC Sentinel*, vol. 1, no. 3, 2008, 20–2.

22 *Id.*, 'Islamist', 703–6; *id.*, 'Violence', 108–12.

23 *Id.*, *The Failure of Jihad in Saudi Arabia*, Occasional Paper Series, Combating Terrorism Center at West Point, 25 February 2010, 12–13; *id.*, 'Islamist', 707–9; *id.*, 'Violence', 113–15.

of a safe haven from which they could operate, causing the organisation to rethink its strategy and focus on Saudi Arabia, whose ties with the United States had been a source of anger to Bin Laden for several years.[24]

For these and other reasons, QAP was founded in Saudi Arabia in 2002 on the orders of Bin Laden. The direct reasons behind launching attacks in 2003 are somewhat unclear, but may have had to do with al-ʿUyayri's alleged lack of preparedness at an earlier stage[25], an attempt to capitalise on anti-American feelings resulting from the war in Iraq that had just been launched or as a response to several events taking place at that time.[26] Whatever the precise reason, from May 2003 on, QAP launched an unprecedented series of attacks on mostly Western targets inside Saudi Arabia that would last until 2004 but petered out in 2005.[27] Although scattered attacks occurred after that, the organisation as a major force was effectively thwarted[28] until several years later, when Saudis who had fled their country to Yemen, along with native Yemenis, re-launched the group from that country.

While the QAP campaign was successful at first, the Saudi authorities eventually gained the upper hand through an increasingly effective counterterrorism strategy.[29] QAP further failed because of both a lack of support among the Saudi population and the war in Iraq, which proved to be an alternative jihad that absorbed much of the human and financial resources that might otherwise have been invested in the struggle in Saudi Arabia itself.[30] This ended – for now, at least – QAP's organised and violent campaign. The group, although made up of a diverse

[24] Anthony H. Cordesman and Nawaf Obaid, *Al-Qaeda in Saudi Arabia: Asymetric Threats and Islamist Extremists*, Washington, D.C.: Center for Strategic and International Studies, 2005, 3–4; Hegghammer, 'Islamist', 709; *id.*, 'Violence', 115.

[25] *Al-Riyāḍ*, 27 September 2005.

[26] Hegghammer, *Failure*, 13; *id.*, 'Islamist', 710; *id.*, 'Violence', 116.

[27] See also Jonathan R. Bradley, 'Al Qaeda and the House of Saud: Eternal Enemies or Secret Bedfellows?', *Washington Quarterly*, vol. 28, no. 4, 2005, 141; International Crisis Group, *Saudi Arabia backgrounder: Who are the Islamists?*, ICG Middle East Report no. 31, Amman, 21 September 2004, 12–14; Riedel and Saab, 'Al Qaeda's', 35–7.

[28] Michael Knights, 'The Current State of al-Qaʿida in Saudi Arabia', *CTC Sentinel*, vol. 1, no. 10, 2008, 7–10.

[29] Cordesman and Obaid, *Al-Qaeda*, 11–20; Joshua Teitelbaum, 'Terrorist Challenges to Saudi Arabian Internal Security', *Middle East Review of International Affairs*, vol. 9, no. 3, 2005, 5–7.

[30] Hegghammer, 'Islamist', 712–13. For more on the Saudis who did go to Iraq, see *id.*, 'Combattants saoudiens en Irak: modes de radicalisation et de recrutement', *Cultures & Conflits*, no. 64, 2006, 111–27.

membership[31], had effectively rallied around the goal of trying to expel the non-Muslims from the Arabian Peninsula. The extent to which a man like al-Maqdisi, whose writings concentrated almost exclusively on the struggle against 'apostate' Muslim regimes rather than non-Muslim 'occupiers', influenced this group (as well as the visitors to Bayt Shubrā) is what we will turn to now.

Adopting al-Maqdisi's Frame

It is clear that the group of youngsters that gathered at Bayt Shubrā did not dedicate the time they spent together to meticulously reading, studying and analysing Juhayman's or al-Maqdisi's books.[32] There was, however, a process of radicalisation taking place. Their inclination towards the *ahl al-ḥadīth* moved them away from major twentieth-century Saudi scholars such as Ibn Baz and Ibn al-ʿUthaymin because they believed that these *ʿulamāʾ* were not true Salafis, who shunned following any particular *madhhab*, but rather Hanbalis who had deviated from the tradition of Ibn ʿAbd al-Wahhab.[33] As such, they were more attracted to the methods of al-Albani, who also rejected the various schools of law, and – in at least some cases – certain Bedouin, who not only refused to follow a particular *madhhab* but also shunned modern society and the Saudi state.[34] It is therefore not surprising that Juhayman, who had held similar beliefs, became something of a role model to them. In fact, Bayt Shubrā itself was meant as an imitation of a similar house used by Juhayman, Bayt al-Ikhwān (house of the brotherhood).[35]

Just as Juhayman eventually became politicised and radicalised, so did some visitors to Bayt Shubrā also start combining their pietistic isolation from the Saudi state and its institutions with criticism of the regime that was increasingly framed in terms of Islamic/un-Islamic. Their strict views, linked with the growing sense in the early 1990s that Saudi Arabia was not the pious state it claimed to be, resulted in a willingness to apply *takfīr* to the rulers or even to civil servants working for the government. It was

[31] Thomas Hegghammer, 'Terrorist Recruitment and Radicalization in Saudi Arabia', *Middle East Policy*, vol. 13, no. 4, 2006, 42–8; International Crisis Group, *Saudi*, 14–17; Meijer, '"Cycle"', 289–99, 301–11.

[32] Interview with al-Sarḥān, London, 2 July 2008.

[33] Interviews with al-Dawsarī, Riyadh, 25 November 2008; al-Dhāyidī, Riyadh, 8 November 2008; al-ʿUtaybī, London, 1 August 2008.

[34] Interview with al-ʿUtaybī, London, 1 August 2008.

[35] Hegghammer and Lacroix, 'Rejectionist', 104–11, 116–17.

in this context that they came into contact with some of al-Maqdisi's writings (including *Al-Kawashif al-Jaliyya*), which condemned the Saudi state and its laws and policies for being un-Islamic, as we saw in Chapter 4. Consequently, al-Maqdisi became the most important radical scholar for the visitors to Bayt Shubrā, whose books were read by most or all of the youngsters there.[36]

Framing QAP's Jihad

As we saw earlier, several visitors to Bayt Shubrā joined QAP in the early 2000s. The two groups were quite different, however, since they not only came into existence at different times but their 'members' also had different backgrounds. Whereas Bayt Shubrā had some visitors who had been to Afghanistan[37], it was mostly made up of radicalised pietistic young men. QAP, on the other hand, consisted mostly of people who had fought in Afghanistan.[38] This predominance of 'Afghan Arabs' in QAP – whose focus was mostly on fighting either a classical jihad (i.e., against invaders of the *dār al-Islām*) or, later, on a global jihad in which they fought the 'far enemy' such as the United States – may explain why they focussed their violence on Western targets in Saudi Arabia rather than on the regime itself. Indeed, Hegghammer has convincingly shown that almost all attacks launched by QAP were directed against Western targets, in keeping with the organisation's framing of their jihad as aimed at expelling the 'infidels' from the Arabian Peninsula.[39] He states that the preference for violence against non-Muslims at the expense of revolutionary violence directed at the regime in Saudi Arabia can be explained by a relative lack of grievances *vis-à-vis* the state among Saudi Islamists, structural and cultural obstacles to mobilising against the regime, a certain amount of xenophobia inherent to Wahhabism and attempts by the regime to steer Islamist activism outside in order to divert it from the Al Saʿud.[40]

While Hegghammer's reasoning explains why QAP directed most of its attacks at Western targets, he acknowledges that some attacks against Saudi security forces did occur, but claims these were mostly out of revenge for violence used against its own members. Later, however,

36 Interviews with al-Dawsarī, Riyadh, 25 November 2008; al-Dhāyidī, Riyadh, 8 November 2008; al-Shāfī, Riyadh, 11 November 2008; al-ʿUtaybī, London, 1 August 2008.

37 Interview with al-Dhāyidī, Riyadh, 8 November 2008.

38 Hegghammer, 'Terrorist', 45–6.

39 *Id.*, 'Islamist', 705–6; *id.*, 'Jihad', 402–15; *id.*, 'Terrorist', 41; *id.*, 'Violence', 110–12.

40 *Id.*, 'Jihad', 406–15.

the QAP literature levelled more verbal attacks against the regime itself, accompanied by actual premeditated attacks against security forces. Hegghammer mentions that QAP may have had a two-stage strategy in which Western targets would be attacked first in order to focus on the Saudi regime later, but that this had few operational and practical consequences. He therefore concludes that QAP's jihad was not openly and explicitly framed and executed as a revolutionary struggle because it would probably not attract enough followers in Saudi Arabia. The attitude of QAP therefore seems to be summed up in the title of one of Hegghammer's articles, namely 'Jihad [against Western targets in Saudi Arabia], Yes, But Not Revolution [against the Saudi regime]'.[41]

As mentioned, this makes one wonder why al-Maqdisi became an important source of influence to QAP, since he frames 'apostate' Muslim regimes as the main enemy, not the West. Hegghammer's argument is certainly correct in the operational sense: one cannot argue with the fact that most operations launched by QAP in the period 2003–5 were aimed at Western targets in Saudi Arabia. That does not preclude the possibility, however, that an anti-Saudi ideology did exist among the members of QAP. In fact, QAP's campaign against Western targets, while not directly anti-state, was itself a sign of criticism against the Saudi regime, which had invited and allowed these Westerners within its borders. Moreover, it is unlikely that later attacks against Saudi security forces were only inspired by revenge. It seems obvious that the decision to start attacking Saudi security personnel instead of Westerners later on in the campaign must have been accompanied by some justifying discourse in order to legitimise this change of tactics.

I argue that there was indeed an anti-regime ideology underlying QAP's activities and that attempts were made to frame the regime as illegitimate and un-Islamic, even though this was mostly not translated into armed attacks against Saudi targets. Although Hegghammer does not deal with this in any detail, he acknowledges that this may indeed have existed. My argument therefore does not clash with his reasoning but complements his focus on the operational side of QAP by concentrating on the group's anti-Saudi ideological undercurrent, which shows that a strongly anti-regime discourse could indeed be found in QAP's literature during the 2003–4 campaign.[42] In the following section, I argue that al-Maqdisi's writings

[41] *Ibid.*, 404–5.

[42] But also see Joas Wagemakers, 'Al-Qaʿida's Editor: Abu Jandal al-Azdi's Online Jihadi Activism', *Politics, Religion & Ideology*, vol. 12, no. 4, 2011, 355–69.

were an important direct and indirect source of religious legitimisation for QAP in its attempts to justify this anti-Saudi stance, and incorporate his views into its own framing of the situation. This explains how al-Maqdisi's writings, while focussing on 'apostate' Muslim regimes, could still be influential among a group that mostly targeted Westerners.

Reframing QAP's Jihad

As we saw in Chapters 1 and 4, al-Maqdisi's books *Al-Kawashif al-Jaliyya* and (to a lesser extent) *Millat Ibrahim*, both of which indicted Saudi Arabia for its 'un-Islamic' rule, were well-known among jihadis in Peshawar during the 1980s and were smuggled into and spread around the kingdom in the late 1980s and throughout the 1990s. Although this did not result in much direct influence, according to Jamal Khashuqji, a Saudi journalist intimately familiar with Islamism in the 1990s, it did ensure that like-minded Saudis would at least have been aware of these books during that decade.[43] This, in turn, means that when preparations were made for the founding of QAP after 2001, these books were probably still available and known to the militants involved in this process. Their knowledge of al-Maqdisi's writings was further facilitated by the introduction of the Internet in Saudi Arabia in 1999, which made it easier to spread and share books, and the launch of al-Maqdisi's own website shortly afterwards, making his entire oeuvre available to everyone.[44]

QAP expressed the fact that it was influenced by al-Maqdisi's writings through its publications, in which it frequently printed his articles or referred to him. QAP's publications primarily include its biweekly magazines *Sawt al-Jihad* and *Muʿaskar al-Battar*, which were published by QAP's military council (*al-lajna al-ʿaskariyya li-l-mujāhidīn fī Jazīrat al-ʿArab*), as well as books and pamphlets by individual members.[45] It could be argued, of course, that al-Maqdisi was simply a major Jihadi-Salafi scholar and was published and mentioned in these magazines for that reason only. This would mean that his influence on other radical groups was just as great. A search of other Arabic-language non-Saudi jihadi magazines with a comparable number of issues during the same period

43 Telephone interview with Khāshuqjī, 27 November 2008.

44 Abū Muḥammad al-Maqdisī, e-mail message to the author, 11 January 2010.

45 These magazines can be found on www.tawhed.ws/c?i=324 and also on the Prism website (www.e-prism.org/articlesbyotherscholars.html). For more on *Ṣawt al-Jihād*, see Nico Prucha, *Die Stimme des Dschihad – 'Ṣawt al-Jihād': al-Qāʿidas erstes Online-Magazin*, Hamburg: Verlag Dr. Kovač, 2010.

(such as *Sada l-Jihad* and *Majallat al-Ansar*[46]), however, shows that al-Maqdisi was both published and mentioned more often and more extensively in *Sawt al-Jihad* as well as *Muʿaskar al-Battar* than in other magazines.[47] Moreover, other authors whose work was published or mentioned in the two Saudi jihad magazines were often Saudis themselves, senior members of al-Qaʿida or scholars who have written extensively on jihad. The fact that al-Maqdisi fitted none of these categories but was nevertheless considered important enough to publish or mention shows that there was probably some other reason for this.

Al-Maqdisi is not a Saudi, does not hold any rank in al-Qaʿida's hierarchy and, although it is part of the solution he offers to the problems he sees in politics and society, few of his writing focus on jihad. This is probably also why his writings that do deal with jihad are only referred to or published occasionally, and if they are, they are usually simply pieces praising the *mujāhidūn* without offering much strategic, ideological or theoretical insight and seem to be aimed only at boosting morale. Al-Maqdisi is often named, however, by QAP authors or interviewees as an important scholar who has influenced them. Moreover, he is sometimes mentioned in QAP literature as an imprisoned but steadfast shaykh, and his work is also published for this reason, as well as quoted for other purposes.[48] That these were not meaningless references becomes clear if one looks at how some members of QAP refer to al-Maqdisi. One prominent member of QAP, for instance, states:

> There are [several] scholars I benefited from, be it through lessons (*al-durūs al-ʿilmiyya*) or through discussions (*al-munāqashāt*), but the scholar I benefited a lot from through his books and writings and through contacting him via the internet – he is my model in this age (*qudwatī fī hādhā l-ʿaṣr*) – is the imam, the divine scholar Abu Muhammad al-Maqdisi.[49]

Similarly, ʿAbdallah al-Rashid, a scholar affiliated with QAP, writes:

> The official [scholars] of Saudi Arabia (*bilād al-ḥaramayn*) study [Muhammad b. ʿAbd al-Wahhab's] *Kitab al-Tawhid*, they talk about loyalty and disavowal (*al-walāʾ wa-l-barāʾ*), they distinguish the ruler's rule on the basis of something other than what God has revealed [. . .] and recite (*yatlūna bi-alsinatihim*) the verses of jihad. With regard to these, you will not find a difference between most of the

[46] These two magazines are also available on www.tawhed.ws/c?i=324.

[47] See Joas Wagemakers, 'Quietist', 134, note 64.

[48] See *ibid.*, 134–5 for specific references.

[49] 'Liqāʾ maʿa l-Shaykh "Abī ʿAbd al-Raḥmān al-Atharī"', *Ṣawt al-Jihād*, no. 5, Shawwāl 1424/November-December 2003, 25.

writings of Abu Muhammad al-Maqdisi – may God strengthen him and break his captivity (*thabbatahu llāh wa-fakka asrahu*) – and the writings of many of them on matters of belief (*masāʾil al-iʿtiqād*) concerning the fundamental issues, except that he distinguishes himself by his sincerity in what he says.[50]

The most sustained and consistent indication of al-Maqdisi's influence on QAP does not lie in his morale-boosting articles on jihad, his writings on his prison experiences or in praise of his work such as that mentioned here, however, but in the frequent references to his book *Al-Kawashif al-Jaliyya*. This book was mentioned[51], recommended[52], promoted[53] and quoted[54], and part of it was republished in another book[55], which in turn was also promoted by QAP[56]. In fact, an entirely new and condensed version of the book fully in line with the original was published[57] (and subsequently promoted by QAP[58]). The praise of the book found in various QAP publications also indicates that it was an influential source for the organisation and its members. For instance, ʿAbdallah al-Rashud, a frequent contributor to *Sawt al-Jihad*, recalls a conversation he had with someone:

I said to him: 'Do you know anything about the books of the imprisoned shaykh Abu Muhammad al-Maqdisi – may God break his captivity?' He said: 'I have heard of them but I have not read them.' I said to him: 'If I could ask you one thing, it would be that you read one of the books of the same shaykh, *Al-Kawashif al-Jaliyya fi Kufr al-Dawla al-Saʿudiyya*.'[59]

50 ʿAbdallāh b. Nāṣir al-Rashīd, *Hashīm al-Tarājuʿāt*, www.tawhed.ws/r?i=j62533fz, 2003, 44.
51 Abū Jandal al-Azdī, *Al-Bāḥith ʿan Ḥukm Qatl Afrād wa-Ḍubbāt al-Mabāḥith*, www.tawhed.ws/r?i=oz5i7eed, 2002, 8 (footnote 1), 12; 'Liqāʾ maʿa l-Shaykh Abī Jandal al-Azdī', *Ṣawt al-Jihād*, no. 10, Dhū l-Ḥijja 1424/February 2004, 23, 28.
52 'Umm Ḥamza Mithāl li-l-Marʾa al-Mujāhida', *Ṣawt al-Jihād*, no. 9, Dhū l-Ḥijja 1424/January-February 2004, 44.
53 'Kitāb Al-Kawāshif al-Jaliyya fī Kufr al-Dawla al-Saʿūdiyya', *Ṣawt al-Jihād*, no. 6, Shawwāl 1424/November-December 2003, 29.
54 Abū Jandal al-Azdī, *Ḥiwār al-Minbar maʿa l-Shaykh Abī Jandal al-Azdī*, www.tawhed.ws/r?i=u2ysawtb, n.d., 29–30.
55 Muʿjab al-Dawsarī [Ṣāliḥ b. Saʿd al-Ḥasan], *Āl Saʿūd fī Mīzān Ahl al-Sunna*, www.tawhed.ws/c?i=141, 2003, 18–20.
56 'Min Iṣdārātinā', *Muʿaskar al-Battār*, no. 17, Rajab 1425/September 2004, 6; 'Qarīban ʿalā Mawqiʿ "*Ṣawt al-Jihād*"', *Ṣawt al-Jihād*, no. 9, Dhū l-Ḥijja 1424/January-February 2004, 47.
57 Muʿjab al-Dawsarī, *Tahdhīb al-Kawāshif al-Jaliyya fī Kufr al-Dawla al-Saʿūdiyya*, www.tawhed.ws/r?i=inbgjtyj, 2003.
58 'Iṣdārāt Jadīda', *Ṣawt al-Jihād*, no. 7, Dhū l-Qaʿda 1424/December 2003-January 2004, 42.
59 ʿAbdallah b. Muḥammad b. Rāshid b. Muḥammad al-Rashūd al-Sabīʿī, *Al-Tatār wa-Āl Saʿūd*, www.tawhed.ws/c?i=141, 2004, 23 (footnote 28, continued from previous page).

The book is also mentioned as 'one of the most famous books circulating on the Internet'[60] and praised by the author of its 'refined version' as a visionary book written 'about ten years ago' but that nevertheless stated what was wrong with Saudi Arabia even then.[61]

The information given here shows that *Al-Kawashif al-Jaliyya* was indeed an important and influential book in the QAP literature. One could argue, however, that this had nothing to do with al-Maqdisi's role in reframing QAP's jihad as an indirect struggle against the Saudi regime itself but could simply be explained by pointing to *Al-Kawashif al-Jaliyya*'s in-depth treatment of the American influence in Saudi Arabia. It is true that this was an important issue to QAP and al-Maqdisi's writings were indeed used to explain that existing Saudi treaties with the United States need not be honoured, thereby opening the way for QAP to fight the Americans.[62] The most important topic mentioned by QAP in relation to *Al-Kawashif al-Jaliyya*, however, was al-Maqdisi's attack on the Saudi regime itself and particularly its so-called 'man-made laws', a ubiquitous issue in his writings. QAP's anti-Saudi stance was expressed in many of its publications, some clearly referring to the allegedly 'un-Islamic' system of laws it applied.[63]

Importantly, the literature of QAP shows that it not only shares al-Maqdisi's conclusion with regard to the Saudi state (i.e., that it is an 'un-Islamic' state), but also frequently uses his writings to show that this is the case. In fact, one might possibly even say that almost every time the alleged *kufr* nature of Saudi Arabia needs to be shown in QAP's literature, al-Maqdisi's work is mentioned or quoted. Al-Maqdisi's writings in which he openly describes Muslim regimes as *ṭawāghīt* are published or quoted by members of QAP[64], for instance, also when he explicitly refers to

See also *id.* (but name given as ʿAbdallāh b. Muḥammad al-Rashūd), 'Al-Tatār wa-Āl Saʿūd fī Naẓrat Shaykh al-Islām Ibn Taymiyya', *Ṣawt al-Jihād*, no. 14, Ṣafar 1425/April 2004, 25 (footnote 1, continued from previous page).

60 'Liqā' maʿa l-Shaykh Abī Jandal al-Azdī', 26.

61 Al-Dawsarī, *Tahdhīb*, 1.

62 See, for instance, the review of al-Maqdisī's *Barā'at al-Muwaḥḥidīn min ʿUhūd al-Ṭawāghīt wa-l-Murtaddīn* in *Ṣawt al-Jihād*, no. 2, Shaʿbān 1424/October 2003, 11. This treatise is also referred to in – for instance – al-Azdī, *Nuṣūṣ*, 4–5; and quoted in *id.*, *Al-Āyāt wa-l-Aḥādīth al-Ghazīra ʿalā Kufr Quwwat Dirʿ al-Jazīra*, www.tawhed.ws/r?i=cnfiic2g, n.d., 2–4.

63 See, for instance, al-Rashūd, *Al-Tatār*.

64 Al-Azdī, *Al-Āyāt*, 2–4; Abū Muḥammad al-Maqdisī, 'Al-ʿIbra bi-l-Ḥaqā'iq wa-l-Maʿānī lā bi-l-Asmā' wa-l-Mabānī', *Muʿaskar al-Battār*, no. 10, Rabīʿ al-Awwal 1425/May 2004, 4–5; *id.*, 'Fasād al-Furūʿ Natīja Ḥatmiyya li-Fasād al-Uṣūl', *Muʿaskar al-Battār*, no. 18, Rajab 1425/September 2004, 4–5.

Saudi Arabia as such[65]. His work is cited when explaining what *kufr* really is[66], and one author states:

> This evil state (*al-dawla al-khabītha*) – the state of the Al Saʿud – which corrupts the people's religion for them, does not differ from its other sisters and loved ones (*ʿan ghayrihā min shaqīqātihā wa-ḥabībātihā wa-akhawātihā*) who do not apply Islamic law (*ghayr al-sharʿiyyāt*) from among the other Arab and Gulf *ṭāghūt* regimes (*al-anẓima al-ʿArabiyya al-Khalījiyya al-ṭāghūtiyya al-ukhrā*) that the shaykhs of the Āl Saʿud – sometimes – attack for their rule according to man-made laws. Whoever wants to know the truth about this infidel apostate state (*hādhihi l-dawla al-kāfira al-murtadda*) should read the book *Al-Kawashif al-Jaliyya fi Kufr al-Dawla al-Saʿudiyya*.[67]

Another scholar affiliated with QAP agrees and writes, partly with reference to *Al-Kawashif al-Jaliyya*:

> Among the greatest contemporary [scholars] who make a case [against the Saudi regime] is the imprisoned shaykh Abu Muhammad al-Maqdisi [. . .] His books and writings contain abundant knowledge (*al-ʿilm al-jamm*) and deep-rooted fundamentals (*al-taʾṣīl al-rāsikh*) that only an arrogant or ignorant person or an agent of the *ṭawāghīt* would deny.[68]

Interestingly, members of QAP do not only mention or quote al-Maqdisi's work when they want to show that Saudi Arabia is a *kufr* state but they are also careful not to go too far in their *takfīr*, and – again – use al-Maqdisi's books to make their case. This desire to wage jihad on a doctrinally sound basis separates QAP from some of the Jordanian jihadis that we will deal with in Chapters 8 and 9. This can probably be explained by the strongly religious Wahhabi background of QAP. Being Saudi, these men grew up and were educated in an environment in which doctrinal purity in every sphere of life was highly important but waging jihad much less so, unlike Jordanian jihadis, who were often more concerned with fighting than with the Salafi creed.[69] It is thus not surprising that some of al-Maqdisi's meticulous writings critical of certain practices among jihadis that caused some Jordanians to accuse him of 'moderation' and 'revisionism', as we will see in Chapter 9, were widely mentioned and

65 See, for instance, the appendix to al-Azdī, *Nuṣūṣ*, 26–33, which al-Maqdisī wrote.

66 See, for instance, al-Azdī, *Al-Bāḥith*, 49 (footnotes 1–2); Sulṭān b. Bijād al-ʿUtaybī, *Risāla fī l-Ṭawāghīt*, www.tawhed.ws/r?i=5z02q0kh, 2002, 14–16.

67 Al-Azdī, *Al-Āyāt*, 5.

68 Al-Rashūd, *Tatār*, 24 (footnote 29, continued from previous page); *id.*, 'Al-Tatār', 25 (footnote 1).

69 This was also confirmed by al-Maqdisī himself. Interview with al-Maqdisī, Amman, 13 January 2009.

quoted by Saudi jihadis as important warnings against extremism in *takfīr* and jihad.[70] It is likely that the greater familiarity with doctrinal details made the Saudi QAP more susceptible to and more appreciative of the more nuanced writings by al-Maqdisi than some Jordanian jihadis, who dismissed them as recantations of his earlier, supposedly more radical work. Several Saudi QAP-affiliated authors stated that the best book one could possibly find against extremism in *takfīr* is al-Maqdisi's *Al-Risala al-Thalathiniyya*.[71]

The combination of using al-Maqdisi's writings for the legitimisation of fighting the Saudi regime as well as for refraining from doing so in an extreme and indiscriminate way becomes very clear with regard to the issue of killing Saudi soldiers. In a Q & A section of QAP's *Sawt al-Jihad* magazine, the question is asked about whether jihad operations against Western targets on the Arabian Peninsula are allowed since one could also hurt Saudi soldiers. The answer refers to al-Maqdisi's writings to make clear that the 'crimes' (*al-jarāʾim*) of the '*anṣār al-ṭawāghīt*' (here: Saudi soldiers) are actually worse than those of the '*ṭawāghīt*' themselves (here: the Saudi regime) since the latter do not actually carry weapons that they turn against the jihadis and that soldiers may therefore be targeted.[72] In other writings by Abu Jandal al-Azdi[73], one of the major ideologues of QAP, it is pointed out that while Saudi soldiers may indeed be killed, it should not be done indiscriminately but according to the *sharīʿa*, and one should take into account that not every soldier is necessarily an infidel, again with reference to al-Maqdisi's books.[74]

70 See, for example, al-Azdī, *Al-Āyāt*, 46, 57 (footnote 101, continued from previous page); *id.*, *Ḥiwār*, 6; *id.*, *Al-ʿAlāqāt al-Dawliyya fī l-Islām*, 3 vols., www.tawhed.ws/a?a=6sbcw2ch, n.d., vol. I, 28–30, 38; Abū Muḥammad al-Maqdisī, 'Al-Ḥidhr wa-l-Kitmān bayna l-Ifrāṭ wa-l-Tafrīṭ', *Muʿaskar al-Battār*, no. 16, Jumādā l-Thānī 1425/August 2004, 5–8; 'Fa-s'alū Ahl al-Dhikr: Fatāwā fī l-Jihād wa-l-Siyāsa al-Sharʿiyya', *Ṣawt al-Jihād*, no. 26, Shaʿbān 1425/October 2004, 51.

71 Al-Rashīd, *Hashīm*, 51; Farḥān b. Mashhūr al-Ruwaylī, 'Iṣlāḥ al-Ghalaṭ fī Fahm al-Nawāqiḍ (1): Al-Taḥdhīr min al-Takfīr Muṭlaqan', *Ṣawt al-Jihād*, no. 18, Rabīʿ al-Thānī 1425/June 2004, 14.

72 'Tasāʾulāt ḥawla Jihād al-Ṣalībiyyīn fī Jazīrat al-ʿArab: Al-Ḥalqa al-Sābiʿa', *Ṣawt al-Jihād*, no. 15, Rabīʿ al-Awwal 1425/April 2004, 22.

73 For more on al-Azdī, see Nico Prucha, 'Jihad on the Internet – The Anomalous Case of Abu Jandal al-Azdi', *Journal for Intelligence, Propaganda and Security Studies*, vol. 2, no. 2, 2007, 44–6; Madawi al-Rasheed, 'The Local and the Global in Saudi Salafi-Jihadi Discourse', in: Roel Meijer (ed.), *Global Salafism: Islam's New Religious Movement*, London: Hurst & Co., 2009, 310–13; *id.*, 'The Local and the Global in Saudi Salafism', *ISIM Review*, no. 21, 2008, 8–9; Wagemakers, 'Al-Qaʿida's', 355–69.

74 Al-Azdī, *Al-Āyāt*, 74–7; *id.*, *Al-Bāḥith*, 28–32, 45–6.

From the foregoing, it is clear that al-Maqdisi was a great source of influence on QAP and has played an important role in reframing the group's position towards the Saudi state. It may very well be, however, that al-Maqdisi's impact on QAP was even greater than the preceding suggests since some arguments used by certain scholars – particularly Abu Jandal al-Azdi, who was strongly influenced by him[75] – look a lot like al-Maqdisi's and may have originally been taken from him but are not attributed as such.[76] Moreover, *Al-Kawashif al-Jaliyya* may have served as a sort of reference work for jihadis in Saudi Arabia in a way that does not always make clear that the book was actually used. One QAP-writer, for instance, cites numerous fatwas by the former Saudi Grand Mufti Muhammad b. Ibrahim Al al-Shaykh. What is interesting is that the author only selected fatwas that al-Maqdisi had mentioned earlier in *Al-Kawashif al-Jaliyya*. Considering the fact that Ibn Ibrahim had produced literally thousands of fatwas, and that al-Maqdisi did not number them consecutively but that they are nevertheless used in exactly the same way by the author, it seems that the latter selected the fatwas on the basis of *Al-Kawashif al-Jaliyya*, or may not even have consulted the original work at all.[77]

A final indication of al-Maqdisi's influence on QAP lies not in what he or his fellow jihadis have written but in how his ideological enemies have responded to his books. The Saudi government and many Saudi scholars have made huge efforts to counter extremism and terrorism through counter-radicalisation schools, but also by writing ideological tracts criticising the jihadis' ideas. While most of these have focussed on the phenomenon in general, several books have been dedicated specifically to al-Maqdisi's book *Al-Kawashif al-Jaliyya*[78] or *Millat Ibrahim*[79]. These books try to refute the ideas expressed in al-Maqdisi's writings – particularly *Al-Kawashif al-Jaliyya* – that Saudi Arabia is a *kufr* state because of its ties with the United States and its alleged man-made

[75] See also *Al-Waṭan*, 8 August 2004.
[76] See, for example, al-Azdī, *Nuṣūṣ*, 2–3.
[77] Al-ʿUtaybī, *Risāla fī l-Ṭawāghīt*, 3–12.
[78] Muḥammad al-Kalīlī, *Al-Radd ʿalā l-Kawāshif al-Jaliyya*, www.alradnet.com/epaper/article.php?id_net=74 (accessed 25 February 2010), 2004; ʿAbd al-ʿAzīz b. Rayyis al-Rayyis, *Tabdīd Kawāshif al-ʿAnīd fī Takfīrihi li-Dawlat al-Tawḥīd*, http://islamancient.com/books,item,39.html, 2003.
[79] Muḥammad b. ʿUmar Bāzmūl, *Al-Radd ʿalā Kutub Mashbūha*, www.salafikurd.com/files/pdf/bazmwl/alrdalameltebraheem.pdf (accessed 25 February 2009), n.d.

laws.[80] They are highly relevant because they show that al-Maqdisi's writings were apparently considered dangerous enough by the Saudi regime to allow (or even encourage) government-supported scholars to write refutations of them. In fact, an unpublished Saudi government-sponsored survey conducted in 2004 shows that among thousands of Saudi 20–30-year olds who had been to Afghanistan or had sympathised with or had even been members of QAP, *Millat Ibrahim* and *Al-Kawashif al-Jaliyya* were considered very important books. In a related question asking what non-Saudi scholar had influenced them most, al-Maqdisi was (a very close) second only to ʿAbdallah ʿAzzam.[81] Moreover, the books refuting al-Maqdisi's writings were not written in the 1990s, when – as we saw in the previous chapter – the authorities must at least have been aware of al-Maqdisi's work, but in 2003 and 2004. The reason for this probably lies in the increased violence at that time and the fact that the influence of these books became so apparent that it could no longer be ignored and something had to be done about it, as Madawi al-Rasheed has observed.[82] This underlines my thesis that al-Maqdisi's writings were important in stimulating anti-Saudi thought in the 1990s but did not have much concrete influence until the early 2000s. Exactly why they had so much influence is the final question of this chapter.

A Wahhabi to the Wahhabis: Explaining al-Maqdisi's Influence

The description just given may create the impression that al-Maqdisi was the only scholar quoted and mentioned in articles produced by QAP. This was not the case, of course. Other authors, including many Saudi jihadis and scholars as well as Ayman al-Zawahiri, Osama bin Laden and ʿAbd al-Qadir b. ʿAbd al-ʿAziz, were cited too. As stated before, however, al-Maqdisi – unlike the other authors mentioned – had not written much about jihad or war against the West, was not a member of al-Qaʿida and was also not a Saudi himself. This begs the question as to how such a scholar who, moreover, did not have the solid religious education that many Saudi shaykhs did enjoy could possibly be so influential. To answer

80 Abū ʿUmar Usāma b. ʿAṭāyā b. ʿUthmān al-ʿUtaybī, *Al-Ḥujaj al-Qawiyya ʿalā Wujūb al-Difāʿ ʿan al-Dawla al-Saʿūdiyya*, http://otiby.net/book/open.php?cat=1&anbook=18 (accessed 25 February 2010), n.d.

81 Interview with al-Hadlaq, Riyadh, 26 November 2009.

82 Al-Rasheed, *Contesting*, 122.

this, we once again have to look to al-Maqdisi's framing of his criticism of Saudi Arabia.

Conditions for Frame Alignment

In the previous chapter, we saw that a frame should ideally indicate the problem, suggest a solution and call for action in a way that resonates with the public it targets. Al-Maqdisi's framing of the Saudi regime in terms of unbelief and apostasy to be countered by jihad clearly did not resonate fully with the *ṣaḥwa*-led opposition in the 1990s. It has become clear throughout this chapter, however, that the visitors to Bayt Shubrā, as well as QAP, did draw conclusions similar to al-Maqdisi's with regard to the Saudi regime, the legitimacy of fighting it and – in isolated cases – even concretely attacking its soldiers.

Although al-Maqdisi's specific interpretation of the core framing tasks indicates why the visitors to Bayt Shubrā and QAP were attracted to his writings in the first place – they would obviously not have used the writings of someone they completely disagreed with – there is more to be said about the reason of al-Maqdisi's influence. After all, the incorporation of diagnosis, prognosis and motivation into one's frame may be essential for frame alignment but is no recipe for guaranteed success. Snow and Benford have given a detailed explanation of how – ideally – frames should be constructed that goes beyond these core framing tasks and that has been substantiated by other scholars.[83] They have distinguished five factors that determine the degree to which a frame aligns with the views of its target audience. The first is centrality, referring to the salience of the movement's or actor's frame in the public's larger belief system. If the frame deals with central issues, its chances of alignment are better than when it only deals with marginal ones.[84] The second factor, range and interrelatedness, is connected to the breadth of the frame (i.e., its applicability in more than one situation) and the extent to which it is connected with other important aspects of people's beliefs.[85] Third, the frame as well as the framer have to be credible in the eyes of the target

[83] See Wagemakers, 'Quietist', 141–3.

[84] Sarah Babb, '"A True American System of Finance": Frame Resonance in the U.S. Labor Movement, 1866 to 1886', *American Sociological Review*, vol. 61, 1996, 1039–43.

[85] A frame can be overstretched, too. See Nicole Youngman, 'When Frame Extension Fails: Operation Rescue and the "Triple Gates of Hell" in Orlando', *Journal of Contemporary Ethnography*, vol. 32, no. 5, 2003, 533–42.

audience.[86] A fourth factor is referred to as 'experiental commensurability', meaning that a frame needs to suggest answers and solutions that are congruent with the conditions in which the audience finds itself and with how it experiences the situation.[87] Finally, a frame needs to have narrative fidelity.[88] This entails that it resonate with people's cultural, religious and national or ethnic narrations.[89]

If a frame adheres closely to the conditions for frame alignment formulated and applied by the various scholars mentioned earlier, it stands a good chance of resonating once it reaches the target audience. It is important to realise that the theory explained here does not entail that people are influenced solely by ideas without looking at the context in which these are expressed. By incorporating aspects such as empirical credibility and narrative fidelity, framing takes the social, political and cultural circumstances in which influencing takes place into account and thereby shows how people are influenced through a dialectical exchange of ideas and context, rather than either of these separately.

Al-Maqdisi's Frame Resonance

If we compare the conditions for frame alignment given here with al-Maqdisi's portrayal of himself and Saudi Arabia in his book *Al-Kawashif*

[86] Jiping Zuo and Robert D. Benford, 'Mobilization Processes and the 1989 Chinese Democracy Movement', *The Sociological Quarterly*, vol. 36, no. 1, 1995, 140–3. See also William A. Gamson, 'The Social Psychology of Collective Action', in: Aldon D. Morris and Carol McClurg Mueller (eds.), *Frontiers in Social Movement Theory*, New Haven & London: Yale University Press, 1992, 69–70. For framers' credibility, see chapter 9.

[87] Timothy J. Kubal, 'The Presentation of Political Self: Cultural Resonance and the Construction of Collective Action Frames', *The Sociological Quarterly*, vol. 39, no. 4, 1998, 540, 550–1; Tracey Skillington, 'Politics and the Struggle to Define: A Discourse Analysis of the Framing Strategies of Competing Actors in a "New" Participatory Forum', *British Journal of Sociology*, vol. 48, no. 3, 1997, 501–2.

[88] Gary Allen Fine, 'Public Narration and Group Culture: Discerning Discourse in Social Movements', in: Hank Johnston and Bert Klandermans (eds.), *Social Movements and Culture*, Minneapolis: University of Minnesota Press, 1995, 127–38; William A. Gamson, *Talking Politics*, Cambridge: Cambridge University Press, 1992, 135–62; Michael J. McCallion and David R. Maines, 'The Liturgical Social Movement in the Vatican II Catholic Church', in: Michael Dobkowski and Isidor Walliman (eds.), *Research in Social Movements, Conflicts and Change*, vol. XXI, Stanford, CT: JAI Press, 1999, 131–2; Elena Zdravomyslova, 'Opportunities and Framing in the Transition to Democracy: The Case of Russia', in: Doug McAdam, John D. McCarthy and Mayer N. Zald (eds.), *Comparative Perspectives on Social Movements: Political Opportunities, Mobilizing Structures, and Cultural Framings*, Cambridge: Cambridge University Press, 1996, 126–36.

[89] Snow and Benford, 'Ideology', 205–11; Benford and Snow, 'Framing', 619–22.

al-Jaliyya, we find that his influence among visitors to Bayt Shubrā and QAP is likely due to the fact that his framing meets these quite accurately. In relation to the concept of centrality, we saw in Chapter 4 that al-Maqdisi's criticism of Saudi Arabia mostly concentrates on three issues: the country's reliance on 'man-made laws', its ties with regional and international organisations that are based on secular systems instead of the *sharīʿa* and the strong Saudi-U.S. relationship. As became clear in the previous chapter, al-Maqdisi frames the first two issues as being related to the worship of *ṭawāghīt*. Since al-Maqdisi sees the application of and adherence to 'man-made laws' as idolatry, he can portray 'un-Islamic' legislation as a grave violation of *tawḥīd*, which is not only a central concept in the Wahhabi version of Salafism but the very basis of Islam. This way, al-Maqdisi can portray Saudi legislative policy as contrary to the fundamentals of Islam around which everything else revolves, which also applies to the kingdom's ties with the United States, dealt with more specifically in Chapter 6.

Al-Maqdisi's frame also meets the conditions mentioned earlier with regard to its range and interrelatedness. Since a broad and radical interpretation of *tawḥīd* is the basis of his entire reasoning, his arguments flow naturally from that point to related concepts such as *takfīr* and jihad, allowing him to use the concept to comment on religious as well as political affairs. Because of this, al-Maqdisi's criticism of Saudi Arabia is embedded in and strongly related to his critique of other countries' policies and legislation, described in Chapter 2. As such, al-Maqdisi uses the concept of *tawḥīd* as a consistent starting point from which to draw a large number of interrelated and broadly applicable conclusions.

The two factors mentioned, though very important, are probably present in the writings of most radical Muslim scholars writing about legislative systems. Indeed, early radical scholars such as Sayyid Qutb and Muhammad ʿAbd al-Salam Faraj also connected the issue of legislation with *tawḥīd* and used that concept as a starting point for their arguments, as we saw in Chapter 2, although not as often and as systematically as al-Maqdisi. Where al-Maqdisi really distinguishes himself from Qutb, Faraj and other radical scholars, however, is in the last three factors that are conducive to strong frame resonance. The credibility of his frame (i.e., the extent to which it can actually be 'proven'), for instance, was quite high. It has to be remembered that al-Maqdisi wrote *Al-Kawashif al-Jaliyya* in 1989, a year before the Gulf War. In that book, as we have seen, he wrote extensively on the close Saudi-U.S. ties, the enormous sales of American weapons to the kingdom and why, despite this, the Saudi army was nevertheless weak and incompetent. He even mentioned the number of American soldiers on Saudi soil and warned that this number might increase in the future. The fact that all of this was meticulously documented in his book and that only a year later the Saudi regime not only turned out to be too weak to take on the Iraqi military threat but invited 500,000 soldiers from its long-time ally America must have supported the book's credibility in the eyes of its readers.

The experiental commensurability of al-Maqdisi's frame was also there. Whereas in the early 1990s, people may have felt that a change in the system was possible through petitions and non-violent protests, this notion was quickly dispelled when the *ṣaḥwa* was repressed, co-opted or exiled, as we saw earlier. This means that while al-Maqdisi's calls for *takfīr* and jihad may have struck many as unnecessary and extreme in the early 1990s, this was probably much less so once the perceived reality of national stalemate and international 'war against Islam' after '9/11' had sunk in and a new and more violent group of fighters had returned from Afghanistan.

Finally and most importantly, *Al-Kawashif al-Jaliyya* – though not written by a Saudi – had a distinctly Saudi Wahhabi flavour to it, showing a close adherence to the Saudi and Wahhabi national, historical and religious narratives. The book was first released under the pseudonym 'Abu l-Baraʾ al-Najdi', thereby invoking the heartland of Wahhabism, Najd. As has been stated before, this 'reflected a desire to authenticate this revolutionary theology by anchoring it in the heart of the Arabian Peninsula, the land of Wahhabiyya'[90]. Al-Maqdisi must have had similar reasons for stating:

> So that the reader knows before he reads this book of mine: I am not a communist, nor a Rāfiḍī[91] Shiite but – may God be praised – a Sunni Arab adherent to *tawḥīd* (*muwaḥḥid*) who is originally from Najd (*Najdiyyan ʿArabiyyan aṣīlan*). [...] I disavow [*atabarraʾa*] to God exalted [communists and Shiites] and their infidel deviant beliefs. I declare my *ʿaqīda* to be the creed of the *ahl al-Sunna wa-l-jamāʿa*, on the basis of the Prophet [...] and the pious predecessors from among his companions and their followers from the best generations. I declare this so

90 Al-Rasheed, *Contesting*, 121.

91 The term Rāfiḍī (rejector) is a derogatory term used by Salafīs for Shiites. For more on this term and the anti-Shiite discourse of many Salafīs, see Guido Steinberg, 'Jihadi-Salafism and the Shiʿis: Remarks about the Intellectual Roots of anti-Shiʿism', in: Roel Meijer (ed.), *Global Salafism: Islam's New Religious Movement*, London: Hurst & Co., 2009, 107–25; Joas Wagemakers, 'Soennitische Islamisten en de Erfenis van de Islamitische Revolutie', *ZemZem: Tijdschrift over het Midden-Oosten, Noord-Afrika en Islam*, vol. 4, no. 3, 2008, 55–9.

that I prevent (*asuddu l-ṭarīq*) the evil scholars (*ʿulamāʾ al-sūʾ*), the scholars of the Al Saʿud, from slandering me because of this or something else.[92]

Al-Maqdisi goes on to recount the story of the Ikhwan, whom the first king of the present Saudi state, ʿAbd al-ʿAziz, defeated at the Battle of Sibilla in 1929. Al-Maqdisi not only clearly sides with the Ikhwan against the king, thereby placing himself in a longer tradition of Wahhabi-inspired opposition against the Al Saʿud, but also claims that the latter have betrayed the original pact between Muhammad b. Saʿud and Muhammad b. ʿAbd al-Wahhab that was the basis of the first Saudi state. He juxtaposes the strict teachings of Ibn ʿAbd al-Wahhab on dealing with non-Muslims with the policies of King Fahd and concludes that 'there is no difference between this state and the other Arab *ṭāghūt* regimes'.[93] He goes on to make his case against Saudi Arabia using Wahhabi concepts (such as *al-walāʾ wa-l-barāʾ*, which we will deal with in the next two chapters) and sources and shows that he is clearly knowledgeable about Wahhabi writings. Moreover, his detailed arguments, particularly in books such as *Al-Risala al-Thalathiniyya*, show that he follows a Salafi and even Wahhabi way of thinking that clearly goes beyond the relatively shallow reasoning of Qutb and Faraj.

In interviews with former visitors to Bayt Shubrā and experts on Islamism in Saudi Arabia, it turned out that – apart from the content of al-Maqdisi's frame as expressed in his diagnosis, prognosis and motivation – the five factors distinguished earlier were indeed very important in explaining al-Maqdisi's influence. Although nobody mentioned the importance of *tawḥīd* and the relationship of everything al-Maqdisi writes to this concept, considering the fact that his followers are all Wahhabi-Salafis, it must be assumed that this was indeed important. The range and interrelatedness of his writings were explicitly acknowledged, however, with one Islamist saying that al-Maqdisi's books are very coherent, never contradict themselves and are argued from a single starting point.[94] The empirical credibility and the experiental commensurability of his frame were also important factors, with interviewees referring to his argument about the American soldiers and his willingness to openly mention broadly acknowledged problems in the current Saudi state as examples. Similarly, al-Maqdisi's own credibility was not in doubt either, not so much because he was seen as a great scholar but

92 Al-Maqdisī, *Al-Kawāshif*, 8.
93 *Ibid.*, 9–14. The quote is on 13.
94 Interview with al-Faqīh, London, 11 March 2008.

because of his clear appearance as a Wahhabi-Salafi 'knowledge seeker' (*ṭālib ʿilm*), unlike someone such as Qutb.[95]

The most important of the five factors, however, was al-Maqdisi's close adherence to the Saudi-Wahhabi intellectual tradition. The fact that he used Wahhabi sources, arguments and concepts, placed them in the context of the history of Saudi Arabia and openly showed his own Najdi roots was acknowledged as an explanation for his influence among both the visitors to Bayt Shubrā and the members of QAP.[96] Some mentioned that al-Maqdisi made the ideas of *takfīr* of the Saudi state 'acceptable' to Saudi jihadis[97] and that the latter would simply not have been receptive to Egyptian or Syrian ideas.[98] In fact, one interviewee told me that al-Maqdisi, unlike major Saudi scholars such as Ibn Baz, represented the real Wahhabi tradition of the *aʾimmat al-daʿwa al-Najdiyya* (the imams of the Najdi propagation of Islam).[99] Al-Maqdisi's use of major Wahhabi scholars in his case *against* the Wahhabi state, was therefore mentioned as an embarrassment for the Saudi government.[100]

In conclusion, we can say that al-Maqdisi proved a major source of influence on the visitors to Bayt Shubrā with regard to their ideas of the *takfīr* of the Saudi regime as well as on QAP in relation to their ideological justification for an anti-Saudi discourse, although this did not translate into a sustained policy of armed attacks against the Saudi state. The reason for people's susceptibility to his specific writings lay in his framing of the situation in a way that concurred with theirs on the one hand and the fact that his frame met all the conditions of a successful frame on the other, in which his being 'a Wahhabi to the Wahhabis' played a major role. This latter aspect again shows that al-Maqdisi adhered closely to a form of Salafism that was used mostly among quietists. His adoption of many of its sources, detailed arguments and concepts makes clear once

95 Interviews with al-Daynī, Jeddah, 13 November 2008; al-Dhāyidī, Riyadh, 8 November 2008; al-Hadlaq, Riyadh, 26 November 2008; al-Masʿarī, London, 10 March 2008; al-Shāfī, 11 November 2008; al-ʿUtaybī, London, 1 August 2008.

96 Interviews with al-Dawsarī, Riyadh, 25 November 2008; al-Daynī, Jeddah, 13 November 2008; al-Dhāyidī, Riyadh, 8 November 2008; al-Hadlaq, Riyadh, 18 November 2008; al-Rājiḥī, Riyadh, 18 November 2008; al-Shāfī, Riyadh, 11 November 2008. Al-Nuqaydān, e-mail message to the author, 6 December 2008. See also 'Liqāʾ maʿa l-Shaykh Abī Jandal al-Azdī', 23; 'Millat Ibrāhīm li-l-Shaykh al-Asīr Abī Muḥammad al-Maqdisī ʿĀṣim al-ʿUtaybī', *Ṣawt al-Jihād*, no. 14, Ṣafar 1425/April 2004, 32.

97 Interview with al-Hadlaq, Riyadh, 18 November 2008.

98 Telephone interview with Khāshuqjī, 27 November 2008.

99 Interview with al-Dawsarī, Riyadh, 25 November 2008.

100 Interview with al-Faqīh, London, 11 March 2008.

again that al-Maqdisi can be seen as a quietist Jihadi-Salafi, who despite his calls for jihad against the rulers does not turn his back on the quietist tradition but embraces it to a large degree. One of the concepts with which he did this is *al-walāʾ wa-l-barāʾ*, which we will now look at in greater detail.

PART III

AL-MAQDISI'S INFLUENCE ON THE DEVELOPMENT OF *AL-WALĀʾ WA-L-BARĀʾ*, 1984–2009

6

The Revival of *al-Istiʿāna bi-l-Kuffār*

In the previous chapters, we have regularly come across the term *al-walāʾ wa-l-barāʾ* as a distinctly Salafi and – particularly – Wahhabi concept, without actually dealing with it in any greater detail. This chapter and the next are meant to do just that. In what follows, I will focus on the notion of *al-istiʿāna bi-l-kuffār*, a dimension of *al-walāʾ wa-l-barāʾ* that is rooted in Islamic tradition, particularly in its Wahhabi version. The inadmissibility of asking 'infidels' for help as reasoned by Wahhabi scholars, particularly against other Muslims during a time of war, was rediscovered by Abu Muhammad al-Maqdisi, and it is likely that through his work a revival of the concept was set in motion.

This chapter starts by giving a historical overview of the concept of *al-walāʾ wa-l-barāʾ* from its pre-Islamic beginnings to its reinterpretation in nineteenth-century Wahhabi discourse, with special attention to the dimension of *al-istiʿāna bi-l-kuffār*. It then deals with al-Maqdisi's rediscovery of the Wahhabi version of this notion and how this was picked up and developed further by Saudi-Wahhabi scholars and activists. Finally, the chapter seeks to explain through the use of framing why al-Maqdisi's rediscovery of *al-istiʿāna bi-l-kuffār* was probably used and built upon by several Saudi Wahhabis. As will become clear, the fact that al-Maqdisi, just as we saw in Chapter 5, made his case by relying on scholars of the Wahhabi-Salafi tradition, who – as we will see – had used *al-walāʾ wa-l-barāʾ* mostly for quietist purposes, once again underlines his credentials as a quietist Jihadi-Salafi.

From *Jāhiliyya* to *Wahhābiyya*: The Development of *al-Walā' wa-l-Barā'*

It is not clear whether *walā'* and *barā'* were initially connected or that they only came to be seen as two different sides of the same coin later on. In any case, the two terms that make up *al-walā' wa-l-barā'* have been translated and explained in different ways. One of the most common meanings of *walā'* (or linguistically similar terms such as *wilāya*) is 'devotion' or 'loyalty' and it is also used to denote patronage in Islam.[1] *Barā'* (or related words like *tabarru'*) is mostly linked with 'being free or innocent', 'denunciation' or 'disavowal' and the term also seems to have been used as such in the *jāhiliyya*, where tribes were often allies of one another and sometimes had to expel one of their members if he or she endangered an alliance. One of the terms used for such an act of expulsion was *tabarru'*, with the tribe declaring itself *bāri'* (innocent or free) of that particular person.[2]

Both terms also seem to have entered the Islamic lexicon as meaning 'loyalty' and 'disavowal', with the latter apparently being used by Muslims to – amongst other things – disassociate themselves from treaties with non-Muslims dating from pre-Islamic times.[3] Throughout the Qur'ān, both terms are used to indicate similar meanings. For example, Q. 3: 28 states: 'Let not the believers take the unbelievers for friends (*awliyā'*, i.e. people to whom one shows *walā'*), rather than the believers.' With regard to *barā'*, Q. 60: 4 reads: 'We are quit of you (*bura'ā'u minkum*).'[4] Both terms have been adopted as 'loyalty' and 'disavowal' by different Islamic trends. These include the Khawārij and the group's more moderate Ibāḍī off-shoot[5], who used *al-walā' wa-l-barā'* to show loyalty towards their own group and disavow outsiders[6], as well as Shiites, for whom loyalty

[1] An extensive treatment of *walā'* in early and classical Islam as patronage can be found in Monique Bernards and John Nawas (eds.), *Patronate and Patronage in Early and Classical Islam*, Leiden & Boston: Brill, 2005.

[2] Wagemakers, 'Transformation', 82–91.

[3] Uri Rubin, 'Barā'a: A Study of some Quranic Passages', *Jerusalem Studies in Arabic and Islam*, vol. 5, 1984, 13–32.

[4] Wagemakers, 'Defining', 348–71.

[5] Etan Kohlberg, 'Barā'a in Shī'ī Doctrine', *Jerusalem Studies in Arabic and Islam*, vol. 7, 1986, 142–4; Werner Schwartz, *Die Anfänge der Ibaditen in Nordafrika*, Wiesbaden: Otto Harrassowitz, 1983, 56–66.

[6] Josef van Ess, *Theologie und Gesellschaft im 2. und 3. Jahrhundert Hidschra*, 6 vols., Berlin & New York: Walter de Gruyter, 1992, vol. II, 224–31.

to their imams and disavowal of the first three caliphs and other 'enemies' became an article of faith[7].

Al-Walāʾ wa-l-Barāʾ *in Salafi Writings*

What the descriptions of *al-walāʾ wa-l-barāʾ* mentioned here have in common is that they indicate a desire to enhance solidarity among and maintain homogeneity of the 'in-group' on the one hand and create a clear distinction with the 'out-group' on the other. Considering the strictness and purity that Salafis strive for in their doctrine, it is not surprising that its scholars seem to have adopted *al-walāʾ wa-l-barāʾ* precisely for this reason. Since the concept is a tool to separate right from wrong and insiders from outsiders, it is perfectly suited to steer Salafis away from *bidaʿ*, *kufr* and *shirk* and the people that espouse such sinful ideas, while at the same time increasing the loyalty to their own *ʿaqīda*. This can be seen in many Salafi writings, and is clearly expressed in the work of one contemporary Wahhabi author, who states:

> Loyalty (*al-muwālāt*) and enmity (*al-muʿādāt*) have a strong connection with the creed of the Muslim (*ʿaqīdat al-Muslim*) and [have] the effect of not being ignorant (*la yankaru*) of his behaviour because the Islamic peoples represent one community (*umma*), the community of Islam. There is a commitment for every individual Muslim who is a brick (*labina min labināt*) of this community that he does not separate from or leave the community of the Muslims (*jamāʿat al-Muslimīn*) and that his loyalty and devotion (*walāʾuhu wa-ikhlāṣuhu*) are to God the Exalted, his messenger and his Muslim community (*li-jamāʿatihi l-Muslima*).[8]

A Salafi scholar who was instrumental in incorporating the idea behind *al-walāʾ wa-l-barāʾ* to Sunni Islam was the Hanbali scholar Ibn Taymiyya. He has devoted an entire book to calling on Muslims to refrain from religious innovations, particularly in the celebration of religious festivals, and adhere to 'the straight path' (*al-ṣirāṭ al-mustaqīm*) or risk sullying

7 Ignaz Goldziher, *Introduction to Islamic Theology and Law* (transl. Andras and Ruth Hamori), Princeton, NJ: Princeton University Press, 1981, 182; Kohlberg, 'Barāʾa', 144–51. Mouline states that *al-walāʾ wa-l-barāʾ* was adopted by "certain Islamic currents" from Judaism "at one point or another in their historical trajectory". Although this is an interesting theory, Mouline only cites some secondary sources indicating that a concept similar to *al-walāʾ wa-l-barāʾ* may have existed in Judaism. He offers no evidence, however, of how or why this concept was adopted by Islamic groups. See Mouline, *Les clercs*, 107.

8 Al-Jawhara bt. ʿAbdallāh, *Waqfa ḥawla l-Walāʾ wa-l-Barāʾ fī l-Islām*, Riyadh: Dār al-Ṣamīʿī li-l-Nashr wa-l-Tawzīʿ, 1991, 11.

the purity of their religion. This does not just involve inner beliefs but also what one says and does, what one eats and the clothes one wears, among other things.[9] Ibn Taymiyya believes that participating in the outward customs of non-Muslims may lead to a situation where one can no longer distinguish between Muslims and 'infidels'.[10] 'If resembling [Jews and Christians] in worldly matters (*umūr dunyawiyya*) leads to affection (*al-maḥabba*) and loyalty (*al-muwālāt*) to them', Ibn Taymiyya asks, 'what about resembling [them] in religious matters (*umūr dīniyya*)?' He subsequently answers his own question by stating that this will result in 'a type of loyalty that is greater and stronger. Affection and loyalty to them is incompatible with faith'.[11] He spends much of the rest of his book warning Muslims about the Jewish and Christian feasts that may lead to such loyalty.

Ibn Taymiyya's book is not only important because it incorporated the concept of *al-walā' wa-l-barā'* into Sunni – or, more specifically, Salafi – Islam but also because it indicated the direction that the concept would take: just as in Ibn Taymiyya's book about this subject, subsequent Salafi scholars dealing with the concept focussed heavily on ritual purity, manners and keeping one's distance from non-Muslims. Ibn Taymiyya's student Ibn Qayyim al-Jawziyya (1292–1350), for example, dealt extensively with the proper ways to greet non-Muslims[12], while the North-African scholar al-Wansharisi (d. 1508 or 1509) wrote that it is forbidden for Muslims to settle among non-Muslims, and stated that it is compulsory for them to emigrate to the *dār al-Islām*.[13] It was also as such (i.e., in a quietist, purity-focussed way) that the concept was dealt with by major nineteenth- and twentieth-century Wahhabi scholars, including contemporary ones such as Ibn Baz, Ibn al-ʿUthaymin and al-Fawzan. Issues such as greeting non-Muslims, emigrating to the *dār al-Islām* and not resembling Muslims in clothing, names or celebrating holidays are

[9] Aḥmad b. ʿAbd al-Ḥalīm b. ʿAbd al-Salām b. Taymiyya, *Iqtiḍā' al-Ṣirāṭ al-Mustaqīm li-Mukhālafat Aṣḥāb al-Jaḥīm*, ed. Nāṣir b. ʿAbd al-Karīm al-ʿAql, 2 vols., n.p.: Dār al-Ishbīliyā li-l-Nashr wa-l-Tawzīʿ, 1998, vol. I, 92.

[10] *Ibid.*, 94.

[11] *Ibid.*, 550.

[12] Shams al-Dīn Abī ʿAbdallāh Muḥammad b. Abī Bakr b. Qayyim al-Jawziyya, *Aḥkām Ahl al-Dhimma*, 3 vols., Dammam/Beirut: Ramādī li-l-Nashr/Dār Ibn Ḥazm, 1997, vol. I, 409–26.

[13] Aḥmad b. Yaḥyā al-Wansharīsī, *Asnā l-Matājir fī Bayān Aḥkām Man Ghalaba ʿalā Waṭanihi l-Naṣārā wa-lam Yuhājir wa-mā Yatarattabu ʿalayhi min al-ʿUqūbāt wa-l-Zawājir*, www.tawhed.ws/c?i=233, 1491.

all dealt with extensively in Wahhabi writings on *al-walāʾ wa-l-barāʾ*, as well as in other Salafi ones.[14]

Al-Istiʿāna bi-l-Kuffār *in Nineteenth-Century Arabia*

In spite of Salafis' overwhelming application of *al-walāʾ wa-l-barāʾ* to ritual matters, it is not clear whether this is also the way the concept is described in the Qurʾān and the Sunna. There are indications that *walāʾ* may have been used to indicate loyalty to one's own group during a time of conflict, – for example, in Q. 60: 1[15] – meaning that the term may have been more political in nature than many works on the concept suggest. Indeed, the idea that it is forbidden to ask non-Muslims for help during a time of conflict is already present in a *ḥadīth* about the Battle of Uhud (625).[16] It may therefore be the case that *walāʾ* (perhaps in combination with *barāʾ*) in early Islam primarily referred to choosing sides between two political entities during times of war, and that it was later conflated with the inadmissibility of resembling non-Muslims (*tashabbuh al-kuffār* or *al-mushābaha li-l-kuffār*), which is how most Salafi authors seem to interpret *al-walāʾ wa-l-barāʾ*. Although this is a point that needs further research, it is clear that *al-istiʿāna bi-l-kuffār* as an aspect of *al-walāʾ wa-l-barāʾ* was important among certain Wahhabi authors in the nineteenth century.[17]

The inadmissibility of *al-istiʿāna bi-l-kuffār* in Wahhabi discourse can arguably be traced back to the eighteenth-century writings of Ibn ʿAbd al-Wahhab himself.[18] It became particularly pronounced, however, in certain nineteenth-century Wahhabi writings. The first important document[19] with regard to this issue was written by Sulayman b. ʿAbdallah Al al-Shaykh (d. 1818), a grandson of Ibn ʿAbd al-Wahhab,

14 Wagemakers, 'Transformation', 88–90; *id.*, 'Framing', 5–7; *id.*, 'The Enduring Legacy of the Second Saudi State: Quietist and Radical Wahhabi Contestations of *al-Walāʾ wa-l-Barāʾ*', *International Journal of Middle East Studies*, vol. 44, 2012, 93–110.

15 Wagemakers, 'Defining', 353–66.

16 Cited in Khadduri, *Islamic*, 90.

17 For more on 'resembling' non-Muslims, see M.J. Kister, '"Do not Assimilate Yourselves…" *Lā Tashabbahū…*', *Jerusalem Studies in Arabic and Islam*, vol. 12, 1989, 321–71.

18 Muḥammad b. ʿAbd al-Wahhāb, *Mufīd al-Mustafīd fī Kufr Tārik al-Tawḥīd*, www.tawhed.ws/a?a=3yk8awwg, n.d.

19 ʿAbd al-Raḥmān b. Muḥammad b. Qāsim al-ʿĀṣimī al-Najdī al-Ḥanbalī (henceforth Ibn Qāsim) (ed.), *Al-Durar al-Saniyya fī l-Ajwiba al-Najdiyya*, 16 vols., n.p., 2004 [7th ed.], vol. VIII, 121–43, which reproduces the text. The document is also available separately. See Sulaymān b. ʿAbdallāh Āl al-Shaykh, *Al-Dalāʾil fī Ḥukm Muwālāt Ahl al-Ishrāk*, www.tawhed.ws/r?i=bm4wz4za, n.d.

who wrote at a time of Al Saʿud-Ottoman conflict, when some Arabians were siding with the Ottoman-supported Egyptian army, and asked them to invade the Arabian Peninsula.[20] As a response to this betrayal of the Arabian rulers, Sulayman stated in his treatise that it was not allowed to show loyalty to the 'polytheists' – a group in which he included the Ottoman invaders of the Arabian Peninsula – and that if one did, one was like them (i.e., polytheist), quoting verses like Q. 5: 51 ('O believers, take not Jews and Christians as friends; they are friends of each other. Whoso of you makes them his friends is one of them') to support his case.[21] This became even clearer when, in the late nineteenth century, the Arabian ruler ʿAbdallah asked the 'polytheistic' Ottomans for help in defending himself against his brother Saʿud, who claimed the throne for himself. Although this call for Ottoman help was supported by the majority of Wahhabi scholars at the time as a necessity, several prominent *ʿulamāʾ* were vehemently against it. These included Hamd b. ʿAtiq (d. 1883 or 1884) and the leader of the Wahhabi scholars, ʿAbd al-Latif b. ʿAbd al-Rahman Al al-Shaykh (d. 1876). The former dedicated an entire treatise to this question of loyalty to 'infidels' and especially the Ottomans (*al-Atrāk*). Just like Sulayman, he condemns loyalty to non-Muslims but stresses the necessity of *barāʾ* more. He states that one can only be a true Muslim if one disavows *shirk* and proclaims one's own *tawḥīd*, which is done by openly stating one's enmity of *mushrikīn*.[22]

Apart from the clear political dimension that these Wahhabi scholars add to *al-walāʾ wa-l-barāʾ*, there is also another important element in their writings on this subject. Whereas Ibn Taymiyya and others wrote about *al-walāʾ wa-l-barāʾ* as a tool to remain pure in one's faith, Wahhabi authors – particularly Ibn ʿAtiq – turned the correct *walāʾ* and *barāʾ* into conditions for being a Muslim. By equating *walāʾ* to polytheists with 'being like them', and by claiming that *barāʾ* is a necessary prerequisite of one's faith, they essentially increased the value of these terms. In other words, whereas Ibn Taymiyya and others used *al-walāʾ wa-l-barāʾ* in order to establish a clear separation between the Muslim 'in-group' and the non-Muslim 'out-group', Wahhabi authors did the same but drew the line elsewhere by including some people usually seen as part of the 'in-group' in the 'out-group'. This attempt to change *al-walāʾ wa-l-barāʾ* from

20 Commins, *Wahhabi*, 33–6.
21 Ibn Qāsim, *Al-Durar*, vol. VIII, 127.
22 Ḥamd b. ʿAlī b. ʿAtīq, *Sabīl al-Najāt wa-l-Fikāk min Muwālāt al-Murtaddīn wa-l-Atrāk*, www.tawhed.ws/r?i=mndyzdnz, n.d., 38–9. For more on this issue, see Wagemakers, 'Enduring', 94-7.

a tool to separate Muslims from non-Muslims into an instrument that does the same but also distinguishes 'real' Muslims from their 'apostate' fellow-believers is an important one, to which we will return in Chapter 7. Although this dimension is perhaps implicitly present in Ibn Taymiyya's work as well, the much more explicit ties in Wahhabi writings between *al-walāʾ wa-l-barāʾ* on the one hand and the opposites of *tawḥīd* and *shirk* on the other are clear.[23] Knowing this, it is not surprising that al-Maqdisi, who wanted sources that combined *takfīr* of the state with a Salafi reasoning, was immediately attracted to these writings. In fact, the eye-opening moment mentioned in Chapter 1, in which al-Maqdisi found writings in the Prophet's Mosque in Medina that gave him Salafi answers to his political questions, was based precisely on the Wahhabi writings mentioned earlier.

Reframing *al-Istiʿāna bi-l-Kuffār*

Al-Maqdisi's use of *al-walāʾ wa-l-barāʾ* in general does not represent a clear break with its history. Three different dimensions of the concept can be discerned in his writings. The first dimension is the quietist, purist dimension that is found in most Salafi writings on the subject, expressed in fatwas on whether or not to emigrate to Muslim countries, accept the nationality of an 'infidel' state and inherit from non-Muslims.[24] A second dimension of *al-walāʾ wa-l-barāʾ* found in al-Maqdisi's writings, dealt with extensively in the next chapter, is a legislative interpretation of the concept, using it as an instrument against 'un-Islamic' laws. Finally, al-Maqdisi also re-appropriates the Wahhabi-Salafi version of *al-istiʿāna bi-l-kuffār* by framing it as applicable to modern-day rulers, which this section focuses on.

Al-Maqdisi's Reintroduction of al-Istiʿāna bi-l-Kuffār

Although the legislative interpretation of *al-walāʾ wa-l-barāʾ* is dominant in al-Maqdisi's writings, he makes very clear where he stands on *al-istiʿāna bi-l-kuffār*, mostly in his book *Al-Kawashif al-Jaliyya*. With regard to Saudi Arabia, al-Maqdisi explains that it is forbidden for Muslim states to help 'infidel' countries or call on them for aid, and asks:

[23] This use of *al-walāʾ wa-l-barāʾ* as a sort of litmus test for being a Muslim is perhaps most clearly and explicitly argued by Sulaymān b. ʿAbdallāh Āl al-Shaykh in his *Awthaq ʿUrā l-Īmān*, www.tawhed.ws/r?i=egtcjv74, n.d.

[24] Al-Maqdisī, *Majmūʿ*, 90–1, 122, 124, respectively.

'What is the rule (*ḥukm*) of those who help and aid (*naṣara wa-ayyada*) the kings and presidents of the infidels and defend them, be it the European Christians, America or the infidel Arab rulers??'[25] He essentially answers his own question in a later section of the book by quoting Q. 5: 51 ('whoso of you makes [Jews and Christians] his friends is one of them'), just as Sulayman b. ʿAbdallah did, effectively accusing states guilty of *walā'* to non-Muslim countries of being 'infidels' themselves.[26] He also cites *Al-Durar al-Saniyya*, a monumental 16-volume Saudi collection of major Wahhabi writings, as stating that 'defending the infidels and helping them with money, with one's body (*al-badan*) or with advice (*al-ra'y*) is clear unbelief (*kufr ṣarīḥ*) that expels one from Islam (*al-milla al-Islāmiyya*)'. He therefore frames Saudi Arabia as being an 'infidel liar (*kādhiba kāfira*)... because of its loyalty (*muwālātuhā*) to Eastern and Western enemies of Islam (*aʿdā' al-dīn min sharqiyyīn wa-gharbiyyīn*)'.[27]

After giving an overview of how this loyalty takes place in practice, particularly in the form of military co-operation with America and huge sums of money paid to that country[28], al-Maqdisi summarises by stating that this loyalty is expressed in 'the consolidation (*tawthīq*) of ties of brotherhood, friendliness, affection and friendship with them'. Perhaps most worrying for al-Maqdisi is that these ties lead to 'loyalty to them through aid and help' in 'security, military and defence agreements and accords (*ittifāqiyyāt wa-muʿāhadāt amniyya wa-ʿaskariyya wa-difāʿiyya*)'[29], particularly when turned against other Muslims. Quoting Ibn ʿAbd al-Wahhab, who stated that 'supporting the polytheists and helping them against the Muslims' is a nullifier (*nāqiḍ*) of Islam[30], he contrasts Saudi Arabia's loyalty to 'the enemies of Islam' with the kingdom's crackdown on Juhayman al-ʿUtaybi and his followers and the 'true upholders of *tawḥīd* (*al-muwaḥḥidīn al-ḥaqīqiyyīn*)'.[31]

Al-Maqdisi's case against showing loyalty to non-Muslim states, particularly if they fight other Muslims, was not new. What was new, however, was that he employed the Wahhabi-Salafi tradition and an in-depth

25 Al-Maqdisī, *Al-Kawāshif*, 21.
26 *Ibid.*, 79.
27 *Ibid.*, 129–30.
28 *Ibid.*, 84–105. See Chapter 4 for a more detailed description of al-Maqdisī's criticism of Saudi-U.S. ties.
29 *Ibid.*, 141.
30 *Ibid.*, 129.
31 *Ibid.*, 179–83. The quote is on 180.

treatment of *al-walā' wa-l-barā'* to prove his point against modern-day Muslim rulers. Moreover, al-Maqdisi clearly tried to link Saudi Arabia's supposed loyalty to the United States and other 'infidel' countries with the kingdom's own past by not only referring to the nineteenth-century Wahhabi writings arguing against *al-isti'āna bi-l-kuffār* but also by explicitly mentioning the Arabian calls for help from the Ottoman-supported Egyptian army at that time.[32] By reintroducing this dimension, al-Maqdisi essentially frames Saudi-U.S. ties as wrong from a Wahhabi and a Saudi historical point of view, and uses this against Saudi Arabia itself, making it a powerful tool for others to adopt.

The Wahhabi Rediscovery of al-Isti'āna bi-l-Kuffār

In Chapter 4, we saw that al-Maqdisi's book *Al-Kawashif al-Jaliyya* was spread among like-minded scholars and activists in Saudi Arabia in the 1990s. Bearing this in mind, it is quite likely that al-Maqdisi's reintroduction of *al-isti'āna bi-l-kuffār* was known to many Saudis who shared his views, particularly in light of the unmistakable similarities between the nineteenth-century calls for Ottoman help and the request for American military assistance during the Gulf War in 1990. Whereas this section deals with al-Maqdisi's probable influence on Saudi-Wahhabi scholars and activists with regard to *al-isti'āna bi-l-kuffār*, it should not be assumed that they suddenly abandoned the more quietist interpretations of *al-walā' wa-l-barā'*. Wahhabi authors supportive of radical ideas continued to write about the question of greeting 'infidels'[33], for example. From the late 1990s, however, a clear trend of Wahhabi discourse could also be discerned that showed that *al-isti'āna bi-l-kuffār* had been rediscovered as a topical and politically relevant form of inadmissible *walā'*, which is likely to have been directly or indirectly inspired by the work of al-Maqdisi.

The authors who were probably influenced by al-Maqdisi do not actually cite his work. Although that seems surprising, it is in fact not. While *Al-Kawashif al-Jaliyya* is highly detailed in its case against Saudi Arabia, and while al-Maqdisi's writings are full of arguments about the legislative version of *al-walā' wa-l-barā'*, he does not deal with *al-isti'āna bi-l-kuffār* very comprehensively, nor in a very organised or structured way. He does

32 *Ibid.*, 148.

33 See, for example, Sulaymān b. Nāṣir al-'Ulwān, *Ḥukm Bada'a Ahl al-Kitāb bi-l-Salām*, www.tawhed.ws/r?i=6i37pcff, 2000.

not actually explain the concept of *al-istiʿāna bi-l-kuffār*, for example, nor does he clearly distinguish *asking* 'infidels' for help from *giving* them help (*iʿānat al-kuffār*) against other Muslims. Moreover, he uses different forms of *walāʾ* (*muwālāt* and *tawallī*) interchangeably without explaining the difference between them, and even mixes up his references to the nineteenth-century conflicts between the Al Saʿud and the Ottomans.[34] While al-Maqdisi later wrote about this issue in a slightly more organised way[35], *al-istiʿāna bi-l-kuffār* in his writings was never really more than a secondary issue at best. Furthermore, the idea al-Maqdisi was reintroducing was controversial, and scholars who adopted his interpretation of *al-istiʿāna bi-l-kuffār* – particularly the more established scholars – may therefore have felt the need to ground their writings in sources of undisputed reputation rather than in a single book written by a relatively unknown radical ideologue. It is therefore important to stress that it was not so much his writing about this subject as such but rather his rediscovery of its relevance for this day and age that explains his likely influence.

Since no Wahhabi-inspired book on *al-istiʿāna bi-l-kuffār* applied to modern states was available before or directly after[36] the appearance of *Al-Kawashif al-Jaliyya*, and considering that book's 'fame' among radical Saudis in the 1990s, we may carefully assume that attempts to revive the concept after 1990 were at least indirectly inspired by al-Maqdisi's work. The first exponent of this trend of reviving the concept seems to have been the radical Saudi scholar Humud b. ʿUqalaʾ al-Shuʿaybi (1927–2002). It is not entirely clear what accounts for the fact that his book was only written in 1999 – several years after *Al-Kawashif al-Jaliyya* became known in Saudi Arabia – but it appears that the book and its successors build on al-Maqdisi's work, despite the time gap between them. This becomes clear in the way these works all clarify, expand on, deepen, organise and/or develop what al-Maqdisi wrote previously. In the case of al-Shuʿaybi, who has spoken highly of al-Maqdisi[37], is said to have been

[34] Al-Maqdisī, *Al-Kawāshif*, 148.

[35] Al-Maqdisī, *Barāʾat*, 9–12; *id.*, *Al-Risāla al-Thalāthīniyya*, 107–8.

[36] An exception seems to be al-Ḥawālī, *Kashf*. This book deals with *al-istiʿāna bi-l-kuffār* only from a political perspective, however, and should therefore probably not be considered as a source of inspiration to religious scholars using the concept.

[37] See, for example, Abū Humām Bakr b. ʿAbd al-ʿAzīz al-Atharī, *Al-Qawl al-Narjisī bi-ʿAdālat Shaykhinā l-Maqdisī*, www.ansar-jihad.net (accessed 24 April 2009), 2009, 34–7; *id.*, *Al-Sayf al-Muhannad fī Munāṣirat Shaykhinā Abī Muḥammad*, www.muslm.net/vb/showthread.php?t=286633, 2008.

influenced by the latter[38] and has himself received praise from him too[39], this is expressed in his effort to present the inadmissibility of *al-istiʿāna bi-l-kuffār* in a much clearer and more organised way than al-Maqdisi did. The book describes the alleged influence of Jews and Christians from the time of the Prophet Muhammad, through (amongst other things) the Crusades, colonialism and Marxism, to present-day America and how 'the Jews and Christians are behind every corruption and deviance that took place in the Islamic creed'.[40] Because of this, al-Shuʿaybī states, Muslims should follow Muhammad's order to drive Jews, Christians and polytheists out of the Arabian Peninsula. Moreover, 'we refuse to ask them for help or rely on them because asking them for help requires loyalty to them (*tastalzimu muwālātahum*), relying on them (*al-rukūn ilayhim*) and taking them as friends (*awliyāʾ wa-aṣdiqāʾ*)'.[41]

After giving a thorough linguistic explanation of *al-walāʾ wa-l-barāʾ*, al-Shuʿaybi goes on to state that the concept is 'a basis of Islam (*qāʿid min qawāʿid al-dīn*) and a foundation of the faith and the creed (*aṣl min uṣūl al-īmān wa-l-ʿaqīda*) without which the faith of a person is not correct'.[42] He subsequently writes at length about different scenarios in which Muslims can call upon non-Muslims for help (against other 'infidels', against fellow believers, etc.). He dismisses them all as wrong since they lead to loyalty (expressed as affection and friendship) to 'the enemies of Islam', which is forbidden by the Qurʾān (esp. Q. 5: 51 and 60: 1).[43] What is remarkable about this book is that al-Shuʿaybi, despite being a (radical) government-employed scholar in Saudi Arabia, explicitly discusses *al-istiʿāna bi-l-kuffār* with regard to states and not just in general, as others do.[44] He even points out that asking an 'infidel' state for help is even more dangerous than doing so with a single non-Muslim since a state is more powerful.[45]

Al-Shuʿaybi's treatment of *al-istiʿāna bi-l-kuffār* was a much more detailed and organised effort to analyse the concept than al-Maqdisi's

38 Interviews with al-Daynī, Jeddah, 13 November 2008; al-Dhāyidī, Riyadh, 8 November 2008; al-ʿUtaybī, London, 1 August 2008.

39 Abū Muḥammad al-Maqdisī, *Risāla ilā l-Shaykh al-Shuʿaybī*, www.tawhed.ws/r?i=6zipf6cz, 2001.

40 Ḥumūd b. ʿUqalāʾ al-Shuʿaybī, *Al-Qawl al-Mukhtār fī Ḥukm al-Istiʿāna bi-l-Kuffār*, www.tawhed.ws/r?i=ta476k4m, 1999, 11–4. The quote is on 12.

41 *Ibid.*, 14.

42 *Ibid.*, 39.

43 *Ibid.*, 58–96.

44 Sulaymān b. Nāṣir al-ʿUlwān, *Ḥukm ʿIyādat Ahl al-Kitāb*, www.tawhed.ws/r?i=5s4kcqhs, 2000.

45 Al-Shuʿaybī, *Al-Qawl*, 64.

Al-Kawashif al-Jaliyya was, but seemingly built on that book and drew similar conclusions. Moreover, it also represented a renewed look at Wahhabi and Islamic tradition and came up with a host of sources that were reinterpreted in light of the circumstances. Although the author does not mention Saudi Arabia by name – possibly out of fear of the authorities – it does seem that he has that state in mind, particularly when discussing the inadmissibility of allowing Jews and Christians onto the Arabian Peninsula.

The work of al-Shuʿaybi was continued directly after '9/11' by two important radical Saudi scholars. The first of these, Yusuf al-ʿUyayri (d. 2003), was the first leader of al-Qaʿida on the Arabian Peninsula (QAP) and is said to have been influenced by al-Maqdisi[46], which seems likely considering the latter's strong impact on QAP, as we saw in Chapter 5. Al-ʿUyayri appears to continue the trend started by al-Maqdisi by focussing on the question of aiding the *kuffār* or asking them for help against fellow believers[47], by making even more use of Wahhabi sources (including the nineteenth-century ones rediscovered by al-Maqdisi)[48] and, unlike al-Shuʿaybi, by explicitly distinguishing two different forms of *walā'* (*tawallī* and *muwālāt*). As mentioned, al-Maqdisi also referred to these terms in the context of *al-istiʿāna bi-l-kuffār*[49] but made no effort to clarify the difference between them. Al-ʿUyayri, on the other hand, does deal with this subject, pointing out that '*al-tawallī* is more specific than *al-muwālāt*. Every *tawallī* is unbelief. There are forms of *muwālāt* that are unbelief and forms that are less than that.'[50]

While al-ʿUyayri gives a short explanation of the difference between *tawallī* and *muwālāt*, this becomes even clearer in a book by the second radical Saudi scholar who wrote about *al-istiʿāna bi-l-kuffār* right after '9/11': Nasir b. Hamd al-Fahd (b. 1968).[51] He defines *tawallī* as a form of unbelief that involves 'affection for the religion of the infidels and for their victory', which includes 'helping them against the Muslims'. *Muwālāt*, on the other hand, is forbidden but does not reach the level of

46 Interviews with al-Dhāyidī, Riyadh, 8 November 2008; al-Shāfī, Riyadh, 11 November 2008.
47 Al-ʿUyayrī, *Ḥaqīqat*, 74–86.
48 See, for instance, *ibid.*, 70–1, 74–5.
49 Al-Maqdisī, *Al-Kawāshif*, 122, 129–30, 141–2.
50 Al-ʿUyayrī, *Ḥaqīqat*, 67.
51 For more on al-Fahd, see Hegghammer, *Jihad*, 87–9.

kufr, and includes things such as greeting non-Muslims first.[52] This way, al-Fahd, who is said to have been influenced by al-Maqdisi[53] and is even referred to by some as 'a Saudi copy' of him[54], establishes a hierarchy in the different dimensions of *al-walāʾ* and simultaneously accuses those of aiding 'infidels' against other Muslims of being guilty of the gravest form of faulty *walāʾ*. Importantly, al-Fahd's book, which is probably the most extensive and detailed of its kind, clearly switches the subject from *al-istiʿāna bi-l-kuffār* to *iʿānat al-kuffār*. This, as Madawi al-Rasheed points out in her seminal book on the Saudi Islamic opposition, should be seen in the post-'9/11' context, when the U.S.-led 'war on terror' caused many countries (including Muslim ones) to help America in its hunt for al-Qaʿida.[55] Although, as we saw before, this dimension had already been mentioned by al-Maqdisi in *Al-Kawashif al-Jaliyya*, al-Fahd made it the focal point of his book and employed the early Wahhabi scholars' writings to support his case. In fact, he explicitly refers to the late nineteenth-century call for Ottoman help (probably to draw a parallel with modern-day Saudi Arabia)[56], as al-Maqdisi did, and he has even written a separate treatise describing the Ottoman Empire as an infidel state that was branded as such by contemporary Wahhabis.[57] The latter could possibly be seen as a historical study of no great importance but, considering al-Fahd's other work and his radical ideas, should probably be viewed as another implicit attempt to show his readers that Saudi Arabia's present-day ally America is really no different from the 'infidel' Ottoman Empire in the nineteenth century.

After the books mentioned earlier were published, the idea that aiding 'infidels' or asking them for help against fellow-Muslims was a form of *kufr* according to Wahhabi sources seems to have become common knowledge among radical Saudi scholars and activists, and was further developed by them. One fatwa by ʿAli b. Khudayr al-Khudayr (b. 1955), for example, dwells further on the exact difference between *muwālāt*

52 Nāṣir b. Ḥamd al-Fahd, *Al-Tibyān fī Kufr Man Aʿāna l-Amrīkān*, 2 vols., www.tawhed.ws/r?i=3b5bzov8, 2001, vol. I, 42–3.

53 Interview with al-ʿUtaybī, London, 1 August 2008. See also *Al-Waṭan*, 28 February 2003, cited in McCants (ed.), *Militant*, Research Compendium, 283.

54 Interviews with al-Daynī, Jeddah, 13 November 2008; al-Dhāyidī, Riyadh, 8 November 2008.

55 Al-Rasheed, *Contesting*, 139, 141, 146.

56 Al-Fahd, *Al-Tibyān*, vol. I, 69. See also al-Rasheed, *Contesting*, 146.

57 Nāṣir b. Ḥamd al-Fahd, *Al-Dawla al-ʿUthmāniyya wa-Mawqif Daʿwat al-Shaykh Muḥammad b. ʿAbd al-Wahhāb minhā*, www.tawhed.ws/r?i=zdntfe5u, n.d.

and *tawallī* in the context of *al-istiʿāna bi-l-kuffār*.[58] Al-Khudayr, a radical Saudi scholar on whom al-Maqdisi is said to have had an impact and who also praises the latter, also quotes exactly those nineteenth-century Wahhabi sources whose relevance for this issue al-Maqdisi rediscovered.[59] Similarly, when the Saudi scholar ʿAbd al-Muḥsin al-ʿUbaykan issued a fatwa in early 2003 in which he declared certain forms of *tawallī* forbidden but not *kufr* and exonerated Muslims who ask infidels for help in certain circumstances from being *kuffār*, he was quickly rebutted by another scholar, Abu Muhammad al-Najdi. The latter claimed:

> It is known from evidence from the Qur'ān, the Sunna and the consensus (*al-ijmāʿ*) that there is no foundation (*qiwām*) to the religion of Islam except through enmity of its enemies (*bi-muʿādāt aʿdā'ihi*) and disavowal of them (*al-barā'a minhum*). That is the path of the messengers of God, may peace be with them.[60]

The fact that a Saudi scholar saw the inadmissibility of *al-istiʿāna bi-l-kuffār* in times of war as only obvious while it seems to have been unheard of in modern Wahhabi discourse until 1989 perhaps shows that the concept had apparently gained wide acceptance among radical Saudi Wahhabi scholars. This was further confirmed when al-Qaʿida activists, some of them members of QAP (such as Abu Jandal al-Azdi), who had certainly been influenced by al-Maqdisi, started applying the prohibition of help from or to 'infidels' to their local conflicts in Saudi Arabia[61] and Iraq[62]. This showed that the concept had now become so familiar that it could be applied to new situations and conflicts.

Explaining al-Maqdisi's Frame Resonance

The revival of *al-istiʿāna bi-l-kuffār* that al-Maqdisi's *Al-Kawashif al-Jaliyya* seems to have caused should be seen in its proper perspective.

58 ʿAlī b. Khuḍayr al-Khuḍayr, *Al-Ḥadd al-Fāṣil bayna Muwālāt wa-Tawallī l-Kuffār* [sic], www.tawhed.ws/r?i=oioei4uv, n.d.

59 *Ibid.*, 2–3.

60 ʿAbdallāh b. Ibrāhīm al-Saʿwī [Abū Muḥammad al-Najdī], *Naqḍ Fatwā l-ʿUbaykān fī Ḥukm Muẓāharat al-Mushrikīn*, www.tawhed.ws/c?i=31, 2003, 1.

61 Al-Azdī, *Al-Āyāt*, 3; *id.*, *Al-Bāḥith*, 28–31; al-ʿUtaybī, *Risāla fī l-Ṭawāghīt*, 26. See also Ḥamd b. Rayyis al-Rayyis, *Hādhihi ʿAqīdatunā*, www.tawhed.ws/r?i=6hggcba2, 2003, 14–16.

62 Abū ʿUmar al-Sayf, *Ḥukm Muẓāharat al-Amrīkān ʿalā l-Muslimīn: Al-ʿIrāq wa-Ghazw al-Ṣalīb; Durūs wa-Ta'ammulāt*, www.tawhed.ws/r?i=22nwaxca, n.d.

The spreading of his book in the 1990s, the certain acquaintance with al-Maqdisi's work of almost all authors mentioned and the use – in the context of *al-istiʿāna bi-l-kuffār* – of Saudi-Wahhabi terms (*tawallī/muwālāt*), sources and events (the nineteenth-century calls for Ottoman help) suggests that he has influenced all of the scholars and activists previously cited. This is not necessarily the case, however. While it is true that writings on the subject seem to have built on al-Maqdisi's work and have clearly developed from his initial idea to its latest applications, it is not certain that all scholars and activists mentioned were actually directly inspired by *Al-Kawashif al-Jaliyya* in their rediscovery of *al-istiʿāna bi-l-kuffār*. The fact that none of these authors quotes *Al-Kawashif al-Jaliyya* underlines this.

It nevertheless seems likely that al-Maqdisi's book, by reintroducing the Saudi-Wahhabi-inspired concept of help from and to 'infidels' against fellow-Muslims, stimulated others to rediscover their own religious and historical tradition. Because al-Maqdisi's case was rather unorganised and – in the case of his reference to nineteenth-century Arabian-Ottoman conflicts – even factually wrong, it becomes understandable that other authors do not actually mention his work as a source of influence. It therefore seems that al-Maqdisi contribution to the development of *al-istiʿāna bi-l-kuffār* can be summed up by saying that he offered other scholars and activists the tools for reviving the concept, but not the proper way to use them. This was left to the other authors themselves, which leaves only one question: why were they influenced by al-Maqdisi?

Explaining al-Maqdisi's Influence

As we saw in Chapter 4, a successful frame should propose a good diagnosis of the problem, present a viable prognosis and call for action. It became clear that *Al-Kawashif al-Jaliyya* offers all three with regard to Saudi Arabia in general, and the subject of *al-istiʿāna bi-l-kuffār* dealt with in this chapter is no exception. It is very clear that al-Maqdisi condemns asking 'infidels' for help or aiding them against other Muslims, that he openly blames the Muslim rulers for this and, as became clear from Chapters 4 and 5, that he sees jihad as the solution to correct this. Considering the fact that his audience existed of radical scholars and activists whose writings show that their criticism of Saudi Arabia (and other countries) is just as severe as al-Maqdisi's (although QAP-members were much more vocal about this than the more established scholars), his frame probably easily resonated with their views.

The three core framing tasks distinguished by Snow and Benford were not the only aspects of a successful frame, however, as we saw in Chapter 5. Frame resonance also depends on the centrality of the frame in the public's perception, its range and interrelatedness with other important aspects of people's beliefs, the extent to which it conforms to people's experiences, whether it can be verified in reality and its congruence with national, religious and cultural narratives. Firstly, with regard to the centrality of *al-istiʿāna bi-l-kuffār* or, more generally, *al-walāʾ wa-l-barāʾ*, al-Maqdisi's framing of the situation clearly incorporates these aspects. Wahhabi writings from the nineteenth century onwards make it abundantly clear that these concepts are integral parts of Islam and touch its very basis. In the writings of some, *al-walāʾ wa-l-barāʾ* has even become a litmus test for determining whether or not someone is a Muslim. Since *istiʿāna bi-l-kuffār* is considered by several scholars to be a form of *tawallī* (i.e., a *kufr* form of *walāʾ*), the importance of the concept in Wahhabi writings is enormous, and al-Maqdisi taps right into this trend.

Secondly, the range of *al-walāʾ wa-l-barāʾ*, of which *al-istiʿāna bi-l-kuffār* is only one dimension, is very broad. As we saw at the beginning of this chapter, the concept is applied to interpersonal and social relations as well as to politics and is used both in times of peace and war. This broad applicability ensures that a frame such as '*al-istiʿāna bi-l-kuffār* is *kufr*' opens doors to other, strongly related concepts such as *tawḥīd* and *shirk*, the basis of Islam and its antithesis. This connection not only raises its importance but also makes sure that al-Maqdisi's indictments of Saudi Arabia (and other states by implication) are immediately linked to apostasy (*ridda*) and *kufr*, making them all the more devastating.

The experiental commensurability and empirical fidelity of al-Maqdisi's frame, thirdly and fourthly, are important too. Al-Maqdisi's frame questions the legitimacy of political ties, particularly with the United States. Consideration of America's bad reputation in the region – for instance, because of its support for Israel – would have made sure that this resonated with many people's experiences anyway. The Gulf War in 1990 and the wars in Afghanistan and Iraq, widely seen across the Arab world as illegitimate invasions or even attacks on Islam[63], only increased this view. Similarly, it is indeed true that the United States has been aided

[63] See, for example, the Pew Research Center for the People and the Press, *Views of a Changing World: How Global Publics View War in Iraq, Democracy, Islam and Governance, Globalization*, Pew Global Attitudes Project, http://pewglobal.org/reports/pdf/185.pdf, June 2003, 46.

in its 'war on terrorism' by Muslim countries such as Pakistan, but also Saudi Arabia, which remained America's ally after '9/11'.[64] Scholars and activists intent on proving that a Muslim country aided the 'infidels' therefore did not have to go out of their way to look for concrete examples but could simply point to the facts.

Fifthly, and finally, al-Maqdisi, just as we saw in Chapter 5, made extensive use of the Salafi (but especially Wahhabi) concept of *al-walāʾ wa-l-barāʾ* and did so on the basis of Wahhabi sources. Although the authors of the specific sources whose value he rediscovered were known for their strictness – particularly Ibn ʿAtiq – they were nevertheless part and parcel of the Wahhabi tradition, and their (other) work was used extensively by government-employed scholars too. This is important to emphasise since, as Madawi al-Rasheed points out, some radical Saudi scholars were not much inspired by Islamist thinkers such as Qutb since these were 'simply not their reference points'.[65] Using Wahhabi sources therefore seems a necessary condition for influencing them. Al-Maqdisi not only used Wahhabi sources, however, but also appealed to an episode in Saudi history, showing that the modern-day calls for 'infidel' help were not new but had been condemned before. *Ṣaḥwa* activist Muhammad al-Masʿari may therefore only have been exaggerating slightly when he claimed:

> The Wahhabi[s] in contemporary Saudi Arabia do not name the exact ancestors to which we should refer because it would undo their own arguments about authority and obedience. [...] Their writing undermines the position of the al-Saud [sic], so they have been conveniently dropped from the discourse.[66]

Unlike in Chapter 5, it was not possible to speak with the people involved in the process of reviving *al-istiʿāna bi-l-kuffār*, who are all either dead or imprisoned, in order to verify the theoretical explanation given earlier. Several knowledgeable journalists assured me that *al-walāʾ wa-l-barāʾ* was very important in accounting for al-Maqdisi's influence among these scholars and activists[67], however, and it does indeed seem likely that he was at least partly responsible for the start of a revival of *al-istiʿāna*

[64] Roger Hardy, 'Ambivalent Ally: Saudi Arabia and the "War on Terror"', in: Madawi al-Rasheed (ed.), *Kingdom without Borders: Saudi Arabia's Political, Religious and Media Frontiers*, London: Hurst & Co., 2008, 104–10.

[65] Al-Rasheed, *Contesting*, 139.

[66] Okruhlik, 'Making', 258.

[67] Interviews with al-Dhāyidī, Riyadh, 8 November 2008; al-ʿUtaybī, London, 1 August 2008.

bi-l-kuffār for the reasons given here. Because al-Maqdisi adhered so strictly to the tradition of *al-walāʾ wa-l-barāʾ* and Wahhabism, which was overwhelmingly used for quietist purposes, this chapter not only underlines his status as a quietist Jihadi-Salafi but also shows that this has been instrumental in explaining his likely influence in this respect. Al-Maqdisi's use of *al-walāʾ wa-l-barāʾ* was expressed much more, however, in the concept's legislative dimension, which we will deal with in the next chapter.

7

'Salafising' Jihad

Al-Maqdisi is likely to have had a modest but nevertheless important impact on Saudi Salafi-Wahhabi scholars and activists with regard to *al-isti'āna bi-l-kuffār*. This is not the only dimension of *al-walā' wa-l-barā'* in which al-Maqdisi has been influential, however, nor have only Saudis been influenced by him in this respect. This chapter deals with one of al-Maqdisi's main themes, namely *al-walā' wa-l-barā'* as a tool to frame the legislation of 'man-made laws' as *kufr* and the laws and their legislators as *ṭawāghīt* in order to legitimise *takfīr* of and jihad against the rulers. It also shows how and why non-Saudi authors have been influenced by his use of *al-isti'āna bi-l-kuffār*.

The chapter starts with an analysis of al-Maqdisi's views on *al-walā' wa-l-barā'* as a means to frame laws and the rulers that apply them as guilty of un-Islamic loyalty that should be fought by means of jihad. It then deals with the Jihadi-Salafi scholars who have probably been influenced by al-Maqdisi in this respect, as well as with the non-Saudi authors who seem to have adopted his modern-day application of *al-isti'āna bi-l-kuffār*. Finally, the chapter focuses on how al-Maqdisi's influence on both groups can be explained through framing. Throughout the chapter, we will see how al-Maqdisi takes an inherently subversive and thus very un-quietist idea (jihad against Muslim rulers) and incorporates it into his own Salafi discourse through the use of *al-walā' wa-l-barā'*. By reframing the excommunication of and the jihad against the Muslim world's rulers in a Salafi way – indeed by 'Salafising' them – al-Maqdisi again shows his close adherence to quietist ideas, underlining his own position as a quietist Jihadi-Salafi.

Jihad as *Barā'* against 'Infidel' *Walā'*

In Chapter 2, we saw that al-Maqdisi is vehemently against what he sees as un-Islamic rule and legislation, expressed in the adoption of 'man-made laws', particularly if it takes on a systematic form through the exchange of the *sharīʿa* for a secular or otherwise non-Islamic constitution. We also saw that al-Maqdisi, like many other Salafis, believes that the systematic application of *qawānīn waḍʿiyya* is a violation of *tawḥīd* in the legislative sphere and therefore a form of *kufr* on the basis of verses such as Q. 5: 44[1], and that he has adopted the ideas of both the mediaeval Salafi scholar Ibn Taymiyya and the modern-day Qutb to support his case. It has also become clear that al-Maqdisi – just like Qutb – uses Q. 9: 31[2] to support the idea that the rulers applying these 'man-made laws' are not just *kuffār* but also *ṭawāghīt*. Finally, Chapter 2 showed that al-Maqdisi believes that the *kufr* of these supposedly 'infidel' Muslim rulers is even worse than the *kufr aṣlī* of Jews and Christians and that a jihad against them is justified, for which he calls in his writings.

Although there is a logic to his reasoning, it only partly distinguishes itself from the works of Qutb or Faraj, who stated similar things. While al-Maqdisi goes into much greater detail explaining why a jihad against the ruling 'idols' and their 'infidel' laws should be fought, and adheres closely to the Salafi creed in doing so, there is more to his arguments than this. The extra element al-Maqdisi adds in his writings is *al-walā' wa-l-barā'*, thereby giving his arguments a much more Salafi character since the concept is strongly associated with that branch of Islam. Since I have not found this connection between jihad against present-day Muslim rulers for their application of 'man-made laws' on the one hand and *al-walā' wa-l-barā'* on the other in the writings of any other scholar, this can be considered a new ideological development started by al-Maqdisi. How he establishes a link between the two is dealt with in this section.

Connecting Walā' *with Worship*

As mentioned in the Introduction to this book, Salafis distinguish three different forms of *tawḥīd*. One of these, *tawḥīd al-ulūhiyya* or *tawḥīd al-ʿibāda* (respectively the unity of divinity and the unity of worship),

[1] Q. 5: 44: 'Whoso judges not according to what God has sent down – they are the unbelievers.'

[2] Q. 9: 31: 'They have taken their rabbis and their monks as lords apart from God, and the Messiah, Mary's son – and they were commanded to serve but One God; there is no god but He; glory be to Him, above that they associate.'

involves the idea that only God may be worshipped. Although this seems an obvious idea shared by all Muslims, Salafis use this form of *tawḥīd* to claim that practices such as the veneration of so-called saints is, in fact, a form of *shirk*. Muslims involved in this practice probably see themselves as monotheists too, however. The fact that Salafis disagree with this suggests that they have a broader definition of divinity and worship than others, which is indeed the case. This can also be seen in the way al-Maqdisi connects *al-walāʾ wa-l-barāʾ* with legislation.

Al-Maqdisi, as we saw in Chapter 1, was influenced by the ideas of Juhayman al-ʿUtaybi. The latter had used the concept of *al-walāʾ wa-l-barāʾ* before, which he summed up in the term '*millat Ibrāhīm*' (the religion of Abraham). Juhayman states that the *millat Ibrāhīm* is part of 'that which distinguishes the sincere (*al-ṣādiq*) from the pretender (*al-muddaʿī*)'.[3] The characteristics of separating an 'in-group' from an 'out-group' inherent in *al-walāʾ wa-l-barāʾ*, which we saw in Chapter 6, can clearly be discerned here and even more so in Juhayman's definition of the *millat Ibrāhīm*. He claims that it rests on two pillars (*aṣlayn*), namely 'loyalty (*ikhlāṣ*) to the worship of God alone' and 'the disavowal (*al-tabarruʾ*) of polytheism and its people (*al-shirk wa-ahlihi*) and showing enmity (*al-ʿadāwa*) to them'.[4] Unlike other Wahhabi authors, however, Juhayman believes – and his take-over of the Grand Mosque in 1979 showed – that 'disavowal' should not just be expressed in verbal enmity of *shirk* or emigrating to the *dār al-Islām*, but also by withdrawing from the supposedly deviant Saudi society, and 'fighting'.[5]

In his most important book describing *al-walāʾ wa-l-barāʾ*, al-Maqdisi adopts the concept of *millat Ibrāhīm* and defines it as

> loyalty (*ikhlāṣ*) to the worship of God alone in every meaning that the word worship encompasses (*bi-kull mā taḥwīhi kalimat al-ʿibāda min maʿānin*) and the disavowal (*al-barāʾa*) of polytheism and its people.[6]

This definition obviously closely resembles Juhayman's description of the *millat Ibrāhīm* but al-Maqdisi does not attribute it to him. The reason for this may be similar to why, as we saw in Chapter 6, Wahhabi authors apparently adopting al-Maqdisi's interpretation of *al-istiʿāna bi-l-kuffār* do not cite the latter either: like al-Maqdisi's case against

[3] Juhaymān b. Sayf al-ʿUtaybī, *Rafʿ al-Iltibās ʿan Millat Man Jaʿalahu llāh Imāman li-l-Nās*, www.tawhed.ws/r?i=odutomsw, n.d., 4.
[4] *Ibid.*, 5.
[5] *Ibid.*, 16.
[6] Al-Maqdisī, *Millat*, 13–14.

calling the 'infidels' for help, Juhayman's treatment of *al-walāʾ wa-l-barāʾ* is sketchy and unorganised, presenting a new idea but doing so in a superficial manner. Moreover, both al-Maqdisi's modern-day application of *al-istiʿāna bi-l-kuffār* and Juhayman's interpretation of *al-walāʾ wa-l-barāʾ* are controversial and therefore perhaps best grounded in undisputed Wahhabi sources rather than in the writings of relatively unknown radicals. As we saw in Chapter 6, it is probably for these reasons that certain Wahhabis writing about *al-istiʿāna bi-l-kuffār* do not cite al-Maqdisi's work, despite their likely familiarity with it, and it probably also explains why al-Maqdisi does not mention Juhayman in this respect but instead gives the impression of having taken his definition from Ibn ʿAbd al-Wahhab's work.[7]

One could argue that, since the concept of *millat Ibrāhīm* appears several times in the Qurʾān[8] and is indeed used by Wahhabi scholars, al-Maqdisi simply adopted it from these sources. In fact, while al-Maqdisi speaks highly of him in his early writings[9], he downplayed the impact Juhayman had had on his own work when I asked him about it.[10] The fact, however, that his definition of *millat Ibrāhīm* is almost literally the same as Juhayman's, as well as the fact that the name of the chapter in which al-Maqdisi wrote this is exactly the same as the name Juhayman used for his chapter, suggests that the Saudi rebel may have had a greater impact on al-Maqdisi than the latter is willing to admit.[11]

Whatever the case may be, the only significant difference between Juhayman's definition of *millat Ibrāhīm* and al-Maqdisi's is the further specification of the word 'worship' by the latter by adding the words 'in every meaning that the word worship encompasses'. Because al-Maqdisi uses Q. 9: 31 ('they have taken their rabbis and their monks as lords apart from God') to equate the following of non-Islamic laws with worship, he can apply the word 'worship' to 'infidel' legislation. Since he believes loyalty should involve the worship of God alone, following non-*sharʿī* laws is not only an act of *shirk* because it directs worship away from God but also a forbidden form of *walāʾ*, which is also reserved for God

[7] *Ibid.*, 14.
[8] See, for example, Q. 22: 78 and Q. 2: 130.
[9] See, for example, al-Maqdisī, *Millat*, 16; *id.*, *Al-Kawāshif*, 6.
[10] Interview with al-Maqdisī, al-Ruṣayfa, 17 January 2009.
[11] Al-ʿUtaybī, *Rafʿ*, 5; al-Maqdisī, *Millat*, 13. The title of both chapters is '*Fī Bayān Millat Ibrāhīm*'.

only. It is in this context that al-Maqdisi's criticism of 'man-made laws' in countries such as Kuwait, Saudi Arabia and Jordan should be seen.

Considering al-Maqdisi's connection between the 'worship' of other laws and *walāʾ*, it is not surprising that he refers to the total lack of application of the *sharīʿa* he observes in the Muslim world today as 'complete loyalty (*tawallin muṭlaqin*)' to non-Islamic laws, 'in other words, entering the religion of the idols (*dīn al-ṭawāghīt*), worshipping them and taking them as separate lords (*arbāban mutafarriqa*) with their obedience in legislation'.[12] Al-Maqdisi's clear opposition to loyalty to 'man-made laws' is not expressed in detailed descriptions of why adherence to *qawānīn waḍʿiyya* should be seen as *walāʾ*, however, but much more in what he considers the best alternative: *barāʾ*.

Connecting Barāʾ *with Jihad*

In his book *Millat Ibrahim*, al-Maqdisi states:

> Know that the most specific of characteristics of the religion of Abraham and the most important of its requirements in which we see the majority of callers to Islam (*duʿāt*) of our time being enormously negligent (*muqaṣṣirīn fīhā taqṣīran ʿaẓīman*) – in fact, most of them have left it and let it die – are:
>
> - declaring disavowal (*iẓhār al-barāʾa*) of the polytheists and their false objects of worship (*maʿbūdātihim al-bāṭila*);
> - announcing disbelief (*iʿlān al-kufr*) in them and their polytheist gods, methods, laws and regulations;
> - declaring enmity and hatred (*ibdāʾ al-ʿadāwa wa-l-baghḍāʾ*) for them and for their infidel statutes and matters (*li-awḍāʿihim wa-li-aḥwālihim al-kufriyya*) until they return to God, leave [their infidel statutes and matters] entirely, disavow [them] and disbelieve in [them].[13]

Al-Maqdisi then goes on to quote a verse from the Qurʾān (Q. 60: 4) that is not only of great importance in most writings on *al-walāʾ wa-l-barāʾ* but especially in his:

> You have had a good example in Abraham, and those with him, when they said to their people, 'We are quit of you (*innā buraʾāʾu minkum*) and that you serve, apart from God. We disbelieve in you (*kafarnā bikum*), and between us and you enmity (*al-ʿadāwa*) has shown itself, and hatred (*al-baghḍāʾ*) for ever, until you believe in God alone.'[14]

[12] Al-Maqdisī, *Imtāʿ*, 88.
[13] *Id.*, *Millat*, 18.
[14] *Ibid.*

This verse refers to how the example of Abraham's disavowing of idolaters and their gods is a model for Muslims to emulate and can be said to form the basis of al-Maqdisi's discourse on *al-walāʾ wa-l-barāʾ*. As such, it occurs very frequently in his writings.

The need to express disavowal is used by al-Maqdisi in various ways. In his writings, examples can be seen of attempts of his to disavow Shiites[15], Christian ideas on Jesus Christ[16] and certain forms of armed attacks with which he disagrees.[17] What becomes clear from al-Maqdisi's widespread use of the term *barāʾ* is that he considers it an absolute necessity. He once again turns to Abraham to show this by stating that some people think

> that this *millat Ibrāhīm* (i.e., loyalty to worship of God and disavowal of 'polytheism' and its followers) can be realised in this time of ours (*fī zamāninā hādhā*) by studying *tawḥīd* and [having] knowledge of its categories and its three types, [which is] merely theoretical knowledge, while remaining silent about the people of falsehood (*ahl al-bāṭil*) and not announcing and declaring disavowal from their falsehood.[18]

Al-Maqdisi rejects this view, stating that *barāʾ* is of paramount importance in Islam since it is strongly connected with *tawḥīd*[19], which, in turn, is obviously closely linked to the first part of the confession of faith (*shahāda*): 'There is no god but God'. Al-Maqdisi therefore sees *barāʾ* as the necessary expression of this part of the *shahāda*[20] and – just as we saw before in the writings of some Wahhabi scholars – even goes so far as to state that one cannot be a true Muslim without expressing disavowal of the *ṭawāghīt*: 'Know that your Islam and your *tawḥīd* will not be perfected and the meaning of 'there is no god but God' will not be realised and that you will not find your way to Paradise until you disbelieve in and disavow every idol.'[21]

Interpreted as such, al-Maqdisi's foremost application of *barāʾ* is to 'man-made laws' and their legislators in the Muslim world. He states, for

[15] Al-Maqdisī, *Hādhihi*, 13.
[16] *Id.*, *Al-Tuḥfa al-Maqdisiyya fī Mukhtaṣar Tārīkh al-Naṣrāniyya: Bidāyatuhā wa-Muntahāhā*, www.tawhed.ws/t, 1997, 21.
[17] Al-Batīrī, 'Abū', 5.
[18] Al-Maqdisī, *Millat*, 15.
[19] *Id.*, *Barāʾat*, 11; *id.*, *Imtāʿ*, 114; *id.*, *Kashf al-Niqāb*, 16, 19, 106, 110; *id.*, *Al-Kawāshif*, 58, 113.
[20] *Id.*, *Kashf al-Niqāb*, 102, 142; *id.*, *Al-Kawāshif*, 113, 143; *id.*, *Millat*, 21–2, 46.
[21] *Id.*, *Kashf al-Niqāb*, 19.

example, that the true *tawḥīd* rests upon 'the disbelief of the idols, all idols, and the disavowal of their people'. This not only refers to 'idols of stone and wood' but also to 'the idols of ruling according to something other than what God has sent down (*ḥukm bi-ghayr mā anzala llāh*)... the idols of the law'.[22] More specifically, al-Maqdisi writes that one needs to disavow 'all *ṭawāghīt* that you serve besides God [...], be they idols (*aṣnām*) made of stone, the sun, the moon, a grave, a tree or regulations and laws made by man'.[23] Elsewhere, he writes:

> Before everything [else], you have to disbelieve in this idol – the [Kuwaiti] constitution and its laws – hate it, show enmity to it and disavow it and you should only be satisfied with and submit to the rule of God alone. That is in order to realise the meaning of 'there is no god but God' [...] You must also disavow everyone who defends it (*dāfaʿa ʿanhu*), protects its laws (*nāfaḥa ʿan qawānīnihi*) and persists on legislating it (*aṣarra ʿalā taḥkīmihi*) and enslaves mankind to it (*taʿbīd al-ʿibād lahu*).[24]

These last words make particularly clear that *barāʾ* should not just be aimed at the laws themselves but also at those who uphold them, including not just legislators but also the army and the secret service, as we also saw in Chapter 3 with regard to *takfīr*.[25]

Because al-Maqdisi frames 'man-made laws' and their legislators as *ṭawāghīt* and accuses the latter of *shirk* and *kufr* – terms that occur frequently in the Qurʾān, Islamic scholarly tradition in general and particularly in Wahhabi writings on *al-walāʾ wa-l-barāʾ* – he can employ this tradition to support his case, even though these sources and *ʿulamāʾ* do not mention or apply the concept in the way al-Maqdisi does. Although Wahhabi scholars did indeed condemn 'un-Islamic' laws and also wrote extensively about *al-walāʾ wa-l-barāʾ*, they did not connect the two. While al-Maqdisi believes that a legislative dimension was implied in or can at least be justifiably deduced from Wahhabi writings on *al-walāʾ wa-l-barāʾ* and the Qurʾānic verses that deal with this concept, it is clear that he introduces an entirely new connection that he nevertheless tries to ground in Islamic and especially Wahhabi tradition.[26] This creative use of the sources to establish the link between 'man-made' legislation and

[22] *Id.*, *Al-Kawāshif*, 58.
[23] *Id.*, *Millat*, 22.
[24] *Id.*, *Kashf al-Niqāb*, 102–3.
[25] *Id.*, *Al-Maṣābīḥ*, 7.
[26] This is particularly clear in his book *Millat Ibrāhīm*, which is full of references to Ibn Taymiyya, Ibn Qayyim al-Jawziyya, Ibn ʿAbd al-Wahhāb and later Wahhābī scholars. See also Wagemakers, 'Defining', 360–9.

al-walā' wa-l-barā' is perhaps best seen in the foreword to his book *Millat Ibrahim*, where he states:

To the idols in every time and place...
To the idols[:] rulers (*ḥukkāman*), emperors (*qayāṣira wa-akāsira*), faraos and kings...
To their fallacious keepers (*sadanatihim*) and their scholars (*ʿulamāʾihim*)...
To their friends (*awliyāʾihim*), their armies, their police, their secret services and their guards...

To all of them... we say:
'We are quit of you and that you serve, apart from God'
Quit of your rotten laws, methods, constitutions and principles (*qawānīnikum wa-manāhijikum wa-dasātīrikum wa-mabādiʾikum al-natina*)...
Quit of your rotten governments, courts, signs and symbols (*ḥukūmātikum wa-maḥākimikum wa-shiʿārātikum wa-aʿlāmikum al-ʿafina*)...
'We disbelieve in you, and between us and you enmity has shown itself, and hatred for ever, until you believe in God alone'[27]

This addition of al-Maqdisi's own ideological statements to the literal words of Q. 60: 4 makes it look as if this verse was actually also meant to be used against 'apostate' rulers and their 'infidel' laws, which – considering his very frequent use of such interpretations – indeed seems to be what he believes.

Al-Maqdisi's insistence on *barā'* as a condition for true *tawḥīd* notwithstanding, he explicitly does not apply *takfīr* to all people who refrain from disavowing 'infidel' laws or their legislators. He acknowledges that some Muslims may be under great pressure not to confront the rulers with their 'unbelief' by openly disavowing them and declaring them to be infidels, and he excuses such people.[28] He advises Muslims who may not be strong enough to disavow the *ṭawāghīt* openly to move away from them and to raise their children in such a way that they know the *kufr* nature of the rulers and their laws.[29] Al-Maqdisi writes that the Prophet Muhammad stated that people should act only according to their abilities[30], and sums up his views on this issue by stating that those who can, should disavow the *ṭawāghīt* with their hands, or otherwise with their tongues or at least in their hearts.[31] Since it is difficult – if not impossible – to tell what goes on in a person's heart, this implies

[27] Al-Maqdisī, *Millat*, 1.
[28] *Ibid.*, 57–61.
[29] *Ibid.*, 37–8; *id.*, *Kashf al-Niqāb*, 109–14; *id.*, *Al-Kawāshif*, 144–5.
[30] *Id.*, *Tabṣīr*, 142.
[31] *Id.*, *Kashf al-Niqāb*, 107.

a carefulness to judge people's faith if they do not openly disavow the rulers and their laws. As such, al-Maqdisi reconciles his strict views on the necessity of *barāʾ* for every Muslim with his unwillingness to apply *takfīr* to whole groups of Muslims.

Despite al-Maqdisi's accommodation of Muslims who do not denounce the 'apostate' rulers and their laws openly, he makes clear that *barāʾ* in one's heart is not his favoured form of disavowal. He cites Wahhabi scholar ʿAbd al-Rahman b. Hasan Al al-Shaykh, stating that God 'has compelled disavowal from (*al-barāʾa min*) polytheism and polytheists, disbelieving in them, showing enmity to them, hating them and waging jihad against them'[32], thereby connecting *barāʾ* with jihad. Al-Maqdisi further argues that *barāʾ* is embodied by 'enmity' and 'hatred', as mentioned in Q. 60: 4, and finds that nothing expresses this better than jihad. Consequently, he states that people should not only disavow *qawānīn waḍʿiyya* and their legislators but also that 'the highest degree (*aʿlā marātib*) of this disavowal is jihad'[33], which should be aimed at 'destroying these idolatrous regimes and fighting their servants until the entire religion is God's entirely.[34]

By thus connecting *walāʾ* towards 'un-Islamic' laws with worship, and its alternative – *barāʾ* – with jihad, while all the time stressing the necessity of disavowal for all Muslims, al-Maqdisi has turned *al-walāʾ wa-l-barāʾ* from a quietist tool to purify the religion into an instrument for revolution. Although, as we have seen, concepts such as *tawḥīd*, *kufr* and *shirk* have been used for similar purposes before, al-Maqdisi employs the very Salafi concept of *al-walāʾ wa-l-barāʾ* to reach the same conclusion in what may be described as a 'Salafised' call for jihad, seemingly with the Qurʾān (and Wahhabi tradition) firmly on his side.

Al-Maqdisi's reasoning, though rooted in past writings, clearly represents a break with what has been written about *al-walāʾ wa-l-barāʾ* before, however. As we saw in Chapter 6, the concept had always retained its character of separation between the Muslim 'in-group' and the non-Muslim 'out-group'. Some Wahhabi scholars added to this the dimension of using *al-walāʾ wa-l-barāʾ* to separate 'true' Muslims from alleged apostates and hypocrites (i.e., placing some people from the 'in-group' in the 'out-group'), but they nevertheless retained the basic Muslim/non-Muslim dichotomy that was central to the concept. This was also the

[32] *Id.*, *Millat*, 21.
[33] See, for example, *ibid.*, 47; *id.*, *Al-Kawāshif*, 143.
[34] *Id.*, *Al-Kawāshif*, 114. The last words are a reference to Q. 2: 193 and Q. 8: 39.

case with contemporary Wahhabi scholars (including al-Maqdisi) who stressed the inadmissibility of *al-istiʿāna bi-l-kuffār*. Although they often used this dimension of *al-walāʾ wa-l-barāʾ* to accuse Muslim rulers of *kufr*, the underlying idea was still that Muslims should be loyal to their co-religionists while disavowing others. Indeed, the reason Muslim rulers were accused of *kufr* was precisely because they had supposedly violated this understanding. Al-Maqdisi's legislative interpretation of *al-walāʾ wa-l-barāʾ* fundamentally changed this, however. His view that Muslims should be loyal to God and their fellow-believers but should disavow 'man-made laws' and their legislators shifted the separating element of *al-walāʾ wa-l-barāʾ* not just partially but entirely from the Muslim/non-Muslim divide to the 'true' Muslim/'apostate' Muslim one. This meant that al-Maqdisi – in his legislative version of *al-walāʾ wa-l-barāʾ* – completely abandoned the traditional 'in-group' versus 'out-group' dichotomy in favour of a new one. It is likely that this shift by al-Maqdisi is a highly important one, as we will see.

Adopting a 'Salafised' Jihad

In academic literature on Islamism, the concept of *al-walāʾ wa-l-barāʾ* is often immediately connected with the name of al-Maqdisi.[35] This is sometimes confirmed by radical Muslims themselves. The Lebanese radical Muslim scholar ʿUmar Bakri Muhammad, for example, calls *Millat Ibrahim* and *Al-Kawashif al-Jaliyya* 'excellent' books and even refers to al-Maqdisi as a *mujaddid* (renewer)[36] because he was the first to link the excommunication of Muslim leaders for their allegedly un-Islamic rule with *al-walāʾ wa-l-barāʾ*.[37] As we have seen in this chapter and the previous one, al-Maqdisi has indeed contributed to the development and revival of aspects of *al-walāʾ wa-l-barāʾ*. We also saw in the previous chapter, however, that there is less certainty about al-Maqdisi's influence with regard to *al-istiʿāna bi-l-kuffār* among Saudi-Wahhabi scholars and activists. The same can be said for his impact on others regarding his

[35] See, for example, Jarret M. Brachman, *Global Jihadism: Theory and Practice*, London & New York: Routledge, 2009, 22, 48; Kazimi, 'Virulent', 59; Devin R. Springer, James L. Regens and David N. Edger, *Islamic Radicalism and Global Jihad*, Washington, D.C.: Georgetown University Press, 2009, 50.

[36] Based on a *ḥadīth*, the term *mujaddid* is usually applied to scholars who have somehow greatly advanced or unified the Muslim community and are said to appear at the beginning of every Muslim century. See Ella Landau-Tasseron, 'The "Cyclical Reform": A Study of the *Mujaddid* Tradition', *Studia Islamica*, vol. 70, 1989, 79–117.

[37] Telephone interview with ʿUmar Bakrī Muḥammad, 29 August 2008.

connection between legislation and *al-walāʾ wa-l-barāʾ* and the extent to which non-Saudi ideologues have been influenced by his reintroduction of *al-istiʿāna bi-l-kuffār*, both of which are dealt with in this section.

Adopting the Legislative Form of al-Walāʾ wa-l-Barāʾ

Taking into account the fact that al-Maqdisi appears to be the first scholar who connected the inadmissibility of legislating 'man-made laws' with *al-walāʾ wa-l-barāʾ*, we may carefully assume that all authors who made this connection after al-Maqdisi made it in *Millat Ibrahim* (1984) likely adopted this link from him. Also, considering the fact that al-Maqdisi wrote extensively and in a highly detailed way about this issue, unlike what he did with *al-istiʿāna bi-l-kuffār*, we may assume that the scholars and activists who have indeed been influenced by him in this respect actually quote his writings, unless there is a particular reason for their not doing so. Finally, it is obvious that the people who have been influenced by al-Maqdisi on this issue are familiar with him and his work. Taking all of these premises into account, it is difficult to prove that al-Maqdisi's connection between 'un-Islamic' legislation and *al-walāʾ wa-l-barāʾ* has had much impact beyond a few mentions here and there.

When trying to analyse the scope of al-Maqdisi's influence with regard to his legislative version of *al-walāʾ wa-l-barāʾ*, it is striking that only very few authors seem to have adopted this idea in their writings. To be sure, the idea that the rulers of the Muslim world are 'infidels' and that they and their laws are even *ṭawāghīt* is a widely held belief among Jihadi-Salafis in general, and the concept of loyalty and disavowal is often used and applied, as we have seen. Al-Maqdisi's distinct connection between supposedly *kufr* legislation and *al-walāʾ wa-l-barāʾ* is much rarer, however, and cannot always be clearly discerned, particularly in the militant form (jihad as *barāʾ*) that al-Maqdisi proposes.

One of the scholars who seems to have adopted al-Maqdisi's connection is Abu Humam Bakr b. ʿAbd al-ʿAziz al-Athari, a Jordanian friend and student of al-Maqdisi's, who has written several treatises defending the latter from others' ideological attacks.[38] The connection between the two men is clear, but al-Athari does not cite any of al-Maqdisi's works in the treatise relevant here.[39] In this document, he deals with the supposed need of Muslims to 'avoid and denounce' elections and parliamentary

[38] Al-Atharī, *Al-Qawl*; *id.*, *Al-Sayf*.

[39] *Id.*, *Al-Hajr wa-l-Taqbīḥ li-Ahl al-Intikhābāt wa-l-Tarshīḥ*, www.tawhed.ws/r?i=0504094r, 2006.

candidates. The author urges his readers to 'avoid [parliamentary] representatives and not to go to them in their tents (*fī khiyāmihim*) and their parliaments (*majālisihim*)'. The connection between distancing oneself from something on the one hand (*barā'*) and legislation on the other is left implicit here but is further confirmed by the author when he continues by stating that 'the issue of *al-walā' wa-l-barā'* is amongst the most important issues of faith, and its most sublime'.[40] Still, al-Athari does not establish a clear connection between legislation and *walā'*, and this statement is a far cry from al-Maqdisi's clear call for jihad against such legislators as the most important form of *barā'*. It could be that al-Athari feared the Jordanian authorities, who would probably not have tolerated a document openly calling for jihad against its parliamentary representatives, causing the author to refrain from issuing such a call and to limit his message to simply avoiding them. Even so, al-Maqdisi's influence with regard to the legislative version of *al-walā' wa-l-barā'* in this particular text is less than clear.

Only slightly more clarity is given in the writings of Syrian jihad strategist Abu Musʿab al-Suri. In his writings, al-Suri praises al-Maqdisi as an important scholar of jihad[41] and names his books among the writings that have influenced him, stating that his works are 'among the beneficial jihadi intellectual libraries (*al-maktabāt al-fikriyya al-jihādiyya al-nāfiʿa*)'.[42] This is confirmed by Lia, the foremost expert on al-Suri and his writings, who states that al-Suri considered him an important ideologue[43], and probably even wrote al-Maqdisi a letter asking him to advise his former pupil Abu Musʿab al-Zarqawi to be more pragmatic in dealing with the Taliban when he was in Afghanistan.[44] Al-Maqdisi himself also mentions al-Suri as one of the people he met during his own stay in that region while working as a religious instructor in some of the training camps in Khost, teaching the trainees about issues such as *al-walā' wa-l-barā'*.[45]

It is not clear whether al-Suri was one of the recipients of al-Maqdisi's teachings in the Afghanistan/Pakistan region, but it seems he may have picked up some of it. Al-Suri deals with the subject of *al-walā' wa-l-barā'* in a very general way, but modern-day politics can easily be read into

40 *Ibid.*, 5.
41 Al-Sūrī, *Daʿwat*, vol. II, 1052.
42 *Ibid.*, 1130.
43 Lia, *Architect*, 88.
44 *Ibid.*, 269–70.
45 Abū Muḥammad al-Maqdisī, e-mail message to the author, 15 January 2010.

it, particularly since his entire book is about contemporary jihad. In this context he refers to the need to 'adhere to the *millat Ibrāhīm* by complete disavowal (*al-barā'a al-kāmila*) from the unbelievers (*al-kāfirīn*), hating them and showing them enmity', followed by Q. 60: 4.[46] As mentioned, the term *millat Ibrāhīm* goes back at least as far as the Qur'ān itself, and Q. 60: 4 had also been used in explaining *al-walā' wa-l-barā'* long before al-Maqdisi employed it extensively. The latter does seem to have been the first to explain the *millat Ibrāhīm* primarily and almost entirely through this verse, as al-Suri also does here. While this is by no means conclusive evidence of al-Maqdisi's influence on al-Suri, it is interesting to see one of his 'markers' in the writings of another scholar.

Al-Suri also writes that 'appealing (*al-taḥākum*) to ['un-Islamic'] laws and regulations (*qawānīnihim wa-sharā'i'ihim*) is the biggest form of loyalty to them (*akbar ashkāl wilāyatihim*)'. Although the author goes on to cite Ibn Taymiyya, giving the impression that he bases this thought on that scholar's work, the fatwa he quotes – while mentioning 'loyalty (*muwālāt*) to the unbelievers' – does not actually refer explicitly to legislation but to 'appealing (*al-taḥākum*) to [the unbelievers] apart from God's book (*min dūna kitāb Allāh*)'. Moreover, the Qur'ānic verse Ibn Taymiyya mentions (Q. 4: 51[47]) has no direct connection with legislation either.[48] Al-Suri's statement does resemble al-Maqdisi's reasoning a lot, however, and – just as al-Maqdisi does in his work – establishes a direct connection between *walā'* and 'un-Islamic' legislation. Considering al-Suri's praise for al-Maqdisi, their personal acquaintance and the possibility that the former actually took lessons in religious issues from the latter, it is not unlikely that al-Suri took this connection between legislation and *al-walā' wa-l-barā'* from al-Maqdisi. This would also explain why al-Suri does not actually cite al-Maqdisi's work: if he learned this information directly from him, there would be less need to refer to his writings.

As with al-Athari, the evidence of al-Maqdisi's influence on al-Suri is not very conclusive, and we must therefore be careful not to ascribe any impact to al-Maqdisi in this respect with too much certainty. This is different, however, with the writings of Abu Jandal al-Azdi, a leading ideologue of al-Qa'ida on the Arabian Peninsula (QAP) who, as we saw

46 Al-Sūrī, *Da'wat*, vol. I, 157; *ibid.*, vol. II, 967.

47 Q.: 4: 51 reads: 'Hast thou not regarded those who were given a share of the Book believing in demons and idols, and saying to the unbelievers, "These are more rightly guided on the way than the believers"?'

48 Al-Sūrī, *Da'wat*, vol. I, 158; *ibid.*, vol. II, 969.

previously, was heavily influenced by al-Maqdisi. In one of his books, he quotes al-Maqdisi at length, including portions where the latter states with regard to the rulers:

> [The] truth of their office (*waẓīfatihim*), their post (*manṣibihim*) and their work can be summarised in two clear reasons of unbelief. They are:
>
> - helping polytheism (*nuṣrat al-shirk*) – through loyalty (*tawallī*) to the idolatrous
> - infidel legislation and the law (*al-qānūn wa-l-tashrī' al-kufrī al-ṭāghūtī*); and
> - help to the people [of this 'infidel' legislation] and their loyalty (*tawallīhum*) and
> - help (*muẓāharatuhum*) against the upholders of *tawḥīd* (*al-muwaḥḥidīn*).[49]

These two points can be equated respectively with the legislative version of *al-walā' wa-l-barā'* and the concept of *i'ānat al-kuffār*, and thus constitute the two dimensions of loyalty and disavowal for whose development or revival al-Maqdisi has been important. The first point, especially since it is a quote from al-Maqdisi, is an unambiguous sign that al-Azdi adopted the link between legislation and *al-walā' wa-l-barā'*. In fact, right at this point, al-Azdi emphasises this by adding an explanatory note to al-Maqdisi's quote, stating – in the context of his ideological attack on the Saudi security forces: '[The unbelievers'] laws themselves stipulate that the nature of the office of [the security] apparatuses and their chief importance is the protection of the laws (*ḥifẓ al-qawānīn*), their application (*tanfīdhuhā*) and loyalty to its legislators (*muwālāt ahlihā*)'.[50]

Al-Maqdisi's impact with regard to his legislative dimension of *al-walā' wa-l-barā'* can thus be said to be limited. Not only do very few scholars show clearly discernible traces of treating the application and following of 'man-made laws' as a form of *walā'*, but even in the case of those who do we cannot always be certain about al-Maqdisi's influence on them. Moreover, even the scholars who seem to have been influenced by al-Maqdisi in this respect do not frame jihad as the highest form of *barā'*. The fact that even Abu Jandal al-Azdi, who cites al-Maqdisi's work so often, only briefly refers to the link between 'un-Islamic' legislation and *al-walā' wa-l-barā'* makes clear that this connection may have been an original ideological contribution to Salafi ideology, but not one that has had a lot of provable impact. This is slightly different, however, with the

49 Al-Azdī, *Al-Bāḥith*, 29.
50 *Ibid.*

reception of al-Maqdisi's reintroduction of *al-istiʿāna bi-l-kuffār* among non-Saudi scholars.

Non-Saudis Adopting al-Istiʿāna bi-l-Kuffār

As we saw in the previous chapter, al-Maqdisi's influence with regard to *al-istiʿāna bi-l-kuffār* seems to have been important but limited because he reintroduced an idea that appears to have resonated particularly well with Saudi-Wahhabi scholars but was not attributed to him for various reasons. We also saw that, following al-Maqdisi's *Al-Kawashif al-Jaliyya*, *al-istiʿāna bi-l-kuffār* was developed further into a broader, more detailed and more widely applicable concept, seemingly on the basis of elements already present in that book. It seems that non-Saudi scholars have also been part of this process, but joined it at a later time. More specifically, all contemporary non-Saudi writings I have found on this topic were either released after '9/11' or are undated but appear to have been written after September 2001 as well, when several Muslim countries started helping the American-led 'war on terrorism' against al-Qaʿida. Probably as a result of this development, the writings dealt with in this section focus not so much on *asking* 'infidels' for help but *giving* them help against Muslims. This suggests that the international political context has had a similar impact on their writings as in the Saudi authors' case – who had also been influenced by the Saudi call for American help against Saddam Husayn in 1990 – but, since their adoption of the concept happened several years later, caused them to highlight a different aspect of *al-walāʾ wa-l-barāʾ*. As such, it is not surprising that – like their Saudi counterparts – they do not quote al-Maqdisi's work because they joined the development of *al-istiʿāna bi-l-kuffār*'s inadmissibility at a later stage and are thus further removed from al-Maqdisi's *Al-Kawashif al-Jaliyya*, the book that reintroduced the concept.

Abu Basir al-Tartusi (b. 1959), a Syrian-British Jihadi-Salafi scholar who has spoken highly of al-Maqdisi[51] and has written him several critical yet brotherly letters[52], seems to be the first non-Saudi who adopted

[51] Abū Baṣīr al-Ṭarṭūsī, *Dhabban ʿan ʿIrḍ Akhīnā l-Shaykh Abī Muḥammad al-Maqdisī*, www.abubaseer.bizland.com/refutation.htm, 2002.

[52] *Id.*, *Kabwat Fāris: Munāqashat Qawl Abī Muḥammad al-Maqdisī fī Masʾalat al-ʿUdhr bi-l-Jahl wa-l-Radd ʿalayhi*, www.abubaseer.bizland.com/articles.htm, 2000; *id.*, *Taṣwībātunā li-Risālat Hādhihi ʿAqīdatinā li-Akhīnā Abī Muḥammad al-Maqdisī*, www.abubaseer.bizland.com/refutation.htm, 2000. See also Abū Muḥammad al-Maqdisī, *Al-Nukat al-Lawāmiʿ fī Malḥūẓāt al-Jāmiʿ*, www.tawhed.ws/t, 1998; *id.*, *Hādhihi*; *id.*, *Risāla li-l-Shaykh Abī Baṣīr*.

the idea of *iʿānat al-kuffār* in a book released in December 2001. In this work, he generally deals with the question of *hijra* in the context of *al-walāʾ wa-l-barāʾ*, possibly reflecting the fact that he lives in a (partially hostile, post-'9/11') non-Muslim country, from which emigration to the *dār al-Islām* may seem a solution to avoid *walāʾ* to one's 'infidel' environment. This becomes even clearer when he deals with a very specific question that became highly relevant for Muslims in the West after '9/11': is it allowed for them to be soldiers in a Western army and fight fellow-believers? Partially in response to a fatwa by the famous Egyptian Sunni scholar Yusuf al-Qaradawi, who had stated that Muslims were allowed to do so, Abu Basir categorically rejects the idea and states that such an act is 'help and loyalty (*al-muẓāhara wa-l-muwālāt*)' forbidden by the *sharīʿa*, considered a form of 'major unbelief (*kufr akbar*) that expels the person guilty of it from Islam'.[53] He claims that fighting Muslims as part of a Western army not only constitutes 'help to the polytheists (i.e., the Americans) against the Muslims' but would also favour 'loyalty to country and nationality (*al-walāʾ li-l-waṭan wa-li-l-jinsiyya*) over loyalty to the creed of Islam (*ʿaqīdat al-dīn*)'. Moreover, participation in Western armies' wars would make a Muslim soldier 'a partner of the Americans in every crime that they commit against the Muslims in Afghanistan'.[54]

Abu Basir's book clearly reflects the international political context in which he found himself when he wrote it. As such, he applies the concept of helping *kuffār* in fighting other Muslims to a new and highly topical situation and can therefore be said to be part of the broader contemporary development of *al-istiʿāna bi-l-kuffār* and its off-shoots that was started by al-Maqdisi. Like the Saudi scholars and activists dealt with in Chapter 6, he therefore seems to have been indirectly influenced by al-Maqdisi, although – in the absence of more concrete evidence – the latter's impact must be assumed with some care.

A similar attitude is called for when dealing with another non-Saudi ideologue who may have been influenced by al-Maqdisi: al-Qaʿida's Egyptian leader, Ayman al-Zawahiri (b. 1951). He praises al-Maqdisi for his knowledge, which he got to know when the two met in Peshawar, and specifically mentions his 'call to the unity of God (*al-daʿwa li-l-tawḥīd*) and the enmity of the falsehood (*muʿādāt al-bāṭil*) in this time

[53] Abū Baṣīr al-Ṭarṭūsī, *Al-Hijra. Masāʾil wa-Aḥkām*, www.tawhed.ws/r?i=6pydfou2, 2001, 51–2. The quote is on 51.
[54] *Ibid.*, 53.

of ours'.[55] The latter has written a treatise focussing entirely on *al-walāʾ wa-l-barāʾ*, which he starts by framing mankind as being engaged in a battle between 'the forces of unbelief, tyranny and arrogance (*quwā l-kufr wa-l-ṭughyān wa-l-istikbār*) and the Muslim community and its jihadi vanguard (*ṭalīʿatihā l-mujāhida*)'. He states that this conflict 'reached its summit with the two blessed raids on New York and Washington'.[56] Al-Zawahiri quickly moves on to a more general treatment of *al-istiʿāna bi-l-kuffār*, however, and states that 'the *sharīʿa* forbids us to help the *kuffār* against the Muslims' and claims that instead 'it has ordered us to wage jihad against the unbelievers'.[57] After having built his case that asking help from and giving help to 'infidels' is wrong, he rhetorically asks what some of the scholars whose writings he has just cited would have said 'if they witnessed the American planes and armies and their allies that take off from the Gulf states to bomb the Muslims in Iraq?! What would they say if they witnessed the American planes that take off from Pakistan to kill the Muslims in Afghanistan?!'[58]

Al-Zawahiri thus also applies the impermissibility of asking for help from or giving aid to non-Muslims in the context of the 'war on terrorism', and as such is very much part of the trend of developing *al-istiʿāna bi-l-kuffār*. Although he clearly knows and admires al-Maqdisi, there is no indication that al-Zawahiri has been directly influenced by him, and it therefore seems likely that al-Maqdisi has only had an indirect impact on al-Qaʿida's leader as part of the revival of *al-istiʿāna bi-l-kuffār* that he set in motion with *Al-Kawashif al-Jaliyya*.

A similar conclusion seems justified with regard to several other scholars, some of whom simply repeat arguments heard before.[59] Several of these are certainly familiar with al-Maqdisi and his writings, such as the aforementioned Abu Musʿab al-Suri[60], but also Abu l-Walid

55 Al-Atharī, *Al-Qawl*, 42-4; *id.*, *Al-Sayf*, 7.

56 Ayman al-Ẓawāhirī, *Al-Walāʾ wa-l-Barāʾ: ʿAqīda Manqūla wa-Wāqiʿ Mafqūd*, www.tawhed.ws/r?i=xotaoud8, 2002, 2. See also Stéphane Lacroix, 'Ayman al-Zawahiri, Veteran of Jihad', in: Gilles Kepel and Jean-Pierre Milelli (eds.), *Al Qaeda in its Own Words* (transl. Pascale Ghazaleh), Cambridge, MA, & London: Belknap/Harvard University Press, 2008 [2005], 206–34; Raymond Ibrahim (ed. & transl.), *The Al Qaeda Reader*, New York: Doubleday, 2007, 66–115.

57 Al-Ẓawāhirī, *Al-Walāʾ*, 23.

58 *Ibid.*, 18.

59 Muḥammad Aḥmad, *Akhṭar Ṣuwar al-Muwālāt al-Kufriyya fī hādha l-ʿAṣr*, www.tawhed.ws/r?i=28021003, n.d. See also Abū Humām Bakr b. ʿAbd al-ʿAzīz al-Atharī, *Al-Maṭar al-Wābil fī Ijābat al-Sāʾil*, www.tawhed.ws/c?i=31, 2008, 32.

60 Al-Sūrī, *Daʿwat*, vol. I, 173–6; *ibid.*, vol. II, 964–7, 969–73, 985–9.

al-Ansari[61], who claims he hosted al-Maqdisi and Abu Mus'ab al-Zarqawi in his home in Afghanistan.[62] Others scholars again apply the concept of *i'ānat al-kuffār* to new situations, however. Perhaps in response to certain Iraqis who wanted Western armies to come and overthrow Saddam Husayn, the Kuwaiti Jihadi-Salafi scholar Hamid al-'Ali (b. 1962) is asked 'what the ruling [is] with regard to those who call the American forces for help in their invasion of Muslim countries'.[63] Al-'Ali, who says he does not know al-Maqdisi personally but does praise him[64], states in response that 'if a Muslim helps a *kāfir* with invading Muslim countries he becomes an apostate unbeliever (*kāfiran murtaddan*)'.[65] Other scholars move this discussion further. As the 'war on terrorism' progressed, new regimes were installed and later elected in Afghanistan and Iraq. These governments co-operated with the Americans, prompting one Jihadi-Salafi scholar to warn against 'co-operation with the unbelievers occupying the Muslim countries, be they Americans or others'.[66] Another condemns the *'ulamā'* who 'allow the loyalty (*muwālāt*) of [Afghan President] Karzai and [(former) Iraqi Prime Ministers] 'Allawi, al-Ja'fari and al-Maliki to the Crusaders'.[67]

All of these references to *al-isti'āna bi-l-kuffār* and its offshoots by non-Saudi Jihadi-Salafi scholars seem to be very much part of the concept's revival that was likely started by al-Maqdisi's book *Al-Kawashif al-Jaliyya* and further developed by various Saudi scholars. There are three significant differences with the writings of the Wahhabi *'ulamā'* that we dealt with previously, however. Firstly, as mentioned, the non-Saudi scholars joined the revival of condemning helping or asking for help from *kuffār* at a later stage, and applied it to different situations. Secondly, some of the details added to the concept in Saudi writings, such as the difference between *muwālāt* and *tawallī*, were more or less lost in the works dealt with in this section, perhaps because their authors were less

61 Abū l-Walīd al-Anṣārī, *Ḥukm man A'āna Kāfiran fī Qitāl al-Muslimīn*, www.tawhed.ws/r?i=16011022, n.d.

62 *Id.*, 'Al-Zarqāwī', 26. Al-Maqdisī himself claims that he and his family even lived in al-Anṣārī's house when the latter and his family were away. Al-Maqdisī, e-mail message to the author, 15 January 2010.

63 Ḥāmid b. 'Abdallāh al-'Alī, *Ḥukm I'ānat al-Kuffār 'alā Ghazw al-Muslimīn wa-l-Du'ā' lahum bi-l-Naṣr*, www.tawhed.ws/r?i=mogga525, 2003, 1.

64 Al-Atharī, *Al-Qawl*, 62.

65 Al-'Alī, *Ḥukm*, 1–2. The quote is on 1.

66 'Abd al-Ḥakīm Ḥassān, *Al-Taḥdhīr min Mu'āwanat al-Kāfirīn*, www.tawhed.ws/r?i=op8hi6db, n.d., 5.

67 'Abd al-Majīd 'Abd al-Mājid, *Ṣafā' al-Manhaj Ahamm min Tabri'at al-Ashkhāṣ*, www.tawhed.ws/c?i=31, 2007, 2–3.

concerned with the concept's theoretical development than with its practical application. Finally, as might be expected, although the non-Saudi authors did make use of Wahhabi sources, and particularly more generally Salafi sources, they made somewhat less use of the specific Wahhabi writings on which al-Maqdisi based himself.[68] In fact, the nineteenth-century conflicts between the Ottomans and the Al Saʿud that caused several of these works to be written are hardly mentioned in the non-Saudi writings dealt with here. This suggests that the contemporary application of *al-istiʿāna bi-l-kuffār* has left the strictly Saudi-Wahhabi realm and has more or less entered 'mainstream' Jihadi-Salafi discourse. While this entails that the links between these non-Saudi writings and the original work by al-Maqdisi have become more tenuous, it should be borne in mind that it was *Al-Kawashif al-Jaliyya* that probably started the revival of this concept. This, in turn, means that although these non-Saudi scholars may not even have consulted that book on this issue, they are nevertheless likely to be ideological heirs to a trend that al-Maqdisi began.

The Acceptance of al-Maqdisi's 'Salafised' Jihad

If we take another look at how al-Maqdisi frames the new or reintroduced dimensions of *al-walāʾ wa-l-barāʾ* and the 'Salafised' jihad emanating from them in his writings, we can see that the three core framing tasks dealt with in previous chapters (diagnosis, prognosis and a call for action) are all there. As we saw in Chapter 6, this was the case with regard to his reintroduction of *al-istiʿāna bi-l-kuffār*, and the same applies to his legislative dimension of *al-walāʾ wa-l-barāʾ*. Al-Maqdisi clearly frames this problem as lying in 'man-made laws' and their legislators. The solution as al-Maqdisi sees it is that Muslims should not show loyalty to them but instead wage jihad against them as the highest form of disavowal, which he calls for frequently. Differences between the frames of these two dimensions of *al-walāʾ wa-l-barāʾ* appear, however, when we look at the actual quality of al-Maqdisi's frames in relation to his audience.

The Quality of al-Maqdisi's Frames

Al-Maqdisi's framing of the legislative dimension of *al-walāʾ wa-l-barāʾ* – 'worship' of 'man-made laws' is *kufr walāʾ* and should be countered by

[68] This is particularly apparent in al-Ẓawāhirī, *Al-Walāʾ*, which does not quote a single Wahhābī scholar. This is odd, since – as we have seen – Wahhābī scholars have been instrumental in the development of *al-walāʾ wa-l-barāʾ*. One can only guess as to why al-Ẓawāhirī decided to do that.

barāʾ in the form of jihad – adheres to some of the conditions for a – theoretically – successful frame. As we saw earlier, al-Maqdisi adopts from certain Wahhabi scholars the idea that *al-walāʾ wa-l-barāʾ* is a litmus test of Muslims' true beliefs, thereby stressing its centrality to the lives of Muslims. Because of this, the concept also has a broad range and can be applied to various subjects, and is closely related to terms such as *tawḥīd*, *īmān*, *kufr*, *shirk* and *ṭawāghīt*. The problem with al-Maqdisi's 'legislative' framing of *al-walāʾ wa-l-barāʾ* may lie in the final three dimensions of what a good frame should be, and these likely explain partly why he has had such limited influence in this respect. Although al-Maqdisi could plausibly establish a link between 'worship' of laws and *walāʾ*, this may have come across as a bit too far-fetched for many scholars. While Q. 9: 31 seemingly provides a Qurʾānic basis for the equation of 'legislators' ('their rabbis and their monks') with objects of worship, such a verse is lacking with regard to al-Maqdisi's attempts to take this analogy even further by incorporating it into the concept of *al-walāʾ wa-l-barāʾ*. As mentioned, the concept had always been applied to separate an 'in-group' from an 'out-group', but al-Maqdisi applied it to laws and their legislators solely to weed out the 'apostates' from the 'in-group'. This clear break with the concept's core meaning may well have seemed unknown and strange to other scholars, who may have felt it was untrue to their religious narrative. Moreover, because this legislative dimension does not appeal to actual events and trends beyond the idea that Muslim rulers apply 'man-made laws' – which al-Maqdisi's audience believes anyway – the connection between *al-walāʾ wa-l-barāʾ* and 'un-Islamic' legislation probably does not resonate well with regard to experiental commensurability and empirical credibility. All in all, al-Maqdisi's framing of *al-walāʾ wa-l-barāʾ* as a concept relevant to legislation may simply have been too ideologically far-fetched for most scholars.

The situation is quite different, however, for the non-Saudi adoption of *al-istiʿāna bi-l-kuffār*. As we saw in Chapter 6, al-Maqdisi's frame in this respect – Saudi Arabia is loyal to the United States and other 'non-Muslim' countries and entities by helping them and asking them for help, which are forms of *kufr* – not only centres around the basis of Islam (*tawḥīd*) but it also has a broad range because of its wide applicability. Precisely because al-Maqdisi ties *al-istiʿāna bi-l-kuffār* to overarching terms such as *tawḥīd* it can be related to other relevant concepts such as *kufr* and *shirk*. Moreover, and unlike al-Maqdisi's legislative dimension of *al-walāʾ wa-l-barāʾ*, his and others' use of *al-istiʿāna bi-l-kuffār* is likely to resonate strongly with a Jihadi-Salafi audience because of its experiental commensurability and empirical fidelity. During the time when the works adopting *al-istiʿāna bi-l-kuffār* dealt with in this chapter were written, the 'war on terrorism' was a very concrete reality for many Muslims, and so was the fact that several Muslim countries helped or assisted the United States and its allies in their efforts. Although non-Saudi scholars applied the concept to other conflicts than the Saudi authors we looked at in the previous chapter did, this only shows that they developed it even further, which again underlines the concept's breadth and wide applicability. Thus, the only real difference between the quality of al-Maqdisi's frame with regard to *al-istiʿāna bi-l-kuffār* among Saudis and non-Saudis is its narrative fidelity. Whereas Saudi authors would probably be attracted to al-Maqdisi's extensive use of Saudi history and Saudi-Wahhabi sources, this was obviously much less the case for non-Saudi scholars, who did not grow up in this tradition, although most of them did use some Wahhabi sources.

Much of the preceding is speculative. Given the absence of personal contact with and relevant information about the people who were likely influenced by al-Maqdisi's ideas on this topic, speculating is the best we can do. Framing theory offers tools, however, with which we can speculate in a way that makes sense and at least gives us an idea of what is likely to have happened. The difference in the reception and adoption of al-Maqdisi's two different dimensions of *al-walāʾ wa-l-barāʾ* dealt with in this chapter is further underlined by another tool that framing theory offers us: frame alignment.

The Resonance of a 'Salafised' Jihad

Both of al-Maqdisi's versions of *al-walāʾ wa-l-barāʾ* dealt with in this chapter take the concept of jihad against the 'apostate' rulers and give it a more Salafi character than it had in the works of Qutb and Faraj. The process of trying to make the frame of such a 'Salafised' jihad resonate with a target audience has been labelled 'frame alignment'. Four different processes of frame alignment have been distinguished. The first of these is frame bridging, denoting 'the linkage of two or more ideologically congruent but structurally unconnected frames regarding a particular issue or problem'.[69] In other words, frame bridging is the process that takes place when the framer and his or her audience are basically in agreement about a certain issue but the latter have just not been mobilised for action (yet). As soon as this happens, a frame has been bridged.[70]

[69] Snow et al., 'Frame', 467.
[70] *Ibid.*, 467–9.

The second form of frame alignment, frame amplification, is slightly more difficult than frame bridging because it stresses one aspect of a particular frame that is likely to resonate with a certain audience, rather than emphasising the entire frame.[71] The third form, frame extension, is the label applied to attempts to extend an existing frame in order to incorporate 'interests or points of view that are incidental to its primary objectives but of considerable salience to potential adherents'.[72] Such efforts may be taken to make a less than fully resonant frame align more with an audience's.[73]

The final and most difficult form of frame alignment is frame transformation. This is the case when 'new values may have to be planted and nurtured, old meanings or understandings jettisoned, and erroneous beliefs or "misframings" reframed'.[74] Since this requires the (partial) transformation of the audience's frame, this process does not involve simply connecting two ideologically congruent frames, as with frame bridging, but actually altering (parts of) the prism through which the public looks at a situation or problem.[75]

If we apply these four different forms of frame alignment to al-Maqdisi's influence with regard to his two versions of *al-walā' wa-l-barā'* discussed in this chapter, we can see that the revival of *al-isti'āna bi-l-kuffār* is clearly a case of the relatively easy frame bridging. In his book *Al-Kawashif al-Jaliyya*, al-Maqdisi frames the rulers of Saudi Arabia (and, by extension, other Muslim countries) as infidels and condemns their ties with, particularly, America. Instead, he advocates cutting these ties and waging jihad against those rulers. The non-Saudi audience dealt with in this chapter may not have been ready to accept the idea that the Al Sa'ud were infidels in 1989, when al-Maqdisi drew this conclusion, but it certainly started believing that after '9/11'[76], condemns their ties

71 *Ibid.*, 469–72.
72 *Ibid.*, 472.
73 *Ibid.*, 472–3; Daniel B. Cornfield and Bill Fletcher, 'Institutional Constraints on Social Movement "Frame Extension": Shifts in the Legislative Agenda of the American Federation of Labor, 1881–1955', *Social Forces*, vol. 76, no. 4, 1998, 1308-11; Scott Davies, 'From Moral Duty to Cultural Rights: A Case Study of Political Framing in Education', *Sociology of Education*, vol. 72, 1999, 14; Wagemakers, 'Framing', 10–14.
74 Snow et al., 'Frame', 473.
75 *Ibid.*, 473–6; Mitch Berbrier, '"Half the Battle": Cultural Resonance, Framing Processes, and Ethnic Affectations in Contemporary White Separatist Rhetoric', *Social Problems*, vol. 45, no. 4, 1998, 436–44.
76 See, for example, www.tawhed.ws/c?i=141, where numerous works can be found – including ones by al-Ṭarṭūsī and al-Ẓawāhirī – that are very critical of Saudi Arabia.

with the United States and favours the same solution. In other words, al-Maqdisi's framing of the situation was congruent with theirs. The only difference was that al-Maqdisi used the concept of *al-isti'āna bi-l-kuffār* to reframe the situation in a more Salafi way. Since this was based on an existing concept and was rooted in sources that had existed for a long time but were rediscovered by al-Maqdisi, it was probably very easy for Jihadi-Salafis to adopt al-Maqdisi's 'Salafised' jihad because they did not have to alter their beliefs in any way. They just needed to adopt a Salafi-Wahhabi concept that was actually part of their own ideological tradition but that had simply lain dormant for some time. Since adopting *al-isti'āna bi-l-kuffār* tied the concept of jihad even more to their own Salafi beliefs, it is likely that this was actually a preferred choice for them.

The situation is different when looking at al-Maqdisi's legislative version of *al-walā' wa-l-barā'*. In this case, al-Maqdisi could not suffice with simply bridging his own frame but actually partly had to transform the frames of others. While his Jihadi-Salafi audience agreed that 'un-Islamic' laws are *kufr* and their legislators are apostates and concurred with his conclusion that – on the basis of Q. 9: 31 – they may even be seen as idols that can be worshipped, which may account for the influence al-Maqdisi probably did have, they had never framed that problem in terms of *al-walā' wa-l-barā'*. This concept had never been used exclusively to distinguish between 'true' Muslims and 'apostates' instead of the traditional divide between a Muslim 'in-group' and a non-Muslim 'out-group'. In other words, for successful resonance of al-Maqdisi's frame to take place, a thorough reframing of their existing ideas on *al-walā' wa-l-barā'* would have been required. This is difficult enough in itself but even more so as it was not even necessary to frame jihad in a more 'Salafised' way by using *al-walā' wa-l-barā'* since the Salafi tradition already offered the tools to do this. For example, al-Maqdisi's own reasoning of *takfīr* of Muslim rulers described in Chapter 2 closely resembles that of quietist Salafis without necessarily referring to *al-walā' wa-l-barā'*. Also, the idea that 'un-Islamic' laws could be seen as objects of worship had been propounded not just by Qutb but also by Salafi scholars long ago[77], ensuring

[77] Ibn 'Abd al-Wahhāb, for example, stated that a *ṭāghūt* is 'anything that is worshipped apart from God'. He distinguished five different main types of *ṭawāghīt*, including 'the one who rules according to something other than what God has sent down' and 'the one who is worshipped apart from God and is satisfied with [this] worship'. Even if one assumes that 'rules' should be interpreted here as what a judge – not a legislator – does, it is easy to read a legislative interpretation into these words. See Muḥammad b. 'Abd al-Wahhāb, *Risāla fī Ma'nā l-Ṭāghūt*, www.tawhed.ws/r?i=8p4ty5r7, n.d.

that Jihadi-Salafi scholars really had no particular need for *al-walā' wa-l-barā'* to 'Salafise' their jihad.

Since all the authors influenced by al-Maqdisi with regard to both versions of *al-walā' wa-l-barā'* treated in this chapter are either dead or in situations where one is virtually unable to interview them, it is difficult to ascertain whether the makeup of al-Maqdisi's frames and his frame alignment were actually the reasons for their being influenced by him. We may carefully assume, however, that these do indeed explain both the scope of and the limits to his impact. Given the ideas that al-Maqdisi introduced or reintroduced, the personal and ideological ties he has with many of the scholars who seem to have been influenced by him, the clear development of *al-isti'āna bi-l-kuffār* by non-Saudi scholars and, finally, the political context in which all of this has taken place, this seems an obvious conclusion. Influence or not, however, al-Maqdisi's attempts to 'Salafise' jihad by tying it to a mostly a-political concept such as *al-walā' wa-l-barā'* again betray his clear desire to adhere to a quietist Salafi trend, thereby showing once more his credentials as a quietist Jihadi-Salafi.

PART IV

AL-MAQDISI'S INFLUENCE ON THE JORDANIAN JIHADI-SALAFI COMMUNITY, 1992–2009

8

Guidance to the Seekers

The aspects of al-Maqdisi's influence we have seen so far have been almost entirely ideological, without his personal presence playing much of a role: he spent little time in Saudi Arabia, stayed briefly in Afghanistan/Pakistan and during his time in Kuwait and Iraq he was still too young to have been of much influence. This changed, however, when al-Maqdisi moved to Jordan in 1992. There, he found himself in a situation where he could start building a network of followers that was not just based on his writings but also on his personal contacts. This chapter and the next focus on how and why al-Maqdisi's presence in Jordan as well as his writings influenced the radical Islamist community there.

In what follows, we will first look at the political context in Jordan, starting with the role of Jordanian Islam as a social and political force in the country, before moving on to an analysis of the period during which al-Maqdisi arrived in the kingdom. We will then turn to how his moving to Jordan initially influenced the radical Islamist community and how he tried to channel its widespread discontent. Finally, we will look at how al-Maqdisi's influence from 1992, when he arrived in Jordan, until 1994, when he went to prison, can be explained using framing. As we will see, the impact of al-Maqdisi and his quietist Jihadi-Salafi message in Jordan at this stage owed much to his ability to provide guidance to seekers of knowledge in need of a spiritual leader.

The Jordanian Political Context

At the time of al-Maqdisi's arrival in Jordan, the country was not unfamiliar with variants of Islam that went beyond the strictly personal sphere and touched political or social issues. In fact, the country has a long history of being engaged with such trends, and its rulers even claim to enjoy a certain religious legitimacy of their own. Before moving on to al-Maqdisi's actual arrival in Jordan, it is therefore necessary to take a closer look at the religious trends and discourses that were present in the country before he came there.

Islam in Jordan

Jordan has always been an overwhelmingly Sunni Muslim country, and the strong relationship between Islam and the Jordanian state actually starts with the ruling royal family itself. The kings of Jordan are descendants of Husayn b. ʿAli (c. 1853–1931), the *amīr* of Mecca and as such the ruler over the Grand Mosque in that city. This position not only carried weight in itself but was further enhanced by Husayn's status as a *sharīf* (descendant of the Prophet Muhammad). Husayn's son ʿAbdallah (1882–1951), the first king of Jordan, could thus claim to be of noble as well as of prophetic descent. Although the title of *sharīf* does not imply religious scholarly authority nor make one entitled to a position of political power[1], the Jordanian Hashimites (i.e., descendants of the Prophet's Hashim clan) do enjoy respect and prestige on the basis of their lineage.[2] The Jordanian state, founded in 1921 by the British as part of their colonial plans for the Middle East, was therefore ruled by a succession of kings that had a certain religious prestige from the very beginning.

Despite this religious legitimacy, the identity of Jordan and its Hashimite royal family is complex, and this is partly related to pre-Jordanian history. Presenting himself as a champion of Arab and Islamic rights, Husayn b. ʿAli co-operated with the British during World War I by launching the Arab Revolt in 1916 against the Ottoman Empire. While the British wanted the ruling Ottomans to be defeated in order to further their colonial ambitions, Husayn was promised independent Arab rule. The Hashimites were unfortunate in their endeavours, however, as their revolt – framed as both Islamic and Arab in character – was not as broadly supported as they had hoped and they lost large areas placed under their control by the colonial powers, including Syria and Iraq,

[1] Gudrun Krämer, 'Good Counsel to the King: The Islamist Opposition in Saudi Arabia, Jordan, and Morocco', in: Joseph Kostiner (ed.), *Middle East Monarchies: The Challenge of Modernity*, Boulder, CO: Lynne Rienner Publishers, 2000, 269.

[2] Asher Susser, 'The Jordanian Monarchy: The Hashemite Success Story', in: Joseph Kostiner (ed.), *Middle East Monarchies: The Challenge of Modernity*, Boulder, CO: Lynne Rienner Publishers, 2000, 87.

as well as the region they had originally come from, the west-Arabian Hijaz.

The Islamic and pan-Arab credentials of the Hashimites, on which they tried to base much of their legitimacy, thus eventually only found expression within the borders of Transjordan, as Jordan was called at the time. Even within this country, however, their sovereignty and identity was challenged. The British, for example, although officially no longer in control after 1946, when Jordan gained its independence, retained much of their power in the country – particularly in military affairs – after that date, challenging Jordanian identity by their presence alone but also complicating the rulers' image as upholders of pan-Arab sovereignty.[3] This ambiguity was underlined during the 1950s and 1960s by the competing and revolutionary pan-Arabism of Egyptian President Jamal ʿAbd al-Nasir. The latter's message was a direct challenge to the more conservative rule of the Jordanian King Husayn (1935–99)[4], who had succeeded his assassinated grandfather ʿAbdallah in 1953 after a brief ruling period by Talal, Husayn's father. Moreover, the presence of hundreds of thousands of Palestinian refugees who had fled or were expelled during the 1948 and 1967 Arab-Israeli wars or had become part of the state through Jordan's seizure of the West Bank of the Jordan river in 1948 further complicated the situation. Their large numbers and their Jordanian citizenship presented a demographic challenge to Jordanian identity, which was (and still is) far from clear.[5] This was further complicated because King Husayn saw himself as their representative, causing conflicts with the Palestine Liberation Organisation (PLO), which made a similar claim.[6]

Amidst these challenges to its national identity, and even legitimacy, King Husayn, who ruled the country during most of Jordan's history, relied on several themes to justify his rule and policies, including pan-Arabism, tribalism and – most important for this study – Islam. As Judith Jolen has shown, the latter was expressed in public quotations from the

[3] Joseph Massad, *Colonial Effects: The Making of National Identity in Jordan*, New York: Columbia University Press, 2001, 100–221.

[4] Uriel Dann, *King Hussein and the Challenge of Arab Radicalism: Jordan, 1955–1967*, Oxford: Oxford University Press, 1989.

[5] Alexander Bligh, *The Political Legacy of King Hussein*, Brighton & Portland: Sussex Academic Press, 2002, 73–93; Laurie A. Brand, 'Palestinians and Jordanians: A Crisis of Identity', *Journal of Palestine Studies*, vol. 24, no. 4, 1995, 46–61; Massad, *Colonial*, 222–75; Shaul Mishal, *West Bank-East Bank: The Palestinians in Jordan, 1949–1967*, New Haven & London: Yale University Press, 1979, 74–91.

[6] Sami Al-Khazendar, *Jordan and the Palestine Question: The Role of Islamic and Left Forces in Foreign Policy-Making*, Reading, UK: Ithaca Press, 1997, 51–91, esp. 67–91.

Qur'ān to legitimise the king's position during the Gulf wars as well as the peace agreement with Israel in 1994; in references to Islamic history to emphasise a shared Palestinian-Jordanian Muslim heritage; and by underlining his Hashimite descent to show his dedication to Muslim and Arab causes, particularly regarding Jerusalem. When, in the late 1980s and early 1990s, King Husayn advocated political and economic reforms, he also added 'democracy' as a legitimising theme to his discourse, claiming that Jordan was a democratic state and that the reforms and political decisions – including the peace agreement with Israel – showed the country's democratic nature.[7]

Perhaps because the country lacked a clear identity of its own, had its legitimacy challenged from the very beginning and was forced to rely so much on Islam to counter these challenges, the first Jordanian King ʿAbdallah decided to give his blessing to the foundation of the Muslim Brotherhood in Jordan, the largest Islamic group in the country. The king, wary of political opposition, may have believed that by allowing the Brotherhood as a religious group, he could thwart their political potential right from the start. He also wanted to offset the increasingly popular revolutionary pan-Arab nationalism, and probably believed he could bolster his own religious credentials as a *sharīf* by supporting an Islamic movement.[8]

Founded in Amman by the Jordanian trader ʿAbd al-Latif Abu Qura in 1945, the Muslim Brotherhood in Jordan immediately enjoyed good ties with the king. Although the latter took a more conciliatory approach towards the issue of Palestine than the Brotherhood did, their relationship was generally good during the 1940s and early 1950s. The king allowed them to pursue their social agenda of preaching and teaching Islam and providing services to the public, while the Brotherhood, in turn, could be relied upon to support the king.[9] The relationship gradually soured, however, as the Brotherhood grew more politicised and critical about

[7] Judith Jolen, 'The Quest for Legitimacy: The Role of Islam in the State's Political Discourse in Egypt and Jordan (1979–1996)', unpublished PhD thesis, Catholic University, Nijmegen, 2003, 155–64, 166–70.

[8] Marion Boulby, *The Muslim Brotherhood and the Kings of Jordan, 1945–1993*, Atlanta, Georgia: Scholars Press, 1999, 46–7.

[9] Ali Abdul Kazem, 'The Muslim Brotherhood: The Historic Background and the Ideological Origins', in: Jillian Schwedler (ed.), *Islamic Movements in Jordan* (transl. George A. Musleh), Amman: Al-Urdunn al-Jadid Research Center & Sindbad Publishing House, 1997, 13–18; Ibrāhīm al-Gharāyba, *Jamāʿat al-Ikhwān al-Muslimīn fī l-Urdunn, 1946–1996*, Amman: Markaz al-Urdunn al-Jadīd li-l-Dirāsāt & Dār Sindbād li-l-Nashr, 1997, 45–57.

contested issues such as British influence and the Palestinian question, leading to increased tension between them.[10] The regime, for its part, employed the Brotherhood for its own purposes. Its relations with Syria, for example, fluctuated during the 1970s and early 1980s, and King Husayn used the Brotherhood to put pressure on Syrian President Hafiz al-Asad when bilateral relations were bad but also repressed them during a period of Jordanian-Syrian rapprochement.[11] Although no large-scale crack-down on the Muslim Brotherhood comparable to those in Egypt in the 1960s and in Syria in the early 1980s has taken place in Jordan, the movement continues to have difficult relations with the regime to this day.

While the Muslim Brotherhood is certainly the largest and most influential Islamic group in Jordan, it is not the only one. Others include the Hizb al-Tahrir al-Islami, a-political groups such as the Jamaʿat al-Tabligh, various Sufi brotherhoods, voluntary welfare associations[12] and, most importantly for this study, Salafis. The Jordanian Salafi movement dates back to the 1970s, when students of Islam – for lack of Jordanian educational facilities – travelled abroad to obtain knowledge and frequently ended up in Syria to study with the prominent Salafi scholar Muhammad Nasir al-Din al-Albani. The latter eventually travelled and even permanently moved to Jordan himself and became the focal point of the country's Salafi movement. The community of Salafis that gathered around al-Albani in the 1980s and the 1990s, which included scholars such as ʿAli b. Hasan al-Halabi and Salim al-Hilali, was overwhelmingly quietist in nature. They did not actively support the Jordanian regime but were vehemently against *takfīr* of the king and his government, strongly rejected any form of violence against the state and adopted a strictly a-political attitude. This not only put them at odds with more radical forms of Salafism, which we will deal with later, but also with the Muslim Brotherhood, whose political style they rejected.[13] As such, quietist Jordanian Salafis can be seen as the polar opposite of the Brotherhood.[14]

10 Abdul Kazem, 'Muslim', 19–22; Boulby, *Muslim*, 50–65.

11 Robert B. Satloff, *Troubles on the East Bank: Challenges to the Domestic Stability of Jordan*, New York: Praeger Publishers, 1986, 40–8, 53–8.

12 See Egbert Harmsen, *Islam, Civil Society and Social Work: Muslim Voluntary Welfare Associations in Jordan between Patronage and Empowerment*, Amsterdam: Amsterdam University Press, 2008.

13 Wiktorowicz, *Management*, 120–1, 123–6, 128; *id.*, 'The Salafi Movement in Jordan', 222–6; *id.*, 'The Salafi Movement: Violence and Fragmentation of Community', 229.

14 Quietist Salafis have started tacit co-operation with the Jordanian regime in the past few years, however. Interview with al-Ḥalabī, Amman, 19 January 2009.

Jordan, as the preceding shows, is a country whose rulers enjoy a certain religious legitimacy but also offers several Islamic societal and political avenues of participation. As we saw in the chapters on Saudi Arabia, however, a religiously sanctioned state and a plethora of opportunities for people to express themselves religiously is, under certain circumstances at least, not necessarily a guarantee against the emergence of radical Islamic groups. A process somewhat similar to what happened in Saudi Arabia also took place in Jordan, where the late 1980s and early 1990s proved to be a particularly turbulent and volatile period in the history of the country. Although the country had certainly known other eventful periods – one need only think of the Arab-Israeli wars – the late 1980s and early 1990s were different because certain specific circumstances were conducive to a radicalisation that played right into the hands of ideologues such as al-Maqdisi.

The Turbulent Late 1980s and Early 1990s

The 1980s were an eventful time for the entire Middle East: the Islamic Revolution in Iran had just taken place and a wholly new regime now ruled that country; the Palestinian intifada against Israeli occupation started in 1987; and the Iran-Iraq war was fought throughout this decade. This troublesome period was preceded by years that had brought unprecedented oil-wealth to some countries, which had led to increased financial help to Jordan from Gulf states as well as a rise in employment possibilities there. The remittances from the Jordanians who had started working in the Gulf added further clout to the Jordanian economy. Both the financial help and the remittances declined sharply, however, when oil prices dropped in the 1980s, leading to grave economic problems in Jordan. In the late 1980s, the government therefore eventually decided to call on the International Monetary Fund (IMF) for loans, and they agreed on a structural-adjustment agreement. The economic reforms this implied caused taxes to be raised and subsidies to be cut, leading to a steep rise in prices, which hit the tribal south of the country – traditionally a pillar of support for the regime – particularly hard. A series of protests followed that were not just directed at the economic hardship but also called for greater democratisation.[15]

[15] Kathrine Rath, 'The Process of Democratization in Jordan', *Middle Eastern Studies*, vol. 30, no. 3, 1994, 537–40; Glenn E. Robinson, 'Defensive Democratization in Jordan', *International Journal of Middle East Studies*, vol. 30, no. 3, 1998, 390–1; Curtis R. Ryan, 'Peace, Bread and Riots: Jordan and the International Monetary Fund', *Middle East Policy*, vol. 6, no. 2, 1998, 55–7.

In order to accommodate the wishes of the people, channel their anger and save his own regime from growing instability, King Husayn announced that national elections would be held in 1989, the first time since 1967.[16] The Islamist opposition, primarily but not entirely made up of the Muslim Brotherhood, was quite successful in the elections and – in a surprise to many – won more than a third of the seats in parliament. During the period that followed, a policy of limited liberalisation was pursued, expressed in more freedom of organisation and the press, and the country's new democratic course was even drawn up in what became known as the National Charter (*al-mīthāq al-waṭanī*) in 1991.[17] It soon turned out, however, that the regime's democratisation was not aimed at achieving full democracy and strong liberalisation[18] but only 'to assure its political longevity, but without altering the core structures of power in Jordan'.[19] This attitude was expressed, for example, in allocating seats to districts in ways unfavourable to the Brotherhood[20] but perhaps most importantly in the changing of the electoral law in such a way that it effectively favoured tribal candidates over others, including Islamists.[21] While the Brotherhood continued to abide by parliamentary rules, it was thus less than successful in its political endeavours[22], and parts of the public – while remaining sympathetic – also became disappointed with them for their lack of achievements.[23] It was therefore not surprising that the next

[16] Kamel S. Abu Jaber and Schirin H. Fathi, 'The 1989 Jordanian Parliamentary Elections', *Orient: deutsche Zeitschrift für den modernen Orient*, vol. 31, no. 1, 1990, 72–4; Hanna Y. Freij and Leonard C. Robinson, 'Liberalization, the Islamists, and the Stability of the Arab State: Jordan as a Case Study', *The Muslim World*, vol. 86, no. 1, 1996, 9–10; International Crisis Group, *The Challenge of Political Reform: Jordanian Democratisation and Regional Instability*, Middle East Briefing, Amman & Brussels, 8 October 2003, 4–5; Curtis R. Ryan, 'Jordan and the Rise and Fall of the Arab Cooperation Council', *Middle East Journal*, vol. 52, no. 3, 1998, 393–4.

[17] Renate Dieterich, 'The Weakness of the Ruled is the Strength of the Ruler: The Role of the Opposition in Contemporary Jordan', in: George Joffé (ed.), *Jordan in Transition, 1990–2000*, London: Hurst & Co., 2002, 131–2, 137–8.

[18] Russell E. Lucas, 'Deliberalization in Jordan', *Journal of Democracy*, vol. 14, no. 1, 2003, 137–44.

[19] Robinson, 'Defensive', 387–410. The quote is on 387.

[20] Jillian Schwedler, 'A Paradox of Democracy? Islamist Participation in Elections', *Middle East Report*, no. 209, 1998, 28.

[21] Abla M. Amawi, 'The 1993 Elections in Jordan', *Arab Studies Quarterly*, vol. 16, no. 3, 1994, 15–17; Frédéric Charillon and Alain Mouftard, 'Jordanie: Les elections du 8 novembre 1993 et le processus de paix', *Monde Arabe Maghreb Machrek*, no. 144, 1994, 45–6.

[22] Glenn E. Robinson, 'Can Islamists be Democrats? The Case of Jordan', *Middle East Journal*, vol. 51, no. 3, 1997, 373–87.

[23] Beverley Milton-Edwards, 'Façade Democracy and Jordan', *British Journal of Middle Eastern Studies*, vol. 20, no. 2, 1993, 198.

national elections, in 1993, resulted in losses for the Brotherhood, which now participated through a separate political party (the Islamic Action Front, IAF), and a parliament that was much more loyal to the king than the previous one.[24]

In addition to this economic and political upheaval, Iraqi dictator Saddam Husayn decided to invade Kuwait in 1990, leading to a large-scale American-led operation to liberate the latter. In the aftermath of this war, King Husayn decided to participate in a peace process with Israel, starting with an international conference in Madrid in December 1991. Three years earlier, the king had officially relinquished Jordanian claims to the West Bank and Jerusalem, opening the way for peace talks with Israel since any attempts by Jordan to hold on to those territories would have been turned down by Israel. These talks ultimately resulted in a peace treaty with the Jewish state in 1994. This, in effect, dealt a further blow to the strongly pro-Palestinian Brotherhood, which – despite its parliamentary presence and widespread anti-Israel feelings among the population as a whole – had not been able to stop this agreement.[25] It was in this context of economic and political crisis, disillusionment about the Gulf War and the Brotherhood's parliamentary impotence that al-Maqdisi arrived in Jordan.

Al-Maqdisi's Arrival in Jordan

As mentioned in Chapter 1, al-Maqdisi was one of the hundreds of thousands of Palestinians who came to Jordan in the aftermath of the Gulf War. Since these people were officially Jordanian citizens, Jordan had to accept them, thereby adding a social problem to the burden of other issues weighing down on that country's society and regime. While earlier crises had probably contributed to a greater radicalisation of and influence by pan-Arab leftists and Muslim Brothers, the turbulent late 1980s and early 1990s, with their much lesser emphasis on Arab nationalism and the parliamentary failure of the Brotherhood, did not.[26] This context of political, economic, diplomatic and social instability over various

[24] Kirk Albrecht, 'Hussein Gets a Loyal Legislature', *The Middle East*, no. 273, December 1997, 15–16.

[25] Interview with Shadi Hamid, Amman, 11 August 2008. See also Jillian Schwedler, *Faith in Moderation: Islamist Parties in Jordan and Yemen*, Cambridge: Cambridge University Press, 2006, 169–76.

[26] See also Al-Khazendar, *Jordan*, 101-69 (esp. 124–31 and 161–9).

issues did, however, contribute indirectly to al-Maqdisi's initial influence among radical Islamists in Jordan.

Stability amidst Instability

As happened in several other Arab states during the late 1980s and early 1990s, many 'Afghan Jordanians' who had finished their fight against the Soviet Union in Afghanistan in 1989 returned to their home country. One of the driving forces of the entire 'Afghan Arab' phenomenon, ʿAbdallah ʿAzzam, was actually a Jordanian of Palestinian descent, but it is not clear if and to what extent this benefited the efforts to stimulate Jordanians to go to Afghanistan. In any case, the exodus of probably hundreds of Jordanian fighters to that country was stimulated or at least tacitly allowed by the Jordanian regime.[27] When they returned, however, they were not treated as heroes who had liberated a Muslim country from Soviet occupation but were frequently looked upon with suspicion, and they often failed to reintegrate into society. With regard to Saudi Arabia, it has been pointed out that the radicalisation and battle-hardened attitudes of the returning 'Afghan Arabs' as well as their economic marginalisation because of their long absence prevented them from fully getting back to their old lives. As a result, they often felt alienated and betrayed by society, and in the end socialised mostly with fellow-'Afghans', thereby further reinforcing their radical ideas.[28] It seems that a similar process took place in Jordan, with many 'Afghan Jordanians' not only remaining unemployed but also seeing a stark contrast between their own pious preferences and the 'sinful' lifestyles of a number of Jordanians.[29]

The generally unstable situation in Jordan as a result of economic, social and both domestic and regional political discontent, as well as the badly facilitated return of the 'Afghan Arabs', created a spirit of disillusionment with the Arab regimes and a sense of loss of control among some individuals. Many non-Palestinian Jordanians, for example, felt strengthened in their belief that their country was falling prey to 'outsiders' as a result of the influx of Palestinians after the Gulf War.[30] The inability

[27] International Crisis Group, *Jordan's*, 3. Interviews with Fāris Brayzāt, Amman, 6 August 2008; ʿUrayb al-Rantāwī, Amman, 12 August 2008.

[28] Hegghammer, 'Terrorist', 51.

[29] Anouar Boukhars, 'The Challenge of Terrorism and Religious Extremism in Jordan', *Strategic Insights*, vol. 5, no. 4, April 2006, 3; International Crisis Group, *Jordan's*, 3–4. Interviews with al-Rantāwī, Amman, 12 August 2008, Samīḥ Khurays, Amman, 14 January 2009.

[30] Brand, 'Palestinians', 56.

of the Muslim Brotherhood and the IAF to tackle any of these problems, as well as the apparent unwillingness of Arab governments (including the Jordanian) to stop the American-led war against Iraq, probably only reinforced that attitude. Although King Husayn himself took the hugely popular decision to remain neutral during the Gulf War, which many interpreted as tacit support for Iraq[31], his stance did not change the attitude of those people so disillusioned with the regime that they considered it illegitimate anyway. Among this group, a search for more radical solutions began.[32]

The attempts to find new answers to the questions that arose during this eventful and turbulent period were expressed in the founding of all kinds of radical groups. The best-known of these is probably Muhammad's Army (Jaysh Muhammad), a group that is said to have been founded by a former Muslim Brother, the 'Afghan Arab' Sami Abu Zaydan, in 1988[33], but there were many more. Some of them attacked supposedly sinful places, such as shops selling alcohol or cinemas, but they do not seem to have had a clear agenda, let alone a guiding ideology. They seem to have been little more than disparate radical groups consisting of former 'Afghan Arabs' as well as others, and although they sometimes clearly posed a threat to parts of society, they hardly constituted a unified opposition to the regime or its interests.[34] Clearly lacking any organisational structure, they were connected by their general discontent about the regime and its policies and rejected the Islamist but generally non-confrontational approach taken by the Muslim Brotherhood, which had yielded very little throughout the decades of Jordanian history. Their discontent was fuelled by grievances caused by the crises discussed earlier as well as by their relatively incoherent religious ideas, which employed the radical beliefs of men such as Qutb but also the Salafi writings of the likes of Ibn Taymiyya.[35]

31 Philip Robins, *A History of Jordan*, Cambridge: Cambridge University Press, 2004, 178–80.

32 Muḥammad Abū Rummān and Ḥasan Abū Haniyya, *'Al-Salafiyya al-Jihādiyya' fī l-Urdunn ba'da Maqtal al-Zarqāwī: Muqārabat al-Huwiyya, Azmat al-Qiyāda wa-Ḍabābiyyat al-Ru'ya*, Amman: Friedrich-Ebert-Stiftung, 2009, 15, 93–5; Abu Rumman, *Muslim*, 12–13; interviews with Ḥasan Abū Haniyya, Marwān Shaḥāda, Amman, 13 January 2009; Yāsir Abū Hilāla, Amman, 7 August 2009; Muḥammad Abū Rummān, Amman, 11 August 2008; Khurays, Amman, 14 January 2009.

33 Beverley Milton-Edwards, 'Climate of Change in Jordan's Islamist Movement', in: Abdel Salam Sidahmed and Anoushiravan Ehteshami (eds.), *Islamic Fundamentalism*, Boulder, CO: Westview Press, 1996, 127.

34 International Crisis Group, *Jordan's*, 6; Milton-Edwards, 'Climate', 127–34.

35 Abū Rummān and Abū Haniyya, *'Al-Salafiyya'*, 15.

In this climate of disillusionment and these groups' search for a radical and clear alternative to what the regime, the quietist Salafis and the Muslim Brotherhood were offering, al-Maqdisi entered the fray. Unlike these radical groups, al-Maqdisi *did* have a well-developed ideology. By the time he arrived in Jordan in 1992, he had already written several books, had briefly studied – albeit clandestinely – in Saudi Arabia and had taught others in Afghanistan/Pakistan for a short while. Although it is clear that he was not yet the major radical scholar that he is considered to be today, ideologically speaking he was clearly well ahead of his new-found Jordanian audience, which may have been aware of his ideas. There are indications that some radical Jordanians were familiar with his writings[36] and it is quite possible that at least some 'Afghan Jordanians' had been introduced to his books when they were in Afghanistan. Whatever the case may be, upon meeting al-Maqdisi himself, they – considering their radical ideas – were most probably enamoured with his framing of the problems in the Muslim world as having to do with the regimes' political apostasy from Islam, expressed in their 'loyalty' to 'man-made laws' and Western countries. Although al-Maqdisi had not written anything about Jordan at that time, his *general* message must have resonated with these men, particularly during this turbulent period in which Arab regimes (perhaps with the exception of Jordan) were severely discredited for their role in the Gulf War and – especially regarding Jordan – a willingness to make peace with Israel.

In this situation of social, economic and both domestic and regional political instability, al-Maqdisi provided the radicals with a sense of purpose, ideological coherence and indeed stability. It was therefore not surprising that he quickly became a leading figure of this disparate community of fellow-radicals by starting a group of his own. Its 'members' apparently saw themselves as strict upholders of *tawḥīd* and thus seem to have adopted the name Jamaʿat al-Tawhid or Jamaʿat al-Muwahhidin (the Group of Upholders of the Unity of God). The security services later applied the name Bayʿat al-Imam to the group, which was the title of a document that al-Maqdisi had once discussed with one of the men who was later arrested with him, and this is also how they became known in the media, but the group's 'members' did not use the name themselves.[37]

36 Ḥusayn, *Al-Zarqāwī*, 85.

37 Abū Rummān and Abū Haniyya, *'Al-Salafiyya'*, 124, note 11. Interviews with Abū Haniyya, Amman, 13 January 2009; al-Maqdisī, Amman, 13 January 2009. See also Abū Muḥammad al-Maqdisī, *Kashf al-Lithām ʿamman Waṣafū bi-Tanẓīm 'Bayʿat al-Imām'*, www.tawhed.ws/r?i=roqaokar, n.d., 5–6.

Notwithstanding the vague and ill-defined ideology of Jordan's radical groups, al-Maqdisi was not the only Jihadi-Salafi scholar in Jordan at the time. There was another radical ideologue of more or less the same stature as al-Maqdisi called ʿUmar Mahmud Abu ʿUmar, better known as Abu Qatada al-Filastini (b. 1960). Being a Palestinian-Jordanian living in Kuwait, he was expelled from that country and went to Jordan just like al-Maqdisi, but also spent time in Afghanistan. When he arrived in Jordan, however, he did not stay for very long but moved to Britain in 1993, where he is said to have helped spread al-Maqdisi's writings[38] and where he is currently under house arrest on terrorism-related charges. Although al-Maqdisi has expressed some minor criticism of Abu Qatada, he clearly agrees with his general ideas and has praised him and has written the introduction to one of his books.[39] While Abu Qatada is said to have founded a Salafi group called Harakat Ahl al-Sunna wa-l-Jamaʿa in Jordan in the early 1990s, the fact that he left Jordan so quickly after arriving there meant that, unlike al-Maqdisi, he cannot have had much direct influence on radical Islamists there through his personal presence.[40] In fact, al-Maqdisi even says that he has never met Abu Qatada in person, although they have been in touch.[41] Thus, in spite of Abu Qatada's being another major Jordanian Jihadi-Salafi scholar, the spiritual leadership of the radical Islamist community in Jordan in the early 1990s was al-Maqdisi's for the taking.

Channelling the Discontent

The preceding chapters have often mentioned al-Maqdisi's position as that of a quietist Jihadi-Salafi for his close adherence to both quietist and Jihadi-Salafi thinking and concepts. These similarities should mostly be seen at the level of *ʿaqīda*. The fact that al-Maqdisi – despite being a Jihadi-Salafi – resembles quietist Salafis in their *manhaj* of dealing with society (*daʿwa*) as well, however, is also clear. This has already been generally described in Chapter 3 but the full implications of al-Maqdisi's quietist Jihadi-Salafi *manhaj* did not become apparent until he moved to Jordan, where his position in this regard was very important in determining who became his follower and who did not, as we will see in the next

38 Abū Rummān and Abū Haniyya, '*Al-Salafiyya*', 24; Weaver, 'Inventing', 94.

39 See al-Maqdisī, *Waqfāt*, 72; *id.*, *Tabṣīr*, 79; Abū Qatāda al-Filasṭīnī, *Ju'nat al-Muṭayyabīn*, www.tawhed.ws/a?a=aheed274, n.d., respectively.

40 Abū Rummān and Abū Haniyya, '*Al-Salafiyya*', 17.

41 Interview with al-Maqdisī, Amman, 13 January 2009.

chapter. The first indications of this, however, could already be seen in al-Maqdisi's actions with the Jamaʿat al-Muwahhidin.

The group that gathered around al-Maqdisi was very diverse, and it is difficult to establish a profile of a 'typical member'. Although it is clear that most of them were young (between 18 and 30 years) at the time, had little education and were generally from poor families, this is as much as one can say with certainty.[42] Important indicators such as whether members had a Palestinian or a non-Palestinian Jordanian background and whether or not they had gone to Afghanistan seem to be more obscure among the early followers of al-Maqdisi. It seems that both Palestinian-Jordanians and 'East Bank' Jordanians were present in al-Maqdisi's group at this time.[43] The same appears to be the case with 'Afghan Arabs', who were definitely part of the group, but probably not all of them had fought in Afghanistan.[44] The exact size of the group is even more difficult to pin down since it was an informally organised club of people that did not have an actual membership. What is clear is that the number of people eventually arrested, charged and imprisoned for belonging to the group was 16.[45]

Since his move to Jordan, al-Maqdisi and the Jamaʿat al-Muwahhidin concentrated on *daʿwa* activities. Although we have already seen al-Maqdisi's emphasis on *daʿwa* in Chapter 3, this may seem strange considering his calls for jihad that we saw earlier. Why does he call for jihad against a Muslim regime in one context (particularly Saudi Arabia) but not in Jordan, especially since the latter is supposedly much more 'un-Islamic' than the former? At least two reasons can be given for this. Firstly, unlike Saudi Arabia, which was partly founded on the basis of a Salafi ideological tradition and whose youngsters were intimately familiar with Wahhabi teachings, Jordan was still relatively new to Salafism, and particularly Jihadi-Salafism, which had largely been unknown until al-Maqdisi's arrival. In other words, whereas Saudi radicals could fight as

[42] Abū Rummān and Abū Haniyya, *'Al-Salafiyya'*, 47; interviews with ʿAbdallāh Abū Rummān, Amman, 15 January 2009; Brayzāt, Amman, 6 August 2008; Ḥusayn, Amman, 5 August 2008; Rabāba, Amman, 12 January 2009; Marwān Shaḥāda, Amman, 13 January 2009; Usāma Shaḥāda, Amman, 12 January 2009.

[43] Interviews with Brayzāt, Amman, 6 August 2008; Rabāba, Amman, 12 January 2009; Usāma Shaḥāda, Amman, 12 January 2009.

[44] Hafez, *Suicide*, 171–2.

[45] Abū Rummān and Abū Haniyya, *'Al-Salafiyya'*, 20; Ḥusayn, *Al-Zarqāwī*, 91; International Crisis Group, *Jordan's*, 9, footnote 63; interviews with Khurays, Amman, 14 January 2009; al-Maqdisī, Amman, 13 January 2009; Marwān Shaḥāda, Amman, 13 January 2009.

Salafis, Jordanian radicals could not, leading al-Maqdisi to focus on first educating people before they could wage a 'proper' jihad. This argument was not a way of excusing his unwillingness to call for jihad in a country where (unlike in Saudi Arabia) he himself would have to suffer the consequences. This can be seen in his attitude that jihad – though perhaps unwise and imperfect – is legitimate in principle, shown for example in his praise for 'martyred' *mujāhidūn* and his blessing for an armed attack in 1994 (see later). Conversely, it can also be seen in his belief that it was not yet time for jihad in the Palestinian territories – where he would not suffer persecution as a result – because there were supposedly no Jihadi-Salafis to do the fighting there.[46] Secondly, al-Maqdisi also takes into account the fact that some contexts are more conducive to jihad than others. Whereas Saudi Arabia has long been a state with a relatively weak army, Jordan has much stronger and fiercer security and intelligence services, making the chances that jihad would simply end in the mass imprisonment (or even killing) of *mujāhidūn* – as happened in Egypt and Algeria in the 1990s – much more likely. Similarly, one reason al-Maqdisi was unhappy to see Jordanian youngsters go to Iraq after 2003 was that he feared they would simply be massacred, as we will see in the next chapter.

Although the ʿAbdallah b. ʿAbbas mosque in the city of al-Zarqaʾ is said to have played a central role in al-Maqdisi's *daʿwa* efforts[47], and most followers of his message seem to have come from the central Jordanian and poverty-stricken towns of al-Zarqaʾ and al-Salt as well as al-Rusayfa, where al-Maqdisi lived, their message was spread all over Jordan. This was done by preaching sermons in mosques and particularly people's own homes[48] as well as by spreading al-Maqdisi's writings. Later, when al-Maqdisi became better-known, youngsters would photocopy his books themselves and spread them on their own. This way, through personal contacts with people interested in the message as well as with family members, the group of adherents to al-Maqdisi's ideology slowly grew.[49]

The radical youngsters who co-operated with al-Maqdisi in spreading his writings probably relied mostly on his existing ideological discourse, but he also wrote new articles in the early 1990s. It is difficult to ascertain which of al-Maqdisi's writings date back to the period between his arrival

46 Interview with al-Maqdisī, al-Ruṣayfa, 17 January 2009.
47 Abū Rummān and Abū Haniyya, *'Al-Salafiyya'*, 98; al-Sharqāwī, 'Abū', 132.
48 Ḥusayn, *Al-Zarqāwī*, 84–90.
49 Abū Rummān and Abū Haniyya, *'Al-Salafiyya'*, 98; interview with Marwān Shaḥāda, Amman, 13 January 2009.

in Jordan and his incarceration (i.e., 1992–4) since many of his books and treatises are undated. Two of them, however, can be traced to this period and give us important information about al-Maqdisi and his role in Jordan during this time. The first is a letter of advice to 'some brothers' (*baʿḍ al-ikhwa*) that warns against certain extremist views that go beyond those al-Maqdisi himself believes to be correct but that are nevertheless ascribed to him. As we saw in Chapters 2 and 7, al-Maqdisi stresses that concepts such as *takfīr* and *barāʾ* – while extremely important to his ideology – should not be used carelessly, randomly or generally. It is precisely against this usage of such concepts that this letter warns. In it, al-Maqdisi tells his readers that he has never believed that Muslim societies are so steeped in unbelief that every single one of its inhabitants is an 'infidel', even though these ideas are ascribed to him.[50] He also mentions that it is said of him that he considers the armies of 'apostate' Muslim states to be 'infidel' institutions themselves. While he acknowledges that this is indeed his view, he also points out that this does not mean that every individual soldier is an apostate, and refers to those who may be in the army to overthrow the regime as examples.[51] The significance of this letter lies not so much in any groundbreaking insights contained in it but in the fact that it constitutes the first of his writings in which he defends himself against the charge of having certain views that he indeed never expressed in his books. Such attempts to warn against ideological extremism (and especially the counter-charge that al-Maqdisi used to think that way too but has become more moderate) only increased as the years went by, as we will see in the next chapter.[52]

The second piece that al-Maqdisi certainly wrote while in Jordan but before he went to prison is a book specifically written against democracy. Though undated, the book makes clear that it was written around the time of the parliamentary elections and therefore probably dates from 1993.[53] Some of his arguments against democracy are based on views we have already seen before: taking power and sovereignty away from God (by putting it in the hands of the people) constitutes a violation of his absolute unity as expressed in *tawḥīd*, for which it should be condemned as unbelief and as an entirely different and un-Islamic religion of its own.[54] What makes this book different from what he had written before,

50 Al-Maqdisī, *Risālat Munāṣaḥa*, 1–2.
51 *Ibid.*, 2–5.
52 Wagemakers, 'Reclaiming', 523–39.
53 Al-Maqdisī, *Al-Dīmuqrāṭiyya*, 3.
54 *Ibid.*, 4–15.

however, is that he attacks Islamic arguments in favour of democracy. He rebuts, for example, the claim that working for a non-Islamic system is allowed since it was also done by the Qur'ānic Yūsuf (Joseph), who worked for Pharaoh.[55] He also refutes the idea that democracy is really a modern-day form of the Islamic concept of *shūrā* (consultation)[56]. The book is too detailed to deal with at any great length here, but what is significant is that al-Maqdisi specifically wrote this book in a period in which national elections were being held in Jordan. This shows that al-Maqdisi actively tried to incorporate topical issues into his writings and applied his ideology to current events of great importance to his audience, particularly those who wondered whether voting for the Muslim Brotherhood was the right thing to do. He would do this on several other occasions during his stay in Jordan, as we will see in the next chapter, and thus provided his followers with a detailed ideological framework through which they could vent their discontent against the Jordanian regime and its supporters.

It seems that it was precisely the widespread discontent caused by Jordan's instability, expressed among radical youngsters in an unclear desire to seek a religious solution, that made them susceptible to al-Maqdisi's *daʿwa*. This may seem odd given the background of his followers. Some (or even many) of them – including Abu Musʿab al-Zarqawi – had fought in Afghanistan and had gained important military experience there. They were probably less inclined to stick to the quietist *manhaj* of practising *daʿwa* at the expense of actual jihadi action, particularly since they were preaching a distinctly Jihadi-Salafi message, arguing against the Jordanian system and its rulers. Al-Maqdisi, however, simply saw his own activities as part of what he had done for years, namely preaching his ideology, and does not even distinguish between the activities of the Jamaʿat al-Muwahhidin and his work in Afghanistan and other countries since to him they all served the same purpose.[57] Despite the discrepancy between his views on this issue and what may be assumed to be the preferred *manhaj* of at least some of al-Maqdisi's followers with regard to Jordanian society – jihad – he managed to get these followers involved in spreading his ideas in the early 1990s.

Al-Maqdisi's quietist Jihadi-Salafism was underlined when, in 1994, an Israeli settler called Baruch Goldstein murdered dozens of Palestinians

[55] *Ibid.*, 17–26.
[56] *Ibid.*, 31–7.
[57] Interview with al-Maqdisī, Amman, 13 January 2009.

praying at the al-Ibrahimi Mosque in Hebron in the West Bank. Several of the men who participated in al-Maqdisi's *daʿwa* activities wanted to take revenge by staging an attack against Israel. Although al-Maqdisi had smuggled weapons into Jordan apparently abandoned by the Iraqi army as it left Kuwait after its invasion there[58], and even gave a fatwa permitting the attack against Israel[59], he did so only reluctantly since, while considering it legitimate, he wanted to focus on *daʿwa*.[60] The decision to attack Israel – which seems to have been the only armed action the group ever got involved in – proved to be a fateful one since it was discovered and thwarted by the Jordanian security services, leading to the arrest of al-Maqdisi's group.[61]

After the arrest, the *daʿwa* of al-Maqdisi and his group actually continued during their court case. At the trial that preceded their sentencing, the men about to be convicted used the opportunity to tell the judges, lawyers and the journalists present about their ideas. Al-Maqdisi himself says he very consciously seized this chance to do *daʿwa* against people who represented the law of a country not ruled by the *sharīʿa*.[62] He and the others used the court as a pulpit from which they could spread their message of *takfīr* of the rulers, disavowing their 'man-made laws' and openly showing their rejection of the system on which the trial was based.[63] This attitude of defiance towards those in power as well as their attempts to turn an unfortunate situation to their benefit would characterise their stay in prison, during which they often confronted the authorities, and al-Maqdisi used his time to spread his views. Yet it was also during his followers' prison time that al-Maqdisi's position as a quietist Jihadi-Salafi and the emphasis on the use of *daʿwa* that resulted from this gradually stopped being a unifying factor, as we will see in the next chapter. First, however, we must turn to a full explanation of al-Maqdisi's influence in Jordan in the early 1990s.

58 Abū Rummān and Abū Haniyya, '*Al-Salafiyya*', 19; *al-ʿAṣr*, 10 July 2005; *Al-ʿArabiyya* (www.alarabiya.net/programs/2009/03/01/67515.html, accessed 4 March 2009), 1 March 2009; Ḥusayn, *Al-Zarqāwī*, 92; al-Maqdisī, e-mail message to the author, 18 May 2009.

59 Napoleoni, *Insurgent*, 63.

60 Khāshuqjī and Abū Hilāla, 'Al-Munaẓẓir', 12–13; Abū Muḥammad al-Maqdisī, *Liqāʾ min Khalf Quḍbān al-Murtaddīn 'Sana 1418'*, 4–5, 10–11.

61 Interviews with Abū Haniyya, Amman, 9 August 2008; Ḥusayn, Amman, 5 August 2008; al-Maqdisī, Amman, 13 January 2009.

62 Interview with al-Maqdisī, Amman 13 January 2009.

63 Napoleoni, *Insurgent*, 64–6. See also Ḥusayn, *Al-Zarqāwī*, 60–2; al-Maqdisī, *Al-Zarqāwī*, 2.

A Visionary in the Land of the Blind

From Chapter 4 onwards, we have dealt with the so-called core framing tasks, the three aspects that any good frame should possess. Until now, we have seen how al-Maqdisi's diagnosis of a problem, his prognosis and his call for action were not always congruent with other people's own frames. In the case of Jordan at the beginning of the 1990s, however, al-Maqdisi's target audience, consisting of 'Afghan Jordanians' and other disillusioned radicals who gathered around him and his teachings, had very few clear ideas of its own. Being largely unfamiliar with the doctrines of Jihadi-Salafism in an age when such ideas were not yet widespread by way of the Internet, this meant that any Islamic radical solution preached by a knowledgeable scholar would probably have gone a long way to satisfy them. Al-Maqdisi's framing of the rulers of the Muslim world as *kuffār*, his solution of *takfīr* of and jihad against them and his frequent calls for Muslims to act upon this 'duty' to disavow their political leaders will therefore have been an attractive one to young Jordanian radicals hungry for an alternative. In that sense, al-Maqdisi's return to Jordan can be characterised as an arrival in 'the land of the blind'. Al-Maqdisi was not a 'one-eyed man', however, but a scholar with clear ideas of his own who could more accurately be described as a visionary wanting to lead others to 'true Islam'. This meeting between a scholar and a disgruntled group of radicalising youngsters at the right time finds a more explicit theoretical explanation in the concept of cognitive liberation.

Cognitive Liberation

As will be recalled from Chapter 4, McAdam coined the term cognitive liberation to refer to the realisation among the public that the time for contentious action has come. This realisation is said to be caused on the one hand by so-called 'cognitive cues' provided by political opportunities (i.e., openings that allow contention to achieve actual results) and on the other by social movements' capitalisation on these cognitive cues by encouraging people to take action. Cognitive cues mentioned by McAdam include ideological or cultural contradictions (i.e., events or decisions that show a stark contrast between something many people hold dear and what takes place in practice); suddenly imposed grievances, which change an audience's perception of a situation that they previously accepted; and dramatisations of system vulnerability, showing the weak spots of a regime or government. Although others have debated whether it need necessarily be social movements that capitalise on cognitive cues – arguing that external actors can also facilitate the process of cognitive liberation or that even individual members of the public can do this themselves – these authors have not fundamentally changed McAdam's theory.

The idea that cognitive cues partly cause cognitive liberation has been pointed out by others too. Jasper and Poulson have shown that what they refer to as 'moral shocks' can cause people to join protest movements – in their case, animal rights groups and anti-nuclear protestors.[64] They also show that the single event of *Roe v. Wade* (1973), the U.S. Supreme Court decision that stated that abortion was not in violation of the American constitution, caused larger numbers than usual to join the anti-abortion movement.[65] Similarly, Wiktorowicz has argued that crises such as alienation, discrimination or even the death of a family member can cause 'cognitive openings' – that is, a state of mind in which one becomes open and susceptible to new ideas.[66] Such cognitive openings, in the case of religious people (and perhaps also in the case of others), can lead to what Wiktorowicz refers to as 'religious seeking', which most likely occurs when 'an individual's religious views and/or established religious institutions seem inadequate in addressing concerns'.[67] Of course, as Wiktorowicz points out, many find answers to pressing questions triggered by crises in previously held beliefs or at least within the mainstream of religious ideas. Others, however, go beyond these because they find the already available answers wanting. Religious seekers will start taking action of whatever kind once their cognitive openings are filled with ideas they are receptive to and that call for this. As such, social movements, other external actors or the individuals themselves play a role in capitalising on religious seekers' cognitive openings, similar to what McAdam and other scholars have shown.[68]

If we compare the preceding to al-Maqdisi's arrival in Jordan and his influence there in the early 1990s, we can see some very clear parallels. There were indeed several crises going on in Jordan in the late 1980s and early 1990s, as we have seen, which can all be seen as cognitive cues that shocked and contradicted existing beliefs. The IMF-inspired economic

[64] James M. Jasper and Jane D. Poulson, 'Recruiting Strangers and Friends: Moral Shocks and Social Networks in Animal Rights and Anti-Nuclear Protests', *Social Problems*, vol. 42, no. 4, 1995, 493–512.

[65] *Ibid.*, 498.

[66] Quintan Wiktorowicz, *Radical Islam Rising: Muslim Extremism in the West*, Lanham, MD: Rowman & Littlefield, 2005, 5, 20.

[67] *Ibid.*, 21.

[68] *Ibid.*, 85–7.

measures that led to protests, the failed democratisation, the inability of Arab and Muslim states to stop the U.S.-led coalition from attacking the Iraqi army after its occupation of Kuwait, the influx of hundreds of thousands of Palestinians and, finally, the peace process with Israel all constituted crises on their own, and all the more so when taken together. As we have seen, these did indeed lead to the search for new and more radical answers among various Jordanians, particularly those who had returned from fighting the Soviet Union in Afghanistan, only to find that they were not really welcome anymore. What is also clear is that these 'religious seekers' did not find their answers in mainstream Jordanian religious discourse. They did not join the Muslim Brotherhood, which was the accepted Islamist opposition movement, and their views of the Islamic Action Front will not have improved after that party failed to stop the peace agreement with Israel.

If we try to assess al-Maqdisi's role in this situation, we can see that he was instrumental in translating the cognitive openings caused by the various crises in Jordan – which acted as cognitive cues – into action, which in his case was a radical *daʿwa* across the country. By providing guidance to these religious seekers, he gave them answers to the questions that had arisen. Al-Maqdisi can therefore be seen as responsible for capitalising on the cognitive openings among some of Jordan's radical Islamists in the early 1990s. It is important to understand, however, that while these religious seekers lacked a clear ideology and religious agenda of their own, they were not apathetic actors waiting for someone to come and fill their heads with ideas they could not think of themselves. In this respect, it needs to be repeated that several of these radical youngsters had already taken the initiative to establish various groups, and some had even taken action by attacking 'sinful' places in cities such as al-Zarqaʾ. Although together these hardly constituted a coherent and organised plan based on a comprehensive ideology, it does show that al-Maqdisi was only partly responsible for turning cognitive openings into cognitive liberation and contentious action. Similarly, after the murder of dozens of Palestinians in Hebron – itself perhaps a 'moral shock' causing a cognitive opening – several 'members' of the Jamaʿat al-Muwahhidin decided to take action independently of al-Maqdisi's ideological input. Nevertheless, al-Maqdisi's influence was certainly important. He provided the religious seekers with a comprehensive ideology that fitted the times and the context in which they found themselves and gave them a sense of direction that they had lacked before he came.

'Filling the Gap'

Cognitive liberation and its related concepts on the framing of ideas and the capitalisation on others' search for them thus suggests that al-Maqdisi played an important role in the radicalisation of a loose group of youngsters known as the Jamaʿat al-Muwahhidin. This is confirmed by the people involved in these events at the time. Many informants did indeed state that al-Maqdisi was the person responsible for leading a disparate group of radicalising youngsters into a clearly Jihadi-Salafi direction, albeit one with quietist overtones through its stress on the *manhaj* of *daʿwa*.

Several former fellow-prisoners of al-Maqdisi's, for example, pointed out that some people in Jordan in the early 1990s were looking for a radical alternative to the Muslim Brotherhood and the entire Jordanian system and found this in al-Maqdisi and his teachings.[69] Similarly, several Jordanian journalists intimately familiar with radical Islam in Jordan also believed this to be the case.[70] Finally, this view was likewise expressed by Jordanians who held extremist ideas at the time and were closely involved with radical groups themselves, but have now rejected this ideology.[71] Al-Maqdisi, one former radical and prominent Jordanian journalist told me, 'filled the gap' left by the ideas of the Muslim Brotherhood, which had clearly been discarded by the youngsters that later followed al-Maqdisi. As such, he came along at exactly the right time to capitalise on their search for something entirely different.[72]

This chapter has shown that al-Maqdisi's frame of anti-regime ideas expressed in religious terms found a willing audience in the radicalising youngsters searching for alternative answers to their questions in Jordan in the early 1990s. His clearly expressed and coherent ideas provided an ideological basis for their shared grievances. We have also seen, however, that it was not their specific preference for the details of his ideology but rather their much more general search for radical Islamic ideas that caused them to accept al-Maqdisi's quietist Jihadi-Salafism, expressed here in his stress on a quietist way of dealing with society through *daʿwa*.

69 Interviews with Abū Haniyya, Amman, 13 January 2009; ʿAbdallāh Abū Rummān, Amman, 15 January 2009; Rababa, Amman, 12 January 2009.

70 Interviews with Marwān Shaḥāda, Amman, 13 January 2009; Usāma Shaḥāda, Amman, 12 January 2009.

71 Interviews with Abū Haniyya, Amman, 13 January 2009; Muḥammad Abū Rummān, Amman, 11 August 2008.

72 Interview with Muḥammad Abū Rummān, Amman, 11 August 2008.

Despite the fact that many of them had fought in Afghanistan and were therefore probably more inclined to favour a Jihadi-Salafi *manhaj* of fighting the Jordanian regime, they accepted al-Maqdisi's way, probably because al-Maqdisi's ideas and methods were the best thing on offer at that moment. This suggests that once the situation changed and ideas and methods became clearer, some of these youngsters would start contesting al-Maqdisi's approach. This is indeed precisely what happened, as we will see in the final chapter.

9

The Leader of the Jordanian Jihadi-Salafi Community?

Throughout this study, we have seen that al-Maqdisi's adherence to his own combination of a quietist and a Jihadi-Salafi *ʿaqīda* and *manhaj* was instrumental in explaining why he had an impact in certain political contexts and not in others. This final chapter focusses on Jordan in the period 1994–2009, when al-Maqdisi's quietist Jihadi-Salafi *manhaj* of support for jihad against Muslim rulers in principle, but with a strong preference for *daʿwa* against them, not only became clear among radical Jordanians but also split them in more or less two groups with regard to this position. While several factors contributed to these divergent views of al-Maqdisi, I argue that his quietist Jihadi-Salafi *manhaj* is the overarching concept through which these factors should be explained and that accounts for the fact that al-Maqdisi is a major figure among Jihadi-Salafis in Jordan but is not their undisputed leader.

We will start by looking at al-Maqdisi's experiences in prison from 1994–9 and the period afterwards, during which his position as a quietist Jihadi-Salafi became clear, causing differences of opinion to emerge and eventually to become expressed in severe criticism of al-Maqdisi. We then move on to al-Maqdisi's numerous writings from the period 1994–2009, during which he specifically set out his ideas about his ideological enemies, including the Jordanian state and certain quietist Salafis on the one hand and 'extremist' Jihadi-Salafis on the other. Finally, we will look at how al-Maqdisi's quietist Jihadi-Salafi framing of his enemies amidst the growing tensions in the Jordanian radical Islamist community accounts for both his influence as well as his lack thereof.

The Prison Experience and Beyond

The failed attempt by some followers of al-Maqdisi to take revenge on Israel for the murder of dozens of Palestinians in 1994 by an Israeli settler was the direct cause for the group's arrest and incarceration. Their imprisonment does not seem to have dealt a blow to their Islamist ideals, however. One might expect some 'members' of the group to blame the perpetrators of the attack on Israel for getting caught, leading to the imprisonment of the whole group and perhaps causing some to become disillusioned with their radical ideas altogether, but this does not appear to have happened. Instead, the prison experience not only confirmed their views of the Jordanian regime as an 'un-Islamic' system but also further radicalised them in ways that went beyond the quietist Jihadi-Salafi *ʿaqīda* and *manhaj* that al-Maqdisi preferred.

Growing Rifts

It seems that the Jamaʿat al-Muwahhidin more or less continued its *daʿwa* activities inside prison as if nothing had changed but their new environment was obviously entirely different. The closed and confined space of prison limited their *daʿwa* to a smaller group of people and, importantly, intensified the contacts between the 'members' of the group itself. This enabled their ideas to take definite shape and thus eventually brought differences to the surface among al-Maqdisi's followers that had remained hidden during the pre-prison period, when they were still searching for a clear ideology and believed they were provided with one in al-Maqdisi's teachings.[1] Initially, however, the group still seems to have been led by al-Maqdisi's ideas. This is shown, for example, in the sermons preached by ʿAbd al-Hadi Daghlas[2], one of al-Maqdisi's followers who had also been one of the people behind the failed attack on Israel in 1994. His message in these prison sermons from the same year seems to have been inspired by al-Maqdisi, with its generally radical tone, its emphasis on *tawḥīd* and its attention for 'un-Islamic' legislation clearly bearing the marks of Jamaʿat al-Muwahhidin's spiritual leader.[3]

The message preached by al-Maqdisi and his followers was clearly not accepted by all other prisoners, who included adherents to and members

[1] Abū Rummān and Abū Haniyya, '*Al-Salafiyya*', 23–4; interview with Abū Haniyya, Amman, 13 January 2009.

[2] ʿAbd al-Hādī Daghlas, *Majmūʿa min Khuṭab al-Akh al-Mujāhid ʿAbd al-Hādī Daghlas – Abū ʿUbayda Raḥimahu llāh*, www.tawhed.ws/c?i=31, 2009.

[3] *Ibid.*, 7–8, 19, 34.

of various Islamist trends and groups, such as Hizb al-Tahrir, as well as ordinary criminals. Secular or more nationalist-oriented prisoners are said to have been much less influenced by al-Maqdisi's message[4], and one such inmate even wrote and published an article while he was still in prison that pointed out how radicals such as al-Maqdisi would tear society apart[5]. The Islamist prisoners, particularly if they belonged to the Muslim Brotherhood or Hizb al-Tahrir, may have had more fixed and less Salafi ideas than al-Maqdisi and also did not always agree with his message. In fact, fierce conflicts are said to have raged sometimes, even leading occasionally to *takfīr* of others.[6]

Daʿwa was thus initially very important among the 'members' of the Jamaʿat al-Muwahhidin, even inside prison, and al-Maqdisi was the one who led it. As we saw in Chapter 1, however, his leadership did not last very long, since al-Zarqawi took over after a while. Three reasons can be given for this. Firstly, there was an important difference between the two men regarding personality. As mentioned before, whereas al-Zarqawi was known for his toughness, leadership abilities and his strict discipline inside prison, al-Maqdisi had a more scholarly, much friendlier and less confrontational personality.[7] This was complemented by the social background of the two men: whereas al-Zarqawi was an uneducated man from a poor family in al-Zarqa', al-Maqdisi was clearly middle class, had attended university and grew up in the Gulf. Given the background of their followers, most Jihadi-Salafis who were with them in prison could probably relate more to the experiences of the former than to those of the latter.[8] Secondly, as time went by, ideological differences started to appear between al-Maqdisi and al-Zarqawi. While the latter became more and more interested in direct confrontation of the 'enemies of Islam', preferably abroad, al-Maqdisi maintained that *daʿwa* was the correct approach at that time and that it should concentrate on Jordan.[9] One supporter of al-Zarqawi's approach who wanted to remain anonymous told me that al-Maqdisi was a real Wahhabi who was always concerned about

4 Interviews with Ḥusayn, Amman, 5 August 2008; Rabāba, Amman, 12 January 2009.
5 Interview with ʿIkrima Gharāyba, Amman, 15 January 2009.
6 *Al-Sharq al-Awsaṭ*, 8 March 2004.
7 Abū Rummān and Abū Haniyya, *'Al-Salafiyya'*, 23, 45–47; Brisard, *Zarqawi*, 44–51; Ḥusayn, *Al-Zarqāwī*, 14–17; Napoleoni, *Insurgent*, 66–76; Weaver, 'Inventing', 93–4.
8 Abū Rummān and Abū Haniyya, *'Al-Salafiyya'*, 46–7.
9 *Ibid.*, 25–6; interviews with Abū Haniyya, Amman, 13 January 2009, and an Islamist who wished to remain anonymous, Amman, 10 January 2009.

tawḥīd and *sharʿī* (Islamic legal) issues, whereas al-Zarqawi wanted to fight. While this is something of an exaggeration of the difference between the two men – al-Maqdisi also supported various types of jihad in principle and al-Zarqawi did not simply ignore doctrinal issues altogether – it does point to an important source of conflict between them. Thirdly, and strongly related to the choice between armed action and a less confrontational approach, there was the issue of experience in jihad and the authority derived from this. As we have seen in Chapter 1, al-Maqdisi did spend time in Afghanistan and Pakistan but only to teach, not to fight, unlike al-Zarqawi, who did participate in fighting there. As time went by, the issue of jihadi credentials expressed by fighting experience in Afghanistan became more and more important among the radical inmates.[10]

It seems obvious that in the context of a prison in which inmates are often treated badly and many prisoners have radical Islamist backgrounds and even experience in fighting the Soviets in Afghanistan, al-Zarqawi was more attractive as a leader than al-Maqdisi. The former's tougher personality, his preference for a confrontational and violent approach and his actual experience in fighting made him the likely candidate for such a task. Although the choice of al-Zarqawi as the new leader of the group did not necessarily entail a complete rejection of al-Maqdisi and his ideas, the change in leadership did reflect a growing unease with al-Maqdisi's quietist Jihadi-Salafi *manhaj* of a radical *daʿwa* against Muslim regimes in favour of a more purely Jihadi-Salafi method of fighting only.

Considering this growing divergence in preferred methods, it is not surprising that when the group was released as part of a royal amnesty on the occasion of the ascension to the throne of King ʿAbdallah II after King Husayn's death in 1999, al-Zarqawi and many others went to Afghanistan and other countries to train and wage jihad there.[11] It is clear that there were push-factors causing radicals to go abroad. Like other Arab countries such as Egypt and Algeria, Jordan had cracked down on radical Islamists in the 1990s and kept a close eye on them. Staying in Jordan was therefore bound to be difficult and could easily lead to renewed imprisonment.[12] In fact, al-Maqdisi discussed this issue with ʿAbd al-Hadi Daghlas, who also went to Afghanistan, and when he told

10 Interview with ʿAbdallāh Abū Rummān, Amman, 15 January 2009. See also Wagemakers, 'Invoking', 14–17; *id*., 'Reclaiming', 529–33.

11 Brisard, *Zarqawi*, 55–60.

12 *Ibid*., 59; interviews with Abū Haniyya, Amman, 9 August 2008; Muḥammad Abū Rummān, Amman, 11 August 2008; al-Rantāwī, Amman, 12 August 2008.

him that going there would weaken the *daʿwa* in Jordan, the latter asked al-Maqdisi how he could possibly stay amidst the increasing scrutiny, searches and investigations he and his family were under.[13] At the same time, however, the global jihad preached by al-Qaʿida since the late 1990s may well have acted as a pull-factor for jihadis seeking action[14], which only increased once America launched its 'war on terrorism' after '9/11' and invaded Afghanistan and Iraq in 2001 and 2003, respectively.[15]

Al-Zarqawi's and others' move to Afghanistan to wage a jihad there thus went against the wishes of al-Maqdisi, who felt that they needed to focus on *daʿwa* in Jordan.[16] This was not so much a rejection of al-Maqdisi personally as it was a dismissal of his quietist Jihadi-Salafi *manhaj*. Although it is quite possible that al-Maqdisi and al-Zarqawi were still on good terms when they were in prison together, both of them later became symbols of their respective methods of radical *daʿwa* in Jordan and jihad abroad, leading to an increasingly vocal dismissal of al-Maqdisi's quietist Jihadi-Salafi *manhaj* among some.

Quietism Haunts al-Maqdisi

Although al-Maqdisi continued his *daʿwa* activities after leaving prison in 1999, it should once again be pointed out that his methodological differences with al-Zarqawi and others did not mean he was against jihad. He has long preached in favour of jihad against the Muslim world's own regimes, has praised – as we saw in Chapter 2 – the terrorists directly involved in '9/11' and has spoken highly of some of his former cellmates who had gone to wage jihad in countries such as Afghanistan and Iraq.[17] Al-Maqdisi did not oppose his cellmates' wishes to go abroad and wage jihad for ideological or doctrinal reasons but simply because he felt the time was not right for that and the emphasis should be on *daʿwa* at

[13] Daghlas, *Majmūʿa*, 2. Al-Maqdisī wrote the introduction to this collection of sermons by Daghlas.

[14] Interview with Muḥammad Abū Rummān, Amman, 11 August 2008.

[15] International Crisis Group, *Jordan's*, 11.

[16] Al-Maqdisī, *Al-Zarqāwī*, 4.

[17] See, for instance, Abū Muḥammad al-Maqdisī, *Al-Mujāhidān al-Baṭalān: al-Sarḥān wa-Rafīquhu l-Suwayrikī*, www.tawhed.ws/r?i=8shfqfqc, n.d.; *id.*, *Fī Dhikrā Maqtal Ikhwāninā l-Mujāhidīn al-Arbaʿa fī Kurdistān*, www.tawhed.ws/r?i=0526wy4i, 2002; *id.*, *Al-Akh al-Mujāhid al-Baṭal: Jamāl Rifʿat Rāghib*, www.tawhed.ws/r?i=5snqdcg2, 2004; *id.*, *Kawkaba min al-Abṭāl*, www.tawhed.ws/r?i=mmqsxjyc, 2004; *id.*, *Abū Anas al-Shāmī: Baṭal Qaḍā Naḥbahu taḥta Liwāʾ al-Tawḥīd*, www.tawhed.ws/r?i=0qzxwdo8, 2004.

this stage to educate people. As such, al-Maqdisi continued his missionary work in a situation that was characterised by increasing violence in Jordan, particularly after '9/11', and he was even re-arrested and – though acquitted – imprisoned once again in 2002.[18]

Once in prison, al-Maqdisi produced several important writings, which will be discussed later. He did not really get much media attention again, however, until he was released in late June 2005, when he gave several interviews in which he criticised al-Zarqawi's actions in Iraq. The latter had become the leader of al-Qaʿida in the Land of the Two Rivers (Iraq) during this period and was widely considered to have been responsible for killing many Iraqi civilians – including Shiites – as well as the beheading of the American Nicholas Berg.[19] Al-Maqdisi's criticism of his former pupil included the charges that al-Zarqawi wrongly considered certain (Muslim) civilians to be *kuffār* who may be targeted and also that he used methods that damaged the image of Islam.[20] These rebukes of al-Zarqawi caused some Jordanian radicals to become (more) critical of al-Maqdisi for what they saw as his insults to a brave *mujāhid*. As we saw in Chapter 1, al-Maqdisi's criticism of al-Zarqawi and the latter's response have been dealt with extensively. Yet, what is less apparent from existing publications is that al-Maqdisi's critique – though strongly related to the issue of *takfīr* – was ultimately rooted in the belief that his former cellmates should not have gone abroad to wage jihad in the first place. What spurred his critique of his former pupil was therefore not just the latter's attacks against certain people but also al-Zarqawi's use of jihad at a time when al-Maqdisi considered *daʿwa* the most appropriate *manhaj*. Although these are – strictly speaking – two different issues, al-Maqdisi's critics later conflated them more and more, possibly because they felt that criticising al-Maqdisi's unwillingness to wage jihad himself was a more effective line of attack. In other words, when al-Maqdisi criticised 'extremism in *takfīr*' (*ghulūw fī l-takfīr*, i.e., excommunicating more Muslims than he and like-minded scholars consider justified), it was often interpreted by his critics in light of his earlier preference for *daʿwa* over jihad and, as such, as a stab in the back of *mujāhidūn* in general and al-Zarqawi in particular.

18 Abū Rummān and Abū Haniyya, *'Al-Salafiyya'*, 27–9.

19 '"Zarqawi" beheaded U.S. man in Iraq', http://news.bbc.co.uk/2/hi/middle_east/3712421.stm, 13 May 2004.

20 *Al-ʿArab al-Yawm*, 5 July 2005; *Al-Ghad*, 5 July 2005; *Abū Muḥammad al-Maqdisī. Al-Salafiyya al-Jihādiyya*, www.aljazeera.net/channel/archive/archive?ArchiveId=129776, 6 July 2005.

The interviews in which al-Maqdisi criticised al-Zarqawi led to his renewed imprisonment, only a week after his release, and the beginning of a long, quiet period. It seems that he did not release a single text for almost three years. In the meantime, the war in Iraq went on with an ever-increasing number of killed and wounded. One of those was al-Zarqawi, who was killed in an American attack in 2006. The admiration al-Zarqawi had come to enjoy among his cellmates during his time in prison because of his strength, his confrontational nature and his willingness to fight had presumably grown during his leadership of al-Qaʿida in Iraq, and became even greater once he died as a 'martyr'. As mentioned, after al-Maqdisi's criticism of al-Zarqawi a growing number of Jihadi-Salafis in Jordan came to resent the fact that the former had not only refrained from joining the jihad after his release in order to continue his *daʿwa* but had also criticised a man who did take up arms to fight for the cause of Islam. The anger towards al-Maqdisi over this issue, combined with their conflation of his criticism of 'extreme *takfīrī*s' with his dim view of a wholly jihadi *manhaj*, apparently remained below the surface while he was imprisoned but erupted with a vengeance after he was released in 2008.

In the autumn of 2008, when al-Maqdisi had been out of prison for some months, it appeared that several treatises were circulating among Jordanian Jihadi-Salafis (including postings on radical internet forums) that were critical of him. The direct reason for these writings seems to have been the release of a book by Nur al-Din Bayram, a student of al-Maqdisi's, in August 2008. In this book, Bayram warns against extremism in *takfīr* among some Jihadi-Salafis and claims that one should stay away from them and reject their teachings.[21] Although Bayram states that these people do not apply *takfīr* to Muslims who are only guilty of non-*kufr* sins, as the early Islamic extremist Khawārij did, he nevertheless feels justified in labelling them as such because they do apply excommunication more easily than Salafis are supposed to.[22] It seems that the authors of the critical pamphlets about al-Maqdisi interpret Bayram's criticism as meant for them, and, since al-Maqdisi wrote the introduction to his book, they start deriding both men. Interestingly, while Bayram's critique refers only to 'extremism in *takfīr*', the writings rebutting this charge focus also on his supposed opposition to jihad and its proponents, and, because of this,

[21] Nūr al-Dīn Bayram, *Faṣl al-Maqāl fī Hajar Ahl al-Bidaʿ wa-l-Ḍalāl*, www.tawhed.ws/c?i=31, 2008.

[22] *Ibid.*, 19.

use al-Zarqawi as a symbol to make their case. One of these treatises states:

> [Bayram] is one of those who went to wage jihad in Iraq during the life of shaykh Abu Musʿab [al-Zarqawi], may God accept him, stayed in Iraq for six months and went back to Jordan the way he came (i.e., without fighting there). He has [nevertheless] described the *mujāhidūn* as ignorant and as ones who excommunicate people, shed forbidden blood and take people's possessions.[23]

Another author sarcastically refers to Bayram as 'the hero Nur' and chides him for supposedly fleeing from the jihad in Iraq, which the writer describes as a sin in itself, and for treating the ones who did fight as extremists.[24]

Despite this criticism of Nur al-Din Bayram, it is clear from the authors' critique that they view his negative description of certain Jihadi-Salafis as part of what al-Maqdisi expressed before about al-Zarqawi. Their documents show that it is really al-Maqdisi's *daʿwa* at the expense of jihad that irritates them. One author blames him for focussing on missionary activities and states that when al-Maqdisi is asked about jihad, 'he says it is not allowed because of the absence of a caliphate and that there is no profit in emigrating [to wage jihad] in such circumstances'.[25] In what should probably be interpreted as a sign of disdain for those advocating *daʿwa* over jihad, the author advises al-Maqdisi to realise that the *mujāhidūn* 'are the ones who write knowledge with their blood (*bi-dimāʾihim*) and not with their pens (*bi-aqlāmihim*)'.[26] Another critic states that he remembers al-Maqdisi's critique of al-Zarqawi 'and then he went on to bless and write the introduction to articles of a person we all know' (i.e., Bayram), whom the author accuses of fleeing from jihad 'under false pretences and lies' (*bi-daʿwā wa-akādhīb bāṭila*).[27] One author even mocks the claim that he and like-minded Jihadi-Salafis are Khawārij by telling al-Maqdisi:

> Yes, we have seceded (*kharajnā*) from your rotten ideas (*afkārika l-ʿafina*) [. . .] We have seceded from your deceit (*kidhbika*) over [al-Zarqawi,] the leader of the martyrdom-seekers (*amīr al-istishhādiyyīn*).[28]

23 Abū l-Qaʿqāʿ al-Shāmī, *Kalimat ʿItāb*, n.p., 2008, 2.

24 Al-Yamān ʿAbd al-Karīm b. ʿĪsā al-Madanī, *Al-Ijtihād fī Ḥukm al-Farār min Sāḥāt al-Jihād*, www.almedad.com/vb (accessed 21 April 2009), 2008.

25 Al-Shāmī, *Kalimat*, 3.

26 *Ibid.*, 7.

27 Abū l-Qāsim al-Muhājir, *Al-Maqdisī Yataqaddamu li-l-Warāʾ*, www.muslm.net/vb/archive/index.php/t-315439.html (accessed 20 April 2009), n.d.

28 Abū l-Qaʿqāʿ al-Shāmī, *Naʿam Kharajnā*, www.al-amanh.net/vb/showthread.php?p=7086 (accessed 21 April 2009), 2008.

The criticism levelled at al-Maqdisi continued into 2009, when one al-Mihdar, a regular contributor to radical Internet forums, claimed al-Maqdisi had posted a document on his website without giving credit to its author. Although al-Maqdisi quickly rebutted the accusation[29], this relatively minor issue caused the criticism of his preference for *daʿwa* over jihad at this stage to continue. Once again, the accusations used against al-Maqdisi regularly focussed on his practical opposition to jihad, often invoking al-Zarqawi in doing so. Although many participants on radical Internet forums, particularly Midad al-Suyuf[30], engaged in criticising al-Maqdisi for his supposed disrespect for jihad and *mujāhidūn*, none did so more than al-Zarqawi's brother-in-law Abu Qudama Salih al-Hami, who clearly romanticised the jihad in Afghanistan in the 1980s, at which time he was a reporter there.[31] He states that al-Maqdisi 'represented the *daʿwa* trend', whereas al-Zarqawi 'represented the trend of jihad and its jurisprudence'.[32] 'Al-Zarqawi differed from al-Maqdisi', Abu Qudama writes, 'in the concept (*al-taṣawwur*), the method (*al-manhaj*) and his vision and connection with life and the reality towards jihad [. . .] Al-Zarqawi and al-Maqdisi each had their own *manhaj* and concept towards jihad.'[33] Considering his strong admiration for al-Zarqawi, who had become the antithesis of al-Maqdisi in the minds of some, he states about the latter that 'with regard to jihad and fighting, I do not praise him. Practically, he is no different from the rest of the callers to Islam (*duʿāt*) of our Muslim community [. . .] The jihad of shaykh al-Maqdisi is the jihad of *daʿwa*, not the jihad of fighting', only to add that it would have been better for him to have fought than to concentrate on writing *Al-Kawashif al-Jaliyya* in Afghanistan/Pakistan, which he claims people had no need for anyway.[34]

Some of the things Abu Qudama claims about al-Maqdisi are clearly not true, such as when he denies that al-Maqdisi has had any influence on al-Zarqawi or when he states that he was an adherent to the ideas

[29] Abū Muḥammad al-Maqdisī, *Radd al-Shaykh al-Maqdisī ʿalā Suʾālāt Muntadā Midād al-Suyūf*, www.tawhed.ws/r?i=badmedad, 2009.

[30] Joas Wagemakers, *Midad al-Suyuf and al-Maqdisi: Sworn Enemies?*, www.jihadica.com/midad-al-suyuf-and-al-maqdisi-sworn-enemies/, 2010.

[31] See, for instance, Abū Qudāma Ṣāliḥ al-Hāmī, *Fursān al-Farīḍa al-Ghāʾiba: Al-Zarqāwī wa-l-Jihād al-Afghān* [sic], n.p., 2007, 3–7. I would like to thank Will McCants for providing me with this document.

[32] *Ibid.*, 203.

[33] *Id.*, *Al-Zarqāwī: Al-Jīl al-Thānī li-l-Qāʿida – Dirāsa Manhajiyya wa-Naqdiyya*, n.p., n.d., 48.

[34] *Ibid.*, 167–168, 170.

of the Egyptian extremist group al-Takfir wa-l-Hijra but later recanted these beliefs.[35] The distinction Abu Qudama makes between al-Maqdisi's and al-Zarqawi's *manhaj* is a correct one, however, and it is therefore not surprising that some Jihadi-Salafis were not deterred when several scholars and activists[36] defended al-Maqdisi. When one of these, the Saudi-British radical activist Muhammad al-Masʿari, tried to stand up for him, citing a *ḥadīth* stating that the best jihad is speaking a word of truth to a tyrannical leader, and claiming that al-Maqdisi has been a steadfast proponent of such a jihad[37], he was quickly refuted. One Sina' stated on a radical Internet forum that jihad was really all about fighting and that al-Maqdisi had never participated in that, claiming that 'he has not thrown so much as a stone at the Zionists!!'[38]

Thus, al-Maqdisi's strong preference for his quietist Jihadi-Salafi *manhaj* of expressing his radical ideas through *daʿwa* eventually not only caused some Jordanians to flock to al-Zarqawi but, after his criticism of the latter, also became something that certain people held against him. This meant that al-Maqdisi's quietist tinge – particularly as expressed in his critique of al-Zarqawi – eventually came to haunt him, leading to great enmity among some of Jordan's Jihadi-Salafi community. Indispensable for getting a full view of the situation of al-Maqdisi's influence, however, is his large number of writings throughout the period 1994–2009.

Framing Jordanian Opponents

Al-Maqdisi's preference for radical *daʿwa* at the expense of a *manhaj* of waging jihad only can clearly be discerned in his writings in the period 1994–2009, which show that he remained as radical as he had always been but also that he had become more concerned about the excesses of unbridled *takfīr* and jihad. Similarly, al-Maqdisi's writings

35 *Id.*, *Waqfāt maʿa Thamarāt al-Jihād: Dirāsa Manhajiyya wa-Naqdiyya*, www.muslm.net/vb/showthread.php?t=335818, 2009, 7, 93, respectively.

36 Al-Atharī, *Al-Sayf*; *id.*, *Al-Qawl*; Hānī al-Sibāʿī, *Bayān Markaz al-Maqrīzī bi-Sha'n al-Miḥḍār*, www.almaqreze.net/bayanat/arc1068.html (accessed 2 February 2009), 2009; Abū Baṣīr al-Ṭarṭūsī, *Al-Tafrīq bayna l-Tanāṣuḥ wa-l-Tarāju'*, www.abubaseer.bizland.com/articles.htm, 2009.

37 Muḥammad b. ʿAbdallāh al-Masʿarī, *Bayān min Abū* [sic] *Mājid Muḥammad b. ʿAbdallāh al-Masʿarī*, 'Al-Siyāsa al-Sharʿiyya' section, Shabakat Midād al-Suyūf, www.almedad.com/vb/forumdisplay.php?2 (accessed March 2009), 26 February 2009.

38 Sinā', *Risāla Maftūḥa ilā Faḍīlat al-Duktūr Abī Mājid al-Masʿarī min Ibnatikum al-Mukhallaṣa Sinā'*, 'Al-Siyāsa al-Sharʿiyya' section, Shabakat Midād al-Suyūf, post no. 1, www.almedad.com/vb/forumdisplay.php?2 (accessed 25 January 2010), 26 February 2009.

also show that his quietist Jihadi-Salafi *manhaj* had become ever more contested, expressed in his increasingly defensive treatises against his fellow-Jordanian detractors. All these different trends are reflected in the change in general focus of his writings, moving from a sharp critique against the Jordanian state and certain quietist Salafis more or less in the period 1994–9 to increasingly frequent rebukes of 'extremism in *takfīr*' after that period.

The State and Its Salafi Supporters

As we saw in Chapter 8, one of the aspects that al-Maqdisi's *da'wa* focussed on after he arrived in Jordan was providing a topical and practically relevant application of his general beliefs. This was expressed in his book on democracy before the Jordanian parliamentary elections in 1993, and this trend continued after he was imprisoned in 1994. A year after his incarceration, for example, al-Maqdisi wrote a treatise in which he presented a shortened version of his book *Millat Ibrahim* (1984).[39] His message in this text is similar to the one in the original version of the book – stressing the need for *barā'* of idols (which include 'legislation, laws and constitutions'[40]) as 'the most important mark of [the messengers'] *da'wa*'[41] – but his writing is more specific with regard to certain issues. He pays more attention, for instance, to why it is forbidden to help the authorities who base their rule on 'man-made laws', and goes into greater detail than in the original book to explain to what extent Muslims should disavow government jobs and what the judgement is about those who work for the regime.[42] Although this treatise does not offer insights that al-Maqdisi has not explained before elsewhere, it does give a more concrete application of his ideas on these issues, making it more useful.

Al-Maqdisi's practical application of more general ideas expressed before became even clearer in a summarised version of his book *Kashf al-Niqab 'an Shari'at al-Ghab*, which deals with the issue of 'un-Islamic' legislation and why this is a form of *kufr*, as we have seen. This time, he applies the shortened version of the book specifically to Jordan. While repeating his claim that modern-day laws in Muslim countries are comparable to the Mongol legislation condemned by Ibn Taymiyya,

[39] Abū Muḥammad al-Maqdisī, *Hidāyat al-Ḥalīm ilā Ahamm al-Muhimmāt fī Millat Ibrāhīm*, www.tawhed.ws/r?i=g6xpo32c, 1995.

[40] *Ibid.*, 6.

[41] *Ibid.*, 3.

[42] *Ibid.*, 15–16.

he singles out 'the Jordanian *yāsiq* of open unbelief (*al-kufr al-bawāḥ*) and clear polytheism (*al-shirk al-ṣurāḥ*)'.[43] The reason for this specific focus, al-Maqdisi explains, is 'to ease [*Millat Ibrahim*'s] understanding and its circulation among our *tawḥīd*-upholding brothers (*ikhwāninā l-muwaḥḥidīn*), that is in order to clarify the falsehood of these man-made laws (*hādhihi l-qawānīn al-waḍ'iyya*) [. . .] for the callers to *tawḥīd* (*du'āt al-tawḥīd*)'.[44]

Al-Maqdisi goes on to state that, whereas he used his original book to discuss Kuwait's 'man-made laws', he now wants to 'show the stupidity (*safāha*) of [Jordan's] man-made constitution'.[45] He does this by giving a detailed treatment of the Jordanian constitution, criticising it for its articles prescribing supposedly un-Islamic taxes, guaranteeing various types of freedom and equality al-Maqdisi considers incompatible with Islamic law[46], as well as the whole system of separation of powers it underpins[47]. His conclusion, not surprisingly, is no different from what he had said before about other Muslim regimes, whose rulers he accused of making themselves equal to God because of their 'un-Islamic' legislation: he calls the Jordanian king an idol (*ṭāghūt*) and condemns all those who actively uphold the king's regime legislatively, militarily or politically.[48]

Presumably because al-Maqdisi had settled down in Jordan permanently, he was now confronted with questions from youngsters that went deeper than the broad ideology he had described in his books. These questions touched on issues that al-Maqdisi had probably not encountered before since he had never become part of any society so much throughout his adult life. Thus, al-Maqdisi gave extensive advice to youngsters about issues such as co-operation with the Muslim Brotherhood in Jordan[49] and the Islamic legal status of the Jordanian army and police.[50] He also gave more detailed advice about elections while he was in prison. It was clear from his writings that he believed the regime and democracy to be expressions of *kufr* and *shirk*, but now al-Maqdisi dealt specifically with the question of people who run for parliament or vote in elections.[51]

43 *Id.*, *Mukhtaṣar*, 3.
44 *Ibid.*
45 *Ibid.*, 4.
46 *Ibid.*, 6–11.
47 *Ibid.*, 12–18.
48 *Ibid.*, 25–6.
49 *Id.*, *Ḥusn al-Rifāqa fī Ajwibat Su'ālāt Suwāqa*, www.tawhed.ws/t, 1996, 5–10.
50 *Id.*, *Al-Ishrāqa fī Su'ālāt Suwāqa*, www.tawhed.ws/t, n.d.
51 *Id.*, *Ḥukm al-Mushāraka fī l-Intikhābāt*, www.tawhed.ws/t (accessed 2 March 2010), 1997; *id.*, *Al-Jawāb al-Mufīd bi-anna l-Mushāraka fī l-Barlamān wa-ntikhābātihi Munāqaḍa li-l-Tawḥīd*, www.tawhed.ws/c?i=270, 1997. See also *id.*, *Majmū'*, 10–24.

Al-Maqdisi also gave advice to youngsters on what Islam teaches them about what they should do when caught by the authorities, fleeing from them when summoned to surrender to the police[52] and on helping the authorities in their struggle against drugs.[53]

Although al-Maqdisi did not just pay detailed attention to framing the Jordanian state and its institutions as forms of *kufr* between 1994 and 1999, it was the most important theme of his writings in this period. Another important subject he wrote about during this time was quietist Salafism in Jordan. As a movement that was doctrinally close to his own ideology but one that advocated staying away from political discourse entirely, quietist Salafism presented al-Maqdisi with a challenge. While it is not clear whether quietist Salafism draws its adherents from the same parts of society as Jihadi-Salafism[54], it is certain that Jordanian quietist scholars have been engaged in an ideological struggle with more radical and violent forms of Islam for years. They have produced many books and articles that reject the mixing of Islam and politics, denounce *takfīr* of the rulers of the Muslim world and often refer to Jihadi-Salafis as Takfīrīs or Khawārij.[55] Moreover, quietist Salafi scholars enjoy strong financial support from Saudi Arabia, giving them the financial power that Jihadi-Salafis clearly lack.[56] All of these factors make quietist Salafis a force to be reckoned with in the ideological battle for Jordanian religious seekers, forcing al-Maqdisi to deal with them.

To counter the ideological challenge presented by quietist Salafi scholars – and particularly the label of Khawārij that they apply to Jihadi-Salafis – al-Maqdisi started applying the term 'neo-Murjiʾa' (*Murjiʾat al-ʿaṣr*) to his quietist opponents. He claims that just as the original Murjiʾa used to postpone judgement regarding Muslims' sins, quietist Salafis today also refrain from applying *takfīr* to the Muslim world's rulers, even if the latter are guilty of major unbelief through their systematic 'un-Islamic' rule. Al-Maqdisi had already written a book about this subject in a general way several years before he came to Jordan[57],

52 *Id.*, *Lā Taḥzun inna llāh maʿanā*, www.tawhed.ws/t, 1994.
53 *Id.*, *Ḥukm al-Taʿāwun maʿa Anṣār al-Ṭawāghīt li-Muḥārabat Tujjār al-Mukhaddirāt*, www.tawhed.ws/r?i=hdfesdsw, 2008.
54 Interview with Brayzāt, Amman, 6 August 2008.
55 See Mūsā b. ʿAbdallāh Āl ʿAbd al-ʿAzīz (ed.), *Al-Maqālāt al-Manhajiyya fī 'Ḥizb al-Taḥrīr' wa-l-Jamāʿāt al-Takfīriyya*, Riyadh: Dār al-Buḥūth wa-l-Dirāsāt al-Muʿāṣira wa-l-Tarājim, 2006; Muḥammad Nāṣir al-Dīn al-Albānī, *Fitnat al-Takfīr*, www.mahaja.com/library/books/book/116, 1992; ʿAlī b. Ḥasan al-Ḥalabī, *Al-Tabṣīr bi-Qawāʿid al-Takfīr*, Cairo: Dār al-Manhaj, 2005.
56 Wiktorowicz, *Management*, 125–6.
57 Al-Maqdisī, *Imtāʿ*.

and even wrote a shortened version of this book when he was imprisoned, which he tried to spread among his cellmates[58], but he now started applying the term 'neo-Murji'a' to several Jordanian scholars. Specifically, he responded to a book written by the famous Jordanian quietist Salafi scholar Muhammad Nasir al-Din al-Albani and collected, introduced and edited by his student ʿAli b. Hasan al-Halabi.[59] Al-Maqdisi claims that this book attacks 'the religion of the Muslims, the *tawḥīd* of the lord of all being and the *daʿwa* of the prophets and messengers and describes its followers as Takfīrīs and [claims] they follow the religion of the Khawārij'[60]. The reason for this, al-Maqdisi writes, is that these 'neo-Murji'a', 'even though they disagree with the original Murji'a [...], agree with them on many requirements [...] They clearly say that *takfīr* is only allowed [if the culprit has] conviction and rejection in [his] heart (*al-iʿtiqād wa-l-juḥūd al-qalbī*).'[61]

Applying *takfīr* only when it is accompanied by clear evidence that a Muslim has stopped believing in his or her heart means in practice that very few people – let alone Muslim rulers – will be excommunicated since they would have to admit explicitly that they have stopped believing, which they will not do. This entails, al-Maqdisi explains, that quietist Salafi scholars such as al-Albani and al-Halabi, by setting unbelief in someone's heart as a condition for *takfīr*, essentially postpone judgement over Muslim rulers in a similar way to what the original Murji'a did. Al-Maqdisi spends much of the rest of his book rebutting al-Albani's and al-Halabi's claims and trying to show how the latter consistently twists and misquotes the words of other scholars to make his case.[62] This way, al-Maqdisi tries to show that while he does not consider them *kuffār* in principle[63], quietist Salafi scholars are certainly wrong, should not be followed in their way of thinking and incorrectly label Jihadi-Salafis – who do have the right ideas about *takfīr* – as Khawārij.[64]

58 *Id.*, *Kashf Shubhāt*, 1–2.

59 ʿAlī b. Ḥasan al-Ḥalabī (ed.), *Al-Taḥdhīr min Fitnat al-Ghulūw fī l-Takfīr, Bīr Nabālā*, Palestine: Sharikat al-Nūr li-Ṭibāʿa wa-l-Nashr wa-l-Tawzīʿ, 2002 [1996].

60 Al-Maqdisī, *Tabṣīr*, 11.

61 *Ibid.*, 23–4.

62 *Ibid.*, 13–103. For a discussion of how al-Maqdisī does this, see Wagemakers, 'Transformation', 99–101.

63 Al-Maqdisī, *Tabṣīr*, 174.

64 For more on 'Murji'a' and 'Khawārij' as labels, see Joas Wagemakers, '"Seceders" and "Postponers"? An Analysis of the "Khawarij" and "Murji'a" Labels in Polemical Debates between Quietist and Jihadi-Salafis', in: Jeevan Deol and Zaheer Kazmi (eds.), *Contextualizing Jihadi Thought*, London: Hurst & Co., 2012, 143–65.

Al-Maqdisi thus framed the Jordanian state and the quietist Salafi scholars who implicitly supported the regime by accepting the political status quo as *ṭawāghīt* and Murjiʾa, respectively. While maintaining this radical stance towards the state and quietist scholars after his release from prison in 1999, from that year onward a shift in al-Maqdisi's writings can be discerned. Although this shift was neither absolute nor immediate and also did not constitute a revision of earlier-held beliefs, it is nevertheless clear that al-Maqdisi's attention turned more towards a new group of ideological opponents from 1999 onward.

'Extremist' Jihadi-Salafis

As mentioned earlier, the 1990s saw a large-scale crackdown on Islamist groups in countries such as Egypt, Algeria and Jordan. While there are several reasons why this happened, one reason in Algeria was that some Islamists there applied *takfīr* to ever-larger groups of people, leading to increasing numbers of casualties among civilians.[65] It appears that the news of what was happening in Algeria and elsewhere spurred al-Maqdisi to write a forceful critique against 'extremism in *takfīr*', and in late 1998 or early 1999 he finished what is perhaps his most thorough study of all, *Al-Risala al-Thalathiniyya*. As we saw in Chapter 2, this book, written while al-Maqdisi was still in prison, is a sustained attack on 'extremism in *takfīr*' and presents both a comprehensive set of rules that should be followed before using excommunication against other Muslims as well as dozens of cases in which one should be careful not to apply *takfīr* too hastily.[66]

While he had not expressed his criticism of 'extremism in *takfīr*' as forcefully before *Al-Risala al-Thalathiniyya*, al-Maqdisi had earlier shown his concern about the way some radicals were using *takfīr*[67], especially if they attributed their ideas to him[68]. This was strictly a question of doctrine and was not necessarily related to al-Maqdisi's preference for *daʿwa* over jihad in Jordan in the 1990s and afterwards. As shown earlier, however, this was how some of al-Maqdisi's critics interpreted it after he expressed his criticism of certain jihadi practices,

65 See, for example, Mohammed M. Hafez, 'Armed Islamist Movements and Political Violence in Algeria', *Middle East Journal*, vol. 54, no. 4, 2000, 572–91; Quintan Wiktorowicz, 'Centrifugal Tendencies in the Algerian Civil War', *Arab Studies Quarterly*, vol. 23, no. 3, 2001, 65–82.

66 Al-Maqdisī, *Al-Risāla al-Thalāthīniyya*.

67 See, for example, *id.*, *Al-Ishrāqa*, 1–2.

68 See, for example, *id.*, *Hādhihi*, 1–2.

particularly those of al-Zarqawi. While the content of his writings dedicated to his criticism of jihadi practices[69] has been dealt with in Chapter 3, we must now look at how al-Maqdisi's quietist Jihadi-Salafi *manhaj* is the source from which this criticism sprang. In his only book dedicated to jihad, for example, al-Maqdisi mentions *daʿwa* throughout the text and points out that on many occasions, for example in confronting manifestations of supposedly sinful behaviour such as cinemas and sports clubs, jihad is unnecessary and illegitimate. Such sinful places, al-Maqdisi states, should be targets of *daʿwa* so as to bring the people engaged in activities there back to Islam. Moreover, though these people may be sinners, they do not deserve to be killed through armed attacks.[70]

Because jihad may not always be the right or even the legitimate *manhaj* to apply one's *ʿaqīda*, al-Maqdisi stresses the continued need for *daʿwa* among Jihadi-Salafis. This is further underlined by his belief that jihad cannot be effective without *daʿwa* and that the two must go together. Considering the two as complementary, al-Maqdisi believes that any jihad that discards *daʿwa* will quickly become nothing more than isolated attacks that do not bring about true change. He therefore states that jihadi groups and movements ignore *daʿwa* at their peril and advises them to make a constant and sustained effort at confronting their enemies by calling them to Islam. This way, people may actually adopt these beliefs, thus ensuring that the goals of jihad may be consolidated through the use of *daʿwa*, leading to a more positive and lasting effect in the form of a truly Islamic state.[71]

The question of consolidating the gains of jihad is clearly related to the issue of *qitāl al-nikāya* (fighting to hurt the enemy or its interests) and *qitāl al-tamkīn* (fighting to consolidate one's presence in a certain territory) that we saw in Chapter 3. These concepts and al-Maqdisi's strong preference for the latter should be seen through the prism of his quietist Jihadi-Salafi *manhaj* expressed in his tendency to favour radical *daʿwa* over fighting only. Whereas fighting opens up new territories to (the Jihadi-Salafi version of) Islam, *daʿwa* can ensure that their inhabitants also embrace this religion, thus effectively turning the area in question into part of the abode of Islam. Al-Maqdisi even goes so far as to say that

69 *Id.*, *Waqfāt*; *id.*, *Al-Zarqāwī*.
70 *Id.*, *Waqfāt*, 8. See also al-Batīrī, 'Abū', 5.
71 Al-Maqdisī, *Waqfāt*, 33–4, 80–91, 114, 129.

Muslims should preferably only abandon *da'wa* in favour of a jihad that transcends the level of *qitāl al-nikāya*. In other words, he deems *da'wa* so important that the possibility of staging hurtful but fruitless attacks – irrespective of their legitimacy – is no excuse to abandon it.[72] His remark in 2005 that 'every period has priorities and I do not want Iraq or some other place to become a crematory of the sons of this [Jihadi-Salafi] trend'[73] should thus be interpreted as rooted in al-Maqdisi's attempts to encourage radical youngsters to engage in useful *da'wa* instead of wasting their efforts on a jihad that is only going to get them killed.

Despite al-Maqdisi's consistent quietist Jihadi-Salafism throughout his life as a radical ideologue, his books critical of certain jihadi practices made some journalists claim that he had revised his earlier and supposedly more radical views, a process that some say started with *Al-Risala al-Thalathiniyya*.[74] As we have seen throughout this book, however, al-Maqdisi has always qualified his views on issues such as *takfīr* and *barā'*, and these nuances do not just go back a few years but can even be traced to his works in the mid-1980s. Moreover, al-Maqdisi has expressed clear support and even praise for *mujāhidūn* who he felt did have the chance to consolidate their gains earned through jihad, primarily in the Caucasus, thereby again showing that he did not reject jihad in principle.[75]

What ultimately has been and presumably will be much more damaging to al-Maqdisi's reputation than journalists' claims of revisionism are the accusations from fellow Jihadi-Salafis in Jordan that he has betrayed jihad and the *mujāhidūn*, particularly al-Zarqawi. It is therefore not surprising that al-Maqdisi made a sustained effort to disprove these accusations against him. While his quick re-arrest in 2005 did not offer him any chances to do so in that year, he did try to rebut his opponents' claims when he was released again in 2008. Interestingly, while his opponents conflated his criticism of 'extremism in *takfīr*' with his choice for *da'wa* and against jihad and countered the former with a critique of the latter,

[72] *Ibid.*, 55–6.

[73] *Abū Muḥammad al-Maqdisī. Al-Salafiyya al-Jihādiyya*, www.aljazeera.net/channel/archive/archive?ArchiveId=129776, 6 July 2005.

[74] *Al-Ghad*, 7 July 2005; *Al-Ḥayāt*, 13 March 2008; Muḥammad Abū Rummān, 'Al-Maqdisī. wa-stiḥqāq al-Taṣḥīḥ (3)', *Majallat al-'Aṣr*, 11 July 2005; Marwan Shehadeh, 'Weakening al-Qaeda: Literature Review Challenges its Authority', *Arab Insight*, vol. 2, no. 6, 2009, 27–8. See also Lahoud, 'Search', 209, 214.

[75] See, for example, Abū Muḥammad al-Maqdisī, *Risālat Nuṣra wa-'tizāz bi-Imārat wa-Mujāhidī l-Qawqāz*, www.tawhed.ws/r?i=07090901, 2009. See also *id.*, *Risālat Nuṣra li-l-Mujāhidīn fī l-Ṣūmāl wa-Kashf Shubhāt Mashāyikh al-Dajjāl*, www.tawhed.ws/r?i=05100905, 2009.

as we saw before, al-Maqdisi in effect did the exact opposite. He tried to refute those who accused him of betraying jihad and *mujāhidūn* by labelling them as 'extremists in *takfīr*' (*ghulāt al-takfīr*). This was not just ironic given the fact that al-Maqdisi himself had been accused of being a Takfīrī or a Khārijī by quietist Salafis but it probably also showed that he was rather unwilling to address what was perhaps the core issue: his quietist Jihadi-Salafi *manhaj* of radical *da'wa* in favour of jihad. Just as his opponents may have felt they had a strong line of attack with this issue, al-Maqdisi was possibly uncomfortable discussing his jihadi credentials and therefore chose to focus on the topic of *takfīr*, which he knew provided him with a stronger case.[76]

Thus, al-Maqdisi started his own defence by pointing out that, despite accusations to the contrary, he had never revised his views and never would, 'even if my entire family died one by one: my mother, my children, my wives and my brothers'.[77] Quickly after, he addressed the critics whose writings circulated in Jordan in the autumn of 2008. These critics' treatises, as we saw earlier, tried to rebut al-Maqdisi's and Nur al-Din Bayram's claims that they were extremists in *takfīr* but also focussed strongly on the two accusers' lack of jihad experience and supposed betrayal of jihad, the *mujāhidūn* and al-Zarqawi. The communiqué issued by al-Maqdisi and several of Jordan's most important Jihadi-Salafi scholars (including Bayram) to counter these critics' accusations does not focus on the latter charge, however. It simply accuses the writers of the anti-Maqdisi pamphlets of being 'extremists in *takfīr*'.[78] The communiqué – in what seems to be a reference to the accusations levelled at Bayram and al-Maqdisi himself – does state that al-Maqdisi's critics 'sometimes accuse some of the *muwaḥḥidīn* brothers of holding back from jihad, slandering the *mujāhidūn*, fleeing the fronts of jihad, calling the *mujāhidūn* Khawārij and Takfīrīs and fabricating things and lying about the *mujāhidūn*'.[79] This criticism is, however, simply dismissed by saying that 'all of these are false allegations (*da'āwā kādhiba*) for which there is no evidence'.[80]

[76] Wagemakers, 'Invoking', 15–16.

[77] Al-Maqdisī, *Al-Thabāt*, 5–6.

[78] *Barā'a min Fi'at al-Ḍalāl Ghulāt al-Takfīr wa-Mu'taqidātihim al-Zā'igha*, www.tawhed.ws/r?i=t555vdqa, 2008, 1–3. See also Abū Muḥammad al-Maqdisī, *Al-Ghulūw Yamḥaqu l-Barakāt wa-l-Rifq mā Kāna fī Shay' illā Zānahu*, www.tawhed.ws/r?i=24100923, 2009, 1–3.

[79] *Barā'a*, 1–2.

[80] *Ibid.*, 2.

In a later treatise, al-Maqdisi did become more specific by pointing out once again that his criticism of certain jihadi practices was not meant as criticism of jihad itself. The key question of his own unwillingness to wage jihad and his conscious choice for *daʿwa*, however, was again left unaddressed.[81] This does not mean al-Maqdisi is an opportunist or a hypocrite, however. On the contrary, his recent views on this issue are entirely consistent with his long-held beliefs, and his critics can indeed be accused of only reading his books superficially. They are nevertheless correct to point out that al-Maqdisi has not engaged in jihad himself, and his unwillingness to fully address this issue suggests that he realises this. Although al-Maqdisi has also written about topics entirely unrelated to this after his release in 1999, such as international law[82], American foreign policy[83] and Christianity[84], the contentious issue of his quietist Jihadi-Salafi *manhaj* has dominated much of the past decade. That his quietist Jihadi-Salafism is indeed the central factor explaining his (lack of) influence among Jordanian radicals is what we must turn to now.

A New Generation of Quietist Jihadi-Salafis?

Unlike in Saudi Arabia, about which al-Maqdisi simply wrote a (long-uncontested) book criticising its religious credentials without his personal presence playing any role, al-Maqdisi faced stiff ideological competition in Jordan throughout the period 1994–2009. This obviously came from the state's official rhetoric about the rulers' Islamic and Hashimite credentials but more clearly from quietist Salafis and Jihadi-Salafis critical of al-Maqdisi. Such attempts to frame concepts or situations (in this case the Jordanian state and aspects of Islam) in opposition to other framers have been described as counterframing, together making up what is referred to as a frame dispute. These can take place between different groups[85],

[81] Abū Muḥammad al-Maqdisī, *Al-Laghw fī l-Dīn*, www.tawhed.ws/r?i=05040950, 2009, 4–7.

[82] *Id.*, *Al-Sharʿiyya al-Dawliyya wa-Munāqaḍatuhā li-l-Sharīʿa al-Islāmiyya*, www.tawhed.ws/r?i=m2x63u00, 2002.

[83] *Id.*, *Mashrūʿ*.

[84] *Id.*, *Man Kāna Baytuhu min Zujāj fa-lā Yarmī ghayrahu bi-Ḥajar*, www.tawhed.ws/t, 2008; *id.*, *Ilā ʿAbd al-Ṣalīb*, www.tawhed.ws/r?i=0605091a, 2009.

[85] Anne W. Esacove, 'Dialogic Framing: The Framing/Counterframing of "Partial-Birth" Abortion', *Sociological Inquiry*, vol. 74, no. 1, 2004, 70–101; Deana A. Rohlinger, 'Framing the Abortion Debate: Organizational Resources, Media Strategies, and Movement-Countermovement Dynamics', *The Sociological Quarterly*, vol. 43, no. 4, 2002, 479–507.

in opposition to the state's framing[86] or within a single movement. In this section, I argue that – apart from contextual factors – al-Maqdisi's specific (lack of) ideological influence on Jordanian Jihadi-Salafis can be explained by analysing his efforts at counterframing his opponents' views.

One's position in frame disputes and one's success in counterframing others' portrayals of events, persons or situations depends on two factors: the frame itself and the framer. Regarding the former, we can see why al-Maqdisi's ideas did not appeal to all Jihadi-Salafis. Although al-Maqdisi's initial identification of the problem (the Jordanian state's 'un-Islamic' system and its quietist Salafi 'neo-Murji'a' supporters) can be presumed to have been broadly acceptable to them, his solution of engaging in *daʿwa* in Jordan and his frequent calls for this cannot. As we have seen, al-Maqdisi's stress on *daʿwa* in Jordan became a major source of contention among Jordanian radicals' preferring jihad abroad, and their support for his frame was in certain cases half-hearted at best. This ambiguity towards al-Maqdisi's views becomes even clearer when we look at his position as a framer with regard to the state and quietist Salafis as well as to 'extremist' Jihadi-Salafis.

Successful Counterframing

Wiktorowicz has distinguished two different processes in the establishment of 'sacred authority' in framing disputes: crediting and discrediting, which respectively refer to emphasising one's own credibility and attacking one's opponent's authority.[87] The former has to do with the framer's knowledge of his surroundings and the topics on which he or she speaks, his or her character (morality, honesty, reputation, etc.)[88] and the logic

[86] Roberta L. Coles, 'Peaceniks and Warmongers' Framing Fracas on the Home Front: Dominant and Opposition Discourse Interaction during the Persian Gulf Crisis', *The Sociological Quarterly*, vol. 39, no. 3, 1998, 369–91; Robert M. Entman and Andrew Rojecki, 'Freezing Out the Public: Elite and Media Framing of the U.S. Anti-Nuclear Movement', *Political Communication*, vol. 10, 1993, 155–73; David S. Meyer, 'Framing National Security: Elite Public Discourse on Nuclear Weapons During the Cold War', *Political Communication*, vol. 12, 1995, 173–92.

[87] Robert D. Benford, 'Frame Disputes within the Nuclear Disarmament Movement', *Social Forces*, vol. 71, no. 3, 1993, 677–701; Quintan Wiktorowicz, 'Framing Jihad: Intramovement Framing Contests and al-Qaeda's Struggle for Sacred Authority', *International Review of Social History*, vol. 49, supplement 12, 2004, 164.

[88] Marvin E. Goldberg and Jon Hartwick, 'The Effects of Advertiser Reputation and Extremity of Advertising Claim on Advertising Effectiveness', *Journal of Consumer Research*, vol. 17, 1990, 173–4.

and consistency of his or her arguments.[89] Discrediting, on the other hand, is often a process of vilification of one's opponents and of name-calling in order to decrease or diminish the other's credentials.[90]

Among some Jihadi-Salafis in Jordan, al-Maqdisi has clearly been successful in conveying his counterframe. Although this chapter has dealt with much criticism of al-Maqdisi, this should not obscure the fact that he does indeed have many followers and people who admire him. The preceding suggests that al-Maqdisi is thus considered by these young men to be a knowledgeable person with a strong character and logical and consistent arguments who is good at vilifying his opponents. My fieldwork in Jordan has shown that his followers do indeed feel this way about their spiritual leader. They admire him as a scholar, his ability to express difficult things in an easy way, his clear knowledge about the reality in which they live and his translation of old ideas into detailed answers to topical and practically relevant questions. Similarly, his character is also admired by his followers, who like his friendliness, his ability to remain steadfast in his ideas in the face of imprisonment and his willingness to speak truth to power. Finally, and unlike some others, al-Maqdisi's followers also believed in the internal logic and consistency of his writings and rejected any claims that he had revised or moderated his earlier views.[91]

Conversely, his vilification of the Jordanian state and quietist Salafis was also appreciated by his followers. Since his audience consisted of youngsters who rejected the regime, this was obvious regarding the Jordanian state. With respect to major quietist Salafi scholars, however, this

[89] *Ibid.*, 168. See also R. Glen Hass, 'Effects of Source Characteristics on Cognitive Responses and Persuasion', in: Richard E. Petty, Thomas M. Ostrom and Timothy C. Brock (eds.), *Cognitive Responses in Persuasion*, Hillsdale, NJ: Lawrence Erlbaum Associates, 1981, 141–72; Carl I. Hovland and Walter Weiss, 'The Influence of Source Credibility on Communication Effectiveness', *Public Opinion Quarterly*, vol. 15, 1951, 635–50.

[90] Wiktorowicz, 'Framing', 164–6. See also Dawn McCaffrey and Jennifer Keys, 'Competitive Framing Processes in the Abortion Debate: Polarization-Vilification, Frame Saving, and Frame Debunking', *The Sociological Quarterly*, vol. 41, no. 1, 2000, 41–61; Marsha L. Vanderford, 'Vilification and Social Movements: A Case Study of Pro-Life and Pro-Choice Rhetoric', *Quarterly Journal of Speech*, vol. 75, no. 1, 1989, 166–82.

[91] Interviews with Abū Haniyya, Amman, 9 August 2008 & 13 January 2009; ʿAbdallāh Abū Rummān, Amman, 15 January 2009; Muḥammad Abū Rummān, Amman, 11 August 2008; Marwān Shaḥāda, Amman, 13 January 2009; various students of al-Maqdisī, al-Ruṣayfa, 17 January 2009. See also Abū Muḥammad al-Maqdisī, *Su'āl ʿan ʿAdad min al-Umūr allatī Nasabat li-l-Shaykh Abī Muḥammad al-Maqdisī baʿda Liqāʾ Ṣaḥīfat al-Sabīl*, www.tawhed.ws/r?i=2506091a, n.d.; *id.*, *Su'āl ʿan Ishkālayn fī baʿḍ Kitābāt al-Shaykh Abī Muḥammad al-Maqdisī*, www.tawhed.ws/r?i=2506091c, n.d.

was less natural. As pointed out earlier, the label al-Maqdisi used for these scholars – 'neo-Murji'a' – is a strong one since it is partly correct, avoids the (in this case) clearly ridiculous label of *kuffār* but nevertheless puts a negative stamp on them and is too complicated to be easily refuted. Al-Maqdisi's ability to confront quietist Salafis on their own terms – with Salafi arguments and concepts – was mentioned as a major asset in his attacks on them, just like his forceful refutation of them in their ideological disputes.[92] The fact that his followers apparently accepted al-Maqdisi's quietist Jihadi-Salafi teachings perhaps suggests that they themselves had also been strongly influenced by quietist Salafism prior to encountering al-Maqdisi's teachings. While there need not be a strict correlation between support for al-Maqdisi and a quietist background, most of his students I spoke to did indeed have roots in quietist Salafism and told me that al-Maqdisi's closeness to quietism was instrumental in his being attractive to them.[93]

Failed Counterframing

Al-Maqdisi's quietist Jihadi-Salafi counterframing thus explains much of his influence on those who admire him. As we have seen, however, al-Maqdisi was subjected to a lot of criticism among some Jordanian Jihadi-Salafis. This can also be explained through his position as a quietist Jihadi-Salafi counterframer. With regard to his knowledge, it may be expected that some of al-Maqdisi's critics at least accept that he is a scholar. On the Midad al-Suyuf forum, however, al-Maqdisi is regularly dismissed as someone who lacks any scholarly credentials. One thread on this forum, for example, states that 'I have not found anyone with knowledge who follows al-Maqdisi'[94], while a participant cites a treatise stating:

> Shaykh al-Maqdisi is a scholar to the people of ignorance (*ahl al-jahāla*) that do not know what knowledge is [...] Anyone who says al-Maqdisi is a *mujāhid* is crazy (*aḥmaq*) and anyone who says that he is the theorist (*munaẓẓir*) of Jihadi-Salafism is stupid (*akhraq*) and so is anyone who claims al-Maqdisi is a *mujāhid* scholar.[95]

92 Interviews with Abū Haniyya, Amman, 13 January 2009; Rabāba, Amman, 12 January 2009; Usāma Shaḥāda, Amman, 12 January 2009; various students of al-Maqdisī, al-Ruṣayfa, 17 January 2009.

93 Interview with various students of al-Maqdisī, al-Ruṣayfa, 17 January 2009.

94 Hosam_one, *Lam Ajid Aḥadan Yatbaʿu l-Maqdisī dhū* [sic] *Baṣīra*, 'Al-Siyāsa al-Sharʿiyya' section, Shabakat Midād al-Suyūf, post no. 1, www.almedad.com/vb/showthread.php?t=11932 (accessed 7 January 2010), 23 March 2009.

95 Anas al-Shamrī, *Al-Shaykh al-Maqdisī ʿĀlim ʿinda Ahl al-Jahāla (bi-qalam: al-Gharīb al-Muhājir)/Wa-Ṭalaba l-Gharīb Munāẓarat al-Maqdisī*, 'Al-Siyāsa al-Sharʿiyya' section,

This remark, as well as those mentioned before in this chapter, make clear that it is not so much al-Maqdisi's 'bookish' knowledge that his critics want but his 'jihadi knowledge'. In this respect, he is regarded as ignorant, and this is clearly held against him, especially in light of his criticism of others, as we have seen. Moreover, the steadfast and upright character his admirers ascribe to him contrasts with the image of al-Maqdisi as a liar and an opportunist that his critics claim he is, particularly when contrasted with their hero al-Zarqawi, who was known for his toughness and perseverance.[96] Finally, at least some of his critics believe al-Maqdisi has revised his views or is at least inconsistent in his writings, damaging the logic of his arguments.[97]

It may be assumed that his critics agreed with his counterframes of the Jordanian state and quietist Salafis but they obviously disagreed with his attacks on certain radicals as Takfīrīs and Khawārij, particularly if those included al-Zarqawi and others who had spent time in prison with him but who later went abroad to wage jihad. These men's decision to go to Afghanistan or Iraq in order to fight instead of remaining in Jordan to engage in *daʿwa* essentially constituted a rejection of al-Maqdisi's quietist Jihadi-Salafi *manhaj*, perhaps suggesting that they, unlike al-Maqdisi's current followers, did not have a background in quietist Salafism. Although, again, there is not necessarily a connection between having no roots in quietist Salafism and waging jihad abroad, it is clear that none of his students who went off to wage jihad after being released in 1999 had quietist Salafi backgrounds.[98]

Thus, there is a clear distinction between al-Maqdisi's quietist Jihadi-Salafi *manhaj* of emphasising *daʿwa* and the more purely Jihadi-Salafi *manhaj* of fighting only. While adherents to both methods support jihad, those favouring the latter are perhaps more inclined to view jihad as a goal in itself, regardless of the outcome. This difference in *manhaj* not only once again illustrates al-Maqdisi's status as a quietist Jihadi-Salafi but also that this has both helped and prevented his influence in

Shabakat Midād al-Suyūf, post no. 1, www.almedad.com/vb/showthread.php?t=12654 (accessed 7 January 2010), 13 July 2009.

96 Ḥusayn, *Al-Zarqawī*, 98–9. Interviews with ʿAbdallāh Abū Rummān, Amman, 15 January 2009, and an Islamist who wished to remain anonymous, Amman, 10 January 2009.

97 See, for example, Fayṣal, *Maṭrūḥ li-l-Niqāsh: Ishkālāt fī Fikr al-Maqdisī*, 'Al-Radd ʿalā Firaq wa-l-Milal wa-l-Naḥl al-Ḍāla' section, Shabakat Midād al-Suyūf, post no. 1, www.almedad.com (link no longer available), n.d.

98 Ḥasan Abū Haniyya, Abū Muḥammad al-Maqdisī, e-mail messages to the author, 26 May 2009.

Jordan. Whereas among some in Saudi Arabia, and with regard to certain aspects of *al-walā' wa-l-barā'*, al-Maqdisi's adherence to quietist ideas, concepts and sources was an asset, as it was among some in Jordan, it clearly became a liability to others. This not only shows that al-Maqdisi's message is received differently in different contexts but it also makes clear that there are limits to what his quietist Jihadi-Salafism can achieve. Consequently, one could indeed speak of a new generation of quietist Jihadi-Salafis in Jordan (and elsewhere) who look to al-Maqdisi as their leader. His and their particular ideas and methods, however, are likely to remain contested and disputed for years to come.

Conclusion

This final chapter summarises the book's contents and draws conclusions about both al-Maqdisi's quietist Jihadi-Salafism and broader ones that can be drawn from the preceding chapters. As such, this chapter shows that despite the book's focus on one individual ideologue, a close and detailed look at his writings and his influence makes clear that there are wider implications.

This book deals with the Palestinian-Jordanian ideologue Abu Muhammad al-Maqdisi, whose guiding ideology – Salafism – plays an important role throughout the book. Salafis are referred to as such because they feel the duty to emulate the first three generations of Muslims – *al-salaf al-ṣāliḥ* – as meticulously and in as many spheres of life as possible. They believe this can be achieved by adhering closely to a strict *ʿaqīda* and its correct *manhaj* of application in various contexts. By emphasising *tawḥīd*, rejecting alleged *bidaʿ*, advocating a literal reading of the Qurʾān and *ḥadīth*s and dismissing *taqlīd* of the *madhāhib* in favour of *ijtihād* when no conclusive textual answer can be found, Salafis believe they can live up to the supposed ideal embodied by the *salaf*. This seemingly clear-cut ideological basis obscures huge disagreements between Salafis, however. To clarify these disagreements, three different types of Salafis have been distinguished: quietists or purists, who advocate a peaceful and non-political *manhaj* in society through education and *daʿwa*; politicos, who engage in political debates and sometimes even participate in elections; and jihadis, who combine Salafi ideology with the belief that jihad is not limited to waging war on non-Muslims but may also mean fighting against supposedly apostate Muslim rulers. This study argues that this distinction is a useful one but also that it obscures the differences within and the similarities between the individual categories, and that this does not just apply to *manhaj* but also to *ʿaqīda*. Al-Maqdisi is a prime example of this, combining a Jihadi-Salafi basic creed and method with a strong preference for sources, arguments, concepts and methodological applications rooted in the quietist tradition. This is why al-Maqdisi may be more accurately referred to as a 'quietist Jihadi-Salafi'.

Salafism has its roots in the general Sunni tendency to model their behaviour after the life of the Prophet Muhammad but particularly in a historical trend of Islamic scholars who relied on *ḥadīth*s of his and his companions' lives to discern rules at the expense of other devices used to build an Islamic jurisprudence. This trend is usually ascribed to scholars such as Ahmad b. Hanbal (780–855) and Taqi l-Din b. Taymiyya (1263–1328), whose ideas find expression in various Salafi groups and trends, perhaps most successfully in Wahhabism, the form of Salafism that emanated from the central-Arabian region of Najd through the writings of Muhammad b. ʿAbd al-Wahhab (1703–92). Because Wahhabism became the state version of Islam in Saudi Arabia, it found a solid base there, from which it was subsequently spread with the use of the country's oil wealth as a conservative alternative to the revolutionary rhetoric from Egypt's President Nasser and Iran's revolutionary regime in the 1960s and 1980s, respectively. Because of this and because of the many Arab workers who moved to the Gulf to work in its oil industry and adopted the conservative form of Islam applied there, the Wahhabi version of Salafism spread across the Arab world. At the same time, the decline of Nasser's pan-Arabism after the Arab losses to Israel in 1967 led to a greater susceptibility to religious alternatives, creating openings for (Wahhabi-)Salafism. Combined with the spread of radical ideas such as those of Sayyid Qutb (1906–66), this led to forms of radical Salafism expressed, for example, in the violent and anti-state groups in Egypt responsible for assassinating Egyptian President Anwar al-Sadat in 1981. The move of many of these radicals (as well as others) to Afghanistan after it was invaded by the Soviet Union in 1979 militarised them further and gave them important networks and contacts. These, together with other radicalising factors such as the rejection by society of 'Afghan Arabs' returning to their home countries and the American invasion of Iraq in 1990, would later be instrumental in founding al-Qaʿida and its offshoots in various countries. The influence of al-Maqdisi and his quietist Jihadi-Salafi ideology on the development of some of these radical trends form the subject of this study. In particular, it tries to answer the question of why al-Maqdisi has been influential on certain radical Islamists.

Against the backdrop just mentioned, Chapter 1 shows that al-Maqdisi, born in the West Bank in 1959 and raised in Kuwait, was influenced by friends and local Islamist preachers to become more religious and critical of Muslim rulers, and slowly drifted towards the quietist Jihadi-Salafism that characterised his writings later on. During the 1970s and early 1980s, he was influenced by the Muslim Brotherhood, the writings of Sayyid Qutb and the ideas of Juhayman al-ʿUtaybi (d. 1980) as well as by the books of major quietist Salafi scholars such as Muhammad Nasir al-Din al-Albani (d. 1999) and ʿAbd al-ʿAziz b. Baz (d. 1999). Because of this mix between criticism of Muslim rulers and Salafism, al-Maqdisi was initially attracted to the writings of Muhammad Surur, who combined a Brotherhood-inspired critique of politics with Salafi sources. After finally realising his dream of studying in Saudi Arabia, however, al-Maqdisi discovered the Wahhabi religious tradition and found that it was fully Salafi in nature but also offered him the tools with which to excommunicate the political rulers. With this intellectual and religious baggage, he moved to Afghanistan and Pakistan, where he discovered that – his support for jihad notwithstanding – he was really more suited to practise a radical *daʿwa*.

Al-Maqdisi's strong preference for Salafi writings rooted in a mostly quietist tradition such as the Saudi-Wahhabi one, as well as his tendency to favour *daʿwa* over jihad for himself and – in many situations – for others too, shows his quietist Jihadi-Salafism in both *ʿaqīda* and *manhaj*. To al-Maqdisi, as well as to many of his Wahhabi-Salafi role models, there was no contradiction between calling on others to wage jihad and staying away from the battlefields oneself. This attitude, rooted in his quietist Jihadi-Salafism, was not easily accepted by everyone, however, particularly in Jordan, where he moved in 1992 and still resides today.

Chapter 2 shows that the quietist Jihadi-Salafi ideology that al-Maqdisi gravitated towards during his life can also be discerned in his writings. Although he has not written much about his specific ideas on jihad, it is clear that he supports the classical form of jihad described extensively in writings on the *sharīʿa*, which was waged between the *dār al-Islām* or *dār al-īmān* on the one hand and the *dār al-ḥarb* or *dār al-kufr* on the other. He holds the same view of Osama bin Laden's global jihad, which involves attacking the Western supporters of the 'apostate' regimes in the Muslim world, primarily the United States, and it is therefore not surprising that al-Maqdisi praises al-Qaʿida and '9/11'. The most important dimension of jihad described in al-Maqdisi's writings, however, is the fighting aimed at overthrowing the *murtaddūn* ruling the Muslim world.

Though partly inspired by Qutb's political writings, al-Maqdisi's ideas on what constitutes *kufr* are very close to or even identical with what some quietist Salafi scholars believe. Al-Maqdisi states that God's *tawḥīd* – the basis of Islam as expressed by its confession of faith – should also be found in legislation. In practice, this means that in his view, all laws applied in a country should comply with the *sharīʿa*. If rulers occasionally deviate from Islamic law by mistake or because they were bribed to do so, this only makes them guilty of *kufr aṣghar*, which is no cause for excommunication. As soon as rulers apply 'man-made laws' as a result of *jaḥd* of the *sharīʿa*, the *iʿtiqād* that other laws are better or their *istiḥlāl* of non-*sharʿī* rules, however, or even go so far as to exchange Islamic law for a different legislative system altogether, this changes the situation. Al-Maqdisi considers such a conscious or far-reaching application of laws other than God's a violation of *tawḥīd* and therefore an act of *shirk* and *kufr akbar*. This reasoning, as well as the conclusion that *kufr akbar* justifies *takfīr* of the person guilty of it, is shared by some major quietist Salafi scholars. Al-Maqdisi further concludes that all Muslim rulers – whom he refers to as *ṭawāghīt* for their supposed assumption of divine legislative tasks – may be fought through jihad. While quietist Salafi scholars disagree with this conclusion, there is nevertheless a strong resemblance between al-Maqdisi's and their *ʿaqīda* with regard to the important topic of *kufr*.

Even though quietist Salafi scholars disagree with al-Maqdisi's *manhaj* towards politics and society, expressed in his calls for jihad against the Muslim rulers, Chapter 3 shows that they are still closer to him than the preceding suggests. That chapter points out that, while al-Maqdisi supports jihad in principle, he strongly emphasises the need for *daʿwa*, the preferred *manhaj* of quietist Salafis. His stress on the importance of *daʿwa* besides or even instead of jihad is also related to al-Maqdisi's belief that fighting should be well-organised and should not just be aimed at hurting the enemy and his interests (*qitāl al-nikāya*) but also at consolidating the gains of military victory by setting up a safe haven for 'true' Muslims or even an Islamic state (*qitāl al-tamkīn*). Since he considers *daʿwa* to be the ideal tool to bring people in conquered territories to the 'true' Islam, he believes jihad and *daʿwa* cannot be seen separately.

Al-Maqdisi's call against a sole reliance on jihad is also related to his belief that violence is not always necessary and should be used with the utmost care. He warns against the targeting of women and children, although he does believe that if they help *kuffār* against Muslims during a war, they do become combatants and thus legitimate targets. Unlike other Jihadi-Salafis such as Osama bin Laden, who try to expand the definition of combatants in order to justify and legitimise their attacks against civilians such as on '9/11', al-Maqdisi mostly tries to expand the number of targets of jihad within his own preferred struggle against the Muslim world's regimes. By describing those who help the rulers by supporting or defending their 'un-Islamic laws' as *anṣār al-ṭawāghīt*, al-Maqdisi effectively expands his definition of targets of jihad in such a way as to include military officers, customs officials and diplomats, among others. He is careful, however, to point out that not everyone working for 'infidel' regimes should be excommunicated since, he states, most people do not actively uphold or defend the rulers' legislative system and many do not even realise its sinful nature. This careful application of *takfīr* as well as his strong emphasis on the *manhaj* of *daʿwa*, once again show that al-Maqdisi is quite close to quietist Salafism.

Chapter 4 shows that al-Maqdisi also adhered to his quietist Jihadi-Salafism with regard to a specific issue such as the state of Saudi Arabia. That country is obviously not a regular Muslim country since its application of Wahhabism sets it apart in the eyes of many as a truly (or perhaps even overly) Islamic state. Throughout the twentieth century, there has nevertheless been Wahhabi opposition against the Saudi regime for its supposed failure to live up to its own religious credentials. Chapter 4 deals with one example of this: the *ṣaḥwa* (awakening). This revivalist trend has its roots in the 1960s, when foreign Muslim Brothers who had been expelled from their home countries, as well as like-minded Saudis, provided Wahhabism with some politically inspired zeal, thereby creating a much more politicised form of Wahhabism than had existed until then. This trend became especially apparent immediately after the Gulf War in 1990, when Saudi Arabia invited 500,000 U.S. soldiers to protect the kingdom from a potential attack by the Iraqi army, which had just occupied neighbouring Kuwait. This invitation created such anger among many that a popular protest movement came about that was mostly guided by *ṣaḥwa* scholars and activists.

Shortly before the anti-U.S. protests erupted in 1990, al-Maqdisi had written a book on Saudi Arabia in which he harshly criticised the country for its 'un-Islamic laws', its ties with 'infidel' organisations and states and its strong relations with the United States. Instead of praising the regime for its piety, al-Maqdisi claimed that Saudi Arabia was an 'infidel' state and – importantly – he did so on the basis of sources that were firmly rooted in Saudi-Wahhabi history and its quietist tradition, which once again underlined his quietist Jihadi-Salafi credentials. The book in which he wrote these things was spread among 'Afghan Arabs' in the late 1980s and early 1990s and was subsequently smuggled into the country by returning fighters. Although the book's harsh religious conclusions about Saudi Arabia went too far for the politically inspired *ṣaḥwa*, it did enter the country at a time of heightened criticism of the state and was spread among many of the state's critics. As such, it made a modest contribution to the general formation of anti-Saudi views in the early 1990s. Moreover, Saudi Arabia's focus on combatting the non-violent but seemingly dangerous *ṣaḥwa* allowed al-Maqdisi's book to spread across the country relatively easily, becoming well-known among more radical Saudi activists not yet mobilised against the state.

The importance of the spreading of al-Maqdisi's book about the kingdom throughout the 1990s becomes clear in Chapter 5, which shows that radicalised pietistic youngsters who gathered in dwellings such as Bayt Shubrā, a house in Riyadh, as well as the later al-Qaʿida on the Arabian Peninsula (QAP), were heavily influenced by al-Maqdisi. Some members of the group that met at Bayt Shubrā launched an attack in Riyadh in 1995, killing several people, and QAP was responsible for several deadly attacks in the period 2003–5. Most of these attacks were aimed at American targets, but one may nevertheless assume that they were supported by an underlying anti-Saudi discourse since the Americans had been invited in, or were at least allowed in, by the Saudi authorities, making attacks against U.S. targets implicitly anti-Saudi too. Chapter 5 shows that the principal use of al-Maqdisi's writings – particularly his book critical of the Saudi regime – to Bayt Shubrā and especially QAP was his providing them with a justification and a legitimisation of this anti-Saudi ideological undercurrent. Although this did not translate into many attacks against Saudi targets, it did lead to an anti-Saudi discourse that was clearly and to an important extent fuelled by al-Maqdisi's writings.

Whereas al-Maqdisi's radical conclusions about the Saudi state went too far for the *ṣaḥwa*, they were embraced by the visitors to Bayt Shubrā, and particularly QAP. This can be explained by their greater radicalism but also because al-Maqdisi's descriptions of what was wrong with the regime and what should be done about it conformed neatly with the situation in which both groups found themselves. Al-Maqdisi portrayed the Saudi state's 'un-Islamic laws' and ties with 'infidel' organisations and countries as a direct violation of *tawḥīd*, a concept of supreme importance in Wahhabi discourse, emphasised the state's controversial and widely resented relations with the United States and supported his arguments with detailed numbers and figures. Moreover, and perhaps most importantly, al-Maqdisi made extensive use of Saudi history and the Wahhabi religious tradition to accuse Saudi Arabia, effectively showing to his audience that – in his view – the kingdom could not even live up to its own standards and was indicted by its own history and tradition. Al-Maqdisi thus appealed to deeply felt and widely valued feelings and sensitivities, thereby expressing his quietist Jihadi-Salafism to an audience that was highly susceptible to it.

An explanation similar to the one mentioned in Chapter 5 can be given for al-Maqdisi's influence with regard to asking 'infidels' for help, especially against other Muslims during times of war, as is shown in Chapter 6. *Al-istiʿāna bi-l-kuffār* is an aspect of *al-walāʾ wa-l-barāʾ*, a concept dating back to pre-Islamic times but that is nowadays used to indicate that Muslims should be loyal to the 'in-group' of fellow-believers whilst shunning and even hating the 'out-group' of non-Muslims and, in the case of Wahhabism, even other 'apostate' Muslims. This concept has long been used in a quietist, a-political way, and the notion of *al-istiʿāna bi-l-kuffār* as applied by several nineteenth-century Wahhabi scholars with regard to the impermissibility of asking 'infidel' armies for help when fighting other Muslims had long lain dormant. During al-Maqdisi's stay in Saudi Arabia in the early 1980s, however, he rediscovered the concept of *al-walāʾ wa-l-barāʾ* (including *al-istiʿāna bi-l-kuffār*) and saw its value as a tool to indict present-day Muslim regimes for their military ties with contemporary 'infidel' states and armies.

Several years after the Gulf War in 1990, when the Saudi call for American help against Iraq looked similar to the nineteenth-century events that had caused some Wahhabi scholars to write about *al-istiʿāna bi-l-kuffār* in the first place, several Saudi scholars picked up the concept and seemingly started developing it from where al-Maqdisi had left it. The latter, though probably responsible for the concept's rediscovery, had made a rather shoddy case for the notion's revival. He did not explain the concept very clearly – for example, nor did he specify its different shades of meaning, and he even mixed up his references to nineteenth-century Saudi history. Other scholars corrected these mistakes, however, and each in his own way dealt with the different interpretations of the concept, adapting it to new situations and applying it to new conflicts probably by building on al-Maqdisi's seminal but imperfect earlier work. As mentioned, this can be explained by al-Maqdisi's extensive use of the very concepts that those Wahhabi scholars most probably influenced by him hold dear. His emphasis on *tawḥīd*, the broad range and applicability of *al-istiʿāna bi-l-kuffār*, its relevance for contemporary conflicts and al-Maqdisi's close adherence to Saudi and Wahhabi historical, cultural and religious tradition together explain his likely influence and also show once more his mix between quietist and Jihadi-Salafi sources and arguments.

Irrespective of al-Maqdisi's influence with regard to *al-istiʿāna bi-l-kuffār*, he has actually written much more about another dimension of *al-walāʾ wa-l-barāʾ*, namely its legislative interpretation, as becomes clear in Chapter 7. This dimension of *al-walāʾ wa-l-barāʾ* seems to be an original contribution to the concept by al-Maqdisi and is explained by viewing the following of 'man-made laws' as a form of worship and thus as a sinful form of *walāʾ*. This should be countered, according to al-Maqdisi, by *barāʾ* of the persons guilty of this misplaced loyalty, preferably in its highest form: jihad. This way, *al-walāʾ wa-l-barāʾ* is turned from an instrument to separate the Muslim 'in-group' from the non-Muslim (or, in some Wahhabi cases, 'apostate') 'out-group' into a revolutionary tool that focusses solely on dividing 'true' Muslims from their deviant fellow-believing rulers. As such, al-Maqdisi does not just partially but entirely abandons the core meaning of the concept it has had over the centuries. This is probably also the reason why very few radical scholars have clearly adopted this interpretation of *al-walāʾ wa-l-barāʾ*: although they shared his critical view of Muslim rulers and agreed that jihad against them was justified, using *al-walāʾ wa-l-barāʾ* to justify this may have seemed odd and disconnected from their religious narratives.

Al-Maqdisi's likely influence was greater with regard to *al-istiʿāna bi-l-kuffār* among non-Saudi scholars, which is also dealt with in Chapter 7. Their adoption of this concept after '9/11' and their application of it to new conflicts and situations but without referring to Saudi-Wahhabi tradition and its different shades of meaning suggests that this dimension of *al-walāʾ wa-l-barāʾ* has more or less become 'mainstream' among Jihadi-Salafi scholars. It also means that the links between their writings and al-Maqdisi's reintroduction of the concept have become more tenuous, but it should be kept in mind that it was al-Maqdisi's rediscovery that probably started the concept's revival in the first place, thus making these non-Saudi scholars distant heirs of al-Maqdisi's work. The reason for this lies not so much in al-Maqdisi's use of Saudi-Wahhabi sources, which were probably less important to these non-Saudi scholars, but possibly in the fact that al-Maqdisi was offering his audience a more Salafi version of something they agreed with anyway: *takfīr* of and jihad against Muslim rulers. Whereas al-Maqdisi's legislative version of *al-walāʾ wa-l-barāʾ* had to break with tradition to achieve this, and was probably less successful as a result, his rediscovery of *al-istiʿāna bi-l-kuffār* was firmly rooted in Wahhabism and, to a lesser extent, Islamic tradition in general. Thus, his adherence to the quietist Wahhabi tradition once again probably caused him to be influential among fellow Jihadi-Salafis.

As mentioned, al-Maqdisi moved to Jordan in 1992, a move that is dealt with in Chapter 8. Though Jordan is not like Saudi Arabia, it nevertheless has a strong tradition of mixing Islam with politics and/or society, both by its Hashimite royal family, who claim to be descendents of the Prophet Muhammad, and the well-established Jordanian Muslim Brotherhood as well as other Islamist groups, including quietist Salafis. When al-Maqdisi arrived in Jordan, he entered a country that was deeply mired in economic, political and regional crises. This caused a shock among many Jordanians, and some of them, particularly those who had returned from Afghanistan only to find that they were not really welcome anymore, started looking for more radical alternatives than what the regime, the Brotherhood opposition and quietist Salafis were offering. Many of these returnees did not have clear-cut ideological goals but had simply turned against the regime and wanted something new and Islamic to express their contention.

In this context, al-Maqdisi – who obviously did have clear ideas of his own – quickly became the leader of a group of mostly poor and uneducated youngsters. Despite the radical and sometimes violent tendencies of these youngsters, the group concentrated on learning and discussing and spreading al-Maqdisi's books to a wider audience of like-minded men. Although the group was sent to prison in 1994 because several of its members had tried to attack Israel, *daʿwa* was their most important activity in the early 1990s. This way, it became clear that al-Maqdisi adhered closely not only to the quietist *ʿaqīda* but also to its *manhaj*, instead of relying solely on jihad to express his contention. This can be explained by pointing to the ill-defined ideas al-Maqdisi's followers had and his willingness and ability to offer these 'religious seekers' both a radical Islamic alternative that nobody else was giving them and also his own quietist Jihadi-Salafi tendencies.

While al-Maqdisi's distinct creed and method were acceptable to the Jordanian radical youngsters looking for a religious alternative to what they knew in the early 1990s, the prison experience from 1994–9 – dealt with in Chapter 9 – clarified people's ideas and showed that the group was not as united on al-Maqdisi's *manhaj* as it seemed to be. This was most clearly expressed in the youngsters' attitude to al-Maqdisi's famous follower Abu Musʿab al-Zarqawi (1966–2006), whose toughness, confrontational nature and willingness to fight was more popular in prison than, and contrasted sharply with, al-Maqdisi's friendly, more 'bookish' and peaceful demeanour. These differences ultimately – and because of various other factors – culminated in the decision by some to leave Jordan in order to wage jihad when the group was released in 1999, instead of staying in Jordan to practise *daʿwa*, as al-Maqdisi wanted them to do. Al-Maqdisi's strong preference for the quietist *manhaj* was further expressed when he criticised *mujāhidūn* – and al-Zarqawi, who had become the leader of al-Qaʿida in Iraq, in particular – for their reckless use of violence and their targeting of other Muslims. This criticism seems to have created a lasting resentment among several Jordanian Jihadi-Salafis, who not only rejected al-Maqdisi's *manhaj* of radical *daʿwa* in Jordan at the expense of jihad abroad but whose admiration for al-Zarqawi was also hurt when the latter's erstwhile mentor criticised his former student even though he had never participated in any jihad himself. This subsequently caused much criticism to be aimed at al-Maqdisi, which was particularly scathing with regard to his choice of a quietist *manhaj* to express his radical beliefs instead of waging jihad.

In the meantime, al-Maqdisi had facilitated the growth of his group of followers, both inside and outside prison, by writing relevant and topical applications of his general beliefs against the Jordanian state, quietist Salafis and the people he considered extremists in *takfīr*. Although he was considered a powerful critic of the state and quietists, his writings on 'extremists in *takfīr*' sometimes missed the point. While al-Maqdisi's critics interpreted his criticism of excesses in jihad as demeaning to *mujāhidūn*, and especially al-Zarqawi, although it was not meant that way, al-Maqdisi seems to have been too quick to dismiss his own detractors as 'extremists in *takfīr*', even if they only (and rightly) pointed out that he had never participated in a jihad. In post-1994 Jordan, al-Maqdisi's quietist Jihadi-Salafism was therefore both an asset and a liability. While some Jordanian radicals – including many who had roots in quietist Salafism themselves – were attracted to his particular *ʿaqīda* and *manhaj*, others – especially those who had never had ties with quietist Salafism before – dismissed him as a *dāʿī* (caller) instead of a *mujāhid*. Al-Maqdisi's inability to convince his critics that he was part of Jihadi-Salafism too means that his position as the major scholar of the Jordanian Jihadi-Salafi community is contested to this day.

This study has described al-Maqdisi as a Jihadi-Salafi with a particular tendency towards quietist Salafism, expressed in his use of sources, arguments and concepts, as well as in his preferred method of applying this creed to society through *daʿwa*. While this tendency can be seen throughout his life and his writings, it has not always been successful. Whereas Jihadi-Salafis in Saudi-Arabia and many scholars writing about *al-walāʾ wa-l-barāʾ* liked al-Maqdisi's work, others, such as the *ṣaḥwa* and especially some Jihadi-Salafis in Jordan, were less enthusiastic or even openly hostile to him and his writings. This can probably be explained – respectively – by the radical views al-Maqdisi expresses in his books, which went too far for the non-violent and partly institutionalised *ṣaḥwa*, and the strongly doctrinal approach that al-Maqdisi takes in his writings, which was acceptable to Saudi scholars steeped in Wahhabism but unfulfilling to Jordanian action-oriented radicals. This is probably also the reason why al-Maqdisi's combination of support for jihad in principle but generally adhering to *daʿwa* was easily accepted in Saudi Arabia but not in Jordan. In the latter country, al-Maqdisi's critics essentially wanted him to be like ʿAbdallah ʿAzzam (1941–89), the Palestinian Muslim Brother who not only wrote extensively on jihad but, as soon as the opportunity arose, also moved to Afghanistan to organise and facilitate the armed struggle against the Soviets. This shows that al-Maqdisi's quietist Jihadi-Salafism, despite seemingly combining the 'best' of both worlds, clearly has limits.

Strongly related to the limits of al-Maqdisi's quietist Jihadi-Salafism is a conclusion that goes beyond his personal influence and challenges broader notions of the reasons behind Salafism's popularity. Authors such as Olivier Roy suggest that certain Muslims strive for deculturalised and deterritorialised forms of Islam so as to purify their religion from the cultural remnants of, for example, Egypt, Pakistan or Morocco.[1] Since Salafis strive to purify their beliefs from such cultural *bidaʿ*, this seems particularly relevant to Salafism. Indeed, the term 'Salafism' is sometimes also used simply to indicate 'purity' or 'authenticity' in Islam, quite apart from any doctrinal connotations.[2] This study on al-Maqdisi shows, however, that his close adherence to Wahhabi-Salafi teachings was sometimes considered alien by Jordanian Jihadi-Salafis, suggesting different Salafi 'cultures' after all. Similarly, ties between Salafi scholars and the regimes under which they live may create new religious traditions. Saudi scholars such as Ibn Baz, for example, have dedicated several fatwas to discussing the proper way to greet non-Muslims, probably because social relations

1 Roy, *Globalized*, 21–6.

2 Thomas Hegghammer, 'Jihadi-Salafis or Revolutionaries? On Religion and Politics in the Study of Militant Islamism', in: Roel Meijer (ed.), *Global Salafism: Islam's New Religious Movement*, London: Hurst & Co., 2009, 248–9.

between Muslims is one of the few areas that Saudi scholars have a say in. In Jordan, however, where Salafi scholars are not given social leeway in return for political loyalty, I found that issues such as greeting non-Muslims were not considered important at all. As such, the widely divergent reception of al-Maqdisi's writings shows that Salafism is not a universal 'one-size-fits-all' type of Islam that is easily accepted among like-minded Muslims everywhere. Although stripped of cultural baggage in theory, Salafism can acquire new 'cultural' traits and characteristics in practice, making it more acceptable to some than to others.

Moreover, while this study has focussed on an ideologue, it has become clear throughout the various chapters that the radicalisation that al-Maqdisi has influenced is not simply a matter of ideas and ideologies. As Chapters 4–9 have shown, al-Maqdisi's ideas sometimes coincided with changes in politics and society that made people susceptible to them, particularly in the early 1990s in Saudi Arabia and Jordan. This shows that radicalisation does not entail perfectly happy people waking up one day, reading a radical idea and suddenly going off to wage jihad, nor do people radicalise solely through circumstances around them. Instead, this study suggests that it is often a dynamic combination between them, and that neither can simply be dismissed, which is something many academics dealing with ideology have perhaps known for some[3] time but may not have seen in such detail. The successes and failures of al-Maqdisi's attempts to influence others therefore entail that the role of ideology in radicalisation be part of a reciprocal relation between ideas and their political and socio-economic surroundings, a cross-fertilisation of text and context, as it were.

Furthermore, this book also has implications for the study of dynamics in ideology. Movements and their actors are often masters at framing and reframing, appropriating and re-appropriating terms and concepts in different circumstances, while at all times making them seem the definitive interpretations of that particular notion. Throughout this study, we have also seen this phenomenon with regard to terms such as *kufr*, *ṭawāghīt* and, especially, *al-walāʾ wa-l-barāʾ*. The latter term's dynamic change from its pre-Islamic beginnings to its modern-day applications by scholars such as al-Maqdisi attests to the flexibility such ideological concepts have. At the same time, the trajectory of *al-walāʾ wa-l-barāʾ* also suggests that concepts can be overstretched and cannot simply be adapted to mean

[3] Michael Freeden, *Ideologies and Political Theory: A Conceptual Approach*, Oxford: Oxford University Press, 1996, 552.

everything. Al-Maqdisi's use of the term to portray 'man-made laws' as sinful loyalty that should be fought through jihad as the ultimate form of disavowal was hardly adopted by others, probably, as this study maintains, because this interpretation abandoned the concept's core meaning of establishing a strict dichotomy between Muslims and non-Muslims. This suggests that while ideologies and their concepts are flexible, there are limits to which they can be adjusted, and they should not lose their core meaning to avoid becoming altogether meaningless.

The Introduction to this study started by citing an American report that named al-Maqdisi as the most important jihadi scholar alive. Perhaps this is true. Al-Maqdisi has indeed been a major ideologue with regard to *al-walāʾ wa-l-barāʾ* as well as among Jihadi-Salafis in Saudi Arabia, Jordan and, although this is difficult to measure, probably beyond those countries. He has, moreover, been consistent in his beliefs and has not revised or renounced his radicalism, despite possibly being pressured to do so. It is therefore ironic that this man, at the height of the criticism levelled against him in Jordan and on jihad forums, was forced to cite a publication of mine[4], a newspaper article by Saudi journalist (and former follower of al-Maqdisi's) Mishari al-Dhayidi[5] and, indeed, the very American report cited earlier[6] to underline his jihadi credentials. Al-Maqdisi's need to cite these particular sources to assert his credibility is one indication of the ferocity of the debates surrounding his ideas, which, as this study has shown, are often closely related to his quietist Jihadi-Salafism. It also indicates that these debates are not about to end anytime soon.

4 Al-Maqdisī, *Al-Laghw*, 4.
5 *Ibid.*, 8.
6 *Ibid.*, 7.

Bibliography

A non-exhaustive list of sources cited in this study follows. The actual number of sources used is far greater, but for reasons of space, many have been omitted, and only the works referred to in the preceding pages are mentioned. For the same reason, the numerous references to articles in newspapers and weekly or monthly magazines, including Islamist periodicals, blogs, forum posts and *ḥadīth* collections, have also been omitted.

Interviews

During the course of my research, I have learned a lot from informal conversations I had with many people, as well as from prepared interviews with Islamists and others who wished to remain anonymous. These have been omitted from the following list, which only shows the semi-structured interviews of the people who allowed me to use their names.

Muhammad al-Masʿarī, London, 10 March 2008
Saʿd al-Faqīh, London, 11 March 2008
Camille al-Ṭawīl, London, 28 June 2008
Saʿūd al-Sarḥān, London, 2 July 2008
ʿAbdallāh al-ʿUtaybī, London, 1 August 2008
Fu'ād Ḥusayn, Amman, 5 August 2008
Fāris Brayzāt, Amman, 6 August 2008
Yāsir Abū Hilāla, 7 August 2008
Ḥusayn Abū Rummān, Amman, 11 August 2008
Muḥammad Abū Rummān, Amman, 11 August 2008
Shadi Hamid, Amman, 11 August 2008
ʿUrayb al-Rantāwī, Amman, 12 August 2008
Ḥāzim al-Amīn, Beirut, 14 August 2008
ʿUmar Bakrī Muḥammad, by telephone, 29 August 2008

Mishārī al-Dhāyidī, Riyadh, 8 November 2008
Fahad al-Shāfī, Riyadh, 11 November 2008
Yūsuf al-Daynī, Jeddah, 13 November 2008
ʿAbd al-ʿAzīz b. Faysal al-Rājiḥī, Riyadh, 18 November 2008
Muḥammad al-Dawsarī, Riyadh, 25 November 2008
ʿAbd al-Raḥmān b. ʿAbd al-ʿAzīz al-Hadlaq, Riyadh, 26 November 2008
Jamāl Khashuqjī, by telephone, 27 November 2008
Manṣūr al-Nuqaydān, by e-mail, 6 December 2008
Usāma Shaḥāda, Amman, 12 January 2009
Yūsuf Rabāba, Amman, 12 January 2009
Ḥasan Abū Haniyya, Amman, 9 August 2008, 13 January 2009
Abū Muḥammad al-Maqdisī, Amman, 13 January 2009
Marwān Shaḥāda, Amman, 13 January 2009
Samīḥ Khurays, Amman, 14 January 2009
ʿAbdallah Abū Rummān, 15 January 2009
ʿIkrima Gharāyba, Amman, 15 January 2009
Abū Muḥammad al-Maqdisī, Ruṣayfa, 17 January 2009
ʿAlī b. Ḥasan al-Ḥalabī, Amman, 19 January 2009

Websites and Forums

Please note that some of these websites may no longer be accessible.

http://dienoelislaam.web-log.nl
http://islamancient.com
http://otiby.net
http://prostrate4allah.wordpress.com
http://saaid.net
http://tawhid.over-blog.com
http://tibyan.wordpress.com/
http://www.abubaseer.bizland.com
http://www.al-amanh.net
http://www.alarabiya.net
http://www.alhramain.com
http://www.aljazeera.net
http://www.allaahuakbar.in
http://www.almaqreze.com
http://www.almaqreze.net
http://www.almedad.com
http://www.almuslimoon.com
http://www.alradnet.com
http://www.ansar-jihad.net
http://www.binbaz.org.sa
http://www.e-prism.org
http://www.jihadica.com
http://www.mahaja.com
http://www.memri.org

http://www.muslm.net
http://www.qaradawi.net
http://www.salafikurd.com
http://www.salafipublications.com
http://www.tawhed.ws
http://www.ummah.net

Media

Al-ʿArab al-Yawm
Al-ʿArabiyya
Al-Dustūr
Al-Ghad
Al-Ḥayāt
Al-Jazīra
Al-Quds al-ʿArabī
Al-Ra'y
Al-Riyāḍ
Al-Sabīl
Al-Sharq al-Awsaṭ
Al-Wasaṭ
Al-Waṭan
Jakarta Post
Majallat al-Anṣār
Majallat al-ʿAṣr
Majallat al-Jamāʿa
Middle East Times
Muʿaskar al-Battār
Qanāt al-Jazīra
Reuters
Ṣadā l-Jihād
Ṣawt al-Jihād
The Economist
The New York Times
The New Yorker

Books, Articles, Reports and Fatwas

Primary Sources (Arabic, English)

ʿAbd al-Mājid, ʿAbd al-Majīd, *Ṣafā' al-Manhaj Ahamm min Tabri'at al-Ashkhāṣ*, www.tawhed.ws/c?i=31, 2007.

Abū Iyād, *Kufr Can Occur without Believing in Kufr or Desiring it*, www.salafipublications.com, n.d.

———, *Kufr Can Occur without Istihlaal or Juhood*, www.salafipublications.com, n.d.

Aḥmad, Muḥammad, *Akhṭar Ṣuwar al-Muwālāt al-Kufriyya fī hādha l-ʿAṣr*, www.tawhed.ws/r?i=28021003, n.d.

Āl ʿAbd al-ʿAzīz, Mūsā b. ʿAbdallāh (ed.), *Al-Maqālāt al-Manhajiyya fī 'Ḥizb al-Taḥrīr' wa-l-Jamāʿāt al-Takfīriyya*, Riyadh: Dār al-Buḥūth wa-l-Dirāsāt al-Muʿāṣira wa-l-Tarājim, 2006.

Āl al-Shaykh, Muḥammad b. Ibrāhīm, *Risālat Taḥkīm al-Qawānīn*, www.tawhed.ws/a?a=ug3vtxq5, n.d.

Āl al-Shaykh, Sulaymān b. ʿAbdallāh, *Al-Dalāʾil fī Ḥukm Muwālāt Ahl al-Ishrāk*, www.tawhed.ws/r?i=bm4wz4za, n.d.

———, *Awthaq ʿUrā l-Īmān*, www.tawhed.ws/r?i=egtcjv74, n.d.

Albānī, Muḥammad Nāṣir al-Dīn al-, *Concerning Those who do not Rule by what Allaah SWT has Revealed*, www.salafipublications.com, n.d.

———, *Fitnat al-Takfīr*, www.mahaja.com/library/books/book/116, 1992.

ʿAlī, Ḥāmid b. ʿAbdallāh al-, *Ḥukm Iʿānat al-Kuffār ʿalā Ghazw al-Muslimīn wa-l-Duʿāʾ lahum bi-l-Naṣr*, www.tawhed.ws/r?i=mogga525, 2003.

Anṣārī, Abū l-Walīd al-, *Ḥukm man Aʿāna Kāfiran fī Qitāl al-Muslimīn*, www.tawhed.ws/r?i=16011022, n.d.

Arberry, A. J., *The Koran Interpreted*, New York: Touchstone, 1955.

Atharī, Abū Humām Bakr b. ʿAbd al-ʿAzīz al-, *Al-Hajr wa-l-Taqbīḥ li-Ahl al-Intikhābāt wa-l-Tarshīḥ*, www.tawhed.ws/r?i=0504094r, 2006.

———, *Al-Maṭar al-Wābil fī Ijābat al-Sāʾil*, www.tawhed.ws/c?i=31, 2008.

———, *Al-Qawl al-Narjisī bi-ʿAdālat Shaykhinā l-Maqdisī*, www.ansar-jihad.net, 2009.

———, *Al-Sayf al-Muhannad fī Munāṣirat Shaykhinā Abī Muḥammad*, www.muslm.net/vb/showthread.php?t=286633, 2008.

Azdī, Abū Jandal al- [Fāris al-Zahrānī], *Al-ʿAlāqāt al-Dawliyya fī l-Islām*, 3 vols., www.tawhed.ws/a?a=6sbcw2ch, n.d.

———, *Al-Āyāt wa-l-Aḥādīth al-Ghazīra ʿalā Kufr Quwwat Dirʿ al-Jazīra*, www.tawhed.ws/r?i=cnfiic2g, n.d.

———, *Al-Bāḥith ʿan Ḥukm Qatl Afrād wa-Ḍubbāt al-Mabāḥith*, www.tawhed.ws/r?i=oz5i7eed, 2002.

———, *Nuṣūṣ al-Fuqahāʾ ḥawla Aḥkām al-Ighāra wa-l-Tatarrus*, www.tawhed.ws/r?i=nw8coox6, 2003.

———, *Ḥiwār al-Minbar maʿa l-Shaykh Abī Jandal al-Azdī*, www.tawhed.ws/r?i=u2ysawtb, n.d.

ʿAzzam, ʿAbdallāh, *Al-Difāʿ ʿan Arāḍī l-Muslimīn Ahamm Furūḍ al-Aʿyān*, www.tawhed.ws/r?i=x483iubf, n.d.

Barāʾa min Fiʾat al-Ḍalāl Ghulāt al-Takfīr wa-Muʿtaqidātihim al-Zāʾigha, www.tawhed.ws/r?i=t555vdqa, 2008.

Bayram, Nūr al-Dīn, *Faṣl al-Maqāl fī Hajar Ahl al-Bidaʿ wa-l-Ḍalāl*, www.tawhed.ws/c?i=31, 2008.

Bāzmūl, Muḥammad b. ʿUmar, *Al-Radd ʿalā Kutub Mashbūha*, www.salafikurd.com/files/pdf/bazmwl/alrdalameltebraheem.pdf, n.d.

Bint ʿAbdallāh, Al-Jawhara, *Waqfa ḥawla l-Walāʾ wa-l-Barāʾ fī l-Islām*, Riyadh: Dār al-Ṣamīʿī li-l-Nashr wa-l-Tawzīʿ, 1991.

Burjis, ʿAbd al-Salām al-, *A Treatise on Ruling by other than What Allaah has Revealed*, www.salafipublications.com, n.d.

Daghlas, ʿAbd al-Hādī, *Majmūʿa min Khuṭab al-Akh al-Mujāhid ʿAbd al-Hādī Daghlas – Abū ʿUbayda Raḥimahu llāh*, www.tawhed.ws/c?i=31, 2009.

Dawsarī, Muʿjab al- [Ṣāliḥ b. Saʿd al-Ḥasan], *Āl Saʿūd fī Mīzān Ahl al-Sunna*, www.tawhed.ws/c?i=141, 2003.

———, *Tahdhīb al-Kawāshif al-Jaliyya fī Kufr al-Dawla al-Saʿūdiyya*, www.tawhed.ws/r?i=inbgjtyj, 2003.

Fahd, Nāṣir b. Ḥamd al-, *Al-Dawla al-ʿUthmāniyya wa-Mawqif Daʿwat al-Shaykh Muḥammad b. ʿAbd al-Wahhāb minhā*, www.tawhed.ws/r?i=zdntfe5u, n.d.

———, *Al-Tibyān fī Kufr Man Aʿāna l-Amrīkān*, 2 vols., www.tawhed.ws/r?i=3b5bzov8, 2001.

———, *Risāla fī Ḥukm Istikhdām Asliḥat al-Damār al-Shāmil ḍidda l-Kuffār*, www.tawhed.ws/r?i=2gi7siuw, 2003.

[Faqīh, Saʿd al-, Abū Qatāda al-Filasṭīnī and Muḥammad al-Masʿarī], *Al-Niẓām al-Saʿūdī fī Mīzān al-Islām*, www.tawhed.ws/r?i=geijr8cj, 1996.

[Faqīh, Saʿd al-], *The Rise and Evolution of the Modern Islamic Reform Movement in Saudi Arabia*, n.p., n.d.

Faraj, Muḥammad ʿAbd al-Salām, *Al-Farīḍa al-Ghāʾiba*, www.tawhed.ws/a?a=a5ieej5j, n.d.

Fawzān, Ṣāliḥ b. Fawzān al-, *Shaikh Salih al-Fawzaan on Those who Ought to Pronounce Takfir and Establish the Hadd Punishment*, www.salafipublications.com, n.d.

———, *Shaikh Salih al-Fawzan Explains his Words in Kitaab ut-Tawheed on Ruling by other than what Allaah has Revealed*, www.salafipublications.com, n.d.

———, *Why Manhaj?*, www.allaahuakbar.in/aqeedah/manhaj/index.htm, n.d.

Filasṭīnī, Abū Qatāda al-, *Bayna Manhajayn '9'*, www.tawhed.ws/r?i=u33n7szs, n.d.

———, *Juʾnat al-Muṭayyabīn*, www.tawhed.ws/a?a=aheed274, n.d.

Ḥalabī, ʿAlī b. Ḥasan al- (ed.), *Al-Taḥdhīr min Fitnat al-Ghulūw fī l-Takfīr*, Bīr Nabālā, Palestine: Sharikat al-Nūr li-Ṭibāʿa wa-l-Nashr wa-l-Tawzīʿ, 2002 [1996].

———, *Al-Tabṣīr bi-Qawāʿid al-Takfīr*, Cairo: Dār al-Manhaj, 2005.

Hāmī, Abū Qudāma Ṣāliḥ al-, *Al-Zarqāwī: Al-Jīl al-Thānī li-l-Qāʿida – Dirāsa Manhajiyya wa-Naqdiyya*, n.p., n.d.

———, *Fursān al-Farīḍa al-Ghāʾiba: Al-Zarqāwī wa-l-Jihād al-Afghān* [sic], n.p., 2007.

———, *Waqfāt maʿa Thamarāt al-Jihād: Dirāsa Manhajiyya wa-Naqdiyya*, www.muslm.net/vb/showthread.php?t=335818, 2009.

Ḥassān, ʿAbd al-Ḥakīm, *Al-Taḥdhīr min Muʿāwanat al-Kāfirīn*, www.tawhed.ws/r?i=op8hi6db, n.d.

Ḥawālī, Safar b. ʿAbd al-Raḥmān al-, *Kashf al-Ghumma ʿan ʿUlamāʾ al-Umma*, http://saaid.net/book/open.php?cat=84&book=540, 1991.

———, *Ẓāhirat al-Irjāʾ fī l-Fikr al-Islāmī*, 2 vols., www.tawhed.ws/a?a=q3vtcgx3, 1985/6.

Ibn ʿAbd al-ʿAzīz, ʿAbd al-Qādir, *Risālat al-ʿUmda fī Iʿdād al-ʿUdda li-l-Jihād fī Sabīl Allāh*, 2 vols., www.tawhed.ws/a?a=85ud42ss, n.d.

Ibn ʿAbd al-Wahhāb, Muḥammad, *Mufīd al-Mustafīd fī Kufr Tārik al-Tawḥīd*, www.tawhed.ws/a?a=3yk8awwg, n.d.

———, *Risāla fī Maʿnā l-Ṭāghūt*, www.tawhed.ws/r?i=8p4ty5r7, n.d.

Ibn ʿAtīq, Ḥamd b. ʿAlī, *Sabīl al-Najāt wa-l-Fikāk min Muwālāt al-Murtaddīn wa-l-Atrāk*, www.tawhed.ws/r?i=mndyzdnz, n.d.

Ibn Bāz, ʿAbd al-ʿAzīz, *Imaam Ibn Baaz on Tabdeel and Kufr Doona Kufr*, www.salafipublications.com, n.d.

———, *Imaam Ibn Baz on the Manhaj of Correcting the Rulers*, www.salafi publications.com, n.d.

Ibn Qāsim al-ʿĀṣimī al-Najdī al-Ḥanbalī, ʿAbd al-Raḥmān b. Muḥammad (ed.), *Al-Durar al-Saniyya fī l-Ajwiba al-Najdiyya*, 16 vols., n.p., 2004 [7th ed.].

Ibn Qayyim al-Jawziyya, Shams al-Dīn Abī ʿAbdallāh Muḥammad b. Abī Bakr, *Aḥkām Ahl al-Dhimma*, 3 vols., Dammam/Beirut: Ramādī li-l-Nashr/Dār Ibn Ḥazm, 1997.

Ibn Taymiyya, Aḥmad b. ʿAbd al-Ḥalīm b. ʿAbd al-Salām, *Iqtiḍāʾ al-Ṣirāṭ al-Mustaqīm li-Mukhālafat Aṣḥāb al-Jaḥīm*, ed. Nāṣir b. ʿAbd al-Karīm al-ʿAql, 2 vols., n.p.: Dār al-Ishbīliyā li-l-Nashr wa-l-Tawzīʿ, 1998.

Imaam al-Albani and his Argument against Ahl ut-Takfir, www.salafipubli cations.com, n.d.

Imaam Ibn Baaz on Imaan, Kufr, Irjaa and the Murjiʾah, www.salafipublications .com, n.d.

Kalīlī, Muḥammad al-, *Al-Radd ʿalā l-Kawāshif al-Jaliyya*, www.alradnet.com/ epaper/article.php?id_net=74, 2004.

Khuḍayr, ʿAlī b. Khuḍayr al-, *Al-Ḥadd al-Fāṣil bayna Muwālāt wa-Tawallī l-Kuffār* [sic], www.tawhed.ws/r?i=oioei4uv, n.d.

Madanī, Al-Yamān ʿAbd al-Karīm b. ʿĪsā al-, *Al-Ijtihād fī Ḥukm al-Farār min Sāḥāt al-Jihād*, www.almedad.com/vb, 2008.

Maqdisī, Abū Muḥammad al- and Hānī al-Sibāʿī, *Al-Rasāʾil al-Mutabādila bayna l-Shaykh Abī Muḥammad al-Maqdisī wa-l-Duktūr Hānī al-Sibāʿī Ḥafiẓahu llāh*, www.tawhed.ws/r?i=040309ga, 2009.

Maqdisī, Abū Muḥammad al-, *Abū Anas al-Shāmī: Baṭal Qaḍā Naḥbahu taḥta Liwāʾ al-Tawḥīd*, www.tawhed.ws/r?i=oqzxwd08, 2004.

———, *Al-Akh al-Mujāhid al-Baṭal: Jamāl Rifʿat Rāghib*, www.tawhed.ws/r?i= 5snqdcg2, 2004.

———, *Al-Dīmuqrāṭiyya Dīn*, www.tawhed.ws/t, n.d.

———, *Al-Ghulūw Yamḥaqu l-Barakāt wa-l-Rifq mā Kāna fī Shayʾ illā Zānahu*, www.tawhed.ws/r?i=24100923, 2009.

———, *Al-Ishrāqa fī Suʾālāt Suwāqa*, www.tawhed.ws/t, n.d.

———, *Al-Jawāb al-Mufīd bi-anna l-Mushāraka fī l-Barlamān wa-ntikhābātihi Munāqaḍa li-l-Tawḥīd*, www.tawhed.ws/c?i=270, 1997.

———, *Al-Kawāshif al-Jaliyya fī Kufr al-Dawla al-Saʿūdiyya*, www.tawhed.ws/t, 2000/1 [1989].

———, *Al-Laghw fī l-Dīn*, www.tawhed.ws/r?i=05040950, 2009.

———, *Al-Maṣābīḥ al-Munīra fī l-Radd ʿalā Asʾilat Ahl al-Jazīra*, www.tawhed .ws/t, n.d.

———, *Al-Mujāhidān al-Baṭalān: al-Sarḥān wa-Rafīquhu l-Suwayrikī*, www .tawhed.ws/r?i=8shfqfqc, n.d.

———, *Al-Nukat al-Lawāmiʿ fī Malḥūẓāt al-Jāmiʿ*, www.tawhed.ws/t, 1998.
———, *Al-Qawl al-Nafīs fī l-Taḥdhīr min Khadīʿat Iblīs*, www.tawhed.ws/t, n.d.
———, *Al-Risāla al-Thalāthīniyya fī l-Taḥdhīr min al-Ghulūw fī l-Takfīr*, www.tawhed.ws/t, 1998/9.
———, *Al-Sharʿiyya al-Dawliyya wa-Munāqaḍatuhā li-l-Sharīʿa al-Islāmiyya*, www.tawhed.ws/r?i=m2x63u00, 2002.
———, *Al-Thabāt al-Thabāt fī Zaman al-Tarājuʿāt*, www.tawhed.ws/r?i=khlovemo, 2008.
———, *Al-Zarqāwī: Āmāl wa-Ālām (Munāṣara wa-Munāṣaḥa)*, www.tawhed.ws/r?i=dtwiam56, 2004.
———, *Barāʾat al-Muwaḥḥidīn min ʿUhūd al-Ṭawāghīt wa-Amānahum li-l-Muḥāribīn*, www.tawhed.ws/r?i=70q3bqpe, 2002.
———, *Fī Dhikrā Maqtal Ikhwāninā l-Mujāhidīn al-Arbaʿa fī Kurdistān*, www.tawhed.ws/r?i=0526wy4i, 2002.
———, *Hādhihi ʿAqīdatunā*, www.tawhed.ws/t, 1997.
———, *Hidāyat al-Ḥalīm ilā Ahamm al-Muhimmāt fī Millat Ibrāhīm*, www.tawhed.ws/r?i=g6xp032c, 1995.
———, *Ḥiwār al-Shaykh Abī Muḥammad al-Maqdisī maʿa Majallat ʿal-ʿAṣrʾ*, www.tawhed.ws/r?i=j37307wg, n.d. [2002/3].
———, *Ḥukm al-Mushāraka fī l-Intikhābāt*, www.tawhed.ws/t, 1997.
———, *Ḥukm al-Taʿāwun maʿa Anṣār al-Ṭawāghīt li-Muḥārabat Tujjār al-Mukhaddirāt*, www.tawhed.ws/r?i=hdfesdsw, 2008.
———, *Ḥusn al-Rifāqa fī Ajwibat Suʾālāt Suwāqa*, www.tawhed.ws/t, 1996.
———, *Iʿdād al-Qāda al-Fawāris bi-Hajr Fasād al-Madāris*, www.tawhed.ws/t, 1986/7.
———, *Ilā ʿAbd al-Ṣalīb*, www.tawhed.ws/r?i=0605091a, 2009.
———, *Imtāʿ al-Naẓar fī Kashf Shubhāt Murjiʾat al-ʿAṣr*, www.tawhed.ws/t, 1999/2000 [1991/2].
———, *Irshād al-Mubtadī ilā Qawāʿid al-Saʿdī*, www.tawhed.ws/t, 2009 [1983].
———, *Kashf al-Lithām ʿamman Waṣafū bi-Tanẓīm ʿBayʿat al-Imāmʾ*, www.tawhed.ws/r?i=roqaokar, n.d.
———, *Kashf al-Niqāb ʿan Sharīʿat al-Ghāb*, www.tawhed.ws/t, 1988.
———, *Kashf Shubhāt al-Mujādilīn ʿan ʿAsākir al-Shirk wa-Anṣār al-Qawānīn*, www.tawhed.ws/t, 1999 [1995].
———, *Kawkaba min al-Abṭāl*, www.tawhed.ws/r?i=mmqsxjyc, 2004.
———, *Lā Taḥzun inna llāh maʿanā*, www.tawhed.ws/t, 1994.
———, *Liqāʾ min Khalf Quḍbān al-Murtaddīn ʿSana 1418ʾ*, www.tawhed.ws/r?i=j44n2568, 1997.
———, *Liqāʾ min Khalf Quḍbān Sijn Suwāqa ʿSana 1420ʾ*, www.tawhed.ws/r?i=dgxh8xf7, 1999.
———, *Majmūʿ Fatāwā l-Shaykh Abū* [sic] *Muḥammad al-Maqdisī*, n.p.: Muʾassasat Arḍ al-Ribāṭ al-Iʿlāmiyya, 2007.
———, *Man Kāna Baytuhu min Zujāj fa-lā Yarmī ghayrahu bi-Ḥajar*, www.tawhed.ws/t, 2008.
———, *Mashrūʿ al-Sharq al-Awsaṭ al-Kabīr*, www.tawhed.ws/t, 2004.
———, *Millat Ibrāhīm wa-Daʿwat al-Anbiyāʾ wa-l-Mursalīn wa-Asālīb al-Ṭughāt fī Tamyīʿihā wa-Ṣarf al-Duʿāt ʿanhā*, www.tawhed.ws/t, 1984.

———, *Mīzān al-Iʿtidāl fī Taqyīm Kitāb 'Al-Mawrid al-Zulāl'*, www.tawhed.ws/r?i=aerucf47, 2001 [1987].
———, *Mukhtaṣar 'Kashf al-Niqāb ʿan Sharīʿat al-Ghāb': Al-Dustūr al-Urdunnī*, www.tawhed.ws/t, 1996.
———, *Radd al-Shaykh al-Maqdisī ʿalā Su'ālāt Muntadā Midād al-Suyūf*, www.tawhed.ws/r?i=badmedad, 2009.
———, *Risāla ilā l-Shaykh al-Shuʿaybī*, www.tawhed.ws/r?i=6zipf6cz, 2001.
———, *Risāla li-l-Shaykh Abī Baṣīr*, www.tawhed.ws/r?i=qmof80po, n.d.
———, *Risālat Munāṣaḥa wa-Tadhkīr ilā Baʿḍ al-Ikhwa*, www.tawhed.ws/r?i=ggn087z3, 1992/3.
———, *Risālat Nuṣra li-l-Mujāhidīn fī l-Ṣūmāl wa-Kashf Shubhāt Mashāyikh al-Dajjāl*, www.tawhed.ws/r?i=05100905, 2009.
———, *Risālat Nuṣra wa-ʿtizāz bi-Imārat wa-Mujāhidī l-Qawqāz*, www.tawhed.ws/r?i=07090901, 2009.
———, *Risālatān fī Bidaʿ al-Masājid*, www.tawhed.ws/t, 2009 [1986/7].
———, *Sayfān wa-Nakhla*, www.tawhed.ws/r?i=16100901, 2009.
———, *Su'āl ʿan ʿAdad min al-Umūr allatī Nasabat li-l-Shaykh Abī Muḥammad al-Maqdisī baʿda Liqā' Ṣaḥīfat al-Sabīl*, www.tawhed.ws/r?i=2506091a, n.d.
———, *Su'āl ʿan Ishkālayn fī baʿḍ Kitābāt al-Shaykh Abī Muḥammad al-Maqdisī*, www.tawhed.ws/r?i=2506091c, n.d.
———, *Tabṣīr al-ʿUqalā' bi-Talbīsāt Ahl al-Tajahhum wa-l-Irjā'*, www.tawhed.ws/t, 1996.
———, *Wa-hal Afsada l-Dīn illā l-Mulūk wa-Aḥbār Sū' wa-Ruhbānahā*, www.tawhed.ws/r?i=4knoq5e8, n.d.
———, *Waqfāt maʿa Thamarāt al-Jihād*, www.tawhed.ws/t, 2004.
———, *Wujūb Nuṣrat al-Muslimīn fī Afghānistān*, www.tawhed.ws/t, 2001.
———, *Al-Tuḥfa al-Maqdisiyya fī Mukhtaṣar Tārīkh al-Naṣrāniyya: Bidāyatuhā wa-Muntahāhā*, www.tawhed.ws/t, 1997.
———, *As'ila ḥawla ftirā'āt Mansūba li-l-Shaykh Abī Muḥammad al-Maqdisī*, www.tawhed.ws/r?i=gerbashi, 2008.
Masʿarī, Muḥammad b. ʿAbdallāh al-, *Al-Adilla al-Qaṭʿiyya ʿalā ʿadam Sharʿiyyat al-Duwayla al-Saʿūdiyya*, London: Committee for the Defence of Legitimate Rights (CDLR), 2002 [6th ed.].
Mudhakkirat al-Naṣīḥa, www.alhramain.com/text/payan/alnseha/1.htm, 1992.
Muhājir, Abū l-Qāsim al-, *Al-Maqdisī Yataqaddamu li-l-Warā'*, www.muslm.net/vb/archive/index.php/t-315439.html, n.d.
Nājī, Abū Bakr, *Idārat al-Tawaḥḥush: Akhṭar Marḥala Satamurru bi-hā l-Umma*, www.tawhed.ws/a?a=chr30fzr, n.d.
Nine Rules Concerning Kufr and Takfir, www.salafipublications.com, n.d.
Quṭb, Sayyid, *Maʿālim fī l-Ṭarīq*, www.tawhed.ws/a?a=r5kf57rg, n.d.
———, *Milestones*, New Delhi: Islamic Book Service, 2005 [2001].
Rashīd, ʿAbdallāh b. Nāṣir al-, *Hashīm al-Tarājuʿāt*, www.tawhed.ws/r?i=j62533fz, 2003.
Rashūd al-Sabīʿī, ʿAbdallah b. Muḥammad b. Rāshid b. Muḥammad al-, *Al-Tatār wa-Āl Saʿūd*, www.tawhed.ws/c?i=141, 2004.
Rayyis, ʿAbd al-ʿAzīz b. Rayyis al-, *Tabdīd Kawāshif al-ʿAnīd fī Takfīrihi li-Dawlat al-Tawḥīd*, http://islamancient.com/books,item,39.html, 2003.

Rayyis, Ḥamd b. Rayyis al-, *Hādhihi ʿAqīdatunā*, www.tawhed.ws/r?i=6hggcba2, 2003.

Saʿwī, ʿAbdallāh b. Ibrāhīm al- [Abū Muḥammad al-Najdī], *Naqḍ Fatwā l-ʿUbaykān fī Ḥukm Muẓāharat al-Mushrikīn*, www.tawhed.ws/c?i=31, 2003.

Sayf, Abū ʿUmar al-, *Ḥukm Muẓāharat al-Amrīkān ʿalā l-Muslimīn: Al-ʿIrāq wa-Ghazw al-Ṣalīb; Durūs wa-Taʾammulāt*, www.tawhed.ws/r?i=22nwaxca, n.d.

Sayings of the Ulamaaʾ Regarding Ruling by Other than what Allaah has Revealed and the Two Types of Kufr, www.salafipublications.com, n.d.

Shāmī, Abū Anas al-, *Al-Shīʿa*, www.tawhed.ws/a?a=qecrkm8c, 2009.

Shāmī, Abū l-Qaʿqāʿ al-, *Kalimat ʿItāb*, n.p., 2008.

———, *Naʿam Kharajnā*, www.al-amanh.net/vb/showthread.php?p=7086, 2008.

Shaykh Abdul-Azeez ar-Raajihee on Secular Laws, Changing the Whole of the Deen, and the Accusation of Irjaaʾ against Ahl us-Sunnah, www.salafipublications.com, n.d.

Shuʿaybī, Ḥumūd b. ʿUqalāʾ al-, *Al-Qawl al-Mukhtār fī Ḥukm al-Istiʿāna bi-l-Kuffār*, www.tawhed.ws/r?i=ta476k4m, 1999.

———, *Ḥukm mā Jarā fī Amrīkā min Aḥdāth*, www.tawhed.ws/r?i=horoxyam, 2001.

Sibāʿī, Hānī al-, *Bayān Markaz al-Maqrīzī bi-Shaʾn al-Miḥḍār*, www.almaqreze.net/bayanat/arc1068.html.

Sūrī, Abū Muṣʿab al-, *Daʿwat al-Muqāwama al-Islāmiyya al-ʿĀlamiyya*, 2 vols., www.tawhed.ws/a?a=hqkfgsb2, 2004.

Ṭarṭūsī, Abū Baṣīr al-, *Al-Hijra. Masāʾil wa-Aḥkām*, www.tawhed.ws/r?i=6pydfou2, 2001.

———, *Al-Tafrīq bayna l-Tanāṣuḥ wa-l-Tarājuʿ*, www.abubaseer.bizland.com/articles.htm, 2009.

———, *Dhabban ʿan ʿIrḍ Akhīnā l-Shaykh Abī Muḥammad al-Maqdisī*, www.abubaseer.bizland.com/refutation.htm, 2002.

———, *Hādhihi ʿAqīdatunā wa-Hādhā lladhī Nadʿū ilayhi*, www.tawhed.ws/r?i=xdvnxy3h, 2002.

———, *Kabwat Fāris: Munāqashat Qawl Abī Muḥammad al-Maqdisī fī Masʾalat al-ʿUdhr bi-l-Jahl wa-l-Radd ʿalayhi*, www.abubaseer.bizland.com/articles.htm, 2000.

———, *Taṣwībātunā li-Risālat Hādhihi ʿAqīdatinā li-Akhīnā Abī Muḥammad al-Maqdisī*, www.abubaseer.bizland.com/refutation.htm, 2000.

The Creed of Imaam al-Albaanee on Takfir and Apostasy, www.salafipublications.com, 2000.

ʿUlwān, Sulaymān b. Nāṣir al-, *Ḥukm Badaʾa Ahl al-Kitāb bi-l-Salām*, www.tawhed.ws/r?i=6i37pcff, 2000.

———, *Ḥukm ʿIyādat Ahl al-Kitāb*, www.tawhed.ws/r?i=5s4kcqhs, 2000.

———, *Ḥukm Qatl Aṭfāl wa-Nisāʾ al-Kuffār fī l-ʿAmaliyyāt al-Istishhādiyya*, www.tawhed.ws/r?i=enpuzc42, 2001.

ʿUtaybī, Abū ʿUmar Usāma b. ʿAṭāyā b. ʿUthmān al-, *Al-Ḥujaj al-Qawiyya ʿalā Wujūb al-Difāʿ ʿan al-Dawla al-Saʿūdiyya*, http://otiby.net/book/open.php?cat=1&book=18, n.d.

ʿUtaybī, Juhaymān b. Sayf al-, *Rafʿ al-Iltibās ʿan Millat Man Jaʿalahu llāh Imāman li-l-Nās*, www.tawhed.ws/r?i=odutomsw, n.d.

———, *Risālat al-Imāra wa-l-Bayʿa wa-l-Ṭāʿa wa-Ḥukm Talbīs al-Ḥukkām ʿalā Ṭalabat al-ʿIlm wa-l-ʿĀmma*, www.tawhed.ws/r?i=fcchouzr, n.d.

ʿUtaybī, Sulṭān b. Bijād al-, *Risāla fī l-Ṭawāghīt*, www.tawhed.ws/r?i=5zo2qokh, 2002.

ʿUthaymīn, Muḥammad b. Ṣāliḥ al-, *Imaam Ibn Uthaymeen on the Manhaj of Correcting Rulers*, www.salafipublications.com, n.d.

———, *Shaikh Ibn Uthaimeen on Ibn Baz and Albani's Position on Ruling by Other than what Allaah has Revealed*, www.salafipublications.com, n.d.

———, *Shaikh Ibn ʿUthaymeen on al-Hukmu bi-ghayri maa Anzallallaah*, www.salafipublications.com, n.d.

———, *The Muslims* [sic] *Belief*, www.allaahuakbar.in/scholars/uthaymeen/muslims_belief.htm, n.d.

ʿUyayrī, Yūsuf al-, *Ḥaqīqat al-Ḥarb al-Ṣalībiyya al-Jadīda*, www.tawhed.ws/a?a=cfmaghvc, 2001.

Wansharīsī, Aḥmad b. Yaḥyā al-, *Asnā l-Matājir fī Bayān Aḥkām Man Ghalaba ʿalā Waṭanihi l-Naṣārā wa-lam Yuhājir wa-mā Yatarattabu ʿalayhi min al-ʿUqūbāt wa-l-Zawājir*, www.tawhed.ws/c?i=233, 1491.

Zarqāwī, Abū Muṣʿab al-, *Bayān wa-Tawḍīḥ limā Athārahu l-Shaykh al-Maqdisī fī Liqāʾihi maʿa Qanāt al-Jazīra*, n.p., n.d.

Ẓawāhirī, Ayman al-, *Al-Walāʾ wa-l-Barāʾ: ʿAqīda Manqūla wa-Wāqiʿ Mafqūd*, www.tawhed.ws/r?i=xotaoud8, 2002.

Secondary Sources (Arabic, Dutch, English, French, German)

Abdella Doumato, Eleanor, 'Manning the Barricades: Islam According to Saudi Arabia's School Texts', *Middle East Journal*, vol. 57, no. 2, 2003, 230–47.

Abdul Kazem, Ali, 'The Muslim Brotherhood: The Historic Background and the Ideological Origins', in: Jillian Schwedler (ed.), *Islamic Movements in Jordan* (transl. George A. Musleh), Amman: Al-Urdunn al-Jadid Research Center & Sindbad Publishing House, 1997, 13–43.

Abir, Mordechai, *Saudi Arabia: Government, Society and the Gulf Crisis*, London & New York: Routledge, 1993.

Abou Zahab, Mariam, and Olivier Roy, *Islamist Networks: The Afghan-Pakistan Connection* (transl. John King), New York: Columbia University Press, 2004.

Abu Jaber, Kamel S., and Schirin H. Fathi, 'The 1989 Jordanian Parliamentary Elections', *Orient: deutsche Zeitschrift für den modernen Orient*, vol. 31, no. 1, 1990, 76–86.

Abu Rumman, Mohammad Suliman [Muḥammad Abū Rummān], *The Muslim Brotherhood in the 2007 Jordanian Parliamentary Elections: A Passing 'Political Setback' or Diminished Popularity?*, Amman: Friedrich-Ebert-Stiftung, 2007.

Abū Rummān, Muḥammad, and Ḥasan Abū Haniyya, *'Al-Salafiyya al-Jihādiyya' fī l-Urdunn baʿda Maqtal al-Zarqāwī: Muqārabat al-Huwiyya, Azmat al-Qiyāda wa-Ḍabābiyyat al-Ruʾya*, Amman: Friedrich-Ebert-Stiftung, 2009.

Adams, Charles J., 'Mawdudi and the Islamic State', in: John L. Esposito (ed.), *Voices of Resurgent Islam*, New York & Oxford: Oxford University Press, 1983, 99–133.

Ahady, Anwar ul-Haq, 'Saudi Arabia, Iran and the Conflict in Afghanistan', in: William Malley (ed.), *Fundamentalism Reborn? Afghanistan and the Taliban*, New York: New York University Press, 117–34.

Algar, Hamid, *Wahhabism: A Critical Essay*, Oneonta, NY: Islamic Publications International, 2002.

Amawi, Abla M., 'The 1993 Elections in Jordan', *Arab Studies Quarterly*, vol. 16, no. 3, 1994, 15–27.

Amnesty International, *'Your Confessions are Ready for You to Sign': Detention and Torture of Political Suspects*, www.amnesty.org/en/library/info/MDE16/005/2006/en, 23 July 2006.

Ansary, Abdullah F., 'Combating Extremism: A Brief Overview of Saudi Arabia's Approach', *Middle East Policy*, vol. 15, no. 2, 2008, 111–42.

Ashour, Omar, 'Lions Tamed? An Inquiry into the Causes of De-Radicalization of Armed Islamist Movements: The Case of the Egyptian Islamic Group', *Middle East Journal*, vol. 61, no. 4, 2007, 596–625.

Atawneh, Muhammad Al, *Wahhābi Islam Facing the Challenges of Modernity: Dār al-Iftā in the Modern Saudi State*, Leiden: Brill, 2010.

Ayoob, Mohammed, and Hasan Kosebalaban (eds.), *Religion and Politics in Saudi Arabia: Wahhabism and the State*, Boulder, CO, & London: Lynne Rienner Publishers, 2009.

Babb, Sarah, '"A True American System of Finance": Frame Resonance in the U.S. Labor Movement, 1866 to 1886', *American Sociological Review*, vol. 61, 1996, 1033–52.

Baehr, Dirk, *Kontinuität und Wandel in der Ideologie des Jihadi-Salafismus: Eine ideentheoretische Analyse der Schriften von Abu Musʿab al-Suri, Abu Mohammed al-Maqdisi und Abu Bakr Naji*, Bonn: Bouvier, 2009.

Benford, Robert D., and David A. Snow, 'Framing Processes and Social Movements: An Overview and Assessment', *Annual Review of Sociology*, vol. 26, 2000, 611–39.

Benford, Robert D., 'Frame Disputes within the Nuclear Disarmament Movement', *Social Forces*, vol. 71, no. 3, 1993, 677–701.

Berbrier, Mitch, '"Half the Battle": Cultural Resonance, Framing Processes, and Ethnic Affectations in Contemporary White Separatist Rhetoric', *Social Problems*, vol. 45, no. 4, 1998, 431–50.

Bergen, Peter L., *Holy War Inc.: Inside The Secret World of Osama bin Laden*, New York: Free Press, 2002.

———, *The Osama bin Laden I Know: An Oral History of Al-Qaeda's Leader*, New York: Free Press, 2006.

Bernards, Monique, and John Nawas (eds.), *Patronate and Patronage in Early and Classical Islam*, Leiden & Boston: Brill, 2005.

Bligh, Alexander, *The Political Legacy of King Hussein*, Brighton & Portland: Sussex Academic Press, 2002.

Bonnefoy, Laurent, 'Salafism in Yemen: A "Saudisation"?', in: Madawi al-Rasheed (ed.), *Kingdom without Borders: Saudi Arabia's Political, Religious and Media Frontiers*, London: Hurst & Co., 2008, 245–62.

Bonner, Michael, *Jihad in Islamic History: Doctrines and Practice*, Princeton & Oxford: Princeton University Press, 2006.

Bonney, Richard, *Jihād from Qur'ān to bin Laden*, New York: Palgrave Macmillan, 2004.

Boukhars, Anouar, 'The Challenge of Terrorism and Religious Extremism in Jordan', *Strategic Insights*, vol. 5, no. 4, April 2006.

Boulby, Marion, *The Muslim Brotherhood and the Kings of Jordan, 1945–1993*, Atlanta, Georgia: Scholars Press, 1999.

Brachman, Jarret M., *Global Jihadism: Theory and Practice*, London & New York: Routledge, 2009.

Bradley, Jonathan R., 'Al Qaeda and the House of Saud: Eternal Enemies or Secret Bedfellows?' *Washington Quarterly*, vol. 28, no. 4, 2005, 139–152.

Brand, Laurie A., 'Palestinians and Jordanians: A Crisis of Identity', *Journal of Palestine Studies*, vol. 24, no. 4, 1995, 46–61.

Brisard, Jean-Charles, *Zarqawi: The New Face of Al-Qaeda*, New York: Other Press, 2005.

Brooke, Steven, 'The Preacher and the Jihadi', in: Hillel Fradkin, Husain Haqqani and Eric Brown (eds.), *Current Trends in Islamist Ideology*, Washington D.C.: Hudson Institute, 2006, vol. III, 52–66.

Burgat, François, and Muhammad Sbitli, 'Les Salafis au Yémen ou . . . la modernisation malgré tout', *Chroniques yéménites*, no. 10, 2002.

Burke, Jason, *Al-Qaeda: The True Story of Radical Islam*, London & New York: I. B. Tauris, 2003.

Champion, Daryl, *The Paradoxical Kingdom: Saudi Arabia and the Momentum of Reform*, New York: Columbia University Press, 2003.

Charillon, Frédéric, and Alain Mouftard, 'Jordanie: Les elections du 8 novembre 1993 et le processus de paix', *Monde Arabe Maghreb Machrek*, no. 144, 1994, 40–54.

Coles, Roberta L., 'Peaceniks and Warmongers' Framing Fracas on the Home Front: Dominant and Opposition Discourse Interaction during the Persian Gulf Crisis', *The Sociological Quarterly*, vol. 39, no. 3, 1998, 369–91.

Commins, David, *Islamic Reform: Politics and Social Change in Late Ottoman Syria*, New York & Oxford: Oxford University Press, 1990.

——, *The Wahhabi Mission and Saudi Arabia*, London & New York: I. B. Tauris, 2006.

Cook, David, *Martyrdom in Islam*, Cambridge: Cambridge University Press, 2007.

——, *Understanding Jihad*, Berkeley, Los Angeles & London: University of California Press, 2005.

Cook, Michael, 'On the Origins of Wahhābism', *Journal of the Royal Asiatic Society*, vol. 2, no. 2, 1992, 191–202.

Cordesman, Anthony H., and Nawaf Obaid, *Al-Qaeda in Saudi Arabia: Asymetric Threats and Islamist Extremists*, Washington, D.C.: Center for Strategic and International Studies, 2005.

Cornfield, Daniel B., and Bill Fletcher, 'Institutional Constraints on Social Movement "Frame Extension": Shifts in the Legislative Agenda of the American

Federation of Labor, 1881–1955', *Social Forces*, vol. 76, no. 4, 1998, 1305–21.
Dann, Uriel, *King Hussein and the Challenge of Arab Radicalism: Jordan, 1955–1967*, Oxford: Oxford University Press, 1989.
Davies, Scott, 'From Moral Duty to Cultural Rights: A Case Study of Political Framing in Education', *Sociology of Education*, vol. 72, 1999, 1–21.
Dekmejian, R. Hrair, 'The Rise of Political Islamism in Saudi Arabia', *Middle East Journal*, vol. 48, no. 4, 1994, 627–43.
______, 'The Liberal Impulse in Saudi Arabia', *Middle East Journal*, vol. 57, no. 3, 2003, 400–13.
DeLong-Bas, Natana J., *Wahhabi Islam: From Revival and Reform to Global Jihad*, Oxford: Oxford University Press, 2004.
Dialmy, Abdessamad, 'Le Terrorisme Islamiste au Maroc', *Social Compass*, vol. 52, no. 1, 2005, 67–82.
Dieterich, Renate, 'The Weakness of the Ruled is the Strength of the Ruler: The Role of the Opposition in Contemporary Jordan', in: George Joffé (ed.), *Jordan in Transition, 1990–2000*, London: Hurst & Co., 2002, 127–148.
Entman, Robert M., and Andrew Rojecki, 'Freezing Out the Public: Elite and Media Framing of the U.S. Anti-Nuclear Movement', *Political Communication*, vol. 10, 1993, 155–73.
Erickson Nepstad, Sharon, 'The Process of Cognitive Liberation: Cultural Synapses, Links, and Frame Contradictions in the U.S.-Central America Peace Movement', *Sociological Enquiry*, vol. 67, no. 4, November 1997, 470–87.
Esacove, Anne W., 'Dialogic Framing: The Framing/Counterframing of "Partial-Birth" Abortion', *Sociological Inquiry*, vol. 74, no. 1, 2004, 70–101.
Ess, Josef van, *Theologie und Gesellschaft im 2. und 3. Jahrhundert Hidschra*, 6 vols., Berlin & New York: Walter de Gruyter, 1992.
Fandy, Mamoun, 'CyberResistance: Saudi Opposition between Globalization and Localization', *Comparative Studies in Society and History*, vol. 41, no. 1, January 1999, 124–47.
______, *Saudi Arabia and the Politics of Dissent*, New York: Palgrave, 1999.
Farah, Tawfic E., 'Political Socialization of Palestinian Children in Kuwait', *Journal of Palestine Studies*, vol. 6, no. 4, July 1977, 90–102.
Fattah, Hala, '"Wahhabi" Influences, Salafi Responses: Shaikh Mahmud Shukri and the Iraqi Salafi Movement, 1745–1930', *Journal of Islamic Studies*, vol. 14, no. 2, 2003, 127–48.
Figueira, Daurius, *Salafi Jihadi Discourse of Sunni Islam in the 21st Century: The Discourse of Abu Muhammad al-Maqdisi and Anwar al-Awlaki*, Bloomington, IN: iUniverse, Inc., 2011.
Fine, Gary Allen, 'Public Narration and Group Culture: Discerning Discourse in Social Movements', in: Hank Johnston and Bert Klandermans (eds.), *Social Movements and Culture*, Minneapolis: University of Minnesota Press, 1995, 127–143.
Firestone, Reuven, *Jihad: The Origin of Holy War in Islam*, New York & Oxford: Oxford University Press, 1999.
Fox Piven, Francis, and Richard A. Cloward, *Poor People's Movements: Why They Succeed, How They Fail*, New York: Pantheon Books, 1977.

Freeden, Michael, *Ideologies and Political Theory: A Conceptual Approach*, Oxford: Oxford University Press, 1996.

Freij, Hanna Y., and Leonard C. Robinson, 'Liberalization, the Islamists, and the Stability of the Arab State: Jordan as a Case Study', *The Muslim World*, vol. 86, no. 1, 1996, 1–32.

Futrell, Robert, 'Framing Processes, Cognitive Liberation, and NIMBY Protest in the U.S. Chemical-Weapons Disposal Conflict', *Sociological Enquiry*, vol. 73, no. 3, August 2003, 359–386.

Gamson, William A., 'The Social Psychology of Collective Action', in: Aldon D. Morris and Carol McClurg Mueller (eds.), *Frontiers in Social Movement Theory*, New Haven & London: Yale University Press, 1992, 53–76.

———, *Talking Politics*, Cambridge: Cambridge University Press, 1992.

Gerges, Fawaz A., *The Far Enemy: Why Jihad Went Global*, Cambridge: Cambridge University Press, 2005.

Ghabra, Shafeeq, 'Palestinians in Kuwait: The Family and the Politics of Survival', *Journal of Palestine Studies*, vol. 17, no. 2, 1988, 62–83.

Gharāyba, Ibrāhīm al-, *Jamāʿat al-Ikhwān al-Muslimīn fī l-Urdunn, 1946–1996*, Amman: Markaz al-Urdunn al-Jadīd li-l-Dirāsāt & Dār Sindbād li-l-Nashr, 1997.

Goffman, Erving, *Frame Analysis: An Essay on the Organization of Experience*, New York: Harper & Row, 1974.

Goldberg, Marvin E., and Jon Hartwick, 'The Effects of Advertiser Reputation and Extremity of Advertising Claim on Advertising Effectiveness', *Journal of Consumer Research*, vol. 17, 1990, 172–179.

Goldziher, Ignaz, *Introduction to Islamic Theology and Law* (transl. Andras and Ruth Hamori), Princeton, NJ: Princeton University Press, 1981.

Gunaratna, Rohan, *Inside al Qaeda: Global Network of Terror*, New York: Berkley, 2003.

Habib, John S., *Ibn Saud's Warriors of Islam: The Ikhwan of Najd and Their Role in the Creation of the Saudi Kingdom, 1910–1930*, Leiden: Brill, 1978.

Haddad, Yvonne Y., 'Sayyid Qutb: Ideologue of Islamic Revival', in: John L. Esposito (ed.), *Voices of Resurgent Islam*, New York & Oxford: Oxford University Press, 1983, 67–98.

———, 'The Qur'anic Justification for an Islamic Revolution: The View of Sayyid Qutb', *Middle East Journal*, vol. 37, no. 1, 1983, 14–29.

Hafez, Mohammed M., and Quintan Wiktorowicz, 'Violence as Contention in the Egyptian Islamic Movement', in: Quintan Wiktorowicz (ed.), *Islamic Activism: A Social Movement Theory Approach*, Bloomington & Indianapolis: Indiana University Press, 2004, 61–88.

———, 'Armed Islamist Movements and Political Violence in Algeria', *Middle East Journal*, vol. 54, no. 4, 2000, 572–91.

———, 'From Marginalization to Massacres: A Political Process Explanation of GIA Violence in Algeria', in: Quintan Wiktorowicz (ed.), *Islamic Activism: A Social Movement Theory Approach*, Bloomington & Indianapolis: Indiana University Press, 2004, 37–60.

———, 'Jihad After Iraq: Lessons from the Arab Afghans Phenomenon', *CTC Sentinel*, vol. 1, no. 4, March 2008, 1–4.

———, *Suicide Bombers in Iraq: The Strategy and Ideology of Martyrdom*, Washington, D.C.: United States Institute of Peace Press, 2007.

Hamidullah, Muhammad, *The Muslim Conduct of State*, Lahore: Sh. Muhammad Ashraf, 1996 [1935].

Hardy, Roger, 'Ambivalent Ally: Saudi Arabia and the "War on Terror"', in: Madawi al-Rasheed (ed.), *Kingdom without Borders: Saudi Arabia's Political, Religious and Media Frontiers*, London: Hurst & Co., 2008, 99–112.

Harmsen, Egbert, *Islam, Civil Society and Social Work: Muslim Voluntary Welfare Associations in Jordan between Patronage and Empowerment*, Amsterdam: Amsterdam University Press, 2008.

Harnisch, Chris, and Quinn Mecham, 'Democratic Ideology in Islamist Opposition? The Muslim Brotherhood's "Civil State"', *Middle Eastern Studies*, vol. 45, no. 2, March 2009, 189–205.

Hasan, Noorhaidi, 'The Salafi Madrasas of Indonesia', in: Farish A. Noor, Yoginder Sikand and Martin van Bruinessen (eds.), *The Madrasa in Asia: Political Activism and Transnational Linkages*, Amsterdam: Amsterdam University Press, 2008, 247–274.

Hass, R. Glen, 'Effects of Source Characteristics on Cognitive Responses and Persuasion', in: Richard E. Petty, Thomas M. Ostrom and Timothy C. Brock (eds.), *Cognitive Responses in Persuasion*, Hillsdale, NJ: Lawrence Erlbaum Associates, 1981, 141–72.

Haykel, Bernard, 'On the Nature of Salafi Thought and Action', in: Roel Meijer (ed.), *Global Salafism: Islam's New Religious Movement*, London: Hurst & Co., 2009, 33–57.

———, 'The Salafis in Yemen at a Crossroads: an obituary of Shaykh Muqbil al-Wadiʿi of Dammaj (d. 1422/2001)', *Jemen Report*, no. 2, 2002, 28–37.

Hegghammer, Thomas, 'Abdallah Azzam, the Imam of Jihad', in: Gilles Kepel and Jean-Pierre Milelli (eds.), *Al Qaeda in its own Words* (transl. Pascale Ghazaleh), Cambridge, MA, & London: Harvard University Press, 2008 [2005], 81–101.

———, 'Combattants saoudiens en Irak: modes de radicalisation et de recrutement', *Cultures & Conflits*, no. 64, 2006, 111–27.

———, 'Deconstructing the Myth about al-Qaʿida and Khobar', *CTC Sentinel*, vol. 1, no. 3, 2008, 20–2.

———, 'Global Jihadism after the Iraq War', *Middle East Journal*, vol. 60, no. 1, 2006, 11–32.

———, 'Islamist Violence and Regime Stability in Saudi Arabia', *International Affairs*, vol. 84, no. 4, 2008, 701–715.

———, 'Jihad, Yes, but not Revolution: Explaining the Extraversion of Islamist Violence in Saudi Arabia', *British Journal of Middle Eastern Studies*, vol. 36, no. 3, 2009, 395–416.

———, 'Jihadi-Salafis or Revolutionaries? On Religion and Politics in the Study of Militant Islamism', in: Roel Meijer (ed.), *Global Salafism: Islam's New Religious Movement*, London: Hurst & Co., 2009, 244–66.

———, 'Terrorist Recruitment and Radicalization in Saudi Arabia', *Middle East Policy*, vol. 13, no. 4, 2006, 39–60.

———, 'Violence politique en Arabie Saoudite: Grandeur en décadence d'Al-Qaida dans la péninsule arabique', in: Bernard Rougier (ed.), *Qu'est-ce que le salafisme*, Paris: Presses Universitaires de France, 2008, 105–21.

———, *Jihad in Saudi Arabia: Violence and Pan-Islamism since 1979*, Cambridge: Cambridge University Press, 2010.

———, *The Failure of Jihad in Saudi Arabia*, Occasional Paper Series, Combating Terrorism Center at West Point, 25 February 2010.

Hegghammer, Thomas, and Stéphane Lacroix, 'Rejectionist Islamism in Saudi Arabia: The Story of Juhayman al-ʿUtaybi Revisited', *International Journal of Middle East Studies*, vol. 39, no. 1, 2007, 103–22.

Hodgson, Marshall G. S., *The Venture of Islam: Conscience and History in a World Civilization*, 3 vols., Chicago & London: University of Chicago Press, 1974.

Hourani, Albert, *Arabic Thought in the Liberal Age, 1798–1939*, Cambridge: Cambridge University Press, 1983 [1962].

Hovland, Carl I., and Walter Weiss, 'The Influence of Source Credibility on Communication Effectiveness', *Public Opinion Quarterly*, vol. 15, 1951, 635–50.

Human Rights Watch, *Arbitrary Arrest and Detention of ʿIsam al-ʿUtaibi (Abu Muhammad al-Maqdisi)*, www.hrw.org/en/news/2007/12/03/arbitrary-arrest-and-detention-isam-al-utaibi-abu-muhammad-al-maqdisi, 3 December 2007.

———, *Human Rights Watch Letter to Jordanian Prime Minister Dahabi on Detention of ʿIsam al-ʿUtaibi (Abu Muhammad al-Maqdisi)*, www.hrw.org/en/news/2007/12/03/human-rights-watch-letter-jordanian-prime-minister-dahabi-detention-isam-al-utaibi-a, 3 December 2007.

———, *Jordan: Clarifications on World Report Chapter 2008*, www.hrw.org/en/news/2008/02/18/jordan-clarifications-world-report-chapter-2008, 18 February 2008.

———, *Jordan: Rampant Beatings in Prisons Go Unpunished*, www.hrw.org/en/news/2007/08/29/jordan-rampant-beatings-prisons-go-unpunished, 30 August 2007.

Ḥusayn, Fuʾād, *Al-Zarqāwī: Al-Jīl al-Thānī li-l-Qāʿida*, Beirut: Dār al-Khayyāl, 2005.

Ḥusnī, Aḥmad, 'Qirāʾa fī Kitāb *Imtāʿ al-Naẓar fī Kashf Shubhāt Murjiʾat al-ʿAṣr*', *Al-Misbār*, no. 5, May 2007, 167–73.

Ibrahim, Raymond (ed. & transl.), *The Al Qaeda Reader*, New York: Doubleday, 2007.

Ibrahim, Saad Eddin, 'Anatomy of Egypt's Militant Islamic Groups: Methodological Note and Preliminary Findings', *International Journal of Middle East Studies*, vol. 12, 1980, 423–53.

———, 'Egypt's Islamic Activism in the 1980s', *Arab Studies Quarterly*, vol. 10, no. 2, April 1988, 632–57.

International Crisis Group, *Jordan's 9/11: Dealing with Jihadi Islamism*, ICG Middle East Report no. 47, Amman & Brussels, 23 November 2005.

———, *Saudi Arabia Backgrounder: Who Are the Islamists?* ICG Middle East Report no. 31, Amman, 21 September 2004.

———, *The Challenge of Political Reform: Jordanian Democratisation and Regional Instability*, Middle East Briefing, Amman & Brussels, 8 October 2003.

Izutsu, Toshihiko, *Ethico-Religious Concepts in the Qur'ān*, Montreal: McGill-Queen's University Press, 2002 [1959].

Jansen, Johannes J. G., *The Neglected Duty: The Creed of Sadat's Assassins and Islamic Resurgence in the Middle East*, New York & London: Macmillan, 1986.

Jasper, James M., and Jane D. Poulson, 'Recruiting Strangers and Friends: Moral Shocks and Social Networks in Animal Rights and Anti-Nuclear Protests', *Social Problems*, vol. 42, no. 4, 1995, 493–512.

Jolen, Judith, 'The Quest for Legitimacy: The Role of Islam in the State's Political Discourse in Egypt and Jordan (1979–1996)', unpublished PhD thesis, Catholic University, Nijmegen, 2003.

Jones, Toby Craig, 'Religious Revivalism and its Challenge to the Saudi Regime', in: Mohammed Ayoob and Hasan Kosebalaban (eds.), *Religion and Politics in Saudi Arabia: Wahhabism and the State*, Boulder, CO. & London: Lynne Rienner, 2009, 109–20.

Kazimi, Nibras, 'A Virulent Ideology in Mutation: Zarqawi Upstages Maqdisi', in: Hillel Fradkin, Husain Haqqani and Eric Brown (eds.), *Current Trends in Islamist Ideology*, Washington D.C.: Hudson Institute, 2005, vol. III, 59–73.

Kelsay, John, *Arguing the Just War in Islam*, Cambridge, MA, & London: Harvard University Press, 2007.

———, *Islam and War: A Study in Comparative Ethics*, Louisville, KY: Westminster/John Knox Press, 1993.

Kennedy, Hugh, *The Prophet and the Age of the Caliphates: The Islamic Near East from the Sixth to the Eleventh Century*, London & New York: Longman, 1986.

Kepel, Gilles, *Jihad: The Trail of Political Islam* (transl. Anthony F. Roberts), Cambridge, MA: Belknap/Harvard University Press, 2002 [2000].

———, *Muslim Extremism in Egypt: The Prophet and the Pharaoh* (transl. John Rothschild), Berkeley & Los Angeles: University of California Press, 2003 [1985].

———, *The War for Muslim Minds: Islam and the West* (transl. Pascale Ghazaleh), Cambridge, MA, & London: Belknap/Harvard University Press, 2004.

Khadduri, Majid, *The Islamic Law of Nations: Shaybānī's Siyar*, Baltimore: Johns Hopkins University Press, 1966.

———, *War and Peace in the Law of Islam*, Baltimore: Johns Hopkins University Press, 2008 [1955].

Khatab, Sayed, '*Hakimiyyah* and *Jahiliyyah* in the Thought of Sayyid Qutb', *Middle Eastern Studies*, vol. 38, no. 3, 2002, 145–70.

Khazendar, Sami Al-, *Jordan and the Palestine Question: The Role of Islamic and Left Forces in Foreign Policy-Making*, Reading, UK: Ithaca Press, 1997.

Kister, M.J., '"Do not Assimilate Yourselves . . . " *Lā Tashabbahū . . .* ', *Jerusalem Studies of Arabic and Islam*, vol. 12, 1989, 321–71.

Klandermans, Bert, 'Mobilization and Participation: Social-Psychological Expansions of Resource Mobilization Theory', *American Sociological Review*, vol. 49, October 1984, 583–600.

———, 'The Formation and Mobilization of Consensus', in: Bert Klandermans, Hanspeter Kriesi and Sidney Tarrow (eds.), *International Social Movement Research, Vol. I: From Structure to Action – Comparing Social Movement Research Across Cultures*, Greenwich, CT, & London: JAI Press, 1988, 175–96.

Knights, Michael, 'The Current State of al-Qaʿida in Saudi Arabia', *CTC Sentinel*, vol. 1, no. 10, 2008, 7–10.

Kohlberg, Etan, 'Barāʾa in Shīʿī Doctrine', *Jerusalem Studies in Arabic and Islam*, vol. 7, 1986, 139–75.

Kostiner, Joseph, 'On Instruments and Their Designers: The Ikhwan of Najd and the Emergence of the Saudi State', *Middle Eastern Studies*, vol. 21, no. 3, July 1985, 298–323.

Kraemer, Joel L., 'Apostates, Rebels and Brigands', *Israel Oriental Studies*, vol. 10, 1983, 34–73.

Krämer, Gudrun, 'Good Counsel to the King: The Islamist Opposition in Saudi Arabia, Jordan, and Morocco', in: Joseph Kostiner (ed.), *Middle East Monarchies: The Challenge of Modernity*, Boulder, CO: Lynne Rienner Publishers, 2000, 257–287.

Kruse, Hans, *Islamische Völkerrechtslehre*, Bochum: Studienverlag Brockmeyer, 1979.

Kubal, Timothy J., 'The Presentation of Political Self: Cultural Resonance and the Construction of Collective Action Frames', *The Sociological Quarterly*, vol. 39, no. 4, 1998, 539–54.

Lacroix, Stéphane, 'Ayman al-Zawahiri, Veteran of Jihad', in: Gilles Kepel and Jean-Pierre Milelli (eds.), *Al Qaeda in its Own Words* (transl. Pascale Ghazaleh), Cambridge, MA, & London: Belknap/Harvard University Press, 2008 [2005], 206–34.

———, 'Between Islamists and Liberals: Saudi Arabia's New Islamo-Liberal Reformists', *Middle East Journal*, vol. 58, no. 3, 2004, 345–65.

———, 'Between Revolution and Apoliticism: Nasir al-Din al-Albani and His Impact on the Shaping of Contemporary Salafism', in: Roel Meijer (ed.), *Global Salafism: Islam's New Religious Movement*, London: Hurst & Co., 2009, 58–80.

———, 'Islamo-Liberal Politics in Saudi Arabia', in: Paul Aarts and Gerd Nonneman (eds.), *Saudi Arabia in the Balance: Political Economy, Society, Foreign Affairs*, London: Hurst & Co., 2005, 35–56.

———, 'L'apport de Muhammad Nasir al-Din al-Albani au salafisme contemporain', in: Bernard Rougier (ed.), *Qu'est-ce que le salafisme?* Paris: Presses Universitaires de France, 2008, 45–64.

———, *Les islamistes saoudiens: une insurrection manquée*, Paris: Presses Universitaires de France, 2010.

Lahoud, Carine, 'Koweït: salafismes et rapports au pouvoir', in: Bernard Rougier (ed.), *Qu'est-ce que le salafisme?* Paris: Presses Universitaires de France, 2008, 123–35.

Lahoud, Nelly, 'In Search of Philosopher-Jihadis: Abu Muhammad al-Maqdisi's Jihadi Philosophy', *Totalitarian Movements and Political Religions*, vol. 10, no. 2, 2009, 205–20.

———, *The Jihadis' Path to Self-Destruction*, London: Hurst & Co., 2011.

Lamnaouer, Amel, and Romain Caillet, 'De l'usage du jihad: la fin d'une ère en Égypte? Les revisions idéologiques de Sayyid Imam', in: Hadjar Aouardji and Hélène Legeay (eds.), *L'Égypte dans l'année 2007*, Cairo: CEDEJ, 2008, 85–115.

Landau-Tasseron, Ella, 'Is *Jihād* Comparable to Just War? A Review Article', *Jerusalem Studies in Arabic and Islam*, vol. 34, 2008, 535–50.

———, 'Jihād', in: J. Dammen McAuliffe (ed.), *Encyclopaedia of the Qur'ān*, 6 vols., Leiden: Brill, 2003, vol. III, 35–43.

———, *'Non-Combatants' in Muslim Legal Thought*, Research Monographs on the Muslim World, Center on Islam, Democracy and the Future of the Muslim World, Washington, D.C.: Hudson Institute, Series 1, no. 1, 2008.

———, 'The "Cyclical Reform": A Study of the *Mujaddid* Tradition', *Studia Islamica*, vol. 70, 1989, 79–117.

Laoust, Henri, *La Biographie d'Ibn Taimīya d'apres Ibn Kathīr*, Damascus: Institut Français de Damas, 1943.

Lauzière, Henri, 'The Construction of *Salafiyya*: Reconsidering Salafism from the Perspective of Conceptual History', *International Journal of Middle East Studies*, vol. 42, no. 3, 2010, 369–89.

Lawrence, Bruce (ed.), *Messages to the World: The Statements of Osama bin Laden*, London & New York: Verso, 2005.

Lesch, Ann M., 'Palestinians in Kuwait', *Journal of Palestine Studies*, vol. 20, no. 4, 1991, 42–54.

Lewis, Bernard, 'Some Observations on the Significance of Heresy in the History of Islam', *Studia Islamica*, no. 1, 1953, 43–63.

Lia, Brynjar, '"Destructive Doctrinairians": Abu Musʿab al-Suri's Critique of the Salafis in the Jihadi Current', in: Roel Meijer (ed.), *Global Salafism: Islam's New Religious Movement*, London: Hurst & Co., 2009, 281–300.

———, 'Al-Qaida's Appeal: Understanding its Unique Selling Points', *Perspectives on Terrorism*, vol. 2, no. 8, 2008, 3–10.

———, 'Doctrines for Jihadi Terrorist Training', *Terrorism and Political Violence*, vol. 20, no. 4, 2008, 518–42.

———, *Architect of Global Jihad: The Life of al-Qaida Strategist Abu Musʿab Al-Suri*, London: Hurst & Co., 2007.

———, *The Society of the Muslim Brothers in Egypt: The Rise of an Islamic Mass Movement, 1928–1942*, Reading, UK: Ithaca/Garnet, 1998.

Little, Donald P., 'Did Ibn Taymiyya have a Screw Loose?' *Studia Islamica*, no. 41, 1975, 93–111.

Long, David E., *The Kingdom of Saudi Arabia*, Gainsville: University Press of Florida, 1997.

Lucas, Russell E., 'Deliberalization in Jordan', *Journal of Democracy*, vol. 14, no. 1, 2003, 137–44.

Madelung, Wilferd, 'Murdji'a', in: C. E. Bosworth, E. van Donzel, W. P. Heinrichs and Ch. Pellat (eds.), *Encyclopaedia of Islam: New Edition*, 12 vols. Leiden: Brill, 1993, vol. VII, 605–7.

Mandaville, Peter, *Global Political Islam*, London & New York: Routledge, 2007.

Massad, Joseph, *Colonial Effects: The Making of National Identity in Jordan*, New York: Columbia University Press, 2001.

Mayer, Ann Elizabeth, 'War and Peace in the Islamic Tradition and International Law', in: John Kelsay and James Turner Johnson (eds.), *Just War and Jihad: Historical and Theoretical Perspectives on War and Peace in Western and Islamic Traditions*, New York: Greenwood Press, 1991, 195–226.

McAdam, Doug, 'Culture and Social Movements', in: Enrique Laraña, Hank Johnston and Joseph R. Gusfield (eds.), *New Social Movements: From Ideology to Identity*, Philadelphia: Temple University Press, 1994, 36–57.

———, *Political Process and the Development of Black Insurgency, 1930–1970*, Chicago & London: University of Chicago Press, 1999 [1982].

McCaffrey, Dawn, and Jennifer Keys, 'Competitive Framing Processes in the Abortion Debate: Polarization-Vilification, Frame Saving, and Frame Debunking', *The Sociological Quarterly*, vol. 41, no. 1, 2000, 41–61.

McCallion, Michael J., and David R. Maines, 'The Liturgical Social Movement in the Vatican II Catholic Church', in: Michael Dobkowski and Isidor Walliman (eds.), *Research in Social Movements, Conflicts and Change*, vol. XXI, Stanford, Conn.: JAI Press, 1999, 125–149.

McCants, William (ed.), *The Militant Ideology Atlas*, Executive Report & Research Compendium, West Point, NY: Combating Terrorism Center, 2006.

Meijer, Roel (ed.), *Global Salafism: Islam's New Religious Movement*, London: Hurst & Co., 2009.

———, 'Che Guevara van de Jihad: Yusuf al-Ayiri', *ZemZem: Tijdschrift over het Midden-Oosten, Noord-Afrika en Islam*, vol. 3, no. 1, 2007, 126–31.

———, 'Commanding Right and Forbidding Wrong as a Principle of Social Action: The Case of the Egyptian al-Jamaʿa al-Islamiyya', in: Roel Meijer (ed.), *Global Salafism: Islam's New Religious Movement*, London: Hurst & Co., 2009, 189–220.

———, 'Re-reading al-Qaeda: Writings of Yusuf al-Ayiri', *ISIM Review*, no. 18, 2006, 16–17.

———, 'The "Cycle of Contention" and the Limits of Terrorism in Saudi Arabia', in: Paul Aarts and Gerd Nonneman (eds.), *Saudi Arabia in the Balance: Political Economy, Society, Foreign Affairs*, London: Hurst & Co., 2005, 271–311.

———, 'Yūsuf al-ʿUyairī and the Making of a Revolutionary Salafi Praxis', *Die Welt des Islams*, vol. 47, 2007, nos. 3–4, 422–59.

———, 'Yusuf al-Uyairi and the Transnationalisation of Saudi Jihadism', in: Madawi al-Rasheed (ed.), *Kingdom without Borders: Saudi Arabia's Political, Religious and Media Frontiers*, London: Hurst & Co., 2008, 221–43.

Metcalf, Barbara Daly, *Islamic Revival in British India: Deoband, 1860–1900*, Oxford: Oxford University Press, 2002 [1982].

Meyer, David S., 'Framing National Security: Elite Public Discourse on Nuclear Weapons During the Cold War', *Political Communication*, vol. 12, 1995, 173–92.

Milton-Edwards, Beverley, 'Climate of Change in Jordan's Islamist Movement', in: Abdel Salam Sidahmed and Anoushiravan Ehteshami (eds.), *Islamic Fundamentalism*, Boulder, CO: Westview Press, 1996, 123–42.

———, 'Façade Democracy and Jordan', *British Journal of Middle Eastern Studies*, vol. 20, no. 2, 1993, 191–203.

Mishal, Shaul, *West Bank-East Bank: The Palestinians in Jordan, 1949–1967*, New Haven & London: Yale University Press, 1979.
Mitchell, Richard P., *The Society of the Muslim Brothers*, Oxford: Oxford University Press, 1969.
Morabia, Alfred, *Le Gihad dans l'Islam médiéval*, Paris: Albin Michel, 1993.
Motzki, Harald, 'Ist die Gewaltanwendung von Muslimen gegen Nichtmuslime religiös bedingt? Eine Studie der klassischen ǧihād-Konzeptionen', in: Benjamin Jokisch, Ulrich Rebstock and Lawrence I. Conrad (eds.), *Fremde, Feinde und Kurioses: Innen- und Außenansichten unseres muslimischen Nachbarn*, Berlin & New York: Walter de Gruyter, 2009, 417–52.
______, *The Origins of Islamic Jurisprudence: Meccan Fiqh before the Classical Schools* (transl. Marion H. Katz), Leiden: Brill, 2002.
Mouline, Nabil, *Les clercs de l'islam: Autorité religieuse et pouvoir politique en Arabi Saoudite, XVIIIe – XXIe siècle*, Paris: Presses Universitaires de France, 2011.
Moussalli, Ahmad S., *Radical Islamic Fundamentalism: The Ideological and Political Discourse of Sayyid Qutb*, Beirut: American University of Beirut, 1992.
Napoleoni, Loretta, *Insurgent Iraq: Al Zarqawi and the New Generation*, New York: Seven Stories Press, 2005.
Nevo, Joseph, 'Religion and National Identity in Saudi Arabia', *Middle Eastern Studies*, vol. 34, no. 3, July 1998, 34–53.
Niblock, Tim, *Saudi Arabia: Power, Legitimacy and Survival*, London & New York: Routledge, 2006.
Noth, Albrecht, 'Von der medinensischen "Umma" zu einer muslimischen Ökumene', in: Albrecht Noth and Jürgen Paul (eds.), *Der islamische Orient: Grundzüge seiner Geschichte*, Würzburg: Ergon, 1998, 81–134.
Okruhlik, Gwenn, 'Making Conversation Permissible: Islamism and Reform in Saudi Arabia', in: Quintan Wiktorowicz (ed.), *Islamic Activism: A Social Movement Theory Approach*, Bloomington & Indianapolis: Indiana University Press, 2004, 250–69.
Peters, Rudolph, and Gert J. J. de Vries, 'Apostasy in Islam', *Die Welt des Islams*, vol. 17, no. 1, 1977, 1–25.
Peters, Rudolph, *Islam and Colonialism*, The Hague: Mouton, 1979.
______, *Jihad in Classical and Modern Islam: A Reader*, Princeton: Markus Wiener Publishers, 1996.
Pew Research Center for the People and the Press, *Views of a Changing World: How Global Publics View War in Iraq, Democracy, Islam and Governance, Globalization*, Pew Global Attitudes Project, http://pewglobal.org/reports/pdf/185.pdf, June 2003.
Piscatori, James (ed.), *Islamic Fundamentalisms and the Gulf Crisis*, Chicago: The American Academy of Arts and Sciences, 1991.
______, 'Religion and Realpolitik: Islamic Responses to the Gulf War', in: James Piscatori (ed.), *Islamic Fundamentalisms and the Gulf Crisis*, Chicago: The American Academy of Arts and Sciences, 1991, 1–27.
Prucha, Nico, *Die Stimme des Dschihad – 'Ṣawt al-Jihād': al-Qā'idas erstes Online-Magazin*, Hamburg: Verlag Dr. Kovač, 2010.

———, 'Jihad on the Internet – The Anomalous Case of Abu Jandal al-Azdi', *Journal for Intelligence, Propaganda and Security Studies*, vol. 2, no. 2, 2007, 42–7.

Rabbani, Mouin, 'The Making of a Palestinian Islamist Leader: An Interview with Khalid Mishal: Part I', *Journal of Palestine Studies*, vol. 37, no. 3, 2008, 59–73.

Radi, Lamia, 'Les Palestiniens du Koweit en Jordanie', *Monde Arabe Maghreb Machrek*, no. 144, April-June 1994, 55–65.

Rasheed, Madawi al-, 'God, the King and the Nation: Political Rhetoric in Saudi Arabia in the 1990s', *Middle East Journal*, vol. 50, no. 3, 1996, 359–71.

———, 'The Local and the Global in Saudi Salafi-Jihadi Discourse', in: Roel Meijer (ed.), *Global Salafism: Islam's New Religious Movement*, London: Hurst & Co., 2009, 301–20.

———, 'The Local and the Global in Saudi Salafism', *ISIM Review*, no. 21, 2008, 8–9.

———, *A History of Saudi Arabia*, Cambridge: Cambridge University Press, 2002.

———, *Contesting the Saudi State: Islamic Voices from a New Generation*, Cambridge: Cambridge University Press, 2007.

Rath, Kathrine, 'The Process of Democratization in Jordan', *Middle Eastern Studies*, vol. 30, no. 3, 1994, 530–57.

Riedel, Bruce, and Bilal Y. Saab, 'Al Qaeda's Third Front: Saudi Arabia', *Washington Quarterly*, vol. 31, no. 2, 2008, 33–46.

Robins, Philip, *A History of Jordan*, Cambridge: Cambridge University Press, 2004.

Robinson, Glenn E., 'Can Islamists be Democrats? The Case of Jordan', *Middle East Journal*, vol. 51, no. 3, 1997, 373–87.

———, 'Defensive Democratization in Jordan', *International Journal of Middle East Studies*, vol. 30, no. 3, 1998, 387–410.

———, 'Hamas as Social Movement', in: Quintan Wiktorowicz (ed.), *Islamic Activism: A Social Movement Theory Approach*, Bloomington & Indianapolis: Indiana University Press, 2004, 112–39.

Rohlinger, Deana A., 'Framing the Abortion Debate: Organizational Resources, Media Strategies, and Movement-Countermovement Dynamics', *The Sociological Quarterly*, vol. 43, no. 4, 2002, 479–507.

Rougier, Bernard (ed.), *Qu'est-ce que le salafisme?* Paris: Presses Universitaires de France, 2008.

———, 'Fatah al-Islam: Un Réseau Jihadiste au Cœur des Contradictions Libanaises', in: Bernard Rougier (ed.), *Qu'est-ce que le salafisme ?* Paris: Presses Universitaires de France, 2008, 179–210.

———, 'Le Jihad en Afghanistan et l'émergence du salafisme-jihadisme', in: Bernard Rougier (ed.), *Qu'est-ce que le salafisme?* Paris: Presses Universitaires de France, 2008, 65–86.

———, *Everyday Jihad: The Rise of Militant Islam among Palestinians in Lebanon* (transl. Pascale Ghazaleh), Cambridge, MA, & London: Harvard University Press, 2007.

Roy, Olivier, *Globalized Islam: The Search for a New Umma*, New York: Columbia University Press, 2004.

———, *The Failure of Political Islam* (transl. Carol Volk), London: I. B. Tauris, 1994 [1992].

Rubin, Barnett, 'Arab Islamists in Afghanistan', in: John L. Esposito (ed.), *Political Islam: Revolution, Radicalism, or Reform?*, Boulder, CO, & London: Lynne Rienner Publishers, 1997, 179–206.

Rubin, Uri, 'Barāʾa: A Study of some Quranic Passages', *Jerusalem Studies in Arabic and Islam*, vol. 5, 1984, 13–32.

Ryan, Curtis R., 'Jordan and the Rise and Fall of the Arab Cooperation Council', *Middle East Journal*, vol. 52, no. 3, 1998, 386–401.

———, 'Peace, Bread and Riots: Jordan and the International Monetary Fund', *Middle East Policy*, vol. 6, no. 2, 1998, 54–66.

Sachedina, Abdulaziz A., 'The Development of *Jihad* in Islamic Revelation and History', in: James Turner Johnson and John Kelsay (eds.), *Cross, Crescent, and Sword: The Justification of War in Western and Islamic Tradition*, New York: Greenwood Press, 1990, 35–50.

Salem, Elie Adib, *Political Theory and Institutions of the Khawārij*, Baltimore: Johns Hopkins University Press, 1956.

Salem, Isam Kamel, *Islam und Völkerrecht: Das Völkerrecht in der islamischen Weltanschauung*, Berlin: Express Edition, 1984.

Satloff, Robert B., *Troubles on the East Bank: Challenges to the Domestic Stability of Jordan*, New York: Praeger Publishers, 1986.

Schacht, Joseph, *An Introduction to Islamic Law*, Oxford: Oxford University Press, 1982.

Schwartz, Werner, *Die Anfänge der Ibaditen in Nordafrika*, Wiesbaden: Otto Harrassowitz, 1983.

Schwedler, Jillian, 'A Paradox of Democracy? Islamist Participation in Elections', *Middle East Report*, no. 209, 1998, 25–29.

———, *Faith in Moderation: Islamist Parties in Jordan and Yemen*, Cambridge: Cambridge University Press, 2006.

Scott, Rachel, 'An "Official" Islamic Response to the Egyptian al-Jihād Movement', *Journal of Political Ideologies*, vol. 8, no. 1, 2003, 39–61.

Sharqāwī, Ṭāhir al-, 'Abū Muḥammad al-Maqdisī ... Thunāʾiyyat al-Muqaddas wa-l-ʿUnf', *Al-Misbār*, no. 5, May 2007, 131–43.

Shavit, Uriya, 'Al-Qaeda's Saudi Origins: Islamist Ideology', *Middle East Quarterly*, vol. 13, no. 4, 2006, 3–13.

Shehabi, Saeed, 'The Role of Religious Ideology in the Expansionist Policies of Saudi Arabia', in: Madawi al-Rasheed (ed.), *Kingdom without Borders: Saudi Arabia's Political, Religious and Media Frontiers*, London: Hurst & Co., 2008, 183–97.

Shehadeh, Marwan [Marwān Shaḥāda], 'Weakening al-Qaeda: Literature Review Challenges its Authority', *Arab Insight*, vol. 2, no. 6, 2009, 25–36.

Shepard, William E., 'Sayyid Qutb's Doctrine of *Jāhiliyya*', *International Journal of Middle East Studies*, vol. 35, no. 4, 2003, 521–45.

Sirry, Mun'im, 'Jamāl al-Dīn al-Qāsimī and the Salafi Approach to Sufism', *Die Welt des Islams*, vol. 51, no. 1, 2011, 75–108.

Sivan, Emmanuel, *Radical Islam: Medieval Theology and Modern Politics*, New Haven & London: Yale University Press, 1985.
Skillington, Tracey, 'Politics and the Struggle to Define: A Discourse Analysis of the Framing Strategies of Competing Actors in a "New" Participatory Forum', *British Journal of Sociology*, vol. 48, no. 3, 1997, 493–513.
Snow, David A., and Robert D. Benford, 'Ideology, Frame Resonance, and Participant Mobilization', in: Bert Klandermans, Hanspeter Kriesi and Sidney Tarrow (eds.), *International Social Movement Research, Vol. I: From Structure to Action – Comparing Social Movement Research Across Cultures*, Greenwich, CT, & London: JAI Press, 1988, 197–217.
Snow, David A., E. Burke Rochford, Jr., Steven K. Worden and Robert D. Benford, 'Frame Alignment Processes, Micromobilization, and Movement Participation', *American Sociological Review*, vol. 51, August 1986, 464–81.
Springer, Devin R., James L. Regens and David N. Edger, *Islamic Radicalism and Global Jihad*, Washington, D.C.: Georgetown University Press, 2009.
Stacher, Joshua, 'Post-Islamist Rumblings in Egypt: The Emergence of the Wasat Party', *Middle East Journal*, vol. 56, no. 3, 2002, 415–32.
Steinberg, Guido, 'Jihadi-Salafism and the Shiʿis: Remarks about the Intellectual Roots of anti-Shiʿism', in: Roel Meijer (ed.), *Global Salafism: Islam's New Religious Movement*, London: Hurst & Co., 2009, 107–25.
———, 'The Wahhabi Ulama and the Saudi State: 1745 to the Present', in: Paul Aarts and Gerd Nonneman (eds.), *Saudi Arabia in the Balance: Political Economy, Society, Foreign Affairs*, London: Hurst & Co., 2005, 11–34.
———, 'Wahhabi *ʿulama* and the state in Saudi Arabia, 1927', in: Camron Michael Amin, Benjamin C. Fortna and Elizabeth Frierson (eds.), *The Modern Middle East: A Sourcebook for History*, Oxford: Oxford University Press, 2006, 57–61.
———, *Religion und Staat in Saudi Arabien: Die wahhabitischen Gelehrten, 1902–1953*, Würzburg: Ergon, 2002.
Susser, Asher, 'The Jordanian Monarchy: The Hashemite Success Story', in: Joseph Kostiner (ed.), *Middle East Monarchies: The Challenge of Modernity*, Boulder, CO: Lynne Rienner Publishers, 2000, 87–115.
Swidler, Ann, 'Culture in Action: Symbols and Strategies', *American Sociological Review*, vol. 51, April 1986, 273–86.
Teitelbaum, Joshua, 'Duelling for *Daʿwa*: State vs. Society on the Saudi Internet', *Middle East Journal*, vol. 56, no. 2, 2002, 222–39.
———, 'Terrorist Challenges to Saudi Arabian Internal Security', *Middle East Review of International Affairs*, vol. 9, no. 3, 2005, 1–11.
———, *Holier than Thou: Saudi Arabia's Islamic Opposition*, Washington, D.C.: The Washington Institute for Near East Policy, 2000.
Troquer, Yann Le, and Rozenn Hommery al-Oudat, 'From Kuwait to Jordan: The Palestinians' Third Exodus', *Journal of Palestine Studies*, vol. 28, no. 3, 1999, 37–51.
Tschudi, R., 'Die Fetwa's des Schejch-ül-Islâm über die Erklärung des heiligen Krieges, nach dem Tanîn, Nummer 2119 vom 15. November 1914', *Der Islam*, vol. 5, 1914, 391–3.

Vanderford, Marsha L., 'Vilification and Social Movements: A Case-Study of Pro-Life and Pro-Choice Rhetoric', *Quarterly Journal of Speech*, vol. 75, no. 1, 1989, 166–82.

Vassiliev, Alexei, *The History of Saudi Arabia*, London: Saqi Books, 2000 [1998].

Wagemakers, Joas, '"Seceders" and "Postponers"? An Analysis of the "Khawarij" and "Murjiʾa" Labels in Polemical Debates between Quietist and Jihadi-Salafis', in: Jeevan Deol and Zaheer Kazmi (eds.), *Contextualizing Jihadi Thought*, London: Hurst & Co., 2012, 143–65.

———, 'A "Purist Jihadi-Salafi": The Ideology of Abu Muhammad al-Maqdisi', *British Journal of Middle Eastern Studies*, vol. 36, no. 2, August 2009, 283–99.

———, 'A Quietist Jihadi-Salafi: The Ideology and Influence of Abu Muhammad al-Maqdisi', unpublished PhD thesis, Radboud University, Nijmegen, 2010.

———, 'Abu Muhammad al-Maqdisi: A Counter-Terrorism Asset?' *CTC Sentinel*, vol. 1, no. 6, May 2008, 7–9.

———, 'Al-Qaʿida's Editor: Abu Jandal al-Azdi's Online Jihadi Activism', *Politics, Religion & Ideology*, vol. 12, no. 4, 2011, 355–69.

———, 'An Inquiry into Ignorance: A Jihādī-Salafī Debate on *Jahl* as an Obstacle to *Takfīr*', in: Nicolet Boekhoff-van der Voort, Kees Versteegh and Joas Wagemakers (eds.), *The Transmission and Dynamics of the Textual Sources of Islam: Essays in Honour of Harald Motzki*, Leiden: Brill, 2011, 301–27.

———, 'Defining the Enemy: Abū Muḥammad al-Maqdisī's Radical Reading of Sūrat al-Mumtaḥana', *Die Welt des Islams*, vol. 48, nos. 3–4, 2008, 348–71.

———, 'Framing the "Threat to Islam": *Al-Walaʾ wa-l-Baraʾ* in Salafi Discourse', *Arab Studies Quarterly*, vol. 30, no. 4, 2008, 1–22.

———, 'Invoking Zarqawi: Abu Muhammad al-Maqdisi's Jihad Deficit', *CTC Sentinel*, vol. 2, no. 6, June 2009, 14–17.

———, 'Protecting Jihad: The Sharia Council of the Minbar al-Tawhid wa-l-Jihad', *Middle East Policy*, vol. 18, no. 2, 2011, 148–62.

———, 'Reclaiming Scholarly Authority: Abu Muhammad al-Maqdisi's Critique of Jihadi Practices', *Studies in Conflict and Terrorism*, vol. 34, no. 7, 2011, 523–39.

———, 'Soennitische Islamisten en de Erfenis van de Islamitische Revolutie', *ZemZem: Tijdschrift over het Midden-Oosten, Noord-Afrika en Islam*, vol. 4, no. 3, 2008, 55–9.

———, 'The Enduring Legacy of the Second Saudi State: Quietist and Radical Wahhabi Contestations of *al-Walāʾ wa-l-Barāʾ*', *International Journal of Middle East Studies*, vol. 44, 2012, 93–110.

———, 'The Transformation of a Radical Concept: *Al-Walaʾ wa-l-Baraʾ* in the Ideology of Abu Muhammad al-Maqdisi', in: Roel Meijer (ed.), *Global Salafism: Islam's New Religious Movement*, London: Hurst & Co., 2009, 81–106.

Weismann, Itzchak, 'Between Ṣūfī Reformism and Modernist Rationalism – A Reappraisal of the Origins of the Salafiyya from the Damascene Angle', *Die Welt des Islams*, vol. 41, no. 2, 2001, pp. 206–37.

———, 'Genealogies of Fundamentalism: Salafi Discourse in Nineteenth-Century Baghdad', *British Journal of Middle Eastern Studies*, vol. 36, no. 2, 2009, 267–80.

______, *Taste of Modernity: Sufism, Salafiyya, and Arabism in Late Ottoman Damascus*, Leiden: Brill, 2001.

Wiktorowicz, Quintan, 'Anatomy of the Salafi Movement', *Studies in Conflict and Terrorism*, vol. 29, no. 3, 2006, 207–40.

______, 'Centrifugal Tendencies in the Algerian Civil War', *Arab Studies Quarterly*, vol. 23, no. 3, 2001, 65–82.

______, 'Framing Jihad: Intramovement Framing Contests and al-Qaeda's Struggle for Sacred Authority', *International Review of Social History*, vol. 49, supplement 12, 2004, 159–177.

______, 'The New Global Threat: Transnational Salafis and Jihad', *Middle East Policy*, vol. 8, no. 4, December 2001, 18–38.

______, 'The Salafi Movement in Jordan', *International Journal of Middle East Studies*, vol. 32, no. 2, 2000, 219–40.

______, 'The Salafi Movement: Violence and Fragmentation of Community', in: Miriam Cooke and Bruce B. Lawrence (eds.), *Muslim Networks from Hajj to Hiphop*, Chapel Hill & London: University of North Carolina Press, 2005, 208–34.

______, *Radical Islam Rising: Muslim Extremism in the West*, Lanham, MD: Rowman & Littlefield, 2005.

______, *The Management of Islamic Activism: Salafis, the Muslim Brotherhood, and State Power in Jordan*, Albany, NY: State University of New York Press, 2001.

Wiktorwicz, Quintan, and John Kaltner, 'Killing in the Name of Islam: Al-Qaeda's Justification for September 11', *Middle East Policy*, vol. 10, no. 2, 2003, 76–92.

Wright, Lawrence, 'The Rebellion Within: An Al Qaeda Mastermind Questions Terrorism', *The New Yorker* (www.newyorker.com/reporting/2008/06/02/080602fa_fact_wright), 2 June 2008.

Youngman, Nicole, 'When Frame Extension Fails: Operation Rescue and the "Triple Gates of Hell" in Orlando', *Journal of Contemporary Ethnography*, vol. 32, no. 5, 2003, 521–54.

Zdravomyslova, Elena, 'Opportunities and Framing in the Transition to Democracy: The Case of Russia', in: Doug McAdam, John D. McCarthy and Mayer N. Zald (eds.), *Comparative Perspectives on Social Movements: Political Opportunities, Mobilizing Structures, and Cultural Framings*, Cambridge: Cambridge University Press, 1996, 122–137.

Zebiri, Kate, 'Islamic Revival in Algeria: An Overview', *The Muslim World*, vol. 83, nos. 3–4, July-October 1993, 203–26.

Zeghal, Malika, 'Religion and Politics in Egypt: The Ulema of al-Azhar, Radical Islam, and the State (1952–94)', *International Journal of Middle East Studies*, vol. 31, no. 3, 1999, 371–99.

Zuo, Jiping, and Robert D. Benford, 'Mobilization Processes and the 1989 Chinese Democracy Movement', *The Sociological Quarterly*, vol. 36, no. 1, 1995, 131–56.

Index

Lacroix, Stéphane, 123
leadership. *See imāra*
Lebanon, 24, 174
legal scholars. *See fuqahā'*
legal schools. *See madhhab*
legislation. *See taḥkīm*; *tashrī'*
lesser unbelief. *See kufr*
Letter of Demands. *See khiṭāb al-maṭālib*
Lia, Brynjar, 176
loyalty. *See walā' wa-l-barā', al-*
loyalty and disavowal. *See walā' wa-l-barā', al-*

madhhab (pl. *madhāhib*), 4, 5, 56, 127, 237
maḥabba. *See walā' wa-l-barā', al-*
Mahdi, 100
Majallat al-Ansar, 131
majlis al-shūrā, 103
major sins. *See kabā'ir*
major unbelief. *See kufr*
Maktab al-Khidmat, 14, 15, 18
Maliki school of Islamic law, 4. *See also madhhab*
manhaj, 7–10, 24, 50, 52, 66, 74, 75–93, 202, 206, 211, 212, 213, 214, 216, 217, 218, 219, 221, 222, 223, 228, 230, 231, 235, 236, 237, 238, 239, 240, 241, 245, 246
man-made laws. *See qawānīn waḍ'iyya*
Maqdisi, Abu Muhammad al-, vii, viii, 1, 2, 8, 10, 23, 24, 62, 63, 76, 79, 121, 165, 213, 237, 239, 247, 249
  Abu l-Bara' al-Najdi as a pseudonym of, 141
  alleged revisionism of, 49, 83, 134, 135, 205, 229–231
  as a quietist Jihadi-Salafi, 10, 24, 25, 26, 30, 33–41, 49–50, 52, 66, 75, 93, 97, 115, 120, 143–144, 147, 153, 164, 165, 188, 191, 202, 206, 211, 213, 214, 216, 217–222, 223, 227–231, 233–236, 237, 238, 239, 241, 243, 244, 245, 246, 247, 249
  childhood of, 29, 30–33, 239
  criticism of al-Zarqawi, 46–48, 218, 222
  descent of, 29, 30
  earlier publications on, 19–20
  I'dad al-Qada al-Fawaris bi-Hajr Fasad al-Madaris (1986/7), 37
  ideology of, 24, 51–52, 201, 205, 206, 210, 211, 224, 225, 237, 248
  in Afghanistan, 29, 38, 39, 40, 57, 70, 109, 176, 182, 191, 201, 206, 216, 221, 239
  in Iraq, 191
  in Jordan, 25, 41–49, 191, 192, 198
  in Kuwait, 31–32, 40–41, 191, 239
  in Pakistan, 29, 38–40, 191, 201, 239
  in prison, 42–49, 191, 207, 213, 214–216, 217, 218, 219, 224, 226, 227
  in Saudi Arabia, 36–37, 43, 191, 201, 239, 243
  influence of, 1, 2, 10, 15, 20, 22–23, 24, 25–26, 51, 165, 191, 246–247, 248, 249
  influence on *al-isti'āna bi-l-kuffār*, 147, 153–164, 165, 167, 168, 174, 175, 179–188, 243–245
  influence on Jordanian Jihadi-Salafi community, 191, 196, 198–212, 213, 214–236, 245–246
  influence on legislative interpretation of *al-walā' wa-l-barā'*, 165, 166–179, 183–188, 244, 249
  influence on Saudi post–Gulf War Wahhabi opposition, 20, 109–119, 120, 121, 122, 124, 127–144, 241–243
  Kashf al-Niqab 'an Shari'at al-Ghab (1988), 37, 223